John Dunton and the English Book Trade

Garland Reference Library of the Humanities (Vol. 40)

F. Knight Del.t J. Swaine Sc. After M. V.der Gucht

JOHN  DUNTON,

Born 1659: Died 1733

John Dunton and the English Book Trade

A Study of His Career with a Checklist of His Publications

Stephen Parks

Garland Publishing, Inc., New York & London

1976

Library of Congress Cataloging in Publication Data

Parks, Stephen.
John Dunton and the English book trade.

(Garland reference library of the humanities ; v. 40)
Includes bibliographical references and index.
1. Dunton, John, 1659-1733. 2. Book industries and trade--England--History. I. Title.
Z325.D93P37 658.8'09'0705730924 [B] 75-24078
ISBN 0-8240-9965-6

Printed in the United States of America

C O N T E N T S

P R E F A C E

It will be obvious that I have visited many places and talked with many persons; everywhere I have been received with courtesy and kindness, for which I now express my thanks. Without such assistance this study could not have been completed. In particular, however, I am grateful to the late Dr. A. N. L. Munby, whose thoughtful advice began with my pupilage in Cambridge and who was unfailingly generous with material from his own extensive collections. Also to Dr. James M. Osborn, who patiently read an early draft of this study and made a number of critical suggestions which have been gladly adopted.

A few works which have frequently been cited in notes are referred to in abbreviated form. These symbols will be found listed at the end of the introduction to the checklist. *The Life and Errors of John Dunton* has been cited as *Life and Errors* throughout this work. The edition referred to is in each case John Bowyer Nichols's edition of 1818. As copies of the first edition (1705) of the *Life and Errors* are scarce, it was convenient to use Nichols's edition for reference. Nichols bowdlerized the *Life and Errors*, and he altered Dunton's punctuation; but Nichols's edition is substantially complete and for the purposes of this work has been adequate.*

*J. B. Nichols's copy of the 1705 edition of Dunton's *Life and Errors*, marked with his notes and excisions, is in the Osborn Collection, Yale University Library.

CHAPTER I

EARLY LIFE, APPRENTICESHIP, AND BEGINNINGS IN THE TRADE

(1659-88)

To his contemporaries, John Dunton was largely an object of scorn. But scorn was tempered with respect, for many had known the force of Dunton's own satire. Thus to Hearne, Dunton was merely "a poor craz'd silly Fellow" but to Pope "a broken Bookseller and abusive scribler" and to the Earl of Oxford "the author of many libels".[1] Later in the eighteenth century, and in the nineteenth century, Dunton attracted antiquarian interest, and writers developed the image of him which persists today, that of the quaint bookseller and literary hack, with a thousand maggoty projects crowded into his bursting brain. Lemoine called Dunton a "singular genius" but condemned his writings as "exceeding prolix and tedious, and sometimes obscure". To Nichols, who wrote a memoir of Dunton and bowdlerized his Life and Errors, Dunton was an "ingenious but eccentric Bookseller, whose latter years were strongly tinctured with insanity".[2]

In the opinion of Isaac Disraeli, Dunton's "mind had no elegance, and [his] rhimes are doggrel". But Disraeli read Dunton's works closely and was the first of his critics to identify the sources of many of the passages which Dunton adopted without acknowledgment from earlier authors, a practice which has also been followed by recent critics.[3] A writer of the present century, C. A. Moore, who wrote on Dunton as "pietist and imposter", saw him only as a tradesman; "it was mainly for the purpose of supplying himself with ... articles of merchandise" Moore wrote "that he assumed the additional functions of author and publisher".[4] But even to T. M. Hatfield, who wrote more sympathetically than other recent writers, Dunton was simply one of a "host of literary practitioners, now bawdy, now pious as taste demanded, ... venal and licentious scribblers ...."[5]

Each of these assertions has a measure of truth in it, but none is entirely correct. After 1700, Dunton was indeed a broken man: his married life became a wretched brawl, his attacks of the stone grew frequent and excruciating, and his attempts to subsist by writing - political pamphlets, during the reign of Queen Anne, and later, petitions to King George I seeking reward for his services - earned him only ridicule. Of Dunton's life before 1700 - he was forty years old in that year, and had been twenty-five years in the trade - little has been written other than his own _Life and Errors_. Writers have discussed the _Athenian Mercury_ at some length and perhaps have cited a handful of works published by Dunton. But they have generally perpetuated the portrait of the quaint bookseller, cautioning their readers against acceptance of Dunton's own account of his years in the trade. His instability and unreliability as a witness is evidenced, say his critics, by the scurrilous political tracts which he wrote to support himself in the painful last years of his life. No study has been made of John Dunton's career as a bookseller.

Dunton's early years were tinctured with political and religious views firmly held and strongly expressed, with originality of a high order. As an apprentice to the noted Presbyterian bookseller Thomas Parkhurst, Dunton was a prominent Whig among London apprentices. After his marriage to Elizabeth Annesley, he rapidly became successful as a bookseller, dealing at first mainly in sermons and devotional writings. Dunton continued to prosper until the defeat of the Duke of Monmouth caused a "damp on trade". He then closed his London shop and travelled to America, where he sold books and made friends among the noted divines and booksellers of New England. On the coming of the Prince of Orange to England, Dunton again opened a shop in London, where he traded with mixed success and failure for ten years. During this period he published periodicals, literary and historical works, sermons and political tracts, but chiefly the immensely popular _Athenian Mercury_, avidly read in the coffee-houses for nearly six years. After the death of his wife and a disastrous remarriage, Dunton travelled to Ireland. There he lived for a year, holding auction sales in Dublin. Soon after his return to London in 1699, ill health forced him into retirement, and poverty compelled him to write for other booksellers. In these years he produced the political invective which has earned him the reputation for low scribbling persisting today.

Dunton's Life and Errors has been called a forerunner of the autobiographies of Colley Cibber and Rousseau.[6] In it Dunton elaborated upon his own faults as a general moral lesson - but along with the conventional religious sentiments of the Life and Errors, there is a wealth of information and gossip, about the trade and about his contemporaries. Written in 1704-5, the Life and Errors antedates the scurrilous political writings which have stigmatized Dunton's reputation. In fact, it is a much more reliable work than most writers have believed. The years of Dunton's activity in the book trade were marked by widespread political insecurity. Control of printing and publishing, originally a royal prerogative, had been regulated by act of Parliament since 1662. The failure of Parliament in 1695 to continue to renew the Act of 1662, and the ineffectiveness of the Stationers' Company in enforcing regulations, created instability in the trade not rectified until after the Act of 1710. Dunton's professional career, chronicled in his autobiography and documented by the mass of materials he published, neatly spans this period. Viewed in perspective, John Dunton emerges as a bookseller of originality and brash self-confidence, whose reputation has suffered from the misunderstanding so often coupling his name with that of Edmund Curll. Yet his singular variety of experience in the trade - as publisher, as wholesale, retail, and second-hand bookseller, as auctioneer, journalist and hack - and the fascinating trail of evidence which he left behind him, have combined to make Dunton a revealing subject through whom to study the English book trade in the unsettled years of the late seventeenth century.

Dunton's father, grandfather, and great-grandfather had all been called John Dunton and had all been ordained in the Church of England. Nothing is known of the first Reverend John Dunton beyond his great-grandson's statement that he had been a vicar of Little Missenden, Buckinghamshire. His son, however, was inducted vicar of Little Missenden on 22 May 1617 and there, on 9 October 1622, he married Mary Grimsdale.[7] The third Reverend John Dunton was born at Little Missenden on 10 June 1628. Of his three sisters, Anne, who married William Reading, of Dungrove, near Chesham, had six children; Mary, who married Mr. Woolhouse, Minister of Princes Risborough, Bucks., had seven children; and Elizabeth, who married William Pratt, died without issue.[8]

John Dunton, the father of the bookseller, was first taught by his father, and after his death by the schoolmaster of Tring, in Hertfordshire.[9] He was admitted to Trinity College, Cambridge, on 5 July 1645 as a pensioner, became a scholar of the college in 1647, and took his B.A. degree two years later.[10] After travel in Europe, the Reverend John Dunton returned to England to become rector of St. Mary's, Bedford, where he remained for five years, until about 1657.[11] He married, on 3 June 1654, Lydia Carter, the daughter of Mr. Daniel Carter, of Chesham.[12] On leaving Bedford, John Dunton became rector of Grafham, Huntingdonshire, where his only child, the subject of this study, was born on 4 May 1659. "A quarter of a Year after he was Born, Mrs. Dunton dyed of that Tormenting Disease, called the Twisting of the Guts, which Distemper she endured with wonderful Patience, and with an Humble Submission to the Will of her heavenly Father".[13]

After the death of his wife, the Reverend John Dunton vowed not to remarry for seven years, and went with his servant to Ireland, where he acted as chaplain to Sir Henry Ingoldsby.[14] He returned to England sooner than he had originally intended, and on 11 May 1663 he was presented to the living of St. Michael and All Angels, Aston Clinton, by Sir Gilbert Gerard, the Lord of the Manor at Aston Clinton.[15] Shortly thereafter he married Mrs. Mary Lake, the daughter of the Reverend John Marriat, and they had four children, Sarah, Mary, Elizabeth and Lake Dunton.

The Reverend John Dunton's earnest hope was to make a clergyman of his eldest son, and when he went to Ireland he sent him to be tutored by his brother-in-law, William Reading, of Dungrove. Young John was not an apt pupil. In his Life and Errors, he recalled that all he had been able to accomplish, "under ... a whole catalogue of Teachers, was ... to know the rudiments of my mother tongue. I could improve fast enough in any thing but the art of learning, to which I had a strange kind of aversion, both as it kept me confined, and, as I thought, was too difficult and unpleasant".[16] Certainly his teachers took great pains to implant a knowledge of Latin and Greek in their pupil, and in A Voyage Round the World, Dunton was far from soft-spoken about his schooldays. The mere thought of his schooldays, Dunton wrote, made him tremble, and he welcomed his opportunity to scourge his schoolmasters with his pen as they had chastised him with the birch:

> "Farewel Grammar, thou Bug-bear to tender Striplings and Buttocks; how often hast thou steer'd my penitent Posteriours to a Burchen Wood, and made the Butt-end of my Person weep Carnation Tears; nay, made the poor Pedant wear out himself as much as me in running through Thorns and Briars after some fugitive rugged word or other that wou'd not be hoop't into any of his common Rules".[17]

On his father's return to Aston Clinton, John parted from his friends at Dungrove and went to live at the rectory. The Reverend John Dunton still planned a career in the Church for his son. Under his father's direction, John made some progress with Latin, and he resolved to be more diligent in all his studies;

> "but the difficulties of the Greek quite broke all my resolutions; and, which was a greater disadvantage to me, I was wounded with a silent passion for a Virgin in my Father's house, that unhinged me all at once, though I never made a discovery of the flame, and for that reason it gave me the greater torment".[18]

Though John's difficulties with grammar could not be overcome, his father tutored him in metaphysics, logic, and morality; but "neither Aristotle, Herebord, Wendelin, nor all the Ethicks in the world, could work a reformation in my manners".[19] Finally despairing of educating his son to be a scholar or parson, Dunton resolved to bind him apprentice to some trade "that might both be honourable, and suit the peculiarity of my own genius". He selected for him the trade of bookseller, that he might be "at least a friend to Learning and the Muses, if I would not join myself to them by some nearer affinity".[20]

In the summer of 1674, Dunton left Aston Clinton for London, to stay for a trial period in the house of Thomas Parkhurst, who had been recommended to his father as a "religious and a just man".[21] Parkhurst was a good choice as master for the young Dunton; "the most eminent Presbyterian Bookseller in the Three Kingdoms", Parkhurst traded successfully for many years and became master of the Stationers' Company in 1703. To his apprentice, Parkhurst "shewed ... all the kind civilities and tender regards that were possible for him"; but after a few days had passed, Dunton resolved to return home. Ignoring Parkhurst's suggestion that he write first to his father for advice, Dunton "took horse for Aston Clinton" where he stayed at first with friends, fearful of his father's displeasure. The rector, however, merely gave his son a few stern admonitions, presented him with a packet of letters containing the spiritual reflections of his late mother, and returned him to Parkhurst, with this letter:

> Mr. Parkhurst,
> I have returned you my Son, whom I desire you would receive as myself, and as my own bowels. I own that he may justly have given you offence, for which you might very reasonably refuse him; but I hope he comes again to your greater satisfaction, and to do you better service. I resign him entirely to you; for I know there is none will take a more friendly and Christian care of him than yourself, both with respect to this and another world. I will never encourage him to take the same liberty for the future, and you know I was ignorant of his coming home; however, I hope you will pardon him, which I shall acknowledge as done to myself; and which will for ever oblige your real friend and servant.
>
> J. Dunton[22]

In London again, Dunton found that John Laurence had been accepted for trial in his place and occupied his room at Parkhurst's house. Dunton found lodgings with his cousin, John Child, a grocer in the Stocks Market, and within a week, he came down with smallpox, "which were so severe upon me, that it was almost a miracle I survived them". Laurence was bound apprentice to Parkhurst on 7 September 1674. When Dunton had recovered his health ("though I shall carry the pits, and the signatures of that distemper, to my grave"), he rejoined

Parkhurst's household, successfully completed his second trial, and was firmly bound apprentice for seven years on 7 December 1674.[23] In the company of John Laurence, James Collyer, and Laurence Brimley, Dunton passed his apprenticeship with Parkhurst. "If ever an Apprenticeship was easy and agreeable," Dunton later wrote "it was that which I served".[24] A few months later, Parkhurst wrote to Dunton's father an enthusiastic account of his son's progress, and the rector confided to his son that "Thy Master's Letter to me last week gives me great encouragement ... He writes so fully of thy cheerfulness, tractableness, and industry; and that thou art willing to learn and obey; as also of thy honesty, and especially of thy desire and endeavour to know and serve the Lord."[25]

Dunton wrote very briefly about his apprenticeship in his <u>Life and Errors</u>, and, apart from two love affairs, recalled few errors of that stage of his life. Later in 1675, Dunton journeyed again to Aston Clinton to visit his father, whom continual attacks of the stone had brought near to death. The rector gave his son his dying counsel, and returned him to London with renewed spiritual vigour. There, he became inflamed with a passion for the beautiful Rachel Seaton, whom he had met at the Reverend Mr. Doolittle's meetinghouse. Dunton neglected the duties of apprenticeship as he conducted his flirtation, meeting Miss Seaton at Mr. Dawson's dancing school. But he has spared the reader of his Life and Errors a full account of the affair, for to "publish to the world all the extravagance of this amour ... would almost be to commit the same Error over again".[26] Late in the year, Dunton had premonitory dreams of his father's death. He was not therefore surprised to learn that his father had died of the stone on 4 November 1676, and had been interred in the chancel of Aston Clinton church.[27]

Neglect of duty and sloth were Dunton's two chief faults. For many years he was burdened with the accumulated guilt of seven years' commission of these sins. "Want of industry" was the worst crime for an apprentice, Dunton later declared, "for it presently sets a man thinking how to entertain his fancy, and to divert himself with pleasure".[28] Had he to live again his years of apprenticeship, Dunton stated he would have resolved to apply himself with greater diligence to business. Even after the realization of his failings as confessed in his Life and Errors, Dunton was troubled by the accumulated errors of his apprenticeship. He was so troubled, in fact, that he abstained from Communion for several years heedless of the kind entreaties of his friend and companion Mrs. Isabella Edwards.[29] No fewer than three and a half pages of his lengthy will, which he wrote in 1711, were given to his repentance for various unspecified ills he had caused his master during his apprenticeship. Fifty pounds to Thomas Parkhurst for payment of myriad "unknown debts" was intended to be the first legacy paid out of his estate. Dunton had earlier given his first wife instructions to settle with Parkhurst while he travelled in New England, "but she thinking the Losses Mr. Thomas Parkhurst Sustained by me not so considerable as I did deferred doing of it So when I came home again I thought it necessary to leave them a Debt on my Estate."[30] Chief among these "unknown debts", apparently, and the only one specifically cited in his will, was "for all Over-rating my Fathers Library". Dunton's father left him his library, provided that he "shall not take any of my Library into his possession to dispose of for his owne use tel he hath given a bond of Twenty pounds to my wife for his payment of Ten pounds unto my daughter Sarah when she shall come to be fifteen years of age; and if such Security shall not be granted by my Son John then ... my Library should be sold as soon as may be & the money thereof to be given to my daughter Sarah".[31] The library of the Reverend John Dunton was sold by Parkhurst in 1680, four years after his death. No further explanation has been found of the circumstances surrounding the sale of the elder Dunton's library, but we may surmise that whatever arrangements were made between Dunton and his half-sister Sarah, Thomas Parkhurst gained very little from it.

Politics occupied much of Dunton's time during the years of his apprenticeship, and although he later repented of hours lost to philandering, he often recalled with pride his eminence as a Whig apprentice during these years. The Whig faction among the London apprentices had been incensed when the Tory apprentices presented a petition, bearing 5,000 signatures, to the King which reflected "on Parliaments, the Bulwarks (under His Sacred Majesty) of English Liberties: And this was noised to be the general Sense of all the London-Apprentices"; furthermore, "the Caresses and Favours they receiv'd put them to the Vanity of boasting themselves the onely Loyal Young Men of this City".[32] "I thought if the Tory Apprentices did all they could to Ruin their Country ..." Dunton wrote "that 'twas the Duty of the Whig Apprentices to do all they could to Save it".[33]

The Whig apprentices, led by Dunton, met and mobilized themselves to take action: "Joshua Evans and myself were the first that moved in this affair; but the thing ripened at such a rate, that in a small time there were 300 Apprentices engaged in it, that had their frequent meeting at Russel's house in Ironmongerlane. Mr. B---leyh was chosen Speaker of this grave Society, and myself made Treasurer".[34] Dunton and his "Select Number" of apprentices gathered thirty thousand signatures to their "Healing Address", and they presented it to

Sir Patience Ward, the Lord Mayor, on 2 September 1681. Twenty selected apprentices presented the petition, "and we were well received by my Lord Mayor, who promised he would acquaint the King with our Address, and then bid us return home, and mind the business of our respective Masters. However, before we dispersed, we regaled ourselves very plentifully at Russel's house".[35]

Shortly after the affair of the apprentices' petition, Dunton's apprenticeship was concluded with a mock funeral, which he invited a hundred of his friends to celebrate with him, "though it was no more than a youthful piece of vanity; for all such entertainments are expensive, and they are soon forgotten". Dunton was admitted to the freedom of the Stationers' Company on 5 December 1681.[36]

"My Apprenticeship being now over," Dunton wrote "and myself turned out into a wide world, to stand upon my own legs, and to barter for subsistence among the rest of my fellow creatures, the cares of the present life began to break in upon me; and now my notions of things were very different from those I had entertained before".[37] Dunton followed his father's advice to "take a convenient place", and he cautiously took at first only half a shop, a warehouse, and a "fashionable chamber".

The place chosen for his first shop was the Poultry, where he had served at least part of his apprenticeship with

Thomas Parkhurst. Called the Poultry Market for several centuries, the Poultry had long been deserted by the Poulterers and butchers who had given it the name, and also by their successors, haberdashers and glovers. In 1569, John Alde had sold books at the "long shop" near St. Mildred's Church. Richard Keel and Cuthbert Burbie also had shops in the Poultry in the sixteenth century, and "by the middle of the seventeenth century" William Roberts wrote "the Poultry had become the Paternoster Row of the Period".[38] Nathaniel Ponder, at the Peacock in the Poultry, had published The Pilgrim's Progress in 1678, and other booksellers in the Poultry shared Dunton's political and religious views. Among them were John Laurence, Dunton's fellow apprentice, Thomas Malthus (who fled to Holland in 1685)[39], Edward Croft, Thomas Cockerill, Dorman Newman, Jonathan Greenwood, and Benjamin Alsop, who later let his shop to Dunton when he left bookselling for a commission in the Duke of Monmouth's army.

Dunton wisely resolved to forego love and courtship, planning first "to make the experiment whether my trade would carry two, and then to proceed upon a safe bottom". Printing was the young bookseller's chief concern, and no sooner had he begun to trade than "Hackney Authors began to ply me with 'Specimens,'" as earnestly, and with as much passion and concern, as the Watermen do Passengers, with Oars and Scullers".[40]

Dunton scorned these hacks, and with the aid of Parkhurst ("whose concern for me did not expire with my Apprenticeship"), he published his first book. The Lord's Last Sufferings, dated 1682, was published late in 1681, and advertised in the Term Catalogue for Michaelmas 1681. "This Book fully answered my end;" Dunton wrote, providing what has become a standard illustration of the technique of simple exchange among booksellers, "for, exchanging it through the whole Trade, it furnished my Shop with all sorts of Books saleable at that time."[41]

Later in the winter of 1682, Dunton published Stephen Jay's Daniel in the Den and John Shower's Sermon Preacht upon the Death of Mrs. Anne Barnardiston. These works were followed into print by the first of the several collections of his father's works which he published, The House of Weeping, recommended as the "most proper book yet extant to be given on funeral occasions". In The House of Weeping are found two pages of advertisement which testify to Dunton's success in establishing himself through exchange in the trade. The first, advertising "Books Printed for John Dunton", lists the four titles which had been published under his own imprint; the second, advertising "Books Sold by John Dunton", lists twenty-three titles, for the most part sermons and devotional works, which were to form the basis of Dunton's trade for several years.

Confident that he had established a "safe bottom", Dunton's thoughts turned once again to matrimony; "having now ... the whole world before me," Dunton wrote "and my reputation growing with my circumstances, ... my Friends began to persecute me with the subject of Marriage, and were now as warm upon it as I had once been before".[42]

A shrewd friend suggested Sarah Doolittle, daughter of the Reverend Thomas Doolittle, who, it was suggested, "will make a better wife for you by ten degrees, and then you will have her Father's Copies for nothing; and his Book on the Sacrament, you know, has sold to the twentieth edition, which would have been an estate for a Bookseller".[43] "This design" Dunton wrote "was quite lost in the novelty of another", which Dunton failed to pursue because of a formidable rival.

Shortly thereafter, Dunton happened to join Dr. Samuel Annesley's congregation one Sunday, "where, instead of engaging my attention to what the Doctor said, I suffered both my mind and my eyes to run at random ... [and] I soon singled out a young lady that almost charmed me dead".[44] Unfortunately, this young lady was "pre-engaged", and Dunton's friends advised him to consider her elder sister. "And the hint they gave me, ... made a deeper impression upon me than all the recommendations they had given me before". Cautiously, Dunton approached Dr. Annesley, calling on him supported by his friends Isaac

Brinly and Obadiah Marriott. After hearing a testimonial from Thomas Parkhurst, Dr. Annesley gave Dunton his consent to the marriage, "if I could prevail upon his Daughter for her's; which was more than Mr. Cockeril (deceased) could ever obtain, after a long courtship". Dunton spared the reader of his Life and Errors a full account of his courtship, which he conducted throughout the spring and summer of 1682. Finally he gained her consent, "which was the beginning of the greatest happiness I have as yet met with in this life". Throughout the summer, the two lovers exchanged letters, signing themselves Philaret and Iris. Dunton visited Iris and her father at Tunbridge Wells in July. "Please to deny yourself a little luxuriance in your Letters," Iris cautioned her eager suitor, "lest my Father should find them, and be offended with them".[45] On the Annesleys' return from Tunbridge Wells, preparations were made for the marriage. Dunton took a house on the corner of Princes Street, and the date for the marriage was fixed. John Dunton and Elizabeth Annesley were married at the church of Allhallows on the Wall, London, on 3 August 1682. Dr. Annesley himself gave his daughter in marriage ("which I took as a peculiar favour from himself, it being more than some of his sons-in-law could obtain"), "the entertainment [at the dinner] was plentiful enough, and yet gravely suited to the occasion", and Samuel Wesley, whom

Dunton had known as a student at Edward Veal's academy (and who later collaborated with him in the writing of the Athenian Mercury), presented the couple with an epithalamium.[46] "Some days after this" Dunton confessed in his Life and Errors "were fooled away in treats, and unnecessary expence both of time and money ... When we had stayed a little time at my Father-in-law's, I carried dear Iris home, to the large house I had taken at the corner of Princes-street".[47]

Dunton printed his wife's character, composed by a friend, in his Life and Errors:

> "Iris is tall, of a good aspect; her hair of a light chesnut colour, dark eyes, her eye-brows dark and even, her mouth little and sufficiently sweet, her air something melancholy, sweet and agreeable, her neck long and graceful, white hands, a well-shaped body, her complexion very fair ... she is pleasant, witty, and virtuous; and is mistress of all those Graces that can be desired to make a complete Woman".

Beside it he printed his own, described by Iris's sister:

> "Philaret is of a middle stature; his hair black and curled, his eye-brows black and indifferently even, eyes almost black, quick and full of spirit, his nose rises a little in the middle, his lips red and soft ... his body is slender and every way well-proportioned."[48]

Iris was one of twenty-five children of Dr. Samuel Annesley. Disregarding all considerations of beauty, wit, and piety, the young bookseller could hardly have improved himself more than by marriage into the Annesley family. Samuel

Annesley was a nephew of the first Earl of Anglesey; he was educated at Queen's College, Oxford, and later served as naval chaplain to the Earl of Warwick. At the Restoration, he received the living of St. Giles, Cripplegate, worth £700 yearly, which he resigned after the Act of Uniformity in 1662. When Dunton visited the family, they lived in Spital Yard, Bishopsgate, where Dunton met many of the eminent non-conformists whose works he later published. The family of James Foe had exiled themselves from St. Giles with Dr. Annesley. Daniel Defoe, reared in Dr. Annesley's congregation, later contributed to the _Athenian Mercury_ and wrote an elegy on Dr. Annesley which Dunton published.[49] Dunton had known Samuel Wesley for several years, and when Wesley left Exeter College, Oxford, he became another frequent visitor to Spital Yard and in 1690 married Iris's sister, Susannah Annesley.[50] Wesley and Dunton were close friends during this period, and Dunton in 1685 published Wesley's _Maggots, or Poems on Several Occasions_. In the 1690's, Wesley and Dunton collaborated with a third brother-in-law, Richard Sault, in compiling the _Athenian Mercury_.[51]

The greatest asset Dunton gained in Iris was her business sense. While she lived, Dunton's trade prospered; Iris attended to the drudgery of shop-keeping while her husband travelled, and only she was capable of restraining his mercurial spirits and curbing the extravagant fancies which led to his ruin. At the shop in the Poultry, she soon went to work and Dunton then discovered her talents. "Dear Iris gave an early specimen of her Prudence and diligence" he later wrote "... and thereupon commenced Bookseller, Cash-keeper, managed all my affairs for me, and left me entirely to my own _rambling_ and _scribbling_ humours. However, I always kept an eye over the main chance".[52] Fortune smiled on Dunton, and he published several works late in 1682: sermons by John Howe and Timothy Rogers, and Richard Baxter's _Directions to the Unconverted_. In December, Dunton was invited to feast with the Sons of the Clergy in London, and afterwards he published his _Congratulatory Poem, to the Ministers' Sons_.

Early in 1683, Dunton's first apprentice, Samuel Palmer, was bound to him for eight years.[53] Among the books which Dunton published in that year were _A Continuation of Morning-Exercise Questions_, a thick volume of sermons by various preachers collected by Dr. Annesley, _The Devil's Patriarch_, by Christopher Nesse, a number of chapbooks -- _The Blessed Martyrs in Flames_, _The Swagering Damsell_, and _A Necessary Companion for a Serious Christian_ -- Dunton's own _The Informer's Doom: Or, an Amazing and Seasonable Letter from Utopia, Directed to the Man in the Moon_, and Benjamin Keach's _Travels of True Godliness_, of which Dunton published six editions in 1683-4. These slight sermons and chapbooks formed the bulk of Dunton's trade during these years. They were published in quite large editions - Dunton claimed to have lost 2,000 copies of The Arraignment of Mr. Persecution in a fire, and to have printed 10,000 of Benjamin Keach's Travels before the copy was sold to Nicholas Boddington. Dunton entered these works in the Stationers' Register, and he regularly advertised new publications in the Term Catalogues. They were remarkably profitable.

Early in July, Dunton had his first clash with authority. A "Plot Sermon" had been published, and Dunton and Thomas Malthus were arrested. On 7 July 1683, Dunton and Malthus petitioned Secretary Jenkins: "Sir, We being (according to the Sender of the honourable Warrant) yesterday in the evening, taken into custody by one of his majesties messengers and Secured in Mr. Atterbury's House and have ever since attended on the Right Honourable the Lords in Council in order to a hearing, that we are humbly to beseech your honour that we may be brought to a speedy hearing, in regard we are young men, and our livelihoods depend on our trades, and have no body to look after our concerns at home".[54] Two days later, in a hearing before the King and Council, it was recorded that Dunton "refused to join in printing the Plot Sermon. Larkey, a bookseller in Broad-street, prints it. Malthouse says he will be a stop to the Consolācon Sermon. Will bring a copy in and not print it without approval".[55] Dunton left no account of this episode in his Life and Errors. The "Plot Sermon" referred to may have been Truth Will Out, or, a Sermon Preached upon the First Discovery of this New Plot, on the 20th June, 1683, By a London Minister, which Dunton entered on 27 June, 1683. But this sermon was not published under Dunton's imprint.[56]

In 1684, Dunton published a sixteen page catalogue, embellished with an engraving of his signboard, the Black Raven, by Thomas Catlett. Also, three editions of The Compleat Tradesman, Benjamin Keach's The Progress of Sin, which sold three editions in two years; and two collections of his father's works, The Pilgrim's Guide and Dunton's Remains. Dunton's catalogue demonstrates his success, for it advertised no fewer than 168 works, including 14 lately published, as well as "All sorts of Bibles and Bible-Cases, and all sorts of School-Books". Dunton's thriving trade continued through 1684 and 1685, when he published two further works collected from his father's writings, Heavenly Pastime and An Hue and Cry after Conscience. Samuel Wesley's Maggots, Or, Poems on Several Occasions were also published early in 1685, in two editions. "We took several journeys together into the Country," Dunton wrote "and made visits to both our relations; but, look which way we would, the World was always smiling on us".[57] When Dunton's friend Benjamin Alsop left his large shop in the Poultry to accept a commission in the Duke of Monmouth's army, Dunton gave up his shop and took over Alsop's more spacious premises.[58]

The world continued to smile on Philaret and Iris until the summer of 1685, when the economic repercussions of the Duke of Monmouth's defeat caused a "universal damp on trade" which was particularly damaging to business at the Black Raven. As the sum of £500 was owed to Dunton in New England, he determined to go there to collect it personally, taking with him a cargo of books which he had been unable to sell in London. Iris willingly consented to his taking the voyage, and in August Dunton wrote to his father-in-law for advice. "I have a great number of Books that lie upon my hands," Dunton wrote to Dr. Annesley, "as the 'Continuation of the Morning Exercises,' and others, very proper for that place; besides the 500 _l._ which I have there in Debts".[59] Dr. Annesley gave his son-in-law his blessing, cautioning him against extravagant hopes for the voyage, and Dunton prepared to leave his wife and shop and sail to New England. "I was very glad of any excuse" Dunton confessed "that would make my friends more indulgent to my _rambling_ humour".[60]

Having sent quantities of books ahead, Dunton bid a "sorrowful farewell to dear Iris" and other relations, and travelled down river to Gravesend, where before he could embark for America he was arrested for a debt of £50 for which he had agreed to act as surety for Iris's sister, Bethia Annesley.[61] "I became bound," Dunton wrote "with all the freedom in the world, for this 50 *l*. to one Nevet, a Surgeon; and though I was never dunned twice for money upon my own account, yet I was arrested for this 50 *l*. upon my embarking for New-England". Two friends, Mr. R----f and Mr. Astwood, offered to provide bail for him, and Dunton was allowed to proceed to Boston.[62]

At Gravesend, Dunton encountered his friend Thomas Malthus, bookseller at the Sun in the Poultry, who was making his way to Holland ("his circumstances being somewhat perplexed"). Malthus brought him to the *Susannah and Thomas* of Captain Thomas Jenner, a 150-ton ship which was about to sail for Boston, carrying a crew of 16 sailors and 30 passengers - most of whom were "flying for safety upon the rout at Sedgemoor".[63] Dunton divided his venture of books between the *Susannah and Thomas* and another ship, commanded by Captain Moulton. After a certain amount of indecision, Dunton himself boarded Captain Jenner's ship. Late in October, the *Susannah and Thomas* sailed for Boston. Strong winds forced Jenner's ship to stay for some time at the Downs. During a severe storm, Captain Moulton's ship was lost there, taking with it half of Dunton's venture, which he valued at £500.[64] On

2 November, the _Susannah and Thomas_ left the Downs, only to take refuge a day later at Cowes. Dunton and the other passengers toured the Isle of Wight, and in a few days the _Susannah and Thomas_ was once again under way. Thereafter, the crossing was uneventful, except for the sighting of a Virginia merchant ship which was mistaken for a "Sallee-man" - which put Dunton into a cold sweat, and sent him flying below decks, under the pretext of searching for his ruffles.[65] Dunton was accompanied on the voyage by his apprentice, Samuel Palmer, who patiently nursed him through long periods of seasickness.

On 27 January 1686, after nearly three months at sea, the _Susannah and Thomas_ arrived safely at Boston.[66] "After I got safe upon Terra-firma," Dunton wrote "I could scarce keep my feet under me for several days; the Universe appeared to be one common whirlpool, and one would think that Cartes had contrived his vortices immediately after some tedious voyage".[67]

Dunton was made welcome in Boston by Francis Burroughs, a former member of Dr. Annesley's congregation, who gave him a bed, lent him money, and obtained for him the freedom of the city.[68] Dunton was occupied for several weeks with sight-seeing, meeting the clergymen and tradesmen of Boston, and writing a great number of letters to Iris, to his father-in-law, and to other friends in England. At first he considered disposing of his venture _en bloc_ to the Boston booksellers but discarded this idea when one day he paused "at the Door of Mr. Richard Wilkins, (opposite to the Town-house in Boston) 'Twas here in Capital Letters I found, LODGINGS TO BE LET, WITH A CONVENIENT WAREHOUSE. I found 'twas convenient for my Purpose, and so we soon made a Bargain, and Entred into such a Friendship as will scarce end with our Lives".[69]

Mr. Burroughs and other friends of Dr. Annesley helped Dunton socially. Soon he had made many friends and was invited to dine with the Governor and Magistrates in the Town Hall.

Dunton's particular friends in New England included a number of the ladies of Boston, as well as many clergymen. Among these two groups were found his best customers. Apparently Dunton considered settling permanently in Boston and wrote to Iris to suggest it. She replied in May that it was impossible for her to leave London at that time, as she was still struggling to pay debts that Dunton was bound for. "If there is any encouragement for settling in New-England," Iris wrote to her husband "I will joyfully come over to you; but am rather for your going to Holland, to trade there".[70]

As the news of Dunton's venture spread, the Boston booksellers made an attempt to buy him out at wholesale. Mr. Usher was sent to propose the matter to Dunton, but they came to no agreement.[71] Dunton's retail trade flourished, and he was understandably unwilling to allow a wholesale discount to the trade; the works that Dunton had brought to Boston were "well suited to the genius of New England, so that, ... they began to move apace". "Palmer," Dunton wrote "... was very honest and diligent; took the whole charge of my business off my hands, and left me to ramble and divert myself as my fancy would suggest".[72] And so while his apprentice attended to the daily work of the warehouse, Dunton skipped about Boston and New England, sightseeing and making new friends for his venture. He travelled first to Cambridge, where he met Increase and Cotton Mather, and sold books to the students at Harvard College, then to Roxbury, where the Reverend John Eliot presented him with a dozen copies of his Indian Bible and took him to Natick to observe the customs of the Indians.[73] On his return to Boston, Dunton published a copy he had secured from Increase Mather, a sermon which he had heard Mather preach before a condemned man, shortly after his arrival in New England.[74]

In Boston, Dunton was more closely involved in his business than he generally was in London, and he included in his Life and Errors several anecdotes about his Boston customers' exasperating ways. For one, Mrs. Ab--l inquired at his warehouse for The School of Venus; lacking it, Dunton suggested The School of Virtue, "but that was a Book she had no occasion for". Another customer looked aimlessly about the warehouse, until Dunton "asked her in joke, whether she would not buy the History of Tom Thumb? She told me 'Yes.' Upon which I asked her whether she would have it in folio, with marginal notes" To which she only said, 'The best, the best'".[74a] "He that trades with the inhabitants of Boston" Dunton reflected "whould be well furnished with a Grecian Faith; he may get promises enough, but their payments come late".[75]

Palmer had done his job well, but the market in Boston was saturated, and Dunton began to discover the difficulties of collecting the accounts of his enthusiastic customers. On his return from Natick "there were about two thirds of my Venture of Books; gone off; and I was fearful to sell any more at Boston till the old scores were discharged; for, besides all the money I had taken, there was about four hundred pounds owing me, in Boston and the towns adjacent".[76] Dunton therefore decided to send the remainder of his venture north to Salem, where "several Gentlemen have given me great Encouragement, (by their Promises of Assisting me in the Disposal of them) ... and particularly one Mr. Sewel, who is a Magistrate in that Town, has given me Assurance of a Kind Reception there".[77] Dunton found a suitable warehouse in Salem, and the venture of books was again left to Palmer's capable management while Dunton visited his friends in the town and made the acquaintance of the local ministers, "for you know, Reader, they are the greatest Benefactors to Booksellers; so that, my paying them a visit was but, in other words, to go among my Customers".[78]

The remainder of Dunton's venture was easily sold at Salem, and he began to think of returning to London. Palmer, who was unwilling to return to England (having "dabbled" in Monmouth's adventure), remained in Salem. Dunton travelled south to Boston, where he entrusted debts of ₤300 to Richard Wilkins, said farewell to his numerous friends, and boarded Samuel Leg's ship to return to England.[79] Dunton was one of only three passengers on the eastbound crossing, and the sea on the passage home was as singularly calm as on the passage out it had been turbulent. Dunton sailed from Boston on 5 July 1686, and he arrived in London exactly one month later.[80]

Captain Leg's ship lay at anchor at Gravesend for a night, and then proceeded to Ratcliffe, where Dunton disembarked, carrying his trunk and ₤400, which had nearly been stolen at Gravesend. He went first to see his sister Mary, who gave him news of Iris. "I was now afraid that excess of joy might prove fatal to Iris;" Dunton wrote "and therefore I thought it would be more prudent not to discover myself all at once".[81] Accordingly, he walked directly to the Queen's-head

Tavern at Spital Fields and sent word to his wife (presumably at her father's house in Spital Yard) that at the tavern she would find a gentleman who could give her news of her husband. Iris arrived within the hour, and the couple had a joyous reunion.

Dunton's hopes for a life of ease were shattered when he learned that despite Iris's efforts to clear his debts, he was still so deeply involved on behalf of his sister-in-law, that he dared not let his creditors know of his return. For ten months, Dunton lived in confinement (perhaps in his father-in-law's house), unable to attend even Dr. Annesley's meetings. On one occasion only did he venture out of doors, and that adventure nearly had disastrous results. Impatient with his restricted life, especially on Sundays, Dunton determined to hear Dr. Annesley preach, and he contrived

> "that dear Iris should dress me in woman's cloaths, and I would venture myself abroad under those circumstances. To make short of it, I got myself shaved, and put on as effeminate a look as my countenance would let me; and being well fitted out with a large scarf, I set forward; but every step I took, the fear was upon me that it was made out of form. As for my arms, I could not tell how to manage them, being altogether ignorant to what figure they should be reduced. At last I got safe to the Meeting, and sat down in the obscurest corner I could find. But, as I was returning through Bishopsgate-street, with all the circumspection and the care imaginable (and I then thought I had done it pretty well), there was an unlucky rogue cried out, 'I'll be hang'd if that ben't a man in woman's cloaths.' This put me into my preternaturals indeed, and I began to scour off as fast as my legs

> would carry me: there were at least 20 or 30 of them that made after me; but, being acquainted with the alleys, I dropped them, and came off with honour".[82]

By the early summer of 1687, Dunton had endured nearly a year of hiding in his own house, and he determined to leave London for a ramble to the Low Countries. Accompanied by Iris and a few friends, he travelled first to Stratford, and then to Harwich, where he found a packet-boat about to sail for Brill.[83] In Rotterdam, the fugitive lodged with his sister-in-law and her husband, Mr. Richardson, and he soon made the acquaintance of the English ministers resident there, as well as Mr. Leers, the chief bookseller in Holland.[84] Dunton longed for the company of his wife, and he wrote to her of his loneliness. But Dr. Annesley was unwilling to allow his daughter to undertake such a journey, and, moreover, Iris was occupied in adjusting the affairs of her sister which had necessitated her husband's flight.[85]

From Rotterdam, Dunton travelled through Overskirk to Delft, thence to The Hague, and to Leyden, Haarlem, and Amsterdam, where he stayed four months.[86] In Amsterdam, where he lodged in the same house as John Partridge, the astrologer, Dunton encountered supporters of Monmouth's rebellion who had fled there in 1685. Among these was his friend and former neighbour, Captain Benjamin Alsop, who related to him the "secret history of Monmouth's Adventure for the Crown of

England".

"Holland is a very temperate climate for distressed Debtors;" Dunton reflected "for there you cannot throw a man in prison, unless you subsist him; so that there is very little encouragement for the generation of Pettyfoggers, who have done so much mischief in England".[87]

Leaving Amsterdam, Dunton journeyed to Cleves and Rhineberg, through Dusseldorf to Cologne, and finally to Mainz. He wrote very briefly of his European travel in his Life and Errors, as he planned to relate his experiences at length in a "History of My Travels". Although Dunton became acquainted with the chief booksellers in the towns which he visited, the journey had not been undertaken primarily for business. "Let it, therefore," Dunton concluded the account of his ramble, "be sufficient that, when I had gratified my curiosity, and spent my money, I returned to Rotterdam, and embarked for England".[88]

CHAPTER II

MATURITY IN THE TRADE

(1688-98)

When William of Orange landed at Torbay, Devon, on 5 November 1688, John Dunton was _en route_ from Rotterdam to London. After a "long and dangerous passage", he arrived safely in London on 15 November, where he found "dear Iris in health, and all my affairs in peace".[1] Dunton readjusted to the English climate and recovered his appetite after a rough passage. "I was no sooner landed in England," he wrote "but I was straight metamorphosed into a _Quaker_, and sensibly found this climate colder than in Germany. I was now so hungry, that fresh provisions made me eat abundantly; and, ... every meal was from morning till night; .... And it was a merry world with me now, to be sure; for ... it turned round wherever I went; so that for me now to contradict Copernicus's System, ... was to contradict my very senses". Meanwhile, the Prince of Orange and his retinue made their way to Salisbury and then to London. Late at night on 17 December, Dutch guards took charge of St. James's Palace; the following afternoon the Prince himself arrived. On 18 December John Evelyn recorded that

> "All the world go to see the Prince at St. Jamess where is a greate Court, there I saw him & severall of my Acquaintance come over with him: He is very stately, serious & reserved: The Eng: souldiers &c. sent out of Towne to distant quarters: not well pleased: Divers reports & opinions, what all this will end in: Ambition & Faction feared".[2]

John Dunton was probably not among the crowd at St. James's that afternoon, for in the Poultry, he was again trading as a bookseller, under his old sign of the Black Raven. "The humour of *rambling* was now pretty well off with me," Dunton wrote in his *Life and Errors*, and my thoughts began to fix rather upon Business. The Shop I took, with the sign of the Black Raven, stood opposite to the Poultry Compter, where I traded ten years, ... with variety of successes and disappointments. My Shop was opened just upon the Revolution; and, as I remember, the same day the Prince of Orange came to London."[3]

The shop at the Black Raven in the Poultry which Dunton reopened in 1688 was the shop he had taken over from Benjamin Alsop when Alsop left the trade to accept a commission in Monmouth's army.[4] While Dunton had rambled - and hidden from his creditors, Jonathan Greenwood had traded at the Black Raven. Greenwood, formerly apprenticed to Thomas Cockerill, had been made free of the Stationers' Company in March 1680.[5] From Michaelmas 1681 to Michaelmas 1683, Greenwood had advertised in the Term Catalogues from the Crown in the Poultry,[6] and in Hilary Term 1685 he advertised John Tutchin's _Poems on Several Occasions_ as sold by him at the Raven in the Poultry.[7] Greenwood, who was a member of Dr. Annesley's congregation, was favorably mentioned by Dunton in his _Life and Errors_. He retired from trade sometime after 1685, "with as small a pittance of the World as he had to begin it".[8] There appears to have been no further business relationship between Dunton and Greenwood beyond their agreement for Greenwood's use of Dunton's premises during his absence. It is curious that Greenwood abandoned his own signboard for the Raven, but the reputation and accumulated goodwill of the shop at the Raven were doubtless superior to that of the Crown. Although their names never appeared jointly on a title-page or advertisement, Dunton was closely acquainted with Greenwood and apparently admired him greatly. "He deserves the love and esteem of all good men," Dunton wrote of him, "for the worst that can be said of him is, "There goes a poor honest Man'". Although Dr. Annesley and Greenwood's friends in the trade gave him constant encouragement, his diligence went unrewarded.[9]

The fact that Dunton was able to return to England in 1688 and obtain the credit necessary to engage again in publishing, and to acquire a saleable stock of books, must for the most part be attributed to Elizabeth Dunton's skilful and efficient management of his affairs in London. Dunton had not carried his entire stock to New England. He retained his London warehouse, and Iris very capably managed the wholesale trade. Iris's labor to reduce the amount of Dunton's debt is evidenced by a letter she wrote to her husband in New England, regretting that she was prevented from joining him there; it was impossible for her to leave London until she had paid the money for which he was bound.[10] When a few years later Dunton was absent briefly from London, he admitted on his return that his wife had accomplished more in his warehouse in a month than he could have done in a year.[11] Plainly, Mrs. Dunton had a finer head for business than her husband. Apparently, it was not necessary for Iris to sell any of her husband's copyrights to meet his obligations. Later editions published before his retirement of works originally published by Dunton before 1685 still bore his imprint. Furthermore, so large were Dunton's reserves that quantities of a variety of titles remained in stock in 1688 and were used to help re-establish him in the trade. Of fourteen works advertised by Dunton in Stephen Jay's _Tragedies of Sin_, 1689, six had been originally issued by him in 1682 and 1683.[12]

* * * *

In 1712, the anonymous author of <u>A Caveat against the Whiggs</u> wrote that

> "[the Whiggs] have gone farther yet, and in imitation of their elder brothers, the papists, have furnish'd out a new Martyrology of those Holy Ones who died for rebellion and treason, so that they can not only turn religion into rebellion but sanctifie rebellion into religion, and by a dash of their pen change a pernicious crew of rebels and traytors into a noble army of Saints and Martyrs. 'Tis a great pity that highwaymen and housebreakers cannot do the like kindness for their poor, suffering, persecuted bretheren!"[13]

John Dunton, both as bookseller and as part-author, was largely responsible for the "new Martyrology". The details of the publication of this work provide a revealing example of members of the book trade co-operating to take advantage of popular enthusiasm for subjects of topical interest.

<u>The Protestant Martyrs</u> was published early in 1689, printed by J. Bradford, at the Bible in Fetter Lane.[14] Whether

or not Dunton had any share in the production of this tract is not known;[15] but observing its increasing success, Dunton judged that similar works were assured of a ready sale and straightaway issued a collection of speeches of those who suffered under Lord Jeffreys in the "bloody Assizes", followed closely by an additional collection of dying speeches. Dunton, John Harris, William Rogers and Timothy Goodwin shared in the publication of these works, although only the name of Richard Janeway, another bookseller noted for his fanatical devotion to the Whig cause, appeared on the title page with that of John Dunton.[16] These collections of "dying speeches" were in turn followed into print by a life of Lord Jeffreys, The Bloody Assizes. This was printed in quarto, Dunton advertised, that it might conveniently be bound up with those pamphlets already published.

The authorship of these pamphlets cannot be ascribed to any single writer or compiler. It is abundantly evident, however, that with characteristic readiness to satisfy the public appetite for sensational pamphlets, Dunton mustered a team of hackney writers and set them to work compiling the "martyrology". Dunton was never scrupulous about the accuracy or authority of his sources, nor was he reluctant to print whatever material he could gather without payment. In fact, he advertised for contributions from the public, to be sent to him at the Raven for inclusion in a further volume. The chief part in compiling these dying speeches may be assigned to John Tutchin, *alias* Thomas Pitts, who had himself taken part in the rebellion and been tried and sentenced by Jeffreys, who was later bribed to grant him pardon.

A number of writers have discussed these works, but J. G. Muddiman has most clearly illuminated the question of their authorship.[17] Muddiman correctly identified Pitts with Tutchin but failed to observe that Dunton, in his *Life and Errors*, had identified Pitts as part author of *The Bloody Assizes*, with John Shirley, a very accomplished hack, according to Dunton.[18] The dedication, however, of *The Bloody Assizes*, 1689, was signed "James Bent", which most writers have assumed to be a pseudonym of John Dunton. When later in the year all the "Western Transactions" were collected into the *New Martyrology*, Titus Oates, who then lodged with Tutchin in Westminster, joined the team of compilers. This third edition of the *New Martyrology* was issued in the summer of 1689. A fourth, "By Thomas Pitts", appeared in 1693, and a fifth in 1705. *De Bloedige Vierschaar* also was published in Amsterdam in 1689. Perhaps the most instructive picture of the literary assembly-line technique is to be found in Dunton's portrait of John Shirley:

"Mr. Shirley ... is a good-natured Writer as I know. He has been an indefatigable Press-mauler for above these twenty years. He has published at least a hundred bound Books, and about two hundred Sermons; but the cheapest, pretty, pat things, all of them pence apiece as long as they will run. His great talent lies at _Collection_, and he will do it for you at six shillings a sheet. He knows to disguise an Author that you shall not know him, and yet keep the sense and the main scope entire. He is as true as steel to his word, and would slave off his feet to oblige a Bookseller .... After all, he subsists, as other Authors must expect, by a sort of Geometry".[19]

The Bloody Assizes project was a successful venture for all concerned. For his part, Dunton was well pleased; he stated in his _Life and Errors_ that he sold six thousand copies of "Lord Jeffrey's 'Life'".[20] The success of these pamphlets, after less than a year in the trade, had so well established Dunton that he was later able to recall that "In the year 1689 I had no less than thirty Printers, &c. that traded with me".[21] Also in 1689, Dunton took a new apprentice, Robert Wright, who in March was bound to him for seven years.[22]

Once again well underway in business, Dunton had before him nearly ten years of bookselling activity at the Black Raven. Dunton's career reached its peak in 1693 and 1694. In each of these years he was involved in nearly three dozen projects. His volume of publishing declined after that peak, and the lapse of licensing requirements in 1695 resulted in much keener competion, especially in the field of periodicals, in which he was very active. Attacks of the "stone" began to trouble Dunton in those years, and his domestic harmony was shattered in 1697 by the death of his beloved Iris, who alone had been capable of exercising a levelling influence on her flighty spouse. After a brief period of tranquility in retirement, Dunton's life lapsed into chaos shortly after his marriage, in 1697, to Sarah Nicholas, the daughter of a rich widow of St. Albans. Upon learning that his mother-in-law would not be cajoled into placing her fortune at his disposal, Dunton fled London with a cargo of books and passed an unhappy year in Dublin, feuding with booksellers there. During this period Dunton boasted of a great number of successful ventures, and he conveniently rationalised a small number of failures. Dunton's successes and failures may generally be attributed to the same cause: his highly original, but unstable, turn of mind. Whatever funds Iris had been able to accumulate by careful husbanding of his stock, Dunton squandered on new schemes which he believed certain to improve his fortune. But although he was occasionally able to materialise his visions, his fancy had generally leapt to something new before these visions had been fully developed.

Through the decade of the 1690's, Dunton was involved in many highly complex (and often confused) business ventures. The rest of this chapter, and the two chapters immediately following, will examine Dunton's activities in the trade during this period.

Dunton's Publications

Dunton claimed to have published more than six hundred works during his years in the trade.[23] Taking into account his penchant for extravagant personal claims, one finds the figure impressive. The total number of ventures which he engaged in may well have approached that figure, although only a fraction of the total survives. Dunton was not a frequent advertiser in the Term Catalogues, and during the 1690's he advertised only 71 works, 37 of them in his most productive year, 1693. Wing's *Short Title Catalogue* lists 106 separate works with Dunton's imprint.[24] The checklist appended to this work names 185 publications originated by Dunton during this period, including 11 periodicals, as well as 29 new editions of older works. Dunton himself can be identified as author or part-author of about two dozen of these works. These figures compare favourably with those available for two leading booksellers of the eighteenth century, Edmund Curll and Robert Dodsley. In forty years in the book trade, 1706-1746, Curll published over 1,000 items; Dodsley, in 35 years, 1729-1764, issued over 900.[25] Alongside these titans of the trade, Dunton holds his own. The 214 publications which can be assigned to him for the ten years 1689-1698 amount to an impressive output for the period. Curll and Dodsley, it must be remembered, profited from a rapidly growing reading public, in the country as well as in London, which had only begun to develop in the 1690's when Dunton flourished, his activities confined almost entirely to the metropolis of London.

Characterising London booksellers in his Life and Errors, Dunton often mentioned their political and religious connections. These considerations were important in determining a man's fortunes. His former master, Thomas Parkhurst, was "the most eminent Presbyterian Bookseller in the Three Kingdoms .... When Mr. Parkhurst dies, [John Laurence] will be the first Presbyterian Bookseller in England".[26] These men were Dunton's neighbours in the Poultry and his associates in business. Religious works - sermons, devotional books, and works generally of "rich Protestant porridge" - constituted the bulk of Dunton's stock. Dunton published for his father-in-law, Dr. Annesley, and with his help secured the works of many other eminent divines.[27] Dunton's trade was firmly built on small, low-priced, fast-selling works, the profits from which generally found their way back into the business, generally to finance some new "project" for the delight of the "intellectual virtuosi". Chapbooks, "practical books", and periodicals, with their attractive chances of large return for little risk, also sold well for Dunton, and a significant part of his trade was in political and historical works.

Increase Mather, whom Dunton had visited at Harvard College during his New England ramble, was in London late in 1689. When his son Cotton sent him the manuscript of his memorial of Nathanael Mather, he took it for publication to Dunton. _Early Piety, Exemplified in the Life and Death of Mr. Nathanael Mather_, which sold two editions in 1689, was the first of several profitable works by the Mathers which Dunton published in London. While in New England, Dunton had published Increase Mather's _Sermon Occasioned by the Execution of a Man_, 1686, of which he issued a London edition in 1691. Later, Dunton published Increase Mather's _Wonders of Free Grace_ in 1690, and two editions, in 1691 and 1694, of the life of another of Dunton's Boston acquaintances, John Eliot, by

Cotton Mather. Perhaps the most successful of the works that Dunton published as the London agent for Cotton and Increase Mather were their accounts of the New England witch trials. Cotton Mather's Wonders of the Invisible World sold three editions in London in 1693, and Increase Mather prepared A Further Account of the Tryals in the same year. The long and mutually profitable relationship Dunton had with his New England friends was finally brought to an end, in 1697, by Dunton's decision to leave the trade. In William Turner's Compleat History of the Most Remarkable Providences, 1697, Dunton advertised that he had in the press Increase Mather's Dissertation Concerning the Future Conversion of the Jewish Nation, and that Cotton Mather's Church History of New England would be printed in folio, published by subscription, as soon as the manuscript copy came to Dunton's hands. But Dunton retired, and the Dissertation was eventually printed by R. Tookey for Nath. Hillier in 1709.[28] Cotton Mather's Church History, after a great many difficulties, was printed for Thomas Parkhurst in 1702, as Magnalia Christi Americana.[29]

The year 1690 saw Dunton issue the fourth large volume of his father-in-law's popular morning-exercise sermons. Three earlier volumes of Dr. Annesley's Casuistical Morning-Exercises had been printed in 1661, 1674, and in 1683 for Dunton who had a large trade from the distinguished preacher's congregation. Dunton encouraged morality by the publication of William Barlow's Treatise of Fornication, and An Antidote against Lust, by Robert Carr, "a small Poetical Insect, ... [who] has nothing but his chastity to recommend him".[30] Dunton's first best-selling devotional manual was his third edition, in 1690, of Henry Lukin's Practice of Godliness, which had appeared previously in two editions in 1659. This work was astonishingly popular, if Dunton's memory in 1704 may be trusted, as he claimed to have had printed 10,000 copies of this edition.[31] Only Dr. Williams's copy has been located, however, in his library in London.

1691 was a remarkably creative year for Dunton. In addition to launching the Athenian Society (see below, Chapter III) and skilfully putting down several rivals, Dunton issued 19 new works, several of which he compiled himself. Religio Bibliopolae was one of many imitations of the Religio Medici, an obvious attempt by Dunton to profit from the success of Browne's work. It contains no information relevant to a study of the book trade, and a good part of its religious sentiments have been shown to be plagiarised from other sources.[32] Religio Bibliopolae was mainly a labour of collection, in which several hackney authors are known to have had a hand, as well as Dunton. Although the work is ascribed to "Benj. Bridgwater, Gent.", on the title-page, the prefatory note "To the Reader" admits that "The Author of this Treatise not having leisure to finish this Piece as he intended, being call'd aside upon unavoidable Reasons, we have been compell'd to supply that Defect by another Hand, yet with all the care possible to reach the Air, and Stile of the Author". Benjamin Bridgwater has frequently been identified as a pseudonym for John Dunton without reference to Dunton's portrait of Bridgwater in the _Life and Errors_:

> "[Mr. Ben Bridgwater] was of Trinity College in Cambridge, and M.A. His genius was very rich, and ran much upon Poetry, in which he excelled. He was, in part, Author of 'Religio Bibliopolae.' But, alas! in the issue, Wine and Love were the ruin of this ingenious Gentleman".[33]

A copy of _Religio Bibliopolae_ exists, containing a note in a contemporary hand stating that "The first part was written by the son of Albion Bradshaw who was a servitour in Oxford and pupill to Mr. Wull or Wills."[34] Mr. Bradshaw may be identified with William Bradshaw, "the best accomplished hackney-author I have met with", whom Dunton also identified as the author of _The Turkish Spy_.[35] According to Dunton, during the years of writing _The Turkish Spy_ (1687-93), Bradshaw avoided meeting him, as he had abandoned a project for which Dunton had paid him and had supplied writing materials and books. Dunton specifically stated that Bradshaw's disappearance occurred before _The Turkish Spy_ was first published, and that he afterwards had "no more intelligence of Mr. Bradshaw". Dunton wrote in the same paragraph, however, that Bradshaw wrote for him The _Parable of the Magpyes_ - and the _Parable_ was published in 1691, the year of publication of _Religio Bibliopolae_.

Religio Bibliopolae is chiefly remarkable for the candour of its publisher in advertising that it had not been written entirely by the author named on the title-page. The work had surprisingly large circulation. It was reprinted five times in London, before 1750; it was discussed in the Oxford letter of _l'Histoire des Ouvrages des Savans_ for November, 1694,[36] and it was translated into German in 1737.[37]

Though his ordinary publications often involved collection and collaboration, Dunton produced a work of great originality in his _A Voyage Round the World_, written in 1691. But he had second thoughts about it and in 1704 considered it a product of his youthful exuberance which he listed among his seven repented books, solemnly advising that it be burned.[38] Dunton's _Voyage_ was a development of an unsuccessful periodical of 1689, _A Ramble Round the World_. A considerable amount of autobiography was included in this account of the "rare adventures of Don Kainophilus, from his Cradle to his 15th Year, ... [and] During his Seven Years Prenticeship". Although Dunton was masked by the pseudonym Kainophilus

Evander, and the work was printed for Richard Newcome, Dunton's authorship was hardly concealed. The panegyrical verses prefixed to the work included "The Author's Name When Anagramatized is Hid unto None". The work was, in fact, an early sketch of his Life and Errors.

A Voyage Round the World did not pass entirely unnoticed from the world in 1691, nor has it escaped occasional critical comment in recent years. J. M. Stedmond cited it as "an example par excellence of the very Grub Street formlessness which Swift ... claimed to be, in part, satirizing in the Tale [of a Tub]". He tentatively suggested that "it is not outside the bounds of possibility that Dunton's title, so little justified by the actual contents of his book, may even have played some small part in suggesting to Swift the idea of the voyages of Lemuel Gulliver".[39]

The interest of Laurence Sterne in the work is more clearly traceable. The first volume of A Voyage was reprinted, in 1762, as The Life, Travels, and Adventures, of Christopher Wagstaff, Gentleman, Grandfather to Tristram Shandy. The anonymous editor, who added several chapters to the first volume of Dunton's work to complete it in two volumes, reprinted it "as a proof that Shandeism (or something very like it) had an existence in this kingdom long before a late well-known publication". Pointing out similarities between the two works, the editor suggested "either that the author of _Tristram Shandy_ took the hints and grounds of his work from the adventures of _Kainophilus_, his predecessor ... or that the similarity between them is in many instances so very striking, that the matter deserves to be refer'd to the judgment and curiosity of the public".[40] According to Wilbur Cross, "When Sterne was charged with plagiarizing from Dunton, he wrote to a friend to say that he once met with the book in a London circulating Library and took from it 'many of his ideas.' The very copy of Dunton that Sterne read now rests, it is probable, in the Boston Public Library".[41]

Recalling the events of 1692, Dunton wrote: "The World now smiled on me. I sailed with wind and tide, and had humble servants enough among the Stationers, Booksellers, Printers, and Binders: but especially my own Relations, on every side, were all upon the very height of love and tenderness".[42] Dunton's cousin Elizabeth Carter died in 1692, and Dunton inherited two estates in Chesham, Buckinghamshire.[43] "And now the Master and Assistants of the Company of Stationers began to think me sufficient to wear a Livery; and in the year 1692 they honoured me with the Cloathing". Dunton paid his livery fine of £20. A year later he formed a friendly society with John Harris and about fifty other liverymen, pledging to pay twelve shillings annually to the Renter-Warden to provide "a costly Entertainment to the whole Company".[44] The Master and Wardens of the Company then invited Dunton to dine with the Lord Mayor, Sir William Ashurst. "We went in a body from the Poultry Church to Grocers' Hall, where the entertainment was very generous, and a noble Spoon he sent to our Wives".[45] Dunton was greatly impressed by the occasion, and by the Lord Mayor. "To speak the Truth, I do not think Sir William Ashurst ever acted a little or a mean thing in his whole life". Throughout his subsequent misfortunes, Dunton avoided pawning his silver spoon. He still had it in 1711, when he gave it, in his will, to his adopted daughter.[46]

Besides his financial and social success, the year 1692 proved to be an active one in other ways. The Athenian Society flourished, and in 1692 Dunton issued The Young Students Library, The Visions of the Soul, Before it comes into the Body, and A Scheme of Enquiries ... to form a Body of the Natural, Artificial and Civil History of England. Dunton emerged victor from a feud with the compiler of The Works of the Learned, (see below, Chapter IV) and he began The Compleat Library. Daniel Williams's Gospel-Truth Stated and Vindicated involved Dunton in a pamphlet battle. Dunton also issued a strongly anti-Quaker tract by Francis Bugg, sermons by Timothy Rogers, Samuel Annesley and Edmund Hickeringill, and an historical account of earthquakes. The Athenian Mercury assured a querist that books were indeed more properly given at funerals than biscuits, gloves, or rings,[47] and Dunton issued a funeral present, containing a variety of his father's macabre sentiments appropriate to these occasions. A Mourning Ring, In Memory of your Departed Friend, provided a space on the title-page for the inscription of the name of the deceased, and reassuring essays on "The Sick-Mans Passing-Bell", "The Fatal Moment", and "Observations on the Bills of Mortality".

In The Compleat Library for July 1692, the "News of Learning" recorded that in London, there was "in the Press, a new-Piece the like whereof has hardly ever yet seen the Light". The new piece, which appeared late in September, was The Post-Boy Rob'd of his Mail: Or, The Pacquet Broke Open. "Green heads are very ill judges of the productions of the mind ...." Dunton later wrote, repenting of his part in this and several other youthful projects. "Novelties have charms that are very taking, but ... those false lights are dispelled upon a serious review, and second thoughts are wiser than the first".[48] Written by Charles Gildon, the work concerned "a Company of wild, but witty, and not unlearned Gentlemen, meeting by chance with the Post In The Road, to have robbed him in a Frolick, and then going aside to one of their Companions Country Houses, to have read the Letters".[49] As the story went, innocent letters were sent on to their destinations; but those exposing the "hidden tricks and dark intrigues of States-Men [and] the little and great Contrivances too of private men" were printed. The project evidently enjoyed a measure of success, for a second volume appeared in 1693, and the two volumes were reprinted in 1706 and 1719. R. J. Allen has observed that The Post-boy Rob'd is remarkable as an early example of the use of a club framework in fiction. The Athenian Society, as will be shown, made effective use of the club framework as a means of lending authority to their pronouncements on a variety of subjects; Gildon, who had compiled The History of the Athenian Society, derived the club idea from the Athenian Society. He attributed to the anonymous members of his club the authorship of the work in order to disassociate himself from the affair. R. J. Allen praised Gildon's originality, observing that Gildon's "development of a fictitious society of gentlemen credited with authorship is more complete than any attempt of this sort before the device reached its highest form in the essay periodicals".[50]

In 1693, Dunton reached the peak of his activities at the Black Raven. The volume of his trade in that year, including new editions of older works, was twice that of 1692; in 1694, the number of his new publications decreased slightly. Dunton had not previously advertised extensively in the Term Catalogues, but in 1693 thirty-seven works were advertised in his name. Thirty-four new works are identified in the checklist, and eight new editions. During that busy year, Dunton found time to write only one work himself, England's Alarum. But he contributed to his two successful periodicals, The Athenian Mercury and The Compleat Library, and he compiled proposals for three new projects. Dunton published tracts for Francis Bugg and George Keith, and he engaged in further controversy with the Quakers. A sizable number of religious and devotional works appeared at the Black Raven, including sermons by Stephen Lobb and Thomas Whitaker, meditations by Francis Crow, and An Account of the Conversion of Theodore John, a late Teacher among the Jews. Concerned, as always, for the spiritual welfare of the young, Dunton published Samuel Pomfret's Directory for Youth ... Or a Discourse of Youthful Lusts, and An Earnest Call to the Family-Catechising. Cotton Mather's Wonders of the Invisible World proved highly profitable, going through three editions in 1693, and Increase Mather supplied A Further Account of the Tryals of the New-England Witches. Translations were rather more speculative ventures; Dunton issued several substantial translations in 1693, not, in every case, profitably. Gabriel de Foigny's New Discovery of Terra Incognita Australis evidently paid its way, but John Conrad Werndly's translation of the Liturgia Tigurina did not, for "many hundred reams" of that work were later sold to Mr. Tyson, in Redcross Street, "the Waste-paper Stationer of London".[51] Another ambitious project, the translation of Elie Benoit's History of the Famous Edict of Nantes, so pleased Queen Mary that she gave to her "trusty and well-beloved John Dunton" royal licence for the sole printing and publishing of the work, the only royal licence, Dunton proudly claimed, that Queen Mary issued.[52] After a six-months campaign of advertising and distribution of proposals, the first volume appeared late in 1693. Volume two came out in 1694, but Dunton discontinued the project , and once again "many hundred reams" were sold to Mr. Tyson.[53] Dunton also published two works for Sir Peter Pett, his Memoirs of the ... Earl of Anglesey, and the controversial Remains of Bishop Barlow. Another novelty, undertaken by Dunton and John Harris in 1693, was the mathematician William Leybourn's Panarithmologia, Being A Mirror [Breviate, Treasure, Mate] for Merchants [Bankers, Tradesmen, Mechanicks] And a Sure Guide for Purchasers, Sellers, or Mortgagers of Land, Leases, Annuities, Rents, Pensions, &c. This work was described by C. E. Kenney as "undoubtedly the most enduring of all Leybourn's works: the large ready reckoner as we know it today, ... first produced by Leybourn in 1693". The extent to which the public found the volume useful, as Kenney observed, may be judged by the scarcity of surviving copies of the first edition.[54]

Throughout the year 1693, Dunton was involved in controversy concerning a publication which was at the same time his most profitable tract and his most repented project. In December 1692, Richard Sault put into Dunton's hands a manuscript which he claimed to have compiled from notes made by the attending clergyman at the deathbed of "an Atheist who had apostatized from the Christian Religion and died in despaire at Westminster, December 8th 1692". Dunton saw the tract quickly through the press. Publication was announced in the December number of _The Compleat Library_, and on 9 January 1693 _The Second Spira_ was issued. Dunton chose his title well, as the story of the original Spira was widely known and had had a large circulation. Nathaniel Bacon's translation of _A Relation of the Fearful Estate of Francis Spira, 1548_, had been published in 1638. Bunyan's account of Spira in _Grace Abounding_ had undoubtedly had a great influence on its popularity, and thirteen editions of the work were published before 1695.[55] "Nothing had ever so satisfied the morbid desire of English Calvinists to know just how a doomed 'rebrobate,' - a soul predestined _ab aeterno_ to become a vessel of divine wrath - felt at the approach of death", wrote C. A. Moore, "as did a book describing in detail the dying agonies of the Italian lawyer Francis Spira, a sixteenth-century convert to the Protestant religion who finally yielded to the threats of the

Roman Catholic Church, made a recantation, and thereby incurred certain destruction, as of course he was all along pre-destined to do".[56] The Second Spira sold so well that Dunton was able to advertise the fifth edition in March; 30,000 copies, he wrote, were sold in six weeks.[57]

No sooner had The Second Spira become known as a popular success than clergymen and interested laymen called at the Black Raven to query Dunton about the truth of it, and a neighbouring bookseller, Nathaniel Crouch, began to circulate rumours discrediting it.[58] Later editions of the work included testimonials to its authenticity, given by impartial witnesses who had examined the manuscript at Dunton's shop. The Athenian Mercury printed testimonials from Richard Wolley, who asserted that he was "every day more and more confirmed that my Judgment concerning [The Second Spira] had very good grounds" and from Dunton, who wrote at length to refute false reports concerning the work.[59] The preface to The Second Spira was signed J.S., allegedly the initials of the attending clergyman who had given the memoir to Sault. Although Sault identified him as the Reverend Mr. Sanders, he was unable to tell Dunton where Sanders lodged, and Sanders did not come forward to testify to the accuracy of Sault's story. Repenting of the work in his Life and Errors, Dunton stated his belief that Richard Sault himself was the Second Spira, that the letters of J. Sanders were "counterfeits of his own writing", and that he found it "hard to conceive how any man could write such a dismal narrative that did not himself feel what he there relates".[60] Protesting his innocence, Dunton called for Sanders and Sault to come forward and explain. But "if they will not vindicate themselves, I am not obliged to bear them company".[61] One further work by Sault, A Conference Betwixt a Modern Atheist and his Friend, appeared in 1693, but sold only one edition. Sault retired to Cambridge, where he taught algebra until his death in 1702. Dunton later recovered sufficiently from his embarrassment to publish, in 1719, the "thirtieth" edition of the work, to which he added "A Key to the Second Spira", reiterating his innocence in the affair. He included also an essay of his own writing, "Double Hell, or an Essay on Despair; Occasion'd by Mr. Richard Sault (the Second Spira) crying out of Mr. Dunton's hearing, I am Damn'd! I am Damn'd!"

The year 1694 was not quite so active for Dunton as 1693 had been, but he published nearly three dozen works. The translation of The History of the Famous Edict of Nantes finally appeared, but was discontinued after the second volume. However, staple items - sermons, devotional and controversial works - balanced the losses suffered from that ambitious failure. Lord Delamere's Works succeeded, and Roger Coke's Detection of the Court and State of England was highly profitable. William Leybourn's *Pleasure with Profit*, and Richard Sault's *Treatise of Algebra* appeared, impressive mathematical works in folio. Dunton published *Proposals for a National Reformation of Manners* and ministered to youth by *The Knowledge of the World; or, the Art of Well-Educating Youth*, translated from the French. Another profitable translation, Richard Sault's version of Malebranche's *Search after Truth*, involved Dunton in a dispute with Thomas Bennet, who had independently proposed to publish a translation of the same work by Mr. Taylor of Oxford.[62] In 1694, Dunton began a campaign of advertising and proposals for James Tyrrell's *General History of England*, a work which did not appear until 1696. To Sir William Temple, who was known to him as an enthusiastic supporter of the Athenian Society, Dunton wrote asking for advice and assistance with the proposed work. Advice, at least was forthcoming; Thomas Swift replied from Moorpark that Temple "wishes you Good success. He is of Opinion y^{t} ye best & readiest way to compile a good Generall History of England will be to take in all those parts of it wch have allready been writte by any Approved & esteemed Authors. And to write nothing new besides those parts wch have not yet been touched by any authors of name or Estimation ... but for w^{t} you desire of his Reviewing Altering or Correcting Such a Work He must be excused: being not of an Age or a Humour at

Present to engage in such a Trouble".[63]

Concern for the entertainment of the Fair Sex had always been evident in The Athenian Mercury. Regularly, issues of that paper were devoted entirely to answering their queries. After tantalising his readers for nearly a year by advertisement and discussion in the Mercury, Dunton published for the female virtuosi The Ladies Dictionary: Being A General Entertainment for the Fair Sex. Over seven hundred pages in length, this work was sold bound, for six shillings. The initials N. H. which appear under the dedication of the work conceal the fact that The Ladies Dictionary was yet another project of Dunton's literary assembly-line. This project became so large, however, that Dunton's team were not able to work closely together as in other projects, and duplicated a great deal of material. Gertrude E. Noyes, who examined the articles in The Ladies Dictionary in detail, wrote that "Only plural authorship could account reasonably for the constant repetition of items - many being treated twice and some three times - and for other overlapping material". She clearly demonstrated that "Upon scrutiny, The Ladies Dictionary proves to be a literary mosaic in which are pieced together, often maladroitly, information on and sentiments about women from practically every work of the century which specifically discussed that topic".[64]

In September 1694, Dunton moved from the noise and bustle of the Poultry to a house in Jewen Street, a short distance from his former location. He recorded few particulars of his new premises, but it is likely that they were a change to more modest surroundings. "Cloyed with the crowd of business", Dunton required more leisure for study and writing than he was able to find in the Poultry. Probably, also, the attacks of the "stone" which became a serious problem a few years later were beginning to trouble him.[65] After his removal to Jewen Street, Dunton shared a warehouse with his friend John Harris. Edmund Richardson, near the Poultry Church, stocked all of his publications and shared in many of them.[66] Richardson, an old friend and neighbour, was chiefly a binder, who bound most of Dunton's calf-leather books. Richardson took well to bookselling, however, and he, too, soon had a flourishing trade.[67]

The number of new works issued by Dunton in 1695 was a third of that of 1694. He published the second volume of Malebranche's Search after Truth, a translation of Balthazar Bekker's work on spirits, The World Bewitch'd, and a number of translations of sermons preached on the continent on the death of Queen Mary. William Turner's History of all the Religions in the World was the only sizable new work printed in that year. Dunton's restless temperament was satisfied, however.

In January he sold books at Bristol Fair; in August, he relaxed at Tunbridge Wells.[68]

A translation of Gerard Croese's *General History of the Quakers*, a tract by George Keith and a few sermons were published by Dunton in 1696, a year once again much less active than the preceding one, and one which brought the first of Dunton's personal misfortunes. James Tyrrell's *General History of England* appeared also, handsomely printed in folio with folding tables and royal pedigree charts, for Dunton, Henry Rhodes, John Harris and John Salusbury. The *Reliquiae Baxterianae*, with a funeral sermon on Richard Baxter by Matthew Sylvester, were also printed in folio, with an engraved portrait, for Dunton, Thomas Parkhurst, J. Robinson and John Laurence. Elizabeth Singer (later Mrs. Thomas Rowe), who as "Philomela" and as "The Pindarick Lady of the West" contributed a great deal of verse to the ladies' numbers of the *Athenian Mercury*, was at the time engaged in "Platonick Courtship" with Dunton. In 1696 he published her *Poems on Several Occasions*. In August, Dunton again followed the fashionable world to Tunbridge Wells, leaving Iris, as usual, behind the counter at the Black Raven.

William Fuller, scarcely a year out of prison, summered at Tunbridge Wells also in 1696, where he met noted Whigs and compiled his several tracts "discovering" the true mother of the Prince of Wales.[69] Dunton was deceived by this clever imposter, and he lent assistance to Fuller in publishing his tracts. In his autobiography, published in 1703, Fuller admitted that his assertions did not amount to real proof and charged that "the Affair was much improved by Mr. Richard Baldwin, John Dunton, and other Booksellers, who were zealous for the Cause, and as fond of the Gain they reap'd thereby".[70] "Mr. Fuller is not only a Villain," cried Dunton in his Life and Errors "but he is known to be so .... he has been such a mystery of iniquity, that the World had much ado to unriddle him". Dunton hotly denied Fuller's charge, calling it "the most formal lie I have met with, in regard the Copy was printed off before we saw it". But the "honest and innocent" appearance of the youthful charlatan Fuller deceived Dunton further, for he and Robin Hayhurst were persuaded on another occasion to accompany Fuller to Canterbury in search of "some 'State Letters' which were never in being". Fuller's extravagance shortly led him again to prison, and Dunton complained years later that he had not been reimbursed for the expenses of the Canterbury journey.[71]

In 1696, after the final number of the nineteenth volume, Dunton suspended publication of The Athenian Mercury, although the Athenian Society promised to resume it when the prevailing glut of news had abated. Many lively publications had arisen to compete with the rather staid _Athenian Mercury_, and the public followed the way of novelty. The public were no more inconstant than Dunton himself, whose own life was devoted to the pursuit of the original. Before the end of the year, he had begun two new periodicals. About November, Iris fell ill, and although she lingered some seven months, Dunton's trade suffered greatly from the loss of her direction. Yet another disappointment for Dunton, and certainly a blow to Iris, was the death of her father, Dr. Annesley, in December.

Dunton did not profit directly from the death of his eminent father-in-law, as Dr. Annesley's estate was divided among three of his youngest children. Only a shilling each was left to the others who survived of his twenty-five offspring.[72] Indirectly, however, Dunton turned the occasion to his advantage by publishing Dr. Annesley's funeral sermon, preached by Daniel Williams, and an elegy by Daniel Defoe. A few projects that had long been in preparation were completed in 1697, but Iris's illness continued, and Dunton's spirits wilted. Turner's _Compleat History of the Most Remarkable Providences_, announced in 1695, finally appeared, and another project announced for the fair sex in 1694, _The Challenge, ... Or, The Female War_. In May, Dunton revived _The Athenian Mercury_, but only for ten numbers. On 28 May 1697, Iris died.[73]

"Upon this very sad occasion," Dunton wrote "I put

about twenty of my own and Iris's relations into mourning; and she was carried in a hearse, with several coaches attending, to the New Burying-place, where she desired to be interred .... There I leave her till my life is run out; and then I will lie down by her in the dust till the general resurrection".[74] Throughout the Life and Errors, and in other works, Dunton celebrated Iris as an ideal wife, and their life together as a perpetual courtship. Certainly she was a capable steward of the business. While Dunton flew from one enthusiasm to another, Iris tended the shop, kept the accounts and provided constant encouragement for her mercurial husband. Selections from a spiritual diary which she kept for many years were printed with the funeral sermon preached for her by Timothy Rogers, in The Post Angel, and in Turner's Remarkable Providences. Throughout their married life, Iris had remained sympathetic to her husband's wanderlust, and her serenity was undisturbed by his erratic ways. Shortly after her death, Dunton retired from retail trade and resolved to spend his time in study and writing.

Dunton was still relatively young at the time of his wife's death. Then 38 years old, he lived a further 35 years, until 1732. His dependence on the managerial abilities of Iris had been absolute; she had effectively anchored her husband to the reality of earning a living. Incapable of carrying on trade in an ordinary, humdrum way, Dunton spent the remainder of his life as a free lance "projector", bargaining as best he could with the trade and excoriating those whom he considered to be interfering with his projects.

* * * *

Only one method of publication really satisfied Dunton's hankering for novelty: the publication of periodicals. In this enterprise, financial risk was minimal, and it was possible for the bookseller to withdraw before losses became great. Furthermore, profits could be realized much sooner than in book publishing. Many of Dunton's "periodicals" were on the border between serials and connected instalments of a narrative. Dunton's favourite means of testing the market for a project was to issue "Part I" and promise to continue if the project met with encouragement from the public. As was often the case with Dunton, he failed to exploit the wide possibilities of serial publication.

Familiar with the basic elements of publication in fascicules, Dunton was accustomed to printing collections of works with separate title pages, and he accommodated his customers by allowing them to purchase the works singly. But he failed to foresee that the same buyers who spent only sixpence at one time buying sermons piecemeal might be persuaded to purchase Tyrrell's General History of England, for example, at sixpence a sheet. Twenty years after his retirement from the trade, he was still trying to persuade booksellers to issue his tracts, "secret histories", and the like, which he promised to continue in parts, "if the venture meets with encouragement".

While Dunton was re-establishing himself in the trade in 1689, and issuing volumes of dying speeches with Richard Janeway, he wrote, and Janeway published, The True Protestant Mercury, or an Impartial History of the Times. This periodical appeared on Fridays, and ran for ten issues, 6 December 1689 to 7 February 1690. In it, Dunton was the sole advertiser. A Ramble Round the World; or, the Most Pleasant Travels, Voyages, and Adventures of Kainophilus was also printed for Janeway, and issued for only two numbers, 6 and 8 November 1689. Two years later, Dunton enlarged the work and it became A Voyage Round the World, mentioned earlier.

The first translated periodical in which Dunton was concerned was The Present State of Europe, by I. Phillips. This work began in July 1690 and continued for many years. Though Dunton was involved with its early organization, he had the poor judgment to withdraw before it became successful.[75] The Weekly Pacquet of Advice from Ireland was issued twice, in April 1690, and Dunton may have also been concerned in writing it. Only three numbers of The Coffee-House Mercury, written by Dunton, appeared in November 1690.

Late in 1690 or early in 1691, Dunton met with a serious injury. During his convalescence, he had the first inspiration for what was to become his greatest project, "no more than a confused idea, of concealing the Querist, and answering his Question". After his recovery, Dunton considered the project further, and the Athenian Society gradually took shape in his mind. In March, the first number of *The Athenian Mercury* was issued.

Not long after *The Athenian Mercury* was established, Dunton's mind turned again to translations, and he became associated with Thomas Bennet in the publication of Jean de la Crose's *Works of the Learned*. After a prolonged struggle with Bennet and La Crose for control of this work, Dunton continued it as *The Compleat Library*, written by Richard Wolley. Monthly issues of *The Compleat Library* appeared from May 1692 through June 1694. Dunton's battle for control of La Crose's paper will be discussed in Chapter IV.

Dunton's deep involvement with the Athenian Society prevented him from undertaking any original projects for several years, though he announced in 1694 the publication of *Monthly Letters on Education*, translated from the French edition, reprinted at Amsterdam. However, he apparently decided that publication as a complete volume was the best means of printing the letters. In the summer of 1694 they appeared, as *The Knowledge of the World: Or, The Art of Well-Educating Youth*. At the end of this volume, called Volume I, Dunton advertised that " ... we shall surcease printing these Letters, till there be a Number sufficient to make up a Just Volume".

No additional volumes were published.

Probably Pegasus, with News, an Observator, and a Jacobite Courant has been more highly praised than any of Dunton's projects except The Athenian Mercury. Had Dunton's attention to his work not been distracted by Iris's illness, Pegasus might have survived to bring him both profit and distinction in the trade. As was earlier noted, Dunton had suspended publication of The Athenian Mercury in February 1696, because, he said, of the glut of news. When Dunton decided to re-enter the competition for popular readership in June, he conceived a highly original plan for a paper. Pegasus was issued three times weekly, and the first volume was completed in thirty numbers, from 15 June to 21 August 1696. Beginning with the first number of the second volume, it was called Pegasus, with an Observator on Public Occurrences. Publication ceased after Number 10, on 14 September.[76]

Walter Graham in his English Literary Periodicals observed that Pegasus was "the first really good example of a newspaper with features,[77] and Stanley Morison wrote that "Pegasus had, to some extent, anticipated The Tatler by providing what he termed "An Observation", i.e. dissertation or serialised instruction on some moral, political or historical subject of greater or lesser topical interest".[78] Morison gave Dunton an additional compliment, one that is applicable to few of his publications: "[*Pegasus*] is a vastly more agreeable piece of printing than any contemporary newspaper".

After the discontinuation of *Pegasus*, Dunton began one further periodical project in 1696, a project dedicated to the exposure and extermination of vice. An expansion of an article which had appeared in *The Ladies' Dictionary* in 1694, this project was called *The Night-Walker; Or, Evening Rambles in Search after Lewd Women, with the Conferences held with Them*. He announced that it would be published monthly "'til a Discovery be made of all the chief Prostitutes in England, from the Pensionary Miss, down to the Common Strumpet". He dedicated it to "the Whoremasters of London and Westminster". Although ostensibly highly moral, the content of the periodical was in fact mildly salacious. *The Night-Walker* continued for eight months. But Iris fell sick (she died in May 1697) and the April number of *The Night-Walker* advertised that "Some particular reasons have occasioned the Change of the Person concerned in this Undertaking, but 'tis hoped without any disadvantage to it or to the publick, tho we must own that Gentlemans Accomplishments to be very great and not easily matched". R. M. Wiles, who had a single subject in mind, cited *The Night-Walker* alone of Dunton's periodicals, and he mentioned it "only because the matter in the successive monthly pamphlets, each with separate pagination and signatures, has a degree of continuity that puts the work into the borderland between a tenth-rate periodical and a tenth-rate book published in parts".[79]

Dunton's periodicals (especially, as we shall see, The Athenian Mercury and its ancillary projects) certainly had an effect on the public, in accustoming them to buy in parts works which were designed to be retained and bound up in a volume. It also influenced the form and matter of later periodicals, more successful and more highly valued. But Dunton, beginning in 1697, was unable to carry on with any of his projects, for after the death of Iris, his life was uprooted. Then, following his second marriage, he fled London taking with him a cargo of books which he sold in Dublin. The story of Dunton's further periodicals, and his later tracts of religious and political controversy, will be resumed after a consideration of one of his most successful ventures, The Athenian Mercury, as well as his excursion into the field of literary reviews, The Works of the Learned and The Compleat Library.

CHAPTER III

THE ATHENIAN SOCIETY

(1691-1697)

During the reign of William and Mary, John Dunton enjoyed a period of sustained success that was not equalled in his professional life. His trade flourished, and consequently he was able to launch independently a great variety of original ventures. Introducing his projects in his *Life and Errors*, Dunton remarked on his notorious originality: " ... I have been sufficiently convinced that, unless a man can either think or perform something out of the old beaten road, he will find nothing but what his Forefathers have found before him".[1] Originality proved to be both Dunton's fortune and misfortune, for his energies frequently were so dissipated through the reckless pursuit of novelty that they lost direction entirely, leaving the trail-blazer floundering hopelessly in *terra incognita*. In fact, Dunton was so eager to bring forward new projects that he was rarely capable of successfully exploiting those which he had already begun. But never was his originality more deserving of praise than for the creation of his most successful and most original venture, *The Athenian Gazette*.

In his Life and Errors, Dunton explained the source of his idea for the Gazette:

> "I had received a very flaming injury, which was so loaded with aggravations, that I could scarce get over it. My thoughts were constantly working upon it, and made me strangely uneasy; ... Whilst this perplexity remained upon me, I was one day walking over St. George's Fields, and Mr. Larkin and Mr. Harris were along with me; and on a sudden I made a stop, and said, 'Well, Sirs, I have a thought I will not exchange for fifty guineas.' They smiled, and were very urgent with me to discover it; but they could not get it from me. The first rude hint of it was no more than a confused idea, of concealing the Querist, and answering his Question. However, so soon as I came home, I managed it to some better purpose, brought it into form, and hammered out a Title for it, which happened to be extremely lucky, and those who are well acquainted with the Grecian History may discover some peculiar beauties in it".[2]

The principal original elements of the "Question project" were Dunton's invention of a club framework as a means of capturing public credence for his work and the novel device of answering questions submitted by readers. The first of these, the club framework, was the more important of the two, for the history of journalism as well as for the success of The Athenian Gazette. Dunton created the Athenian Society for the practical advantage of its prestige; had it been generally known that a bookseller was the chief organizer of the project, the public would have had no reason to respect the opinions, or to accept the integrity, of the publication. But the public could be encouraged to trust the pronouncements of an anonymous group of authorities. Dunton understood that the success of the project depended on his creating the illusion of a body of learned men engaged in replying to the questions submitted by readers. Thus the Athenian Society, as it developed in the early numbers of the Gazette, was the first appearance of the club framework in literature. Later authors modified and extended the functions of the device: "Defoe saw its value as a vehicle for the criticism of manners, and turned it to advantage in his Scandalous Club papers. The Weekly Comedy and The Female Tatler made experiments in dramatizing ideas by describing the actual meetings of their fictitious societies. In The Spectator all these possibilities were turned to account, with the important addition of lively characterization of the members. Here, too, the club was linked indissolubly with the publication of the periodical and was sustained throughout".[3]

Dunton's question and answer format was also an original journalistic technique. Essentially, The Athenian Gazette was an early forerunner of the modern Notes and Queries. Dunton was a brilliant popularizer, and he had a thorough understanding of the tastes and interests of his audience. The readers of The Athenian Gazette were largely the habitués of London coffee-houses, where debate on current affairs for men of all classes and parties was carried on. Coffee-houses were an important element of Dunton's own life, and in The Athenian Gazette he hoped to profit from the lively spirit of curiosity and enquiry that he knew existed among his contemporaries. The Athenian Gazette was hawked in the streets by Dunton's "Mercury Women" and with other newspapers was generally available to the patrons of the coffee-houses. Although the Gazette contained no current news, it provided much material to provoke comment and debate. Dunton and his Athenian colleagues carefully maintained a lively interchange of controversy with other papers, and directly with their querists. The questions printed in The Athenian Gazette reflect the chief interests of the period; science, religion, superstition and problems of courtship and love are compounded into an astonishing medley of miscellaneous instruction.[4] Yet the Athenians were ostensibly motivated by the most unselfish ideals; their aim was the promotion of knowledge.

Although it must be recognized that Dunton's own interest was not so much knowledge as the popularization and merchandising of it, nevertheless The Athenian Gazette satisfied a public craving for information and instruction presented in an easily digested form. Perhaps the best evidence of the continuing popularity and usefulness of the Gazette is that collections of material from it continued to be printed long after the Gazette itself had ceased publication: four volumes of The Athenian Oracle in several editions, 1703-48, and selections in 1820 and 1893. In 1823, Adam Clarke wrote: "No reader can peruse these volumes [The Athenian Oracle] without profit. They contain many things of great importance and value. When I was little more than a child, an odd volume of the Athenian Oracle, lent me by a friend, was a source of improvement and delight; and I now consult it with double interest, knowing the well nerv'd hand [Samuel Wesley's] by which at least one-third of it was composed".[5] As Beljame observed, The Athenian Gazette "demonstrates better than anything else how willing to learn were the readers of those days, and how much remained to be done towards their education".[6]

On 17 March 1691, John Dunton entered in the Stationers' Register and had licensed The Athenian Gazette, resolving weekly all the most nice and curious questions proposed by the ingenious. On the same day, the first number of the periodical was published. The Gazette was a folio half-sheet, with drop-head title, printed for P. Smart. Readers were invited to submit queries to the editor by penny post letter to Smith's Coffee-House in Stocks Market in the Poultry, and a number of questions were considered as specimens: "Whether 'tis Lawful for a Man to beat his Wife?", "How came the spots on the Moon?", and "Where was the Soul of Lazarus for the four days he lay in the Grave?". Although the authors announced that

The Athenian Gazette was to be published weekly, other details of its publication were not specified, since it was Dunton's custom in launching a new project to publish a first number as a means of testing the public response, promising to continue if popular reception were sufficiently encouraging.

Public reception of The Athenian Gazette was overwhelmingly encouraging, as Dunton indicated in the second weekly number, in reply to a reader who queried whether the author was in league with the General Penny Post Office: "No, but we are in league with their Majesties Interest, having this first Week about forty Penny-Post Letters, which, (with what this number may probably increase to in a little time,) will be a considerable advancement per Annum, to that Branch of their Majesties Revenue".[7] Enthusiasm for the project remained at a high level, and in the third number Dunton announced: "We find the Questions grow so fast upon us, ... that to obviate the Confusion which thence may follow, we intend to Publish our Paper twice a Week, viz. every Tuesday and Saturday. And in the mean time, till we are got clear of those already on our hands, we desire the curious Inquirers to reserve their New Questions, till we shall give publick Advertisement that we have dispatcht all the Old ones, at least such as deserve an Answer."[8] Ladies, apparently, eagerly read the Gazette, and Dunton soon resolved to devote the issue of the first Tuesday in each month entirely to answering the problems of the "fair sex".[9]

The first two numbers of The Athenian Mercury (after the first number, Dunton had been "obliged by authority" to change the title of his paper from Gazette to Mercury)[10] were written entirely by Dunton with the assistance of Richard Sault, the mathematician, who had offered his help with the work.[11] After the success of the first numbers, Dunton and Sault looked for additional assistance. Sault enlisted Dr. John Norris, "the greatest prodigy of Learning he had ever met with". Dr. Norris offered his assistance without pay and was unwilling to become a permanent member of Dunton's board of editors. Norris was "wonderfully useful in supplying hints; for, being universally read, and his memory very strong, there was nothing could be asked, but he could very easily say something to the purpose upon it".[12] Ten days later, Dunton recruited a third member, his brother-in-law, Samuel Wesley. Wesley had written for Dunton a volume of poems while an undergraduate at Oxford and had in 1690 married Susanna Annesley, a younger sister of Dunton's own wife.

On 10 April 1691, Dunton, Sault and Wesley met at Smith's Coffee-House in the Poultry, where they composed and signed the following articles of agreement for the writing of The Athenian Mercury:[13]

Articles of Agreem^{t} between Sam^{el} Wesley Clerk Richd Sault Gent and John Dunton Stationer of London

In p$\overline{\text{ris}}$ That y^{e} s^{d} Wesley and Sault shall deliver into the hands of the s^{d} Dunton two distinct papers every fryday night each paper to make halfe a printed sheet of the Athenian Gazett or Mercury which s^{d} paper is to be a performance of what is promisd in N° 1: and N° 7

Item: That y^{e} s^{d} Dunton shall have power to intermix and place the said Questions as he pleases and shall pay 10s Sterling for every Number in print after N° 4 the acc^{t} to be adjusted once every fortnight and the s^{d} Money not to be demanded before

Item: That the s^{d} Dunton shall be at liberty if he pleases to print but one of the said papers every week which the s^{d} Sault is to continue as he began or the said Dunton is to be at Liberty to throw up the said paper when he pleases giving a fortnights Warning or paying upon demand 20s Sterling a piece to the s^{d} Wesley and Sault upon discontinuing the said paper

Item: That there be a meeting every Fryday in the afternoon in Some Convenient place betwixt the s^{d} Wesley and Sault to consult of what they have done and to receive new Questions for the next week and the party not coming before 3 of ye Clock is to forfeit one Shilling to be spent and the party that has not finisht his paper by that time excepting Corrections shall forfeit one Shilling to be likewise Spent

Item That every Volume which shall be N° 30 shall have a preface and Index to it the preface to be written by the s^{d} Wesley and Sault for which they shall have 10s betwixt 'em

Item The said Wesley and Sault shall not desert the s^{d} undertaking without giving the s^{d} Dunton a fortnights notice or paying upon demand 20s Sterling a piece for discontinuing the writing of the said paper

Item That the s^{d} Dunton shall not take any other person into the s^{d} undertaking without the Consent of the s^{d} Wesley and Sault and y^{t} ye s^{d} Wesley and Sault shall not engage in the like undertaking for any other person but the s^{d} Dunton upon the said Dunton performance of the above second article

Item That if the s[d] Wesley or Sault should leave off the undertaking, the other shall be at liberty to Engrosse the whole or have equall power with the said Dunton in Choosing another partner fitly qualify[d] for the undertaking to continue the s[d] paper and that noe questions shall be put in that have not been seen both by the said Wesley and Sault

Item It was agreed that the said Dunton shall gett translated by another hand the Acta Eruditorum Lipsiae the Journall de Savans the Universall Bibliotheque the Giornali de literati printed at Rome or any other pieces translated and added to every volume in as many distinct Numbers as he pleases provided still that all such translations doe not prevent what they otherwise should write of the weekly paper

In Witnesse whereof the partyes to these present Articles have sett their hands and Seals this tenth of aprill in the Year of Our Lord 1691.

Sealed and delivered in the presence of

James Smith
the Mark of Mary Smith

Sam: Wesley
Richard Sault
John Dunton

The *Athenian Mercury* continued to be published until 1697, when the twentieth volume was half-completed. Wesley, presumably, was responsible for articles on theological and philosophical questions, and Sault for mathematical and scientific questions, with the informal assistance of John Norris and the overall direction of Dunton. The final item of the articles is particularly interesting as it indicates that Dunton, with *The Athenian Mercury* barely under way, was already considering ways of expanding the project. The idea of translating foreign literary periodicals materialized first as the *Supplements* to *The Athenian Mercury*, which accompanied the first five volumes of the Mercury, then as The Young Students' Library, 1692, and finally as The Compleat Library, which was published monthly by Dunton from May 1692 to June 1694.

Another writer who gave informal assistance to the editors of The Athenian Mercury was Daniel Defoe. Defoe was well acquainted with Dunton, since his family had long belonged to the congregation of Dr. Samuel Annesley, Dunton's father-in-law. Through his association with Dunton, Defoe became an occasional contributor to The Athenian Mercury. In fact the Mercury was Defoe's first connection with a periodical, though he was associated during his lifetime with over two dozen periodicals. A few passages in the Mercury have been attributed to Defoe by J. R. Moore: "Among these are a scornful argument against a husband's fighting a duel with his wife's lover, a story from Knolles' History of the Turks, the discussion of an error made by a man in the wine trade, and the detailed account of a young merchant who has done business on a large scale and is desperate to know how to protect his wife and children as well as his creditors. Sometimes these passages show firsthand knowledge of Spain and the wine trade; sometimes they bear traces of Defoe's personal idiom".[14]

Defoe wrote an ode in celebration of the Athenian Society which Dunton prefixed to Gildon's History of the

Athenian Society, and reprinted in The Athenian Oracle. In 1697, he wrote for Dunton an elegy on the death of Dr. Annesley. Dunton considered Defoe to be "a man of good parts, and very clear sense. His conversation is ingenious and brisk enough. The World is well satisfied that he is enterprizing and bold ...." But Dunton was angered when Defoe reprinted, without Dunton's consent, his ode and elegy in his collected works: "And he might have asked me the question, before he had inserted either of them in the Collection of his Works, in regard he writes so bitterly against the same injustice in others".[15]

In 1704, Defoe attempted to increase the circulation of his Review by borrowing the question and answer technique of the Athenian Society, offending Dunton once again, as Dunton was trying desperately to revive his "question project" as a monthly periodical. In 1706 Dunton wrote: "This man has done me a sensible wrong, by interloping with my 'Question-Project.' Losers may have leave to speak; and I here declare, I am 200 l. the worse for De Foe's clogging my 'Question-Project.' His Answering Questions Weekly, ... ruined my 'Monthly Oracle;' for most are seized with the Athenian Itch, and chuse rather to be scratched Weekly, than stay till the Month is out for a perfect cure".[16] Defoe did not reply.

In early Mercuries, no indication was made of the

existence of a Society, although the authors had from the beginning used the plural form in replying to questions. The first specific indication of the existence of the Society is found in _The Athenian Mercury_ for 5 May, where it was announced that "We have now taken into our _Society_ a Civilian, a Doctor in Physick, and a Chyrurgeon, on purpose to be more serviceable to the Age".[17] In later _Mercuries_, the public came to understand that the members of the Athenian Society held formal meetings to frame their replies to questions. A number of separate works were written "By the Athenian Society" or "By a Member of the Athenian Society", and in certain controversies tracts were written to refute the views of this learned body. _The Young Students' Library_, published in June 1692, had for a frontispiece an engraving by F. H. Van Hove, "An Emblem of ye Athenian Society". This "Emblem" depicted the learned Athenians in conclave - a vastly exaggerated view of the Friday afternoon gatherings of Dunton and his colleagues at Smith's Coffee-House. The true composition of the Athenian Society was probably an open secret among the trade, as Elkanah Settle wrote of the engraving:

> "'Tis true our generous _Athenians_ have lately vouchsafed to give us some small Lineaments of theirs in _Miniature_, in a Sculp before their _Young Students Library_. But there alas, they are pleased to wrap their Faces in Mosaic Veils, very magisterially intimating that they are Persons that daily converse so near with Divinity, that their _shining Faces_ are

> too dazling for humane View .... I confess M^{r}. Engraver has made a pretty Jolly Company of 'em: but there indeed the Painter is a little too poetical: and our Athenians have a little strain'd a point: For when the True Muster Roll of that not overnumerous Society shall be examined, ... you must consider that the Veil'd Faces are by way of Faggots to fill up the Troop: And in that fair Convention of divine Enthusiasts you must not take 'em all for the Boanerges of Wit, the Organs of Thunder, but like Guns in a Fireship, a Tire of painted wooden Tools to make up the Show".[18]

On the title-page of the sixteenth Mercury of the second volume, for 18 July 1691, Dunton's imprint appeared for the first time on an individual number, although it had previously been placed on the general title-page for the first volume, issued on 8 June. How the financial support for The Athenian Mercury was arranged is not known; another bookseller may have had a share in the project. P. Smart, the "publisher" of the earlier numbers of the Mercury, need not be considered, as the name was most probably a pseudonym. Richard Baldwin, a close associate of Dunton during this period, must have held some share in the project, for The Athenian Mercury advertised on 13 June that "We Advise all our Querists to read the Contents and 12 Numbers lately Publisht all together by Mr. Baldwin, ... that they may know what Questions we have Already Answer'd".[19] Advertisements on 11 August and on 1 September announced the forthcoming publication, by R. Baldwin, of the complete second volume and its supplement.

The popularity of *The Athenian Mercury* remained at a high level throughout the first year of publication. Dunton's readers continued to be diverted and edified by the Society's authoritative replies to such questions as "Whether the Sky is a Substance, and may be felt?", "Why a Horse with a round Fundament emits a square Excrement?", and "Why does the Scripture forbid us to wear Linsy-Woolsy?".[20] As early in the first volume as No. 8, on 18 April, Dunton advertised that "We shall all along publish every volume (with a *Preface and Index* to it) as soon as ever we have received Questions enough to fill up *Numb*. 30. that so those *Querists* that stay longest for Answers may not think us tedious". It is characteristic of Dunton's sensitivity to the public reception of his work, that during this initial period of enormous enthusiasm for *The Athenian Mercury*, only the first eighteen numbers of the thirty that made up a volume appeared serially. Each volume was completed by the publication of twelve additional numbers, with the title-page, preface, and index. In an advertisement of 3 June, Dunton emphasised the convenience of this practice:

> "By the *8th* of *June* will be finish'd all the 12 Numbers that compleat our *first Volume*, which shall then be publish'd all together, with a *Preface* and *Index* to it, which said *Preface*, *Index*, and 12 *Numbers*, shall be but 12d. price, that so all those Gentlemen that took in the single Sheets from time to time, may have their *Volume entire* for 2s. 6d. And also that those *Coffee-houses* that did the like may then have the whole First Volume stitch'd up by them,

> for the constant entertainment of their Customers, single Sheets being apt to be lost, except pasted in a Book".[21]

A notable controversy occurred in November 1691, when the Athenian Society devoted two entire numbers of the Mercury to answering a great number of questions on the highly combustible subject of infant baptism.[22] Baptists were offended by the Society's position, and the Baptist minister Hercules Collins, who in 1691 had also published Believers' Baptism from Heaven, and of Divine Institution - Infants' Baptism from Earth, and Human Invention,[23] replied in a short tract called Animadversions upon the Responses of the Athenian Mercury, to the Questions about Infant Baptism.[24] An anonymous writer who styled himself "Philalethes Pasiphilus" also replied to the Athenian Society, in a quarto tract called Confidence Corrected, Error Detected, and Truth Defended: Or, Some Further Reflections upon the Two Athenian Mercuries Lately Publish'd about Infant-Baptism.[25] A more substantial reply came from the Calvinistic Baptist Benjamin Keach, himself no stranger to controversy, who in 1688 had been severely criticised for introducing the "carnal formality" of congregational singing to his meeting. Keach's Pedo-Baptism Disproved: Being an Answer to Two Printed Papers called the Athenian Mercury was printed for John Harris, a neighbour of Dunton's in the Poultry, in two editions in 1691.[26]

The last word in this controversy was not written by the Athenian Society when, early in 1692, numbers 19 to 30 of the Athenian Mercury were printed to complete the fifth volume. These twelve numbers were wholly given to A General Reply to all the Anabaptists have written against the Athenian Mercury on Infant-Baptism. The final word belonged to that indefatigable controversialist, Benjamin Keach, who published yet another refutation, The Rector Rectified and Corrected; Or, Infant-Baptism Unlawful: Being A Sober Answer to a late Pamphlet, ... by Mr. William Burkit, ... wherein all his Arguments for Pedo-baptism, are refuted, ... and the People falsely called Anabaptists, are cleared from those unjust Reproaches and Calumnies cast upon them. Together with a Reply to the Athenian Gazette ....[27] As late as 1694, Giles Firmin referred to the controversy in his tract Some Remarks on the Anabaptist's Answer to the Athenian Mercuries.[28]

Dunton proudly noted, in his Life and Errors, the names of prominent men who regularly read The Athenian Mercury and who occasionally submitted questions. George Savile, Marquis of Halifax, once told Dunton "that he constantly perused our 'Mercuries,' and had received great satisfaction from very many of our Answers". Sir Thomas Pope Blount congratulated Dunton on the success of the project, as did Sir Peter Pett. Sir William Hedges, Governor of Bengal, sent several complete sets to friends in India. Later, Dunton dedicated The Athenian Oracle to James, Duke of Ormond, and when he personally presented a set of his Oracles to the Duke, he was flattered by his generous reception of them. Sir William Temple in particular was a friend to the project, and honoured Dunton by his frequent letters and queries.[29]

Temple's enthusiasm for the project was certainly genuine, for Jonathan Swift, who first became acquainted with the Society through Temple, wrote to his cousin Thomas Swift in May 1692, that "S^{r} W^{m} T[emple] speaking to me so much in their Praise made me zealous for their cause".[30] Swift enjoyed the Athenian project wholeheartedly. He composed an "Ode to the Athenian Society" which he submitted to the Society in February 1692, accompanied by an admiring and somewhat diffident letter:

Moor-park, Feb. 14. 1691.

Gentlemen,

Since every Body pretends to trouble you with their Follies, I thought I might claim the Priviledge of an Englishman, and put in my share among the rest. Being last year in Ireland (from whence I returned about half a year ago), I heard only a loose talk of your Society, and believed the design to be only some new Folly just suitable to the Age, which God knows, I little expected ever to produce any thing extraordinary. Since my being in England, having still continued in the Countrey, and much out of Company; I had but little advantage of knowing any more, till about two Months ago, passing through Oxford, a very learned Gentleman there, first shew'd me two or three of your Volumes, and gave me his Account and Opinion of you; a while after I came to this place, upon a visit to [Sir William Temple] where I have been ever since, and have seen all the four Volumes with their Supplements, which answering my expectation. The perusal has produced, what you find inclosed.

As I have been somewhat inclined to this Folly, so I have seldom wanted some-body to flatter me in it. As for the Ode inclosed, I have sent it to a Person of very great Learning and Honour, and since to some others, the best of my Acquaintance, (to which I thought very proper to inure it for a greater light) and they have all been pleased to tell me, that they are sure it will not be unwelcome, and that I should beg the Honour of You to let it be Printed before Your next Volume (which I think, is soon to be published,) it being so usual before most Books of any great value among Poets, and before it's seeing the World, I submit it wholly to the Correction of your Pens.

I intreat, therefore, one of You would descend so far, as to write two or three lines to me of your Pleasure upon it. Which, as I cannot but expect from Gentlemen, who have so well shewn, upon so many occasions, that greatest Character of Scholars, in being favourable to the Ignorant, so, I am sure, nothing at present can more highly oblige me, or make me happier. I am,

(Gentlemen)

Your ever most Humble,

and most

admiring Servant.

Jonathan Swift.[31]

Dunton inserted the ode and the accompanying letter in the supplement to the fifth volume of The Athenian Mercury. The ode was also printed separately, and in 1710 it was reprinted in A Supplement to the Athenian Oracle.[32] The "Ode to the Athenian Society" was Swift's first published work, and he described his delight in a letter to Thomas Swift:

> "... the Poem I writt to the Athen. Society was all ruff drawn in a week, and finishd in 2 days after, and yet it consists of 12 stanza and some of them above

> thirty lines, all above 20, and yet it is so well thought of that the unknown Gentlemen printed it before one of their Books, and the Bookseller writes me word that another Gentleman has in a book calld the History of the Athen Society, quoted my Poem very Honorably (as the fellow calld it) so that perhaps I was in a good humor all the week, or at least S^{r} W^{m} T speaking to me so much in their Praise made me zealous for their cause, for really I take that to be a part of the Honesty of Poets that they can not write well except they think the subject deserves it.[33]

Other critics, however, have not been so kind as Charles Gildon. According to Johnson, the ode provoked Dryden's remark, "Cousin Swift, you will never be a poet".[34] Sir Henry Craik described the ode as "inflated, disordered, often impenetrably obscure, ... it abundantly justifies the criticism of these early efforts of Swift which tradition ascribed to Dryden".[35] "Experience", added Craik, "taught Swift, like the rest of the world, to laugh at [the Athenian Society], but ... youthful enthusiasm and want of judgment led him, in 1692, to pay the current homage". According to Ricardo Quintana, Swift's mind was dominated by a dislike of pedantry, and he was thus misled into wholesale admiration of the aims of the Athenian Society. Four years later, Dunton was satirized, along with many others, in A Tale of a Tub.[36]

But Swift's experience with the Athenian Society was beneficial for him as a writer, as Mrs. William C. DeVane concluded in her study of Swift's relations with the Athenian

Society.[37] The Athenian Society, wrote Mrs. DeVane, "had awakened [Swift] to the possibility of using science as stuff for poetry.... He was to find too that the use he had found for science in his poetry could be transferred to prose, and was equally useful there .... Swift absorbed all sorts of suggestions that he was to make use of in later life ... it supplied him with hints for his imagery, [and] it supplied him with hints for papers". Indeed, the Athenian Society was influential generally in changing the public attitude to poetry. Through The Athenian Mercury, the public learned that popular poetry need not necessarily be associated with frivolity and immorality.

Early in 1692, the Athenian Society were also involved in two minor controversies. On 5 March, the Mercury commented on David Jones's farewell sermon on usury, and their remarks were quickly answered by Mr. David Jones' Vindication Against the Athenian Mercury concerning Usury.[38] Remarks about the Quakers provoked a series of tracts by William Penn, who wrote, in three parts, The New Athenians No Noble Bereans: Being an Answer to the Athenian Mercury of the 7th Instant, in behalf of the People called Quakers. All three were printed for Thomas Northcott in Lombard Street.[39] Another Quaker reply to the Athenian Society was The Holy Scripture Owned, and the Athenians Injustice Detected, by the abused Quaker. This work was signed by the initials of a number of members of that sect.[40] The Athenian Society, in their turn, devoted two numbers of the *Mercury* in June to their replies.[41] Charles Bathurst had the last word in this controversy, in a pamphlet printed for Thomas Northcott called *The Doting Athenians' Imposing Questions no Proofs. In Answer to their Questions, and most apparent Mistakes, about the People Commonly Called* Quakers.[42]

Inevitably, the Athenian Society soon had to contend with a number of imitators. Chief among these was *The London* Mercury (from No. 9, *The Lacedemonian Mercury*) which first appeared on 1 February 1692 and was printed until the end of May 1692. At first *The London Mercury* was printed for T. Jones without Temple Bar, and from Number 8 it was printed for Randal Taylor, near Stationers' Hall. From the beginning, *The London Mercury* was a larkish undertaking, written by Tom Brown and William Pate; Charles Gildon was also concerned with it briefly. The solemnity and high moral tone of *The Athenian Mercury* bored the writers of *The London Mercury*, who proposed a more lively paper:

> "Last night being very restless in my Bed, I thought fit to divert the time with Sporting an Author .... The first Book I laid my hand on, proved some select Comedies of *Aristophanes*; turning them over my Eye, staid on ... his Comedy of Clouds .... I soon forgot the Inquietude of the past Hours, and resolv'd to spend those to come with more Satisfaction,

> by reading the whole Comedy over, which by that time I had done, it grew toward Morning, and that made me think of taking a refreshing sleep ... but the Wit of Aristophanes had banished Sleep from my Eyes, filling my Head with a thousand pleasant Fancies, till Fortune, that took care of my Health, had, by I know not what means, laid one of those Papers, call'd the Athenian Mercury, by me, being destitute of either Opium or Poppy-Water. I had scarce run over one Paragraph, when I found a heaviness descend on my Eyes, the Welcome Harbinger of approaching Slumbers, which soon followed after ..."[43]

Brown and Pate resented Dunton's assumption of proprietorship of the question and answer device, "as if [the Athenian Society] were more firmly establish'd than the East-India Company, and had an uncontrovertible Patent for answering all Queries exclusive of all men else".[44] But Brown and Pate firmly intended The London Mercury to be a competitor of The Athenian Mercury, as well as a burlesque of it, and they invited questions to be submitted to them at the Welsh Coffee-House without Temple Bar. On the following day, the Athenian Society replied: "Yesterday Morning was publisht a Paper interfering with our Athenian Project ... we therefore here give publick notice, That those Questions which he pretends to answer, shall be all answer'd again by us, that so neither our Querists, the Booksellers, nor the London Coffee-houses may be imposed upon by buying Questions twice answered, for they shall always find in our Papers the best of his Thoughts, and our own Improvements upon all his Questions whatever, together with Remarks upon his Errors".[45]

In the second number of The London Mercury, the Athenian Society were lampooned severely. The London Mercury playfully posed questions for the Athenian Society to answer. Queries from the fair sex were referred to the Athenians, as they were especially popular with ladies. "Which do your Worships think to be the best Philosopher," The London Mercury asked, "the Athenian Mercury, that pretends to know all things, or he Who used to say, Hoc solum scio, quod nihil scio?" The tone of The London Mercury was hostile, and the language coarse:

> "Self-nam'd Athenians, let it, pray, be shewn
> (For sure 'tis obvious to your mighty Wits)
> Why Farts burn blew When through a Candle blown,
> And yet that's Yellow which the same Arse shits?"[46]

The Athenian Mercury remained silent about the interloping London Mercury for several numbers, while Dunton was evidently quietly busy undermining their project. After Number 4, The London Mercury did not appear for ten days. When it reappeared, the editors noted that "The Encouragement this Paper found in the World was so great, that one of the first Undertakers has been Brib'd to desert, yet some others have thought fit to continue it". The authors asked the Athenian Society "whether it was worth the while for the Athenian Society to Bribe off the late Undertaker of the London Mercury C. G?"[47] Brown and Pate were close associates,[48] whereas

Charles Gildon was at that time scarcely more than a young literary hack whose services had been cheaply secured by The London Mercury. Hence Dunton probably had little difficulty persuading him to join forces with the Athenian Society. Gildon was secretly put to work writing The History of the Athenian Society, which was printed late in April 1692. On 28 May, the Athenian Society announced that "There are certain Memoirs come to our Hands about the Lives of Mr. Brown and his Friend, which our next Saturdays Advertisements shall tell the World what Use is design'd to be made of 'em".[49] On 30 May, with the first number of the second volume, The Lacedemonian Mercury appeared for the last time. To have the final word, Dunton on 31 May called the author of The Lacedemonian Mercury an "impudent lyar" and promised "in a very little time ... a just and well Attested Character of him, as to the Scandal he has been to Accademians, Schoolmasters, and all the rest of the World he has Convers'd with ... and then I'll leave the World to Judge of his Reputation and mine".[50]

In his Life and Errors, Dunton gave another account of his victory over The Lacedemonian Mercury:

> "The success of Athens growing so very considerable, Mr. Brown and Mr. Pate began to ape our design, in a Paper they intituled 'The Lacedemonian Mercury,' which immediately interfered with us, under a title which, it is true, was pretty and pertinent enough. Upon this, I was resolved one way or other to blow them up, in regard it was both ungenerous and unjust to interlope

> upon a man where he has the sole right and property, for the Children of the Brain are as much ours as those we beget in lawful wedlock.
>
> "I first of all advertised, 'that all the Questions answered in 'The Lacedemonian Mercury' should be answered over again in our "Athenian Mercury,' with amendments; with the Life of Tom Brown, the chief Antagonist.' This news startled them pretty much. At that time I was altogether unacquainted with Mr. Brown; however, one evening he comes to me with all the civility imaginable, and desires to take a glass with me. I sent for my Athenian Brethren; and we went to the Three Cranes, where we discoursed the matter with him at large. But Mr. Sault, being a Gentleman of courage, and a little inclined to passion, was going to draw upon Mr. Brown, for an uncivil reflection; upon which Mr. Brown cried Peccavi, and promised very faithfully 'that he would never meddle any more with The Lacedemonian Mercury!"[51]

Most probably, The Lacedemonian Mercury was given up simply because the labour of producing it brought in a small return.[52]

Finally, on 31 May, Dunton advised his readers that "there is not any one Question in the Lacedemonian Papers but what they'll find Answer'd in our 6th. Volume, or in the 18 Numbers of our 7th. Volume, just now Publish'd. And we Resolve to continue Answering all Questions whatever, that so we may render our Undertaking perfect".[53]

Concerning The History of the Athenian Society, Dunton in his Life and Errors rather disingenuously wrote that "'The Athenian Mercury' began at length to be so well approved, that Mr. Gildon ... thought it worth his while to write 'A History of the Athenian Society'".[54] Charles Gildon's name did not appear on the title-page of the History ("By a Gentleman, who got Secret Intelligence of their whole proceedings"), and the epistle dedicatory was signed R. L. The authors of The Lacedemonian Mercury, reviewing The History of the Athenian Society on 9 May, were quite unaware that their former partner was responsible for compiling it. The History was "Printed for James Dowley", and at first, the Athenian Society disavowed any connection with it. When on 30 April 1692, a reader asked for the name of the author, the Athenian Society replied that

> "the Athenian Society was so far from being concern'd in writing the History he here speaks of, that they heard nothing of it till the 9th. Sheet was going to the Press, at which time one of our Members sent a Letter to the Author of it, shewing our utter dislike of the Undertaking, which Letter (contrary to the Rules of Civility) he has inserted in his History, with Remarks upon it, we must therefore say this of him, that tho his Writings shew him to be a very witty Person, in being able to say so much on so barren a subject, yet we cannot think he has done by us in this Affair as he wou'd have been served himself, neither has that Person who secretly gave him Intelligence of our Proceedings acted less ungenerously".[55]

Ten days later, the History having met with a kind reception, The Athenian Mercury printed an advertisement for it, advising their readers that "This History is printed on the same size with the Athenian Mercury, that it might bind up with the Entire set for the Year 91".[56] In June appeared The Young Students' Library, which completed the Athenian projects for

1691, and with it "An Emblem of ye Athenian Society" and a comprehensive index to the five volumes of the *Mercury*, their *Supplements*, and *The History of the Athenian Society*. Later, Dunton advertised the *History* as printed for himself; and in his *Life and Errors*, he admitted that he had had Mr. Dowley publish it for him.[57]

The tone of *The History of the Athenian Society* was extravagant flattery: "*England* has the Glory of giving Rise to two of the noblest Designs that the Wit of Man is capable of inventing, and they are, the *Royal Society*, for the experimental improvement of Natural Knowledge, and the *Athenian Society* for communicating not only that, but all other Sciences to all men, as well as to both Sexes; and the last will, I question not, be imitated, as well as the first, by other Nations".[58] Gildon praised the members of the Athenian Society generously for their contributions to the increase of knowledge, and even to the promotion of printing, "for, as that *Art* contributed extreamly to the spreading and progress of Learning, so has this *Project* made grateful Returns already, to the encouragement at least of the Masters of that Art, witness the Controversie with the *Anabaptists*, the *Quakers*, and with Mr. *Jones* on the Subject of *Usury*". Dunton, finally, was unmasked as the originator of the Athenian Society: "... 'tis fit that the World know its Benefactor; and indeed

Justice requires, that *he* who first design'd and propos'd it, should have that Reputation, that is due to him, and have his Name known to Posterity, ... He therefore who form'd the first Idea of this great, this noble Project, was Mr. *Dunton* the Bookseller, for whom all the *Mercuries* are printed". Gildon forestalled criticism, noting that: "I have heard some of the Wou'd-be-Wits object against this Design, merely because invented by a *Bookseller*; but that is so foolish a Flaw to find in it, that it discover'd their Ignorance as well, as Partiality; for first, several noble Inventions have had more unlikely Authors; ... than one that deals in Wit and Learning, and may well be Supposed to converse with many of those Authors he sells. And next, the Learned know, that *Scaliger* was a Bookseller, and *Stephanus* a Printer".[59]

In addition to the publications which have been mentioned, the Athenian Society published in 1692 two further works. The first of these was *A Discourse Concerning the Antiquity, Divine Original and Authority of the Points, Vowels, and Accents, that are placed to the Hebrew Bible* ... *By a Member of the Athenian Society*. This work, with a separate title-page, accompanied *The Young Students' Library*. Late in the year appeared *The Visions of the Soul, Before It Comes into the Body* ... *In Several Dialogues* ... *Written by a Member of the Athenian Society*. Apparently Dunton was more than usually eager to publish the Visions, for the anonymous author (who was probably Dunton himself) stated in the preface: "Perhaps I have more reason to beg pardon of my Brethren the members of the Athenian Society, than of the world, in that I have only mention'd the Subject to them, without taking their advice in the composure; but my Impatient Bookseller, alledging the nearness of the Term, occasion'd the hurrying it into the Press". The second edition of John Norris's Christian Blessedness also came out in 1692. In it, Norris replied to remarks that had been made by the Athenian Society about his essay on Locke which had appeared in the first edition of Christian Blessedness, in 1690. Later, Norris's Practical Discourses upon the Beatitudes of Our Lord and Saviour Jesus Christ were published in several editions in 1693, reprinting his reply to the Athenian Society.[60] The Athenian Mercury also printed advertisements for Daniel Williams's Gospel-truth Stated and Vindicated, which Dunton published. The Mercury also printed a list of errata for the work and answered at length a number of questions about it. Isaac Chauncy replied, in Neonomianism Unmask'd: or, the Ancient Gospel Pleaded,[61] and Dunton printed Williams's further reply in 1693.

From 26 July to 17 September 1692, The Athenian Mercury did not appear. Dunton later explained that its suppression had been due to offence given to a nobleman by a question which he had printed early in July: "The Earl of ----- was once pleased to frown upon "The Athenian Mercury,' and forced us into silence. But, when men are pleased to make personal application, (for the offence was only taken at a question that was sent us, of 'a Father that had two Daughters'), it is a sign there is a sore place, else they would never wince for the matter".[62]

After 1692, the novelty and excitement of the Athenian Society subsided somewhat, although the Society continued to provoke occasional imitation and ridicule. In its second year of publication, The Athenian Mercury began to print readers' letters, as well as questions and answers. In 1693 Elkanah Settle published a play, The New Athenian Comedy, containing the Politicks, Oeconomicks, Tacticks, Crypticks, Apocalypticks, Stypticks, Scepticks, Pneumaticks, Theologicks, Poeticks, Mathematicks, Sophisticks, Pragmaticks, Dogmaticks, &c. of that Most Learned Society.[63] The New Athenian Comedy, which, according to F. C. Brown, was never actually performed, was a prose satire on the Athenian Society. In the upper room of a London coffee-house, the members of the Athenian Society, Wesley, Norris, Sault, and Dunton - represented as "Obadiah Grub, Divinity and Poetry Professor of the Society", "Jerry Squirt, Casuist and Physician in Ordinary", "Joachim Dash,

Mathematician", and "Jack Stuff, a subtle, ingenious half Author, half Bookseller" - debated the problem "Which is the more Noble Animal, a Louse or a Flea?". "The wit is dull" concluded F. C. Brown "and the language scurrilous".[64]

Another imitator, The Jovial Mercury, began on 14 February 1692 and continued for four numbers.

The Ladies Mercury, an attempt by Dunton to publish a separate work for his numerous female readers, began on 27 February 1692, but lasted only for four numbers.[65] Yet another Athenian lampoon, The Moderator, existed for four numbers from 9 June 1692, and it may have been written partly by Tom Brown.[66] In his Athenianism, published in 1710, Dunton specifically mentioned only four "interlopers"; Tom Brown in The Lacedemonian Mercury, Defoe in The Weekly Review, Povey in The General Remark upon Trade, and H----- in The British Apollo.[67] In the early years of the Athenian Society, The Lacedemonian Mercury was considered the only significant interloper. But in 1710, when Dunton was vainly trying to revive the Athenian Society, he was disturbed by later interlopers who imitated only very slightly, the techniques of The Athenian Mercury.

Until 1696 The Athenian Mercury continued to appear twice weekly. But the project failed to maintain the pace of its early years of publication, and after 1693 the Athenian Society engaged in no significant controversy. The Mercuries were still read widely, but the Society were no longer deluged with questions submitted by an eager public. It was never again necessary for them to ask their readers to forbear submitting queries. Each volume of The Athenian Mercury was completed in single numbers after the sixth volume, no additional supplements appeared, and no further imitators arose. After 1692, only one additional work was announced for publication as written "by a member of the Athenian Society", and it was not a substantial one. On 24 April 1694, The Athenian Mercury advertised that "To Morrow will be Publish'd the Souldiers Manual, or Directions, Prayers and Ejaculations for such as lead a military life. By a Member of the Athenian Society. Price 2d. or an hundred of 'em for 14s. stitcht up in Blew Paper to those Gentlemen (or Officers in His Majesties Army) that buy 'em to disperse".[68] No surviving copy of this leaflet has been traced.

In later volumes of The Athenian Mercury, answers to questions became longer than they had formerly been, in the days when readers had clamoured for satisfaction. Although these extended queries and replies are directly related to the letters of correspondents answered by Steele in the Tatler, no further journalistic innovations issued from the Athenian Society. Compiling the twice-weekly Mercury had become a burden to Dunton and his colleagues, and reading the Mercury had become routine for the public. As the questions increased in length, so did the advertisements, not only for Dunton's own projects, but for a variety of other enterprises. Several numbers of the *Mercury* were in later volumes devoted almost exclusively to advertising a "double chance lottery scheme". Dunton and the other members of the Society had new projects under way, and the attentions of the public were drawn to other periodicals and news letters which had lately arisen.

The policies of William III had made new freedom of expression possible for the press, and during the life of *The Athenian Mercury*, many new papers had appeared to compete for circulation with *The Athenian Mercury*. After the end of licensing, despite a certain initial hesitation, newspapers grew less cautious than they had previously been in reporting political news, and the solemn pronouncements of the Athenian Society were no longer the sensation they once had been. The Society had enjoyed a certain vogue for several years, but having failed to modify their strategy to meet changing public moods and changing market conditions, public interest was allowed to drift towards newer and more fashionable publications. In the final number of the nineteenth volume of *The Athenian Mercury*, on 8 February 1696, Dunton announced that:

> "This is to give notice, that the *Proprietor of the Athenian Mercury* thinks fit, whilst the *Coffee-Houses* have the *Votes* every day and *six New's Papers*

> every week, to discontinue this weekly Paper the 19th Volume being now finisht, and carry on the said design in Volumes, and in pursuance of this Resolution 30 Numbers shall speedily be Printed altogether to compleat the 20th Volume, and after that an intire Volume shall be publisht Quarterly .... This is further to give notice, that besides the quarterly Publication of the said Mercuries in Volumes, that the first Undertaker likewise designs to have it continued again in Weekly Papers, as soon as ever the Glut of News is a little over".[69]

The Society made one further attempt to regain public favour. In 1697 they published ten numbers of the twentieth volume of the Mercury. A "New Method" was announced for the Mercury in the first number of the final volume; not only questions and answers were to be printed, but also original prose and verse submitted by readers. This effort was unsuccessful, and the society disappeared until Dunton tried to form a New Athenian Society in 1703.

Clearly the members of the Athenian Society were not interested in the further possibilities of their club device, and they failed to exploit the full range of likely elaborations of the technique. For Dunton, the Athenian Society had been merely a successful journalistic novelty, and it was left to later writers to expand and develop the idea. Nevertheless, the importance of the Athenian Society is that it originated and proved the general usefulness of a club framework, and that it succeeded as an experiment in popular journalism, satisfying the general curiosity and increasing desire for knowledge in a convenient form. Much valuable miscellaneous information was disseminated by Dunton and his colleagues, and their works were avidly read by a largely non-learned public who delighted in taking a short-cut to knowledge.

While popular journalism developed with the progress of the Athenian Society, a general craving for knowledge appeared in another related form. The literary periodical, of a less popular nature than The Athenian Mercury, was pursuing, on the Continent and in England, its own course of development. John Dunton was aware of this, and soon after The Athenian Mercury was under way, he began to involve himself in the field of learned journalism.

CHAPTER IV

DUNTON AND LA CROSE*

Scarcely a month after the successful debut of The Athenian Gazette, Dunton planned to expand the scope of his periodical. When articles of agreement for the enlarged editorial board were drawn up and signed on 10 April 1691 the final article stated:

> It was agreed that the said Dunton shall gett translated by another hand the Acta Eruditorum Lipsise the Journall de Savans the Universall Bibliotheque the Giornali de literati printed at Rome or any other pieces translated and added to every volume in as many distinct Numbers as he pleases provided still that all such translations doe not prevent what they otherwise should write of the weekly paper.[1]

Although this intention had not been expressed when The Athenian Gazette was first licensed and entered, Dunton entered the work again on 18 April as The Athenian Mercury and declared his intention to add to every volume of the Mercury a supplement containing translations of those four continental periodicals.[2] Thus by uniting his popular question and answer serial with the established form of the 'abstract' serial Dunton proposed to invade the field of the

*An earlier version of this chapter has been printed in The Library, 5th Series, XXIII(1968), 13-24.

learned periodical. Unprotected by copyright, translations were fair game for any enterprising bookseller; and the continental publications which Dunton proposed to translate had enjoyed success for a number of years.

The first 'abstract' serial - i.e. a serial devoted primarily to the printing of abstracts of newly published works - was the _Journal des Savans_, published by Denis de Sallo from 1665. Following the lead of this French work came the _Acta Eruditorum_, 1682, published at Leipzig; the _Bibliotheque Universelle_ of Amsterdam; and the _Giornali de' Litterati_ of Rome. Bayle's _Nouvelles de la Republique des Lettres_ began publication at Amsterdam in 1684. These periodicals were not merely catalogues, as had been the earlier _Mercurius Librarius_, or the _Weekly Advertisement of Books_. Although the brief notices of new books which they printed were not book-reviews in the modern sense, the compilers intended to provide an account of the contents of a work and to print sufficient excerpts from it to serve as a guide to its usefulness. "The bare _Titles_ of Books yearly Printed in our common _Catalogues_," wrote the author of _Weekly Memorials for the Ingenious_, "are somewhat dry things, scarce able to raise in men that gust and appetite to Learning, which we may hope these brief _Accounts_ will give them".[3]

The idea of publishing a periodical of abstracts in English was not original to Dunton. *The Philosophical Transactions of the Royal Society* had commenced publication in 1665. Although at first it was composed entirely of original articles of scientific interest, the editor, Henry Oldenburg, announced his intention to provide "some account of the present undertakings, studies, and labours of the Ingenious in many considerable parts of the world". The *Transactions* later contained abstracts of scientific works. *Weekly Memorials for the Ingenious*, printed at London for Henry Faithorne and John Kersey for one year from 16 January 1682, imitated the *Journal des Savans* in English.

Neither was Dunton the first Englishman to propose to translate continental periodicals. *The Universal Historical Bibliotheque* had appeared for three months, January to March 1687, printed for George Wells, at the Sun in St. Paul's Churchyard. Unfortunately, this straightforwardly written and well-printed periodical was not published after the March number because of the death of George Wells, the bookseller.[4] The compiler of this periodical anticipated Dunton's plans, and he wrote in his preface:

> Our Neighbour Nations having observed, that it was not possible to give Men a satisfactory Account of Books by the bare Titles of them, ... and that men were generally desirous to know more of the

Designs and Scopes as well as of the Qualities and Performances of Authors than could be comprehended in the narrow Limits of a Title-Page, ... have published for some years past divers Accounts under several Titles, some in Latin, and others in French and Italian; which has been thought a very useful Design, and much approved by the Learned Men of all Christendom, and accordingly has met with a very kind reception every where .... I desire the Reader would not measure the Design by this Beginning, which is less complete than I intended it at first, because being taken up on a sudden, it was not possible to get in some Papers that were necessary to the perfection of it ....[5]

In the preface to the second number of this work, the compiler observed:

> The Entertainment the first Month of this Undertaking found in the world, was such as to encourage the continuance of it, and a greater improvement too, if it were as easie to get in the materials as I could desire.

On the completion of each volume of The Athenian Mercury, Dunton promised to issue an index, a general title-page, and an Athenian Supplement. The twelve numbers which completed the first volume of The Athenian Mercury were published on 8 June, and on 30 June Dunton advertised the supplement to the first volume as "just now publish'd".[6]

By October 1691 the Athenian Supplements had become popular with the readers of the Mercury, and Dunton had grown even more ambitious for his current project "for the promotion of learning". Late in October, he issued proposals for The Young Students' Library. In this work, the Athenian Society planned to publish extracts from books printed since 1665. Original extracts compiled by members of the Athenian Society were to be included, as well as translations of earlier numbers of the various continental periodicals that had been included in the Athenian *Supplements*. "So most Books," they advertised "*with the solid Truths*, contain a great Quantity of *Rubbish*; ... to distinguish it wherefrom requires a more than ordinary Judgment and Sedulity. *But in Extracts* they are curiously separated, so the most *unexperienced Reader* may securely peruse them, and reap a great deal of advantage by them".[7]

But Dunton's total domination of the field was short-lived, and during the succeeding months his position was challenged by the compiler of *The Works of the Learned*, a monthly serial which had first been published in August 1691. The 'interloper', as Dunton called him, was Jean de la Crose, and his publisher was Thomas Bennet.

Little is known about the early life of Jean Cornand de la Crose, other than that he belonged to a Protestant family of Grenoble and that he studied theology at the Academy of Geneva in 1681.[8] He apparently lived near Paris until the revocation of the Edict of Nantes, after which he lived in Holland, where he was associated with another Huguenot, Jean le Clerc, in writing the first nine volumes of the *Bibliotheque Universelle et Historique*. La Crose had arrived in England by 1691, for he then compiled *The History of Learning: Or, An Abstract of Several Books Lately Published, as well abroad as at home. By one of the Two Authors of the Universal and Historical Bibliotheque*.[9] This 40-page quarto pamphlet was printed for Abel Swalle and Timothy Childe, at the Unicorn at the West-End of St. Paul's Church-Yard. La Crose aimed not simply to translate foreign periodicals, but to provide "a real Abstract taken from the best Books Lately Printed both at home and abroad ... as may most deserve the perusal of the Studious Reader". He planned to continue the work, "if it finds Encouragement, ... as oft as Matter occurs".[10] No further numbers of this work appeared. La Crose wrote in his foreword to *The Works of the Learned* of his difficulties with his first English publisher, "who thought himself wiser than I, and would over-rule in every thing". The nature of La Crose's difficulty is clear: of the eighteen works discussed in *The History of Learning*, seventeen were works published in England, and of these only four had not been published either by Swalle or Childe. La Crose was unwilling to work as a dependent, employed to encourage the sale of works in which his booksellers had an interest.

In August La Crose found a new bookseller and published the first number of _The Works of the Learned, or an Historical Account and Impartial Judgment of Books newly printed, both Foreign and Domestick_. This work was printed for Thomas Bennet, and sold by Randal Taylor. The design of the new periodical was similar to that of the unsuccessful _History of Learning_; eight numbers of _The Works of the Learned_ were published, from August 1691 to March and April 1692.

In his note "To The Reader" in the August number of _The Works of the Learned_, La Crose stated the purposes of his work; he was in full agreement with the ideals which Dunton expressed in his proposals for _The Young Students' Library_. _The Works of the Learned_ would provide a means of saving both time and money, La Crose stated, stressing the sober nature of his undertaking:

> ... this is the Works of the _Learned_, and ... I cannot mention Plays, Satyrs, Romances and the like, which are fitter to corrupt men's Morals, and to shake the grounds of Natural Religion, than to promote Learning and Piety.

With _The Works of the Learned_, the formerly chiefly abstract periodical assumed new responsibilities; La Crose advanced an argument to support the reviewer's right to state a critical opinion:

> If some Authors and Booksellers pretend to damn this design, and ask by what right I take upon me to give out an impartial judgment over their Books and

> erect my self into an Universal Critick. I'll answer, by the same right as they have publish'd 'em. Is not a Book common as soon as it comes into the world, and may not every Reader say, it is good or bad? Well then, since I may make use of my right as well as another, I shall deal more gently with 'em, if I don't tell it with all the Ill Nature the matter will bear, and am satisfied to give a little touch at those things that shall offend me most. Every one may without fear take the same liberty with me; if they give one wholesom advices, either private or publick, they shall be thanked for it, if they reprehend some material things, I'll mend the faults as well as possible; or if they will have some others enlarg'd and explain'd I will endeavour to give them satisfaction. Otherwise I don't love wrangling and have not much time to lose; and though Scriblers should publish every day a Paper against me, I shall not trouble the world with a word of answer.

Presumably Bennet had agreed to allow La Crose a free hand with the writing of the periodical, and La Crose was confident that he would be allowed to continue writing a journal of independent criticism. He was so confident, in fact, that he announced a policy of disdain for the controversy which he rather expected would follow.

At this stage, Dunton's plan was merely to translate foreign periodicals; new material was not to be included, as it would have been costly to do so. In his Life and Errors, Dunton twice asserted that the idea of translating foreign journals was originally his own.[11] He plainly regarded as interference La Crose's plans to produce an original journal similar to those he was preparing to publish in translation. To Dunton, this was unfair competition. Dunton very shortly branded La Crose an "interloper", and prepared to draw him into a quarrel.

After La Crose parted with Abel Swalle and Timothy Childe, he approached other booksellers with his proposals, among them Dunton, who rejected his offers. Dunton brought this to the notice of his readers, in The Athenian Mercury:

> We ... long before certain Offers were made us by Mr. J. de la Cross, promised in our several Supplements the Design and Scope of the most considerable Books Printed in England.[12]

La Crose had come to an agreement meantime with Thomas Bennet, and in the first two numbers of his periodical he made no reply to Dunton. Dunton therefore continued to taunt La Crose. On 6 October, Dunton threatened greater severity:

> What was mentioned in the Athenian Mercury, Numb. 13. Vol. 3. concerning certain Offers made to our Bookseller by Mr. De la Crose; as it was a great Truth, so 'tis not in the least denyed by him in his Advertisement. The reasons why he does not deny it, he Conceals, but except he's Modester for the future, we shall Publish 'em to the World. -- As for his being concern'd either in our Mercury or our Supplements, let the World compare the late Extract he gave of the Voyage into the World of Descartes with an Extract of the same Book which they'll find in the Universal Historical Bibliotheque, and then let 'em judge whether we cou'd ever be so senseless as to admit him into our Society.[13]

On 10 October Dunton wrote that "Mr. De la Crose has been so Honest to declare that he utterly disapproves his Booksellers late Advertisement, and that he would not suffer it in those Copies that were for his own Use".[14] La Crose's declaration to

Dunton may have been made personally or by letter, as there is no trace of it in The Works of the Learned. But Thomas Bennet's advertisement has survived, in at least one copy of the September number of that periodical.[15] In this advertisement, Bennet declared that "Mr. De La Crose has no concern at all, either in that Mercury, or the Supplement .... And as to the Abstracts they promise to publish weekly, 'tis easie to guess what success such Trifling Abridgments are like to meet with in the world".

On 8 October Bennet registered The Works of the Learned, 'to be published monthly', and on 12 October Dunton registered yet another project, The Young Students' Library, or, an Appendix to the Athenian Mercury. Proposals for this work were issued with the general title-page, preface and index to the third volume of The Athenian Mercury, published about 24 October.[16] In The Young Students' Library, Dunton proposed to publish extracts translated from the foreign journals from their commencement to the date of those he was currently translating. His purpose was to provide an opportunity for a young student "to peruse the Extract of a Book before he sets about Reading the Book it self, which may prove as a Card and Compass to direct him in his Course, and keep him from making Shipwrack of the Truth". As the Athenian Supplements had met with success, Dunton procured earlier numbers of the foreign works for translation (including the Bibliotheque Universelle, which he attributed solely to Le Clerc), to which he planned to add original material contributed by the members of the Athenian Society, "So that this Undertaking will serve as a Library for Young Students, that cannot go to the Price of the several Books themselves, and for them that have not time to Peruse them".[17]

In the October number of The Works of the Learned (published at the beginning of November 1691),[18] La Crose began to retaliate:

> Tho the Compilers of the Athenian Mercury, thinking perhaps it might serve their turn to put my name in their Pamphlets, have done it several times in a disingenuous manner: yet I never would have medled with unknown persons, were it not that they have touched me in the most sensible part of an Author, threatning to translate the first Volumes of the Universal Bibliotheque, of which I made one half to the twelfth part incluse; I do not know what the world of such an uncivil dealing, that I living & writing in England and in the Vulgar tongue, they should undertake to make a translation of my own work in concurrence with myself: however I would not have meddled with them, but that I fear from them the same ill usage that some others of my writings which have been put in English without my knowledge, have met with. To prevent this mischief, I design to translate myself the Universal Bibliotheque, with the consent of M. le Clerc my learned Partner tho not as a bare translator, but be mending and enlarging it ....

Dunton hastened to answer La Crose's gentle rebuke, and characteristically he replied with threats. In an advertisement in The Athenian Mercury for 10 November, Dunton stated that the design of The Young Students' Library had met with considerable success, and that he intended

> as a further Encouragement to Subscribers, that whatever we find Valuable in all the Universal Bibliotheques yet Publisht, ... shall be added in the said Volume, all the Universal Bibliotheques being dearly Purchas'd and Enter'd in the Hall-Book ... (they being No Forreigners Property when Translated into the English Tongue) long before any French-man came to Interlope with our Design: But his Interloping is but a Taste of his Morality, we shall therefore Print a larger Account thereof, with his Reasons for leaving Holland, yet unknown to the World, if he at any time Encroaches upon our Booksellers Property, or makes any more scurrilous Reflections: And after all, our Booksellers having (as is evident) Justice and Equity on his side, shall not want a Legal Satisfaction.[19]

By November La Crose had endured a surfeit of Dunton's baiting, and he replied in a severely critical review of the Athenian Supplements. In view of the indignities which he had suffered, his criticism is mild indeed. La Crose's review of the Supplements was given priority over other material in the November number of The Works of the Learned. He explained that "The Athenian Mercury, and the Supplements to it, have found such a favourable acceptance in the Learned World, (if we may believe the Authors themselves) that none of the Ingenious Writers, whose Works make up our Journal, must take it ill, if we give the first place to this Wonderful Attempt of the Whole Athenian Society".[20] La Crose showed great restraint in dealing with the Athenian Society. Principally he cited examples to demonstrate the "insipid style" of their "tiresome abridgements". It is clear that La Crose was not so resentful of their general insolence as he was of their ignoring him in advertisements concerning the *Bibliotheque Universelle et Historique*:

> I may, I suppose, be allow'd to give one Instance ... of their Envy and Malice against me. In their late Proposals they not only ascribe the *Universal Bibliotheque* wholly to Mons. *Le Clerc*, but even Abstracts taken out of the Eleventh Part, that bears my Name alone, ... which my Partner never saw before they were printed; as he himself testifies in the Preface to the XV. Vol.[21]

Dunton reiterated his case against La Crose in the preface to the fourth Athenian *Supplement*, published early in December:

> It is sufficiently known to the *World* that we were the *First that of late years* undertook to Gratifie the Publock with *Extracts of Valuable Books*; and therefore it might have been justly expected, that our *Bookseller* only should have reapt the *Advantage*, *as he run the Risque* that attended such a Design. But no sooner was our Design, after much Cost and Charges like to take, but a *Frenchman* (after his *Undermining Project* had been rejected by several that we cou'd Name) and his Bookseller, *intrude* upon us with their *Book*, Entituled, *The Works of the Learned*: A Piece, for any thing that we can either observe our selves, or hear from Ingenious Men, that the *Learned* will be very little obliged to: And, no sooner did we mention *Proposals*, for the Printing our *Young Students Library*, but this Gentleman *Spitefully* offers to Interfere with us: Had he undertaken *Either of these Designs* before us, we wou'd never have incroacht (as judging it base so to do) on either his, or his Booksellers Designs. But seeing *our Bookseller* was the *First Undertaker*, and that the Forreign Journals are *no Frenchman's property, when Translated into the English Tongue*: We resolve to prosecute our Design with all Expedition Imaginable

> ... so general the Complaint has been of the False and Trifling Account he gives of Books (and therefore no wonder he was continued no longer as an Assistant to Monsieur Le Clerk;) That we have been Importuned by several Learned Persons to make New Extracts of all those Books he has hitherto, and shall hereafter meddle with; which we Resolve to doe, if he at any time Incroaches upon our Bookseller's late Proposals. But it is not our Design to Expose this Gentleman, or any of his Works ... except he urge us to it; but only to vindicate Our own Right .... As to the Frenchmans apprehensions of being wrong'd in our Translations of the Young Students Library, we shall easily rid him of his Fears, ... we do assure him and all the World that we intend to Translate few or none of those Extracts he made for the little time he was concerned with Monsieur Le Clerk, since we promised the publick to give them only the Extracts of the most Valuable Books, and those best done .... But to pretend that he or Monsieur Le Clerk has any Interest in the Universal Bibliotheques here, is an Encroachment upon our English Liberties.

Dunton's particular reply to La Crose's review of the *Mercury* was compounded of his customary threats and abuse:

> The Frenchman, amongst the Works of the Learned has crowded in 3 leaves of Scandal, a strange entertainment for the expectation of all wise and Good men. We shall by and by shew how grosly he accuses himself of all he has charged us with, and sometimes more.[22]

The struggle was almost won for Dunton, but he grasped the opportunity to make a few further caustic observations about La Crose. If La Crose's animosity should continue,

> we shall not only shew the notorious, false, and imperfect accounts he has given of almost every Book he has medled with, but also shall take off the Calumny from those worthy Persons he has abused, and set his whole performance in so true a light, that no man may be any further imposed on by him, tho' there seems to be no great occasion for this, his

> Book meeting with a very inconsiderable Sale, ... which evidently shews the <u>slight Opinion</u> the Learned have of this Gentlemans undertaking.

Throughout the controversy, while La Crose and Dunton aired their mutual grievances, one man who was directly concerned with the situation had remained silent: Thomas Bennet, La Crose's bookseller. As Bennet had agreed to allow La Crose to exercise full discretion concerning *The Works of The Learned*, he had avoided interfering with La Crose's conduct of his side of the dispute - except for the bookseller's advertisement which had been printed in some copies of *The Works of the Learned* for September. While the quarrel raged about him, Bennet had undoubtedly enjoyed the profitable surge of public interest that it created. But if La Crose had been wounded by Dunton in "the most sensible part of an author", so Bennet stood to suffer - if the tide of battle turned towards Dunton - in the most sensible part of a bookseller, his purse. In that event, Bennet would certainly have been concerned to salvage what he could of his investment in *The Works of the Learned*. Perhaps Bennet, losing confidence, approached Dunton; or perhaps Dunton, supremely confident in the eventual outcome of the controversy and sensing that the suitable moment for bargaining had arrived, approached Bennet with the suggestion that the matter be settled to the benefit of the booksellers. Certainly, prior agreement with Bennet is reflected in Dunton's astonishing volte-face in The Athenian Mercury for 2 January 1692:

> The Accounts that have been sent to us concerning Mr. De la Crose, were undoubtedly drawn up by some malicious hands, for upon Inquiry we find they are but mistakes and misrepresentations, of which we thought fit to give publick notice.[23]

The Athenian Mercury confirmed the settlement on 6 February:

> Mr. De la Crose's Bookseller and ours finding that 'tis impossible for 'em both to continue publishing Extracts of Books without interfering with each other, have therefore agreed to print all the Extracts of Books hereafter made ... together in the same Journal entituled. The Works of the Learned, written by Mr. de la Crose.[24]

Bennet, however, had apparently not entirely abandoned La Crose, and he most probably was responsible for ensuring La Crose's continued authorship of the journal. Bennet and Dunton jointly advertised The Works of the Learned in The Athenian Mercury and in the Term Catalogues.[25] Dunton entered his participation in the Stationers' Register on 22 February.

Dunton's influence on The Works of the Learned soon became evident. In the number for January 1692, La Crose included for the first time an article which he called the "News of Learning". "I did not design to insert an Article of this Nature into my Journal," La Crose wrote, "but some particular Circumstances, and Intreaties of intimate Friends, have compell'd me to it on a sudden, and without giving me time enough to get Answers from abroad". He reported brief notes of intellectual happenings in France, Holland, Oxford, Cambridge and London. Not surprisingly, the chief news of learning in London was the forthcoming publication of The Young Students' Library:

> The Young Students Library ... will be Published in a few Weeks. It consists of Abstracts of Books in several Faculties, ... many of which are Collected out of the Journal des Savans of Paris and the Universal Bibliotheque, and, as I hear, accurately Translated.

La Crose had examined portions of the manuscript, and he wrote in enthusiastic support of the work.[26]

The double burden of single-handedly compiling a monthly periodical and quarrelling with Dunton had obviously been a strain on La Crose. The publication of the February number of The Works of the Learned was delayed, and La Crose apologized, as "A heavy Indisposition, which has hinder'd me from writing, and stirring abroad as often as would be necessary, together with the sharpness of the Weather, have caus'd some delay in the publishing of the last Months. However, I hope to be yet strong enough to finish this Volume, with a Paper double the bigness of this for the next Month". Indeed, the particular difficulty of compiling a work of this nature in England had been noted in 1687 by the author of the English Universal Historical Bibliotheque, who had complained that English authors and booksellers were not so accommodating as those on the continent:

> ... as to the Books Printed in England, I have not yet had that Assistance all Foreigners have from time to time, which is to have Abstracts ready drawn, sent them by the Publishers, or Authors, without which it is not possible for any one Man to go through with such a Task as this is. I attribute this in great part to the newness of the thing, it being not yet sufficiently known, nor taken notice of.[27]

Dunton, however, was not completely satisfied with the situation as it stood. He preferred to exercise a greater control over his publications than was possible with La Crose. He therefore persuaded Bennet to surrender his remaining interest in The Works of the Learned, and he announced in the final number of the first volume for March and April 1692 that

> A Monthly Journal returning too quick, to have it always filled with considerable Books; From this time I shall Print The Works of the Learned only four or five times in the Year .... I don't question but this Method will be very Acceptable; which I found my self obliged to pursue, as well from some Objections against the Works of the Learned hitherto, as the disappointment I met with from Monsieur Le Crose, who is very apt to change his Mind, tho strictly obliged; and I am apt to believe one who has bought my right to a Journal Monthly of Books, will have no better success in it.[28]

Dunton had emerged complete victor from the struggle. Bennet retained only the right to publish a journal called The Works of the Learned, and La Crose, chastened, retired for a time from journalism convinced of the impossibility of finding honesty and plain-dealing among the London booksellers.

"Experience has taught me" he later explained "that the perfect establishing of a Journal, so as I understand it, is not the performance of private men".[29]

Dunton hastened to organize his new venture, and he announced on 10 May that "Having bought of the late Undertaker of the Works of the Learned his right to a Monthly Journal of Books, the said Journal will be now carried on by a London Divine, (under the Title of The Compleat Library, or News for the Ingenious, &c.) who will continue it monthly, beginning with this present May".[30]

Dunton regarded The Compleat Library as a continuation and a perfection of The Young Students' Library, of which no further volumes were published, and the Athenian Supplements ceased to appear after the fifth volume. Richard Wolley was the London divine who compiled The Compleat Library for Dunton, and commencing with the number for February 1693, the title-page bore his initials as author. The Compleat Library enjoyed a certain measure of success for a time, although the numbers for July, August, September and October 1693 were delayed until November, after which it resumed monthly publication. Dunton explained the delay in his preface:

> Times being of late very dead, the number of New Books Published very few, and the universal attention of all mens Minds upon the event of the present War, as likewise their particular Expence towards them being so great, that it would hardly

> afford them leisure to mind, or money to spare to buy Books; This Author resolv'd to suspend his Endeavours in this Kind for some time, with intention to resume them again in some more favourable Conjuncture, when Arts should have a Breathing time from Arms.[31]

In July 1694, Dunton announced that as "Many Gentlemen that were wont constantly to take in the Monthly _Compleat Library_, being now gone into the Country, 'tis designed that the _Compleat Librarys_ for _May_, _June_, _July_ and _August_, shall be Publish'd altogether at the beginning of next term",[32] but these numbers never appeared.

Throughout the publication of _The Compleat Library_, Dunton followed a gentle approach to the advancing of his own projects. Of 147 books reviewed during the period May 1692 to December 1693, only eleven were works published by Dunton; but the monthly article on the state of learning in the world contained much enthusiastic comment on his projects. All things considered, Dunton enjoyed greater success than had Thomas Bennet with a monthly journal of books, but the frequenters of the London coffee-houses were surfeited with popular reading material, and Dunton's own erratic temperament made him ever impatient to leap ahead into new activities.

C H A P T E R V

THE DUBLIN SCUFFLE

(1698)

Dunton's wife Iris had suffered patiently for seven months before her death in May 1697. John Dunton, while genuinely grieved at the loss of his wife, saw the commercial possibilities of the event. Thus, he allowed many of Iris's death-bed sentiments and meditations to be included by William Turner in his History of the Most Remarkable Providences, and by Timothy Rogers in The Character of a Good Woman, the sermon he preached at Iris's funeral. Dunton himself later published Iris's writings, in The Post Angel and in his Life and Errors. "That part of the Diary out of which Mr. Rogers extracted several things he published in her 'Funeral Sermon'", Dunton wrote, "was with great difficulty obtained from her by myself in her last sickness; in which, as she expressed it, 'she thought it her duty to deny me nothing'".[1] With characteristic egotism, Dunton expressed his grief to the world, in An Essay, Proving, We shall know Our Friends in Heaven. Writ by a Disconsolate Widower, on the Death of his Wife, and Dedicated to her Dear Memory. In the preface to his Essay, dated "From Eliza's Grave, July 10th 1697", Dunton wrote that "my Inclinations are at present wholly averse from [a second marriage], because I think it utterly impossible for me ever to find such another as thy self". Nevertheless, Dunton was already searching for a wife. When later in the month Samuel Wesley sent Dunton an epitaph for Iris, he wrote: "... I would fain have sent you an Elegy as well as an Epitaph, but cannot get one to my mind, and therefore you must be content with half your desire; and if you please to accept this Epitaph, it is at your service, and I hope it will come before you need another Epithalamium".[2]

Elizabeth Singer, the Pindarick Lady, was Dunton's first choice for a second wife. Dunton's courting of Mrs. Singer's person, however, was not so successful as his courting of her mind had been, and she chose to remain a Platonic friend. In "The Double Courtship", included in Athenianism, 1710, Dunton described his journey to Mrs. Singer's home in Agford, in September 1697, to propose marriage. Rejected by Mrs. Singer, Dunton returned to London, where his "generous and courteous" friend Mrs. Goodall brought him together with Sarah Nicholas, who then lived with her mother, Mrs. Jane Nicholas of St. Albans, in a house in Bull-head Court, near Dunton's own house in Jewen Street.[3] Dunton and Sarah

Nicholas, whom he called Valeria, were married at St. Albans, on 23 October 1697.[4] Three years later, Dunton published a further personal essay, "A Defense of a Speedy Marriage after the Death of a Good Wife".[5]

With Dunton's remarriage began the marital and financial difficulties from which he was to have no relief during the remaining years of his life. The chief impediment to his happiness with Valeria was Valeria's mother. Jane Nicholas had inherited a sizable estate from her late husband, a former Mayor of St. Albans; that she was a woman of shrewdness and intransigence is seen in her treatment of John Dunton. Certainly she sensed that in her daughter Dunton saw not only a potential helpmate but a potential heiress. Dunton was heavily in debt at the time of his remarriage. He had lost a valuable cargo of books at sea in 1685; he had been put to a great expense for Iris's sister Bethia; several projects, notably the History of the Famous Edict of Nantes, had failed; and Iris's long illness had further depleted his resources. Iris's frugal management of his affairs had deferred financial difficulties, but after her death Dunton's creditors pressed for settlement. Dunton hoped for a new beginning in trade, and in return for his mother-in-law's promise of immediate financial relief, and the expectation of a generous legacy, Dunton agreed to settle on his wife a jointure of the three properties he owned in Buckinghamshire. However, when Dunton presented his mother-in-law with a list of the debts which he hoped she would pay, she withdrew her promise of assistance and so inflamed Valeria against Dunton that Valeria vowed never to release her claims on Dunton's property. Mother and daughter then withdrew to St. Albans, leaving Dunton to get on as best he could. Early in 1698, Dunton published An Essay, Proving We shall know Our Friends in Heaven, which, after remarks on the life and death of Iris, became a tirade - the first of several - against his mother-in-law. Dunton's relations with his wife, and his difficulties with his mother-in-law, were described in tracts which he continued to publish for many years after the death of both women. To all proposals, whether pleading or vituperative, Jane Nicholas remained obdurate; and Dunton's creditors remained unsatisfied.

Dunton met his immediate expenses by selling a few of his successful copyrights. Earlier in the year he had jettisoned Tyrrell's General History of England, and when the long-delayed second volume appeared in 1700, it bore the joint imprint of W. Rogers, Robert Knaplock, Andrew Bell, and Thomas Cockerill.[6] Andrew Bell had also given Dunton and John Harris £30 for the third (and subsequent) editions of Coke's Detection of the court and State of England.[7] Baxter's Poetical

Fragments, Shower's Mourner's Companion, and Williams's Gospel Truth Stated and Vindicated were among those sold later in the year. Editions of these works were printed in 1698 and 1699 (while Dunton was away from London) for some of Dunton's former associates: Thomas Parkhurst, Samuel Crouch, John Lawrence, and Thomas Cockerill.[8] After Dunton's return to London in 1699 he continued occasionally to exchange a copyright for ready money, but as late as 1719 he listed a number of copies to which he claimed title, advising his executrix not to sell them for less than a thousand guineas.[9]

Dunton made his next attempt to regain financial independence early in 1698, when he determined to combine his greatest pleasure, rambling, with bookselling, by travelling to Ireland with a stock of books which he planned to sell by auction in Dublin. He was well acquainted with the auction method of bookselling, which had a few years earlier been introduced to England. During the time of Dunton's apprenticeship, in 1676, William Cooper had held the first sale of books by auction in England. In 1680, Dunton had arranged for his master, Thomas Parkhurst, to sell by auction the library which he had inherited from his father, the late Rector of Aston Clinton.[10] The method of offering books for sale to the highest bidder at public auction quickly won public approval; and not only the novelty but the efficiency of auction-selling appealed to Dunton, who hoped to dispose quickly and profitably of a large stock of books without the tedium of tending a shop or warehouse. "But Shops are of small Account", he later wrote in The Dublin Scuffle, "and I hope to get more by Travelling abroad, than by staying at home".[11] With ten tons of books, which he was confident of selling for at least £1500, Dunton arrived in Dublin in April 1698, and began to make plans for three auctions to be held in the summer and autumn.[12]

No surviving copy has been located of any of the ephemeral printed items - sale catalogues, announcements, and open letters - which Dunton issued in Dublin. Neither does the reprinted Dublin edition of The Flying Post (in which many of the announcements appeared) survive.[13] But Dunton included a number of the letters, and the advertisements from The Flying Post, in The Dublin Scuffle, which he published after his return to London. The Dublin Scuffle will be quoted extensively in the following pages, as Dunton left in it a candid account of his Irish expedition, an account which is not disfigured by the mannered piety of his Life and Errors. In The Dublin Scuffle Dunton frankly confessed his dislike of shopkeeping and his love of rambling. He enjoyed the role of impresario which he played in Dublin, and in The Dublin Scuffle he described his trade, his travels and his conversation with a spontaneity which is lacking in his autobiography.

Immediately upon his arrival in Dublin, late one night in April, Dunton with some difficulty found lodgings with Mrs Lisle, at the Duke's Head Tavern in Castle Street, "the first Place I drank at in *Ireland*".[14] In two days' time he had sufficiently recovered from seasickness (which he patiently tolerated, as "*it endears the sence of God's Goodness to me when I come to Land*, and makes me the more thankful for my Preservation") to go sightseeing. Dunton was an indefatigable tourist; to his female correspondent he wrote: "You wou'd smile, Madam, if you had the *Picture of your quondam friend at the black Raven*, like an over-grown *Oaf* newly come to Town, staring and gazing at all the Signs, and every thing else in the Streets; pacing out their length, and enquiring ever and anon, *What call ye this Street*? *Who dwells in yon great House*? *Whose fine Coach is that*? For thus I rambled through every Street, Alley, and corner of this spacious Town".[15] An early reconnaissance of the city was important; Dunton's flamboyant personality was an obvious asset to trade, and Dunton knew the value of publicity. The booksellers of Dublin naturally had misgivings about the invader from London, and he set out to gain their trust and co-operation. "My business now was to see and be seen" Dunton wrote "[and] I marched very methodically out of my Lodgings with two (I can't say a pair of) Gloves in one hand, and a Cane in t'other".[16] Dunton believed his manner of dress to be important, and he carefully groomed himself for the role he intended to play in Dublin: "Being now, Madam, to Sally out into the City, under a necessity of making my self more particularly known, in respect to the affairs I went about, I will presume to suppose you might be inquisitive to understand what sort of Figure was proper for me to make. As to my Cloaths, I confess I was never over-curious, affecting always to appear more plain and cleanly, than gay and finical .... However, it was both necessary and convenient I should rather appear above than below my Quality".[17] Only to the Dublin Play-house Dunton went dressed "tollerably well; tho' not so much to be seen, as to see the Follies of the Age".[18]

Throughout May and June, Dunton combined sightseeing with the serious business of making friends for his venture. In his "Conversation in Ireland" he included a detailed description of how he passed his first few days in Dublin. On his first day there, he visited the bookseller, Matthew Gun, in Essex Street, who became "a constant and generous bidder" at his auctions.[19] At Gun's shop he met Mr. Bently, whom he later employed to bind books for his sales. Mr. Bently showed Dunton the Change, and after they encountered George Larkin, a friend from London, they walked together to the Tholsel, to view the city. There Dunton met Mr. Dell, who later purchased books from him, and they went together to Dick's Coffee-house, where Dunton had been advised by Richard Wilde to hold his sales. "I ... went up, saw it, and liked it, as proper for my Purpose;" Dunton wrote "Dick shewing me all the Civility I could desire".[20] From Dick's the company proceeded "to the Tavern, where having drank a Bottle or two ... we parted, and went each to our several Lodgings".

On his second day in Dublin, Dunton found more suitable lodgings at Counsellour H----'s house in Wine-Tavern Street.[21] There Dunton met William Wainwright, his "first Acquaintance" in Dublin, "who, tho' he lives a Batcheler, is a Person of strict Modesty, and has the symptoms of a good Christian"; and Mrs. Isabella Edwards, who became (as Climene) Dunton's chief Platonic friend in Dublin, and whom he described in his will as his adopted child.[22] Several pages in Dunton's "Conversation in Ireland" are given to a description of Climene's beauty, wit, and piety and a short paragraph to Mr. Edwards, "a Person of indifferent Stature ... and [who] tho' no Pretender to any extraordinary Perfections, is far from being contemptible".[23] Dunton found the booksellers he met to be friendly, but as his arrival became known, an attempt was made to buy out his venture. "Soon after my coming to Dublin," he later explained "Mr. Norman the Bookseller [and Master of the Booksellers' Company in Dublin] sent one Mr. Rogerson, to invite me to his House; when I came thither, I found his Business was to propose the buying of the Venture I had brought over; in which, though we agreed not, he treated me very kindly, shewing me all his House ... From hence he carried me to a large Ware-house, where he had a large Auction, preparing, as he said, for Sale; though I heard nothing more of it while I stayed in Dublin".[24]

On the whole, Dunton was treated well by the booksellers of Dublin, and he praised many of them in The Dublin Scuffle and in his Life and Errors. He was grateful for the "extraordinary Civility" shown him by Andrew Crook, King's Printer, and for the hospitality of the King's Stationer, Thornton, who shared with him a "Bottle of Excellent Claret".[25] Not all the booksellers of Dublin were so easily won to his side, however. Dunton had minor difficulties with Turner, a bookseller, and Brass, a bookbinder, as well as a major difference with Patrick Campbell. When Dunton first arrived in Dublin, Turner boasted of lending him forty shillings, "thinking I suppose, to lessen my Credit with Printers, Stationers, and Binders ... that so my Venture might sleep in quiet, till this Geud Man had cull'd out my best Books, which I judge he thought ... he shou'd have for a Song".[26] So much stir was created about the forty shillings that news of it reached Dunton's manager, Richard Wilde, who was then in London.[27] More serious problems were caused by one of the men whom Dunton employed to bind books for his auctions, Mr. Brass of Copper Alley: "This Brass knowing the necessity I was under of having my Books bound in order to sale, resolves to make me pay a rate for Binding, not only beyond what was given in London, but even beyond what was given by the Booksellers of Dublin ... There was a Necessity of having my Books bound, and I was forc'd to comply with his unreasonable Rates".[28] When Dunton was overcharged as well, he refused to pay, and Brass served him with a summons to appear before the Lord Mayor, who agreed that the charges originally agreed on were fair and dismissed them both.

Patrick Campbell became the chief enemy to Dunton's venture, and during his first weeks in Dublin Dunton called on him several times, hoping to settle accounts with him for books he had asked to be sent him from London. "I went to see Patrick Campbel," Dunton wrote in his "Conversation", "to whom (by his Order) I had sent several of Mr. Turner's History. He treated me well enough the first time I saw him, giving me my Mornings Draught, and telling me I was welcome to Dublin: But I said nothing then of the Books I sent him, nor he to me; which I thought somewhat strange. The second time I went to him, which was the Week following; after the usual How-dee's were over, I expected he shou'd have took some notice to me of the Books; which he not doing, I took notice of 'em to him; and then it was I perceiv'd he had a Natural Aversion to Honesty; for he began to shuffle at the very mention of 'em. However, resolving to be easie with him, I took my leave of him for that time. The third time I saw him, he shuffl'd about my Books at that rate, that a Stranger in his Shop (to whom I offer'd to refer my Cause) resented it: And from that time forward (only for demanding my own, and telling him how unfairly he dealt by me) he became my Enemy".[29]

While Dunton was making himself known in Dublin, Richard Wilde, whom he had engaged to manage his auctions, was buying additional stock in London, and arranging for its shipment to Dublin.[30] But Dunton's life in Dublin was not entirely devoted to sightseeing and visiting taverns and coffee-houses. "For though I had given the Conduct of my Auctions to Mr. Wilde", he insisted, "... yet was I not so freed from Business my self, as not to have Applications made to me, both by the Binders and other Persons".[31] Dunton changed lodgings once again, moving from Wine-Tavern Street to Mr. Thomas Orson's house in the country, at Arbor Hill, about a mile from Dublin.[32] Soon after his move to Arbor Hill, Dunton was bitten by a mastiff ("who had ... torn me to pieces, had not the drawing my Sword baulk'd his Attempt") and he was grateful for the Orsons' kindness in caring for him, as well as for the "Parental tendernesses" they showed him during a severe illness which he suffered while he stayed with them. Exhausted from the fast pace of life in town, Dunton welcomed country life as an opportunity to pursue his "Private Life" and pass his days in writing and meditation. During his stay in Ireland, he found time to complete his New England letters, titled A Summer Ramble, and compiled his "Conversation in Ireland" which he planned to print on his return to London. Later, Dunton heard from London "the sad News of the death of my Owl ... so out of meer love to this old Servant, I fell to write an Essay in praise of an Owl, and have spent about twenty Sheets in telling the Vertues of poor Madge".[33]

Soon Dunton engaged three printers, Brent, Brocas, and Powel, who were partners in the "Top Printing-House in all Dublin". He again changed lodgings, moving to Mr. Lander's house in Capel Street, in order to be near his sale room; and on 24 June he issued his prospectus of "Three Auctions to be held in the City of Dublin".[34]

"Gentlemen," Dunton addressed the Wise and Learned and Studious citizens of Dublin, "Though the Summer be a Time for Rambling, and the Season of the Year invite all Men abroad, that love to see Foreign Countries, yet 'twas not this alone, but the good Acceptance the way of Sale by _Auction_ has met with from all _Lovers_ of Books, that encouraged me to bring to this Kingdom of _Ireland_, a General Collection of the most valuable Pieces ... that have been Printed in _England_ since the Dreadful Fire in _London_ in 1666, to this present Time". Dunton thanked the booksellers of Dublin for their generous reception, but he was unable to resist taunting Patrick Campbell, "who grins at my Undertaking". Dunton proposed to sell his books in three auctions, the first on 7 July, and catalogues for each sale were to be given out at Dick's Coffee-house in Dublin, and at coffee-houses in Limerick, Cork, Kilkenny, Clonmel, Wexford, Galway, and at other country towns. Dunton promised honest management of his auctions - no "setters" to force up the bidding, and equal opportunity for the trade and for private customers - and directed enquiries to Mr. Wilde, for "my Health [calls] me to _Wexford_ to drink the Waters".[35]

Richard Pue was the proprietor of the coffee-house where Dunton held his first auctions. Dick's coffee-house was a most appropriate place for book sales to be held, since Richard Wilde, who had introduced auctions sales to Dublin, had held several sales there before bringing Dunton to Dublin. Wilde had personally furnished the room where the sales were held, and he owned the shelves on which books were displayed.[36] With his sales in the capable hands of Richard Wilde, and with the assistance of "honest Robinson", "trusty James", Nelson, Dunton's porter, Bacon, and his bookkeeper, Price, there was really very little work remaining for Dunton, who freely admitted that "the toyl of keeping Accounts, was a Labour too tedious for my Mercurial Brains".[37] And so he rambled; "I was no sooner home [from Kilkenney]," Dunton wrote, "and had given some necessary Orders about my Auction, but I rambled to Drogheda, and paid a Visit to the famous Boyn".[38] When Dunton learned that his porter had turned thief, he changed his lodgings again, to Mr. Cawley's house, in Wine-Tavern Street, that he might more closely superintend his sales.[39] To his female correspondent Dunton described his morning appearance at the sale room:

> "When I came there [to the sale room], my first Word usually was, Where's Wild? What Sale last Night? Call Price. Sir, here's your Account ready cast up; Thirty Pounds receiv'd, and here's the discharge on't. Call Nelson, Call Robinson, call James, call Bacon. Are the Bills Printed? And were they dispers'd at the Coffee houses, College, and Tholsel? Thus, Madam, you see I was a Man of Business; and that my Province was, to have a general Inspection over all my Servants; and to stir them up to their Duty with the utmost Application".[40]

It is not surprising that Richard Wilde encouraged Dunton's jaunts to distant parts of Ireland, suggesting itineraries and writing letters of introduction. Later in the day, after dinner and a reflective walk in the fields, it was Dunton's custom to visit his sale room again, incognito:

> "I us'd to make a trip to my Auction, and crowd my self among the Gentlemen that went thither to buy Pennyworths; and so cou'd, unobserv'd, observe how things went. And here, to do 'em Justice, I observ'd that several Gentlemen bid like themselves, and as those that understood the Worth and Value of the Books they bid for. And others as much betray'd their Ignorance, and took no other Measures for their bidding, but from the bulk of the Book, if 'twas large (whatever the worth on't was) they bid accordingly. And yet, to do these Right, if they had but paid for what they had so bought, I have no reason to complain of 'em. Others there were, that in their bidding took their Measures from what they heard another bid before 'em; and two of these happening to meet together, wou'd strive so to out-bid each other, that they wou'd sometimes raise but an indifferent Book to a good Price .... But whatsoever any bid, 'twas their own Act and Deed; for I must do my self that Justice, to assert that I had none of those unworthy ways that have been used in some other Auctions. I had not one Setter (to advance the Price, and draw on unwary Bidders) in any of my five Sales".[41]

Dunton's auctions were disturbed briefly by hecklers, and he was greatly obliged to the "brave and generous" Colonel Butler (to whom he dedicated The Dublin Scuffle) for silencing them: "there was some Persons that had a mind to disturb and banter my Auction; but by [Colonel Butler's] appearing against 'em, and resenting the Affront as done to himself, they quickly cry'd Pecavi".[42]

The date of Dunton's second Dublin auction is not known; but his third auction began on 7 November, and the place of sale was changed to Patt's Coffee-House in High

Street. Patt was "a fair-condition'd Man, and very obliging to all his Customers; Loving to do business without making a noise on't";[43] and at his coffee-house Dunton held his farewell sale in November and his "Packing Penny" in December. To explain the move from Richard Pue's coffee-house, and to argue his charges against Patrick Campbell, Dunton addressed a second letter "to those Gentlemen, who have bought Books at my two former Auctions". Patrick Campbell, Dunton explained, "thinking that the Room where Gentlemen had found such fair Usage in my Auction, would give a Reputation to his", offered Dick a higher rent for his room, and "easie Dick ... finding that 'twas the law of Auctions, that he who bids most is the Buyer, e'en lets the Room to Patrick ... without being so fair as to cry Ten Shillings Once, Ten Shillings Twice, either to my self, or to Mr. Wilde, to whom he promised the Refusal".[44] Dunton continued to protest his innocence of unfair dealing, confidently challenging the perfidious Patrick to a "Paper-war": "... if Campbell Replies to this, I'll Answer his Charge, De Die in Diem, till I have worn my Pen to the Stumps".[45]

After his third auction, Dunton found that he had many books remaining unsold. He therefore announced a "Farewell Sale", to be held through November at Patt's, ending at the latest on 1 December; he intended to embark for London on

5 December. At the end of the Sale, Dunton announced, remaining stocks would be offered to the Dublin booksellers. To them, he advised his customers, they would have to pay higher prices. Many purchases at former sales had not been paid for, and Dunton emphasised his conditions of sale:

> "The Conditions of this last Sale are, That whatever is bought till Thursday Night, be all paid the following Fryday; and for what has been bought in my Three past Auctions, 'tis expected they should be all fetcht away by Saturday the 26th at Patt's Coffee-House, from eight in the Morning till eight at Night".[46]

Difficulties of collecting accounts for purchases, and of disposing of the remaining stock, delayed Dunton's return to London. On 12 December he issued a prospectus of a final sale, which he called his "Packing Penny", to be held on 13 December. These last few books were not to be sold by auction, but over the counter at whatever price might be agreed by Mr. Wilde and the buyer. Dunton concluded his announcement with a further plea for payment, and a further threat to the malicious scandal-mongers who had tried to discourage his customers. When the Packing Penny had ended, Matthew Gun paid Dunton about £100 for the remaining stock.[47]

On 26 December, Dunton addressed his "Last Farewell to my Acquaintance in Dublin, whether Friends, or Enemies", in which he published flattering portraits of the clergymen and laity who had been generous buyers at his auctions, and unflattering portraits of his three enemies, Brass, Turner and Patrick Campbell. Dunton planned to take final leave of the "Non-Paymasters" as well, and he advised them that he had "agreed in the Lump ... with an Honest Lawyer ... and *Two Bailiffs*, who will fear nothing in the just Execution of their office".[48]

Although he had been pressed to return annually to Dublin, Dunton had already made plans for a Scottish ramble, and he had, he announced, engaged Richard Wilde as manager. The first part of Dunton's *Summer Ramble* had been written at his leisure in Dublin, and in his "Last Farewell" he announced that as soon as possible after his return to London he intended to begin publication of his *Summer Ramble, or History of my Travels through Ten Kingdoms*,

> "of which I have seen four ... *Scotland*, *France* and *Italy* make it seven; and when I ha' crost the *Hellespont* ... *Greece*, *China* and the *Holy Land*, are the other three I am bound too, and perhaps (when my hand's in) I may step thence to the *Indies* ... *But Shops are of small account* ... and I hope to get more by Travelling abroad, than by staying at home".[49]

Finally, Dunton gave a farewell dinner for a few of his friends, walked to Copper Alley for a parting glare at Brass and Patrick Campbell, and then embarked on Captain Picknance's ship, the Diamond, and sailed for London.

CHAPTER VI

THE ABUSIVE SCRIBBLER

(1700-1732)

On his return to London in 1699, Dunton was not so fortunate as he had been on his return from New England ten years earlier, when he had found his wife in good health and his affairs settled. In 1699, he found his second wife and her shrewish mother installed at the Black Raven, and his debts unpaid. Dunton's friends had been driven away by the two women, and he himself was forced to find lodgings elsewhere. Before the year's end, he stayed briefly in London, Tunbridge Wells, Newcastle, Huntingdon and York.[1]

Dunton's health failed rapidly after 1699. He suffered from the "incurable putrefaction of some morbid juices in the renal concavities" that had killed his father twenty-five years earlier. During these unhappy years his attacks of the stone also became so frequent and so painful, that he had to be attended constantly. Separated from his wife, Dunton was cared for by his landladies and by numerous female friends. When his pain subsided, Dunton exhausted himself by composing diatribes against his mother-in-law and by dashing about London in attempts to interest booksellers in his new projects. His only income during these years came from writing and from the occasional sale of the copyright of a successful book. With his advancing years his writing became increasingly incoherent. Dunton had never written with clarity or brevity; as early as 1691 he had confessed that "I have got such a trick of making *Digressions*, that I find it is hardly possible for me to hold long to a Point".[2] Among his voluminous and discursive writings after 1700, few met with success, and most served only to convince his contemporaries of his growing madness.

Dunton's career as an "abusive scribbler" does not need to be examined in great detail;[3] deliberately the investigation of Dunton's activities in bookselling and publishing has been the primary object of this study. His writings during this period must be discussed briefly, however, as many of Dunton's later publications illuminate his relationships with former colleagues and demonstrate his attitudes to changing conditions and developments in the trade.

In *The Art of Living Incognito*, 1700, Dunton printed an epitaph he had composed for himself:

> "Here lies his Dust, who chiefly aimed to know
> Himself; and chose to live incognito ....[4]

In fact, Dunton chose to live in concealment only from his many creditors; the most intimate details of his relations with his wife, and his grievances against his mother-in-law, were printed for all the world to read. *The Dublin Scuffle*, which he published in 1699, included an account of his personal difficulties, as had *An Essay, Proving We shall know Our Friends in Heaven*, which he had published in 1698. Late in 1699 Dunton wrote another statement of the charges against his mother-in-law, and early in 1700 his friend Anne Baldwin published *The Case of John Dunton, Citizen of London: with Respect to his Mother-in-law, Madam Jane Nicholas, of St. Albans; and her only Child, Sarah Dunton. With the Just Reasons for Her Husband's Leaving Her*.

Dunton's wife and mother-in-law remained obdurate, and he retired to Tunbridge Wells, where he wrote a series of letters which Anne Baldwin published as *The Art of Living Incognito*. Dunton planned to continue this work indefinitely, but only the second part, containing his essay upon his own funeral, reached the public. In a letter to Dunton at Tunbridge Wells, George Larkin reported that the second part was "a poor Drug ... it neither sells it self nor the first Part moor at all".[5] Later in the year Dunton reiterated his charges against his mother-in-law in a four-page tract called *Reflections on Mr. Dunton's Leaving his Wife. In a Letter to*

Himself.

In 1701, Anne Baldwin published for Dunton a further instalment of the chronicle of his marital difficulties. Hopefully titled The Case is Alter'd: Or, Dunton's Re-marriage to the Same Wife, the work had no influence on the unyielding wife and mother-in-law, and Dunton himself had no more to say on the matter until 1705, when he published his Life and Errors. Further, Dunton began a new periodical in 1701, The Post Angel, of which his friend Anne Baldwin was the publisher. Modelled on The Athenian Mercury, The Post Angel included, as well as answers to questions, notes on the remarkable "providences" of the month, biographical notices of eminent persons who had died during the month, news, and book-reviews - "with a Spritual Observator upon each Head". It was written entirely by Dunton until ill health forced him to return to Tunbridge Wells in July 1702. A "society of clergymen" continued the work until September 1702.

In May 1702, Dunton had begun to publish The New Quevedo; or a Vision of Charon's Passengers from the Creation of the World down to this Present Year 1702, with their Names, Qualities, and Particular Crimes. Two numbers only of this work appeared, and Dunton later wrote in his Life and Errors that he regretted having embarked on it.[6]

In August appeared The History of Living Men: Or,

Characters of the Royal Family, the Ministers of State, and the Principal Natives of the Three Kingdoms. Although he advertised for readers to submit their own characters for inclusion in future volumes, the work met with little success, and no further volumes were issued. Dunton later reprinted many of the characters in his autobiography. Elizabeth Mallet, the publisher of these last mentioned works, also offered in that year a periodical by Dunton, The Secret Mercury, Or the Adventures of Seven Days, of which four numbers were issued in September.

On earlier occasions of financial difficulty Dunton had supplemented his income by selling a few of his successful copies to other booksellers. Dunton continued this practice when necessary during his years of retirement, although he still claimed title to a great number of valuable copyrights as late as 1719, when he objected to several booksellers who intended to publish unauthorized editions of some of them.[7] He sold Religio Bibliopolae to C. Corbett, who published a new edition in 1702, and new editions of A New Martyrology and The Post-Boy Robb'd of his Mail appeared in 1705.[8] Dunton sold the copyright of Thomas Doolittle's The Lord's Last Sufferings, the first work he had published on entering the trade, to Thomas Parkhurst, who published the second edition in 1701.[9]

In one instance, the sale of reprint rights met with

outstanding success and led to the revival of a number of similar projects. At Tunbridge Wells, in the late summer of 1702, Dunton prepared a collection of questions and answers from *The Athenian Mercury*. On his return to London he obtained very good terms for the work from Andrew Bell. The collected questions and answers were to be called *The Athenian Oracle*, and the agreement for publishing this work survives in the Bodleian Library.

> Memorandum
>
> That it is agreed between John Dunton Citizen and Stationer of London, on the one Part, And Andrew Bell of the same, That ye s^{d} Jno Dunton shall sell to ye s^{d} Andr. Bell, a Copy Intitled ye Athenian Oracle &c. Which shall contain in Print of a large octave - Long Primer, betwixt thirty or forty sheets as to ye s^{d} Andr Bell shall seem most Convenient: For each sheet thereof ye s^{d} Andr Bell shall Pay to ye s^{d} John Dunton ten Shillings p^{r} Sheet, at ye finishing or Printing of each six sheets, That it be Put to three Printing Houses that it may be finished if Possible by ye first of January next, and that Mr Grantham be one of ye Printers, Provided his Letter be such as ye s^{d} Andr. Bell approves on, and that he will do it as cheap as another. - And that ye s^{d} Andr. Bell do obleige each Printer to let George Larkin Sen^{or} have ye Correcting of each sheet of ye s^{d} Book, & He be Paid for it by them at ye rate yt is usually p^{d} to other Correctors, That ye s^{d} Andr Bell do give to ye s^{d} John Dunton twelve Books B^{d} in calves Leather as soon as they are Published, That if ye s^{d} Andr. Bell shall think fit to go on w^{t} a second, third or Fourth Vol^{m} Each vol. shall be on ye same terms: and if the s^{d} Andr. Bell shall think fit not to go on w^{t} another vol. that it shall be lawfull for ye s^{d} Jno Dunton in whom ye Propriety of ye s^{d} copy is, to go on w^{t} ye s^{d} copy himself, or dispose of it to any other, after the s^{d} Andr Bell has refused it, In confirmation of wch s^{d}

Articles ye s^d Andr. Bell has given a Guinea for ye Use of ye Proprietor of ye fifteen vol. of ye Athenian Mercuries B^d up together in foll. who has Hereunto subscribed his name this seventh day of Novembr. 1702.

[Signed:] Andrew Bell

[Signed:] Witness George Larkin.[10]

In this carefully detailed agreement Dunton had protected himself for every eventuality but one - he omitted to ask for additional payment for subsequent editions. Presumably he believed that the copy had been sold to Bell outright. However, the detailed arrangements for the publication of further volumes indicate that Dunton was unsure of the success of The Athenian Oracle and wanted to reserve the right to sell it to another bookseller if Bell declined to proceed after the first volume. The first volume of The Athenian Oracle appeared in March 1703, and the second followed in May; even the perpetually optimistic John Dunton must have been astonished at the popular reception of the work. Volume III appeared in 1704, by which time it had been necessary to publish second editions of the two earlier volumes. The first two volumes of The Athenian Oracle were reprinted again in 1706 and 1708, and the third volume reached a third edition in 1716.

A fourth volume was planned in 1707, but because the material in the fifteen volumes given to Bell in 1702 had been exhausted, Dunton was forced to apply to Narcissus Luttrell for the loan of the last volumes of the Mercury, and The History of the Athenian Society, that he might compile a final volume:

> To Mr. Luttrell a Member of Parliament, Liueing ouer against the Three Cupps in Holborn
>
> S^{r}.
>
> I had not presumed to haue troubled you with this Letter but that I am under a Necessity of entreating your Generous assistance towards compleating a work now going to ye Press Viz. I haue all the Volumes of ye Athenian Mercuries saue the 18th and 19th Volum, and The History of ye Athenian Society, and haue searcht in near an Hundred likely Places for them & can't yet find y^{m}. but was yesterday inform'd by Mr. Goodwin Bookseller in Fleetstreet that 'tis very Probable that you haue them (as you haue bin a Good Benefactor to the Booksellers in buying most New Peices) this comes therefore humblely to Entreat, you'd lend to Mr Bell the Bookseller in Cornhill, these 3 Peices before mention'd being all 3 wanted to compleat a Supplement to ye 3 Volumes of ye Athenian Oracle lately Publish'd - S^{r}. your Generosity in this Matter will be a Reall Peice of seruice to ye Publick as I know not where to procure them ('the ye Athenian Mercury was my own Project) and I hope that scarcity will in some measure excuse this Great Presumption. S^{r}. Mr. Bell ye undertaker shall when ye Supplement is Printed Present you with a Compleat Set of the Athenian Oracle for your Generosity in lending this 18th, and 19th. Volum and History of ye Athenian Society & these 3 you lend shall (when Printed) be returned as safe as Gold and 'the there Value was but 6^{s} all 3 when first Publish'd if you desire it ye Bearer hereof shall leaue a Pledge 'till they are return'd - S^{r}. I haue only to ask your Pardon for this Presumption, and leaue to subscribe My selfe -
>
> your Very Humble Seruant
> John Dunton.
>
> From ye Sword in Black Fryars
> Dec: 30th 1707.

6. Januar. 1707/8.

> Received & borrowed then of Mr. Luttrell one book in folio, intitled The Athenian Gazett or Casuistical Mercury beginning 11. July. 1695. Volumn. 11th. & ending. [ ]. 14. June. 1697. in vol. 20th. bound in Cambridge Sort of binding; wch I hereby faithfully promise to return Safe & undammaged upon demand; & have for the Security thereof deposited in ye said Mr Luttrell's hands two guineas. & I [being] intending to make use thereof in ye publicaon of y^{e} [History of] Supplement to ye Athenian Oracle &c. I hereby promise to p^{re}sent ye same Athenian Oracle Compleat to Mr Luttrell gratis, Witnesse my hand
>
> John-Dunton
>
> To ye Sword in Black Fryars.[11]

In 1710, Dunton published the fourth volume of _The Athenian Oracle_, called _A Supplement to the Athenian Oracle_, to which he added Charles Gildon's _History of the Athenian Society_, Swift's "Ode to the Athenian Society", and the essay on learning from _The Young Students Library_. A further edition of _The Athenian Oracle_, in four volumes, reached the public in 1728.

In addition to _The Athenian Oracle_, Dunton wrote in 1703 _A Satyr upon King William_, of which three editions were called for, and _The Shortest Way with Whores and Rogues_, published in two editions.

In 1704 Dunton set about to take advantage of the renewed popular interest in the Athenian Society by publishing several new works under their name. In February, he published

The Athenian Spy, which was made up of letters from his female correspondents, "an intire collection of love-secrets communicated from time to time to the Athenian Society". In June, Dunton exercised the option to continue his question project with fresh material, and he began to issue, in monthly parts, *Athenae Redivivae: or the New Athenian Oracle*. *Athenae Redivivae* contained three departments: "The Divine Oracle", "The Philosophick and Miscellaneous Oracle", and "The Secret (or Ladies) Oracle". The first volume, in six parts, was completed by the end of the year; further volumes, although promised, did not appear. *Athenae Redivivae* failed, Dunton later wrote, because Daniel Defoe "interloped" with his *Review*: "Losers may have leave to speak;" Dunton wrote, "and I here declare, I am 200 *l*. the worse for De Foe's clogging my 'Question-Project.' His answering Questions Weekly put a stop to my 'Monthly Oracle' ..."[12]

In the publication of works such as *Athenae Redivivae*, Dunton came very close to bridging the gap between a periodical and a book published in parts. It was not, in Dunton's conception, really a periodical: the parts were intended to be collected and bound, and they were issued with continuous register and pagination. Separate parts did not have separate title-pages, but simply a heading indicating their position in the sequence. But Dunton came no nearer to serial publication than by this sort of project, "to be continued in this method, till the question-project is compleated".

Later in 1704 Dunton published a new weekly paper, The Athenian Catechism. His announcement for this work shows that he was aware of another element which later contributed to the success of serial publication. "The Athenian Catechism," Dunton announced, "will be sold at A Penny each Numb. that the poorer Sort may be able to buy it". But the poorer sort did not buy it, and The Athenian Catechism was discontinued after 20 numbers. No surviving copy of the work has been located. In July Dunton conceived the New Athenian Society, and under their name he published The New Practice of Piety. This was an expanded version of Religio Bibliopolae, a copy which he no longer owned.

Although The Athenian Oracle had sold well, other projects had failed, and Dunton had been unable to settle his numerous debts. Finally his creditors could be put off no longer, and in December 1704, they distrained upon his goods. The only account of this event which survives is found in a letter Dunton wrote to Mr. Sheafe, a stationer who had supplied him with paper for his Life and Errors.[13] Sarah Malthus and others sought to seize all copies of his Life and Errors, although Dunton protested that "I cou'd not honestly claim any *right in ye books* ... till ye Printers & Stationers were first paid as they trusted me on that condition ...." Hence Dunton consigned all copies of the book in Mr. Sheafe's possession to Sheafe and his partner Merreal, to prevent attachment and protect them from loss. Sarah Malthus was cited as the cause of Dunton's financial collapse, as "ye New Athenian Oracles & New Practice of Piety scarce brought in ye charge of Copy Money & Publishing, for by a narrow search into this matter before ye Attachment came I found there was not so many books sold as Malthus thought there was by some hundreds so that (had not h^e Books bin Attacht) all ye Disappointment you had met with from me was entirely owing to her mistake in sale". During this period, Dunton was for the first time confined in the Fleet Prison. Because the Fleet commitment books for this period are lost it is impossible to know the exact dates of his confinement, but in *Dunton's Whipping-Post*, 1706, he listed several works that had been written since his incarceration and he protested against Mrs. Malthus' calling him a "Bankrupt, Jail-Bird".

When *The Life and Errors* finally appeared, in 1705, it failed to sell. Dunton later wrote that he ascribed its failure to the fact that it had been published under the name of a "Poor Tradesman":

> "Montaign tells us, That there was a Book Publish'd in Paris, that being said to be writ by a Great Lord, Sold to the Ninth Edition; but the Right Author being discover'd to be a Poor Tradesman, the Tenth Impression was waste Paper. I have found much of the like Partiality with Respect to my own Writings; for The Athenian Oracle ... came to a Sixth Edition, by appearing without a Name: And my Anonymous Satyr on King William came to a Fourth Edition in six Weeks; but my Idea of a New Life (being Publish'd with the Author's Name) han't bore the Charge of Paper and Print".[14]

Later in 1705 Dunton published third editions of The New Practice of Piety and The Royal Diary, and two new tracts, Plain French: Or, A Satyr upon the Tackers and A Cat May Look on a Queen: Or, A Satyr on Her Present Majesty.

Only one work appeared under Dunton's name in 1706: Dunton's Whipping-Post, Or, A Satyr upon Every Body. This work had first been projected (as a periodical) in 1705; but in the meantime, William Pittis had "interloped" with the publication of The Whipping-Post, At a New Session of Oyer and Terminer.[15] In addition to "The Whoring-Pacquet", Dunton's work included "The Living Elegy" and "The Secret History of the Weekly Writers". In "The Secret History" he scourged the weekly writers - Defoe, Tutchin, Fonvive, Ridpath, Boyer, Crouch, Buckley, and the author of The London Gazette - in order to "provoke them to a Paper Duel". In "The Living Elegy", Dunton attacked the "interloping Whipster" and attempted to pacify his many creditors. Mrs. Malthus, "that spiteful Woman that hired these fellows to slander me", was held responsible for Dunton's current ill-fortune. He was all the more injured by her actions since he claimed to have given Mrs. Malthus her first start in trade at a time when she was "so low ... as to promise me to even every day, if I would but deal with her".[16]

Dunton estimated his debts at the time to be about ₤200, which he promised to pay when "the sun shines, I mean ... October 10, 1708", as he would then have the reversion of his farm at Chesham.[17] At this time Dunton estimated his personal estate to be worth ₤4000 ("In present possession and reversion"), in addition to ₤6000 owed him by "near relations", and he promised settlement, pound for pound, if his creditors would be patient.[18] Dunton concluded his letter to his creditors with a "Rhyming Elegy", for "My body is besieged with the rheumatism, scurvy, and consumptive cough, &c. (which shews death is not far off): but, in a fit of the stone, I actually stand (as Aaron once did in the camp) betwixt the living and the dead; and, whilst I reflect on myself, I find I participate of both: so that, if a Rhyming Elegy was ever proper for a living person, it is so for me".[19]

In the following year, 1707, Dunton published Bumography: Or, A Touch at the Ladies Tails, a "lampoon (privately) dispers'd at Tunbridge-Wells", The He-Strumpets, a satyr on the "Sodomite-Club", and The Pulpit-Fool, in two parts, which in turn satirized in verse a number of members of the clergy. Dunton also published in 1707 Athenian Sport: Or, Two Thousand Paradoxes Merrily Argued, to Amuse and Divert the Age. This work included items from a number of his earlier publications, as well as from John Donne's Paradoxes and Problems. In another publication, The Phenix, he reprinted "scarce and valuable pieces from the remotest antiquity down to the present times". William Oldys wrote of this collection that "it might have succeeded better, had he [the editor] not been for rambling into foreign, or heavy and unaffecting subjects."[20] A second volume of The Phenix appeared in 1708, and the first volume was re-issued with a new title-page (and one additional tract) in 1721.

From 1707 to 1710, Dunton's chief publisher was John Morphew, although several of his more scurrilous pieces were printed and sold by B. Bragg. Morphew had published The Phenix in 1707, and the second volume also appeared with his imprint in 1708, as well as the second edition of A Cat May Look on a Queen, and the second edition of Bumography, newly titled The Rump. During the summer of 1708, Morphew published two new works by Dunton, of which one failed and the other succeeded. The first of these tracts was Stinking Fish: Or a Foolish Poem, Attempted by John the Hermit. In this volume

Dunton promised "a secret, as well as a public history, of all the fools and knaves in the world". He hoped to continue it until he had "cry'd all his stinking fish", but only a second part appeared.

Dunton's successful work in that year was The Hazard of a Death-Bed-Repentance, a reply to Dr. White Kennet's sermon preached at the funeral of the Duke of Devonshire. As an added attraction, Dunton promised on the title-page an essay called "Conjugal Perjury, or an Essay on Whoredom". "Conjugal Perjury" was one of many essays which Dunton announced on his title-pages but failed to bring into print. Nevertheless, three genuine editions of The Hazard were soon sold, as well as three pirated editions.[21] Two months later, Dunton offered The Hazard of a Death-Bed-Repentance, Further Argued, which included his essay on whoredom, but not "the Secret History of the Author's Failings, or D----- at Confession", which he promised on the title-page.

A long awaited event occurred in October 1708, when Dunton's mother-in-law died, but she left a will which provided for her daughter, for the poor of St. Albans, and for an annual sermon in the Abbey - but not for her son-in-law.[22] Mrs Nicholas "desired to be buried in the Abbey Church; and directed that the annuities she had left might be expressly engraven on her tomb-stone, that the memory thereof might not be lost, but preserved for future ages. It was a wise provision; but, like many other testamentary directions, never attended to, for there appears not the smallest vestige of any of the family through the whole church.[23] Dunton's version of the story was not quite so delicate: "And when her Executor ask'd Mr. H--nt (the Clark to the Abby of St. Albans) where Madam Nicholas's Relations were bury'd, (she desiring by her Will to lye by her Husband) he reply'd, it was no matter where, for she deserv'd rather to be flung on a Dung-hill, than to be bury'd in a Church-yard.[24] Dunton and his wife concurred for once and made an attempt to challenge the will, but they were unsuccessful.[25]

Early in 1709, Dunton launched a new periodical, The Christian's Gazette. In his customary tentative fashion he announced that it would be continued "Occasionally, as the Author's Time and Health will Admit". But no further numbers followed, although he revived the title in 1715. A second edition of The Athenian Spy appeared in 1709, and one new work, The Bull-Baiting: Or, Sach---ll Dress'd up in Fire-Works, Dunton's contribution to the controversy aroused by the trial of Dr. Henry Sacheverell. In the next year, 1710, John Morphew published for him the first volume of a work which was intended to be a mammoth anthology of Dunton's works. The first volume of Athenianism contained twenty-four of the six hundred projects which Dunton hoped to print in the complete collection. A number of Dunton's old pieces were reprinted in *Athenianism*, as well as new ones, and Dunton added a list of thirty-five projects which were to be included in the second volume. Volume II never materialized, but a number of the pieces intended for it were later published separately. *Athenianism* also contained as a frontispiece a portrait of Dunton by Vandergucht.

In *Stinking Fish*, 1708, Dunton had announced the sale to Andrew Bell of the right to continue his question-project, and his resolution that "no Interlopers shall run away with the Profits of continuing the *Question Oracle* .... This is therefore to give Notice, that whatever Questions are answer'd by *Foe*, *Povey*, or *The British Apollo*, shall be all answer'd again ... with the best of their Thoughts, and our own Improvements".[26] In 1710, the project finally reached the public, as *Athenian News: Or, Dunton's Oracle*. Dunton entered *Athenian News* at Stationers' Hall as entirely his own property; it was printed by Thomas Darrack and sold by John Morphew. *Athenian News* met with some measure of success, and it continued to be published twice weekly from 4 March to 16 September 1710, when Dunton was compelled by ill health to call a halt to it.

In 1711 Dunton published nothing, and his financial

affairs became more desperate than ever before. Four letters written to him in February of that year indicate that he was relying on the chance of success in a lottery scheme to resolve his difficulties. Not surprisingly, none of his correspondents was willing to lend him money.[27] His fortunes fell so low that on 9 June, Thomas Darrack, the printer of *Athenianism* and *Athenian News: Or, Dunton's Oracle*, had Dunton arrested for a debt of £110.[28]

Once again in the confinement of the Fleet Prison, Dunton compiled his lengthy will.[29] Maria Jones, Dunton's chief female friend of the period, was named executrix. As residuary legatee, she stood to inherit Dunton's estates in Buckinghamshire and all else remaining after payment of legacies which amounted to nearly £600. Dunton's former master, Thomas Parkhurst, was named to receive £50 in payment for various unspecified losses he had suffered during Dunton's apprenticeship. Further, Dunton's executrix was directed to advertise for his creditors to submit their claims on his estate, that all his obligations might be settled before funds were distributed for the purchase of a great number of mourning rings. In the event of success in the lottery scheme (of which Dunton was confident), Mrs. Jones was instructed to purchase a marble stone to mark Dunton's grave and that of his first wife.

* * * *

The first number of The Monitor, in 1714, complained strongly of the proliferation of low tracts which were currently being written, sparing no one their libellous attacks:

> "... one of the Methods by which the Distractions of the present Times have been brought to such a height, has been the unprecedented Liberty of the Press, whereby printed Pamphlets, and daily Papers appear in all Parts of the Nation; in which such Provocations are given, such Indecencies, and such Expressions are to be found, as no Age can shew the like; such personal treatment is given in Print to Men of all Ranks, of the Greatest Quality, as well as of the Commons; nay even to the Sovereign her self, and that without any Ground or Provocation, as no History can shew us the like ....[30]

In the last years of his life, John Dunton was responsible for a considerable number of works of this nature. In 1712 he published only two tracts, The Preaching Weathercock and High-Church. Both of these works were poisonous libels directed against William Richardson, a Presbyterian minister who in 1711 had been ordained in the Church of England. In 1713, Dunton revived the title of The Christian's Gazette, to which he added The Lame-Post and The Court-Spy. In this year he also wrote Neck or Nothing, one of his best-known tracts, in which he replied to Sir Robert Walpole's Short History of the Parliament. R. Tookey and J. Baker were the printer and bookseller associated with Dunton in publishing The Preaching Weathercock, High-Church, and The Christian's Gazette, and T. Warner published Neck or Nothing, Whigg Loyalty and The Impeachment in 1714. The years 1712 to 1714 mark a final transition in Dunton's life; in these years, he lost the small measure of independence that he had managed to retain in the years after his retirement from bookselling. After 1714, his spirit broken, Dunton came to be employed by a small group of booksellers who made their profits at the expense of the pride of a sick old man whom they encouraged to become the laughing-stock of London.

It is clear, from Dunton's occasional entries in the Stationers' Register, and his difficulties with printers as well as booksellers in the years before 1712, that he had been working as a free-lance projector. Dunton had, in fact, made an effort to realize his dream of trading without the encumbrance of a shop, although he had published no copies but his own. Anne Baldwin, Elizabeth Mallet, Sarah Malthus, and John Morphew, the booksellers whose names had most often appeared on the imprints of Dunton's works, were all long-standing friends, and they had published - that is, distributed - his works through their usual channels of trade. Dunton retained ownership of his copies, occasionally registered them, and made his own arrangements with printers.

After 1712, the situation gradually altered, and Dunton came to work, in 1714, as the hireling of a small group of booksellers. In 1712 Dunton insisted that he was the rightful owner of a considerable estate which unfortunately was still subject to a "Joynture Shackle" (High-Church, 1712, pp. 4-5). T. Tookey, who printed the two libels of 1712, also printed a few later tracts; and the group of booksellers who employed Dunton began with J. Baker, in 1712, and Baker, J. Harrison, A. Boulter, and R. Bond in 1714. Later in 1714, the group was composed of Harrison, Sarah Popping, A. Dodd, and Boulter. Dodd's name disappeared from the imprints of Dunton's tracts in 1716, and later the names of Harrison and Boulter; but Sarah Popping continued to publish Dunton's pieces until 1725.[31]

In 1714, forced into hiding by six warrants that had been issued to seize him, "it was ... no longer adviseable to appear with Materials about Him, [and] He laid them aside most facetiously, and appeared under the Title of a Ghost, in which Capacity He was out of the Reach of the Ministry, and the Messengers they employ'd".[32] Only two numbers of Dunton's Ghost, a weekly periodical, appeared in March 1714. Also in 1714 Dunton published The Impeachment, The Conventicle, the second part of Neck or Nothing (which he called Queen Robin) and The Golden Age, the first of a number of tracts written to flatter George I and to petition the King for reward. Dunton called the tracts of this period "private books", and he advertised that they "are only to be had by sending a letter to the Hanover Coffee-House in Fleet-lane, directed to Mr. John Dunton; and if upon a strict Examination it appears the Letter was no Trick to insnare the Author, whatever Books are writ for, shall be sent to the Place appointed the following Day".[33]

During his life Dunton attained a certain celebrity as a pamphleteer, and though it was not quite the renown that he would have wished, it must have had an effect on the sale of his tracts. By 1713 he had become a laughable figure. In that year, the anonymous author of The Character of Richard S--le, Esq., wrote ironically of Steele: "O! Ye Literati of Button's Coffee-House! Ye ladies of St. James's! ... Behold the Patron of Learning! the Encourager of Arts and Sciences! ... dwindled on a sudden into an Author below the Character of

Dunton! below the Politicks of Ridpath!"[34] Swift, in The Public Spirit of the Whigs, wrote that "Among the present Writers on that Side, I can recollect but Three of any great Distinction, which are the Flying-Post, Mr. Dunton, and the Author of the Crisis .... Mr. Dunton hath been longer and more conversant in Books than any of the Three, as well as more voluminous in his Productions: However, having employ'd his Studies in so great a Variety of other Subjects, he hath I think but lately turned his Genius to Politicks".[35] Dunton was flattered by this tribute, and he called his readers' attention to it in later works.

In 1715, Dunton's four booksellers issued a catalogue of his works, pointing out that "whatever Books are written by Mr. John Dunton, if not publish'd with these Four Names, are imperfect Copies, and consequently a wrong to the Author, as well as the Publick".[36] Bungey: Or the False Brother Prov'd his own Executioner sold three editions in 1715, as did The Hereditary Bastard: Or, The Royal-Intreague of the Warming Pan. Dunton also wrote in 1715 King Abigail and King George For Ever, to which he added "The Neck Adventure; Or, The Case and Sufferings of Mr. John Dunton, for Daring to Detect the Treason and Villany of Oxford and Bolingbroke, whilst they were Reigning Favourites, in his Four Essays, intituled, The Court-Spy, Neck or Nothing, Queen

Robin, and The Impeachment".

Early in 1715, King George rewarded Dunton for risking his neck for the Hanoverian succession. The reward was a gold medal which he proudly wore around his neck, to the amusement of London. The Earl of Oxford wrote of him: "This poor wretch Dunton had a gold medal given him of about the value of 30 l., which he used to wear about his neck; but necessity obliged him for bread to pawn it now and then".[37] Dunton wrote an essay on his medal and was confident of further reward. Later in this year he wrote Ox--- and Bull--- and The Shortest Way with the King, both of which sold three editions, and The Mob-War. He also projected a periodical, Neck Intelligence, which was to be the third edition of The Christian's Gazette, but it never appeared.

Dunton's tracts of 1716 included, as well as numerous editions of earlier works, Frank Scammony: Or, The Restoring Clergy Detected, of which six editions were advertised, and A Trip to the Mug House and The Devil's Martyrs, both of which sold three editions. In addition, he wrote three "loyal ironies", The Manifesto of King John the Second, Dunton's Recantation, and Seeing's Believing: Or, K-ng G--rge Prov'd a Us--per. While hawking Seeing's Believing about London, Dunton was arrested and taken before the Lord Mayor. The incident was reported by Dunton's friend George Ridpath in

The Flying Post:

> "The 1st Inst. Mr. John Dunton, Author of Neck or Nothing, went about with a Devil (for that's the Name given to a Printer's Errand Boy) through the capital Streets of this Metropolis, to the great Terror of the Honest Citizens, and dispers'd (by the said Devil) the Title of a Book writ by himself, call'd Seeing's Believing: Or, K-ng G-rge prov'd a Us-per, &c, for which Mr. Duntonand his Devil were taken up, and carry'd before the Lord Mayor of London, and afterwards before one of his Majesty's Principal Secretarys of State. The Whigs pitied the Man, because he had already ventur'd his Neck for Nothing, and the Torys rejoic'd extreamly, because they thought that Mr. Dunton who had lately set up for the Prentender's Rival, under the Title of King John the Second, had now actually hazarded his Neck; but John's Whig Friends were greatly pleas'd, and the Torys very much mortify'd, when they found the Book was only a cunning Irony to catch the foolish Jacks, and that Mr. Dunton, instead of endangering his Neck, hazarded Nothing".[38]

Later in the year, Dunton reminded the King of what he owed him for his loyal services in Royal Gratitude; (Or King George's Promise Never to Forget his Obligations to those who have Distinguish'd Themselves in his Service) Critically consider'd. At this time, Dunton hoped for a sizeable reward, and he believed it to be imminent; in Royal Gratitude, he advertised:

> "As soon as ever Mr. Dunton has clear'd all his Debts (which he hopes to do in a few Weeks, either by the Royal Bounty of King George, or by the Generosity of those Lords and Gentlemen that resolve to Reward his Public Services, with a Purse of two Thousand Guineas) the World may expect Proposals for the Printing A Compleat and Genuine Collection of all his Writings, which will consist of a Thousand distinct Essays, of which 400 have never yet seen the

> Light, and will all be publish'd under this General Title Athenianism".[39]

No reward, however, was forthcoming from the King; but Popping, Harrison, and Dodd published, under the pseudonym of Philo-Patris, a further plea from Dunton at the end of the year, *Mordecai's Memorial: Or, There's Nothing Done for Him. Being a Satyr upon Some-body, but I name No-body: (Or, in Plainer English, a just and generous Representation of Unrewarded Services, by which the Protestant Succession has been Sav'd out of Danger.)*.

In April 1717, Dunton issued *Mordecai's Last Shift*, which was a proposal for a new project, *The Athenian Library*, which he eventually published in 1725. Later, he wrote *The Pulpit Lunaticks*, a contribution to the controversy aroused by a sermon preached by Benjamin Hoadly, Bishop of Bangor. Six editions were sold. Later in the year, Dunton was again confined in the Fleet, where he wrote *Mordecai's Dying Groans from the Fleet-Prison*.[40] In October he scribbled on the reverse of a letter a draft agreement between himself and Daniel Defoe for the publication of a periodical to be called *The Hanover Spy*.[41] There is no evidence that this proposed collaboration was anything more than a dream; when a work of that title appeared in the following year, it was merely a pamphlet containing two essays by Dunton, "The Secret History of Whiggish Ingratitude: Or, The Case and Sufferings of Mr. John Dunton" and "The Hanover-Spy: Or, The Secret History of St. James's". Also in 1718, an anonymous scribbler addressed to Dunton The Pudding Plot Detected in a Letter to J--n D--t--n author of Neck or Nothing.[42]

Notable among Dunton's publications of 1719 was the "thirtieth edition" of The Second Spira. To this edition Dunton added five essays, including "A Key to the Second Spira", in which he again stated his case against Richard Sault, the author of The Second Spira. The State Weathercocks: Or, A New Secret History of the most Distinguish'd Favourites, both of the Late and Present Reign, included the "twentieth edition" of Neck or Nothing and the second edition of Mordecai's Memorial: Or, There's Nothing Done for Him. To this work Dunton appended an advertisement addressed "To all such Honest Booksellers that wou'd not Print Stoln Copies themselves, or (which is full as Bad) wou'd not Encourage such Theft in others". In this advertisement Dunton listed twenty-nine copies to which he claimed title. He stated that he had been informed that certain booksellers planned to reprint a number of them, and added that he had directed his executor not to sell them for less than a thousand guineas. In particular, he complained of the activities of the "pyrat conger" and of certain other booksellers who had first reprinted his copies and then, at Dunton's insistence, had given him a small payment for the copy. Dunton announced that he intended to punish them all, in an essay to be called "The Shop Thief; or, A Satyr on such Knavish Booksellers and Printers that have Pyrated some of Mr. Dunton's Copies and Projects (under a New or Disguis'd Title) proving such *Book-Theft* a baser Villany than if they had Rob'd him on the High-way". "But to do the *Stationers Company* Justice," Dunton added

> "there are a great many *Honest Booksellers and Printers* to be found in it, or (at least) may be made *honest with good looking after* .... I must say this to the Honour of the Stationers Company, when the several Members of it keep Strictly to *the Golden Rule*, ... "Tis then the most Delightful, Gainful, and best Trade in the City of *London*, and had I an Hundred Sons, I'd make 'em all Stationers, Booksellers, and Printers, and that not only as they deal so much with Men of Letters (or the most Refin'd Part of Mankind) but as 'twas my Reverend Father's Dying Advice, '*That I wou'd never desert that Trade or Calling which I had by God's special Providence* been call'd unto' ...."

In January 1720, Dunton began yet another periodical, *The Athenian Spy*, which included several departments that had formerly appeared in other works - "The Lame Poet", "Athenianism", "The Phenix", and "Intellectual Sport" - and one new department, "A Mad-House, for the Cure of Spiritual Lunaticks". Only the first number of this periodical appeared. In March appeared *A Word without Doors* which, although it appeared with Dunton's name, had been written by his friend and executrix, Maria Jones. In September, perhaps prompted by ill health, Dunton added a codicil to his will.[43]

Nothing is known about Dunton's activities after September 1720, until 1723. The death of Sarah Dunton, in March 1721,[44] ended Dunton's "Joynture Shackle", and presumably he was supported during the subsequent years by money realized from the sale of his farms. Dunton's independence did not last long, however, and in 1723 he published an appeal to the King from prison: An Appeal to His Majesty's Most Gracious Promise ... Or, The Humble Petition of John Dunton, Gent. ... That he might not be left to Starve in a Jail. He still owned many valuable copies, he insisted, which he lacked the funds to reprint. To this pamphlet Dunton appended a list of forty political tracts which he claimed to have written (at the hazard of his neck) in support of King George. In the summer of 1723, he published a pious tract called Upon this Moment Depends Eternity: Or, Mr. John Dunton's Serious Thoughts Upon the Present and Future State, in a Fit of Sickness that was Judg'd Mortal.

Two years later, in 1725, Dunton published The Athenian Library, which he had been planning since 1717. Sarah Popping published the first part of The Athenian Library, but no further parts appeared. Again in the Fleet prison, Dunton complained, for the last time, that he had "gone twelve years unrewarded, for his early, bold, and successful venture of life and fortune", in Mr. John Dunton's Dying Groans from the Fleet-Prison.

Dunton published his last work in 1728, a final scourging of his mother-in-law. In An Essay on Death-Bed-Charity, Dunton argued from the examples of his mother-in-law, of Thomas Guy, and of Francis Bancroft, that "great Misers giving large Donatives to the Poor in their last Wills is no Charity".

In 1729, Dunton's friend and executrix, Maria Jones, died, so he named Richard Nowland, in whose house he then lodged, his executor.[45] Dunton still lodged with Richard Nowland when, on 24 November 1732, he died. On 15 December, Nowland was appointed executor.

The library of "the Eminent Mr. John Dunton" was sold "very cheap ... at R. Montagu's Great Book-Warehouse" on 23 April 1733. But the remainder of the estate had not been administered by Nowland when, on 27 June 1744, administration "of the Goods Chattles and Credits of John Dunton ... was granted to Thomas Darrack a Creditor of the said deceased being first sworn duty to Administrator".[46] Darrack, who had been the cause of Dunton's imprisonment in 1711, finally received settlement.

In 1732 the public had quite forgotten Dunton, and no obituary was published. The sole contemporary notice of Dunton's death came from the pen of his former enemy, the Earl of Oxford, who wrote of him: "He died, as I have been informed, the beginning of 1733.[47]

APPENDICES

AUTHORS, CUSTOMERS AND THE TRADE

1. Dunton and his Authors

"Upon trial" Dryden wrote to Tonson in 1697, "I find all of your trade are sharpers".[1] In his youth, Dunton had disapproved of those writers whose "concern lay more in how much a Sheet, than in any generous respect they bore to the Commonwealth of Learning".[2] But experience altered Dunton's outlook, and the world-wise bookseller later confessed, with unexpected candour, that "unless a man can haggle half an hour for a farthing, be dishonest, and tell lies, he may starve behind his Shop-board, for want of subsistence".[3] In fact, the bookseller had to be sharp; his wits were his only protection. In this respect, his position was not much better than that of the author.

During the seventeen years from the lapse of licensing requirements in 1693 (with extensions, to 1695) to the enactment of the first copyright statute, in 1709, the trade was in chaos. The strongly defensive attitude which the author and bookseller adopted towards each other resulted from the state of anarchy in the publishing business during these years. The Stationers' Company was almost totally ineffective throughout the period, and after many years of steadily declining authority, the end of licensing robbed the Company of the small area of jurisdiction which remained. The Company was the more weakened internally as the booksellers, who traditionally had been aligned simply and informally, according to political, religious, trade, and other factors for the exchange of stock, drew more closely together. This state of lawlessness provided a suitable environment for the development of the power of the booksellers' wholesaling associations. The author, having no experience of trade organisation, was left entirely to his own devices in his fight for subsistence. Informal associations of booksellers for the exchange of stock became, for the first time, *congers*; their influence broadened and they began to function as vigilance committees, offering protection to the bookseller who traded with them, and applying trade sanctions to renegades. Dunton's relations with the trade, and the development of these trade associations, will be discussed in part 4. For the present, we shall examine Dunton's relations with his authors.

A common view of the bookseller was that expressed by Ned Ward in *The London Spy*:

> "See the little blade in a cloak, talking with a parson. He's a bookseller in this City, and has got an estate by starving authors .... I tell you he's as honest a man as ever betrayed his trust, or built his own welfare upon another's ruin .... There is an abundance of such sort of plain-dealing practised among our worthy citizens, for you must know they do not always tell the truth in their shops; or get their estates by honesty".[4]

Some booksellers deserved this scourging; but the contempt that the bookseller felt for the hackney writer resulted to a very great extent from the behaviour of the numerous hackneys, among whom fierceness of competition prevented any sort of decorum. Honesty was rewarded with unemployment, and dignity was forgotten in the scramble for the notice of the bookseller. No sooner had Dunton begun bookselling than he was besieged by hoards of hackney authors, who plied him with specimens, "as earnestly, and with as much passion and concern, as the _Watermen_ do _Passengers_ with _Oars_ and _Scullers_".[5]

Authors' grievances against booksellers were legion, and expressions of this ill-feeling are often encountered; the quarrels of Dryden with Tonson and of Pope with Curll and other booksellers are well-known. Three generations earlier George Wither, in _The Schollers Purgatory_, had given booksellers a notable scourging:

> "... the retailer of bookes, commonly called a Books-seller, is a Trade, which being wel gouerned, and lymited within certaine bounds, might become somewhat seruiceable to the rest. But as it is now (for the most part abused) the Bookeseller hath not

> onely made the Printer, the Binder, and the Claspmaker a slaue to him: but hath brought Authors, yea the whole Common-wealth, and all the liberall Sciences into bondage. For he make all professors of Art, labour for his profit, at his owne price, and vtters it to the Common-wealth in such fashion, and at those rates, which please himselfe".[6]

Wither characterised the "meere Stationer", who

> "vvill not stick to belye his Authors intentions, or to publish secretly that there is somewhat in his new ymprinted books, against the State, or some Honourable personages; that so, they being questioned his vvare may haue the quicker sale. He makes no scruple to put out the right Authors Name, & insert another in the second edition of a Booke; And when the impression of some pamphlet lyes vpon his hands, to imprint nevv Titles for yt (and so take mens moneyes twice or thrice for the same matter vnder diuerse names) is no iniury in his opinion".[7]

Further quantities of literary evidence can be marshalled to demonstrate the predicament of the writer, the victim of the cruel domination of the profiteering bookseller. But this is a one-sided view; few booksellers were moved to write memoirs, and Dunton's Life and Errors provides a rare expression of the bookseller's position. Clearly it would be unjust to assert that the blame for the situation lay wholly on either side. Dunton was singularly well qualified to write on the matter. His activities in the trade were both unusual and various, and during the last half of his life, he moved from behind the counter to join the ranks of anonymous mercenaries who during the early years of the eighteenth century filled the bookstalls with countless tracts of poorly written and badly printed political and religious invective. Although Dunton was not entirely blameless as a bookseller, his relations with his authors were unusually successful. This is evidenced (in many cases) by their duration, and by the regard he had for many of them, as shown in the portraits in his Life and Errors.

The bookseller was a necessary intermediary between the author and the public, and he was capable of maintaining and implementing his position. Although it was possible for an author to circumvent the bookseller and to contract directly with a printer to produce his work, few authors could muster the necessary capital or credit. More important, the writer lacked also the means of publishing his work; were he sufficiently self-confident to attempt to reach the public directly, he found normal retail channels of distribution closed to him. A work printed "For the Author" (according to the title-page), was, in Dunton's case, most often a work which had been published normally, but a work for which the bookseller wanted to emphasize the author's responsibility, or at least a work for which he was unwilling to admit publicly his own. William Fuller's discoveries of the true mother of the Prince of Wales were published in this manner. Fuller admitted to dealing with Richard Baldwin and Dunton, but neither of them was willing to acknowledge his connection with Fuller. Furthermore, the bookseller had means of punishing authors turned booksellers. "Many works may be mentioned that never sold well, whilst the author retained the copy-right," wrote Lackington in his _Memoirs_ "which had a rapid sale after it was sold to the trade; and no wonder, for if the publisher wishes to purchase the copy-right, he sometimes will take care to prevent the sale of the work, in order to make the author out of conceit with the book, and be willing to part with the copy-right for a mere trifle".[8]

Informality was the outstanding characteristic of the bookseller's dealings with the general run of writers. Agreements were deceptively casual, and opportunity for dishonesty was available to the unscrupulous of both trades. A few shillings a sheet, a sheet or two now and again, or room and board for lengthy employment at collection or translation, were common arrangements. Hence it is not surprising that deception was practised. Even the most careful bookseller might easily forget the details of his many arrangements. Once the simple transaction of outright purchase of copy was completed, or the general plan of a work of collection had been outlined, the bookseller often appeared to lose interest in the work, leaving the authors to deliver completed copy directly to the printer. Yet the bookseller sometimes had occasion to regret his lack of continued attention. Dunton cautioned "every Bookseller that concerns himself in Printing, to peruse the Copy as it goes to the press, in regard I have smarted more than once for being too credulous in this respect".[9] The Post-boy Rob'd of his Mail was one of Dunton's own repented projects, for he regretted having trusted Charles Gildon who "sent the Copy to the press as he wrote it off, and in regard I had no suspicion of him, I did not peruse the Letters till it was past time to alter them".[10]

Dunton's extreme distaste for the lowest of the hackney writers is evident:

> "... the Learning itself of these Gentlemen lies very often in as little room as their Honesty; though they will pretend to have studied you six or seven years in the Bodleian Library, to have turned over the Fathers, and to have read and digested the whole compass both of Human and Ecclesiastic History - when, alas! they have never been able to understand a single page of Saint Cyprian, and cannot tell you whether the Fathers lived before or after Christ. And as for their Honesty, it is very remarkable: they will either persuade you to go upon another man's Copy, to steal his Thought, or to abridge his Book, which should have got him bread for his lifetime. When you have engaged them upon some Project or other, they will write you off three or four sheets perhaps; take up three or four pounds upon an urgent occasion; and you shall never hear of them more. I have offered thus much, as a character of these Scribblers, that may give the caution to Booksellers, and take off a most wretched scandal from the Trade in general".[11]

Dunton loved nothing more than a novel project, and his cupidity in this respect often led him into dealings which he later regretted. His relations with his more substantial authors were generally successful; he suffered most from the occasional charlatan who was able to entice him into embarking on a project of questionable honesty, or who extorted money on the promise of producing lively evidence guaranteed to expose one of the vices of the age. Dunton and Baldwin may very well have improved William Fuller's copy in order to make it sell - the accusation is not uncommon; but Fuller fraudulently took payment from Dunton and, as noted earlier, led him to Canterbury in the hope of finding "State Letters" which had never existed. Fuller himself wrote favourably only of Elizabeth Harris, whom he was able to charm into lending him money.

To cite other instances, Dunton was badly treated by William Bradshaw, though he admired him nonetheless:

> "Mr. Bradshaw, [was] the best accomplished hackney-author I have met with. His genius was quite above the common size, and his style was incomparably fine. You could propose to him no design within the compass of Learning, but he knew to go through with it. He designed for the Ministry till he had finished his studies; and then fell off, something like Tom Brown, though the comparison be a little too mean for him. He wrote for me the 'Parable of the Magpyes,' and many thousands of them sold. I had once fixed him upon a very great design, and furnished him both with money and books, which were most of them Historical and Geographical; but my Gentleman thought fit to remove himself, and I am not sure that I have seen him since.... If Mr. Bradshaw be yet alive, I here declare to the world, and to him, that I freely forgive him what he owes both in Money and Books, if he will only be so kind as to make me a visit. But I am afraid the worthy Gentleman is dead,

for he was wretchedly overrun with melancholy, and the very blackness of it reigned in his countenance. He had certainly performed wonders with his pen, had not his poverty pursued him, and almost laid the necessity upon him to be unjust".[12]

Colonel F--- G---, however, was not forgiven; he was one of the "greatest Knaves" Dunton had encountered:

"[Colonel F--- G---] had been formerly a Privy-Counseller in Ireland, and was the next in blood to an Earldom; but his Misses had drained his purse, and he left Ireland upon suspicion of debt. The Colonel coming to London, sent for me to the Dolphin in Lombard-street, where, pretending to help me to 'The Secret History of Ireland,' he did me the honour to do me the kindness to ease me of Twenty Guineas. It is true Mr. Darker and I got him arrested, but it was to no purpose; for he produced a protection from the Lord ----, and, at the request of Sir J--- S---, I freely released him, upon his bare word 'that he would pay me as soon as he could.' A month after this, the Colonel came to my house; and told me he could not pay me in less than a year, but he was well acquainted with the Marquis of ----, and if that would be any kindness to me, he would engage Mr. B--- should be his Chaplain. I was always glad to oblige this Reverend Gentleman; and told the Colonel, 'if he would make good his word, I would own it as an extraordinary favour;' upon which the Colonel introduced B--- to the Marquis of ----; and the next time I saw him it was with a Doctor's scarf, which may be said to have cost me Twenty Guineas".[13]

Many of these writers, of course, were genuinely talented. Dunton respected John Shirley, who was "as true as steel to his word, and [who] would slave off his feet to oblige a Bookseller". Although Shirley wrote more than two-hundred sermons in his lifetime, his "great talent [lay] at Collection, and he will do it for you at six shillings a sheet".[14] Ingenious George Ridpath invented the "Polygraphy, or Writing Engine, by which one may, with great facility, write two, four, six, or more copies of any one thing upon so many different sheets of paper at once. This Writing Engine is likewise attended with this advantage, that, being moved by the foot, while the hand guides the Pens, it keeps the whole body in warmth and exercise which prevents many of the usual inconveniences of a sedentary life, besides the time which the engine saves in dispatch".[15] Shirley, Bradshaw, Ridpath, and many others were always on call when Dunton was hurrying to precede another bookseller into print.

Dunton was highly sensitive to the fleeting enthusiasms of the public - the correspondence of the Athenian Society was a reliable index of this - and when he felt controversy in the air he produced pamphlets to encourage its development. Dunton's resourcefulness in meeting the public demand for dying speeches has already been discussed; and The Ladies Dictionary and Religio Bibliopolae have also been cited - all put together on the literary assembly-line, cribbed from the best authors. Dunton's resourcefulness concerning translations is also noteworthy. Translations formed a large part of Dunton's stock, and he was generous in his praise for those authors - Dr. Miller, Tom Brown, George Ridpath, Charles Gildon, Richard Sault, and a Mr. Philips - who specialised in them. Dunton had for some years an arrangement with Mr. Spademan, of Rotterdam, to send him, on publication, works likely to be profitable in translation. In return, Dunton sent English tracts to his friend in Holland. In addition to numerous works of translation undertaken by the Athenian Society, and the translated excerpts from continental periodicals which made up much of his other periodicals, Dunton published Sault's translation of Malebranche, 1693, Foigny's _Terra Incognita Australia_, 1693, Gerard Croese's _General History of the Quakers_, 1696, and a number of sermons preached in Holland on the death of Queen Mary in 1695.[16]

Few writers rose from the rank and file to achieve individual recognition. An unknown writer was almost totally subject to the bookseller. Many never escaped anonymity, and a few are remembered solely because Dunton wrote about them. Dealing with authors was a twofold problem for Dunton, however, and he had to present one face to the importunate hack and another to the established preacher or gentleman of rank, whose name would add lustre to Dunton's own reputation with the public and whose works could be profitably exchanged in the trade.

Dealing with gentleman-authors was quite the opposite of dealing with hackneys; the bookseller was forced to court the author. Established authors were not paid in shillings a sheet, after extensive haggling; they were generally paid a sum for their work after negotiation, as well as with copies of the work. They could demand difficult terms, and Dunton complained of authors "who either turn themselves into _Half-Booksellers_, or else insist upon such terms for their _Copy_, as than an _Impression_ will scarce answer the prime cost".[17]

Dunton was most highly pleased with his clerical authors, men whose sermons were often printed and who were not generally inclined to make heavy demands on the bookseller. Among Dunton's clerical authors, Mr. Turner, Rector of Walbleton, "would not receive a farthing for his Copy till the success was known".[18] Dunton lost patience with the Rector of Chalgrove, Mr. Barlow, who had "a strange habit of borrowing Money, and deferring the Payment".[19] Dunton scrupulously honoured a contract once made, however, although an author might be expected to wait many years for settlement. Dunton published Edmund Hickeringill's sermon _The Good Old Cause, or The Divine Captain Characteriz'd_ in 1692; but he postponed settlement for many years. Finally in 1711, Dunton in his will directed his executrix to settle with Hickeringill, "for that reason all Mr. Hickeringill's Sermons unsold (intituled the Divine Captain) have been kept by me to this day (and are now in my Custody) I being (as near as I can remember) only accountable to the aforesaid Edmund Hickeringill for so many as were sold ...."[20]

The dubious art of collection was practiced by learned authors as well as hireling writers. Matthew Barker published two volumes of _Flores Intellectuales_, intended for the use of young scholars. "For in my younger dayes," Barker candidly wrote, "to help my memory, I kept by me a Paper-Book, wherein I inserted some of those things which did occurr to me in my Reading as most remarkable, and which I had a desire to treasure in my Memory".[21] Sir William Temple advised Dunton not to get rewritten those parts of his proposed general history of England which had already been treated by eminent authors. Dunton's father's books were collections as well, and they were entirely unacknowledged - and although a country vicar may be allowed a certain freedom in collecting material for his sermons, his son's motives in publishing them were not entirely innocent.

Literary amateurs could be an annoyance to a bookseller in many ways. Relieved of the necessity of earning a living by writing, these authors could be distressingly slow in delivering their finished copy. John Salusbury, John Harris, and Dunton persuaded James Tyrrell to compile a general history of England and issued proposals for the work in

November 1694. The first volume of the work was not completed until 1696, the second in 1700, and the last in 1704. Dunton chose to be patient, however, and he wrote in his Life and Errors that "though [Tyrell's History] was ten months longer in the Press than we expected, yet he was so much disinterested in the matter, that we had no reason to complain".[22] Established writers were just as capable of deceiving the public as the hackneys were, though the bookseller fortunately was not held responsible for their dishonesty. In the matter of Bishop Barlow's Remains, Dunton was not culpable. Sir Peter Pett, not Dunton, was criticised for printing without the consent of the owners, portions of Barlow's papers. William Offley, in whose care they had been placed, wrote his reflections on the publication of the Remains, in which he apologised to the Chancellor of Lincoln Cathedral and accused that "one Sir P. P. and the late Vicar of Bugden, were the confederate Pedlars, that have endeavour'd to impose upon the World so much varnish'd Ware, for the sake of Twenty Guineas gave for the Copy; as his Wife inform'd a Reverend Friend of Mine".[23]

Dunton published little verse other than Elizabeth Singer's Poems on Several Occasions, which was encouraged by the Athenian Society, and Samuel Wesley's Maggots, which were mildly salacious and therefore assured of a measure of popularity. In his Life and Errors Dunton advised against trying to live by writing poetry:

> "... when I see an ingenious man set up for a mere Poet, and steer his course through life towards that Point of the Compass, I give him up, as one pricked down by Fate for misery and misfortune ... one would incline to think there is some indispensable Law, whereby Poverty and Disappointment are entailed upon Poets .... I would not ... dissuade any noble Genius to pursue this Art as a little pretty Divertisement; but where it is made the very Trade of life, I am pretty positive the man is in the wrong box.[24]

Dunton might well have extended his advice to include writers generally. Those who chose to write for amusement were indeed fortunate; those who were compelled to make their living by writing had to learn to subsist, as Mr. Shirley did, "by a sort of Geometry".[25]

2. Dunton and the Trade

Agreements in the trade were by tradition informal; the settling of accounts was frequently long delayed, and generally rather carelessly handled. Adam Black, an apprentice in Edinburgh in the eighteenth century, described this traditional state of confusion:

> "The accounts of some of the booksellers were kept in the most slovenly way, and long unsettled, and there was something slightly roguish in them, besides confusion. I recollect an account we had for years going on with another bookseller, Dickson, which never could be brought to a settlement, till one day the two [i.e., John Fairbairn, to whom Black was apprenticed, and Dickson], along with little Doig and another, agreed to dine at Luckie Baxter's, who kept a tavern down one of the stairs on the South Bridge, and settle the accounts after dinner over some tumblers of toddy. Seeing they could not balance accounts, each maintaining that books charged had been returned, it was at last agreed that each should give the other a full discharge, without further examination. The only house during my apprenticeship that kept their accounts with accuracy was that of Bell and Bradfute, and they were looked upon by the others as disagreeable strict precisionists."[1]

Dunton has been accused of many things, but never of being a disagreeable strict precisionist. Yet he insisted that he settled all his accounts every six months. He claimed that he had "twenty times in Trade restored the over-seen gain of a mistaken reckoning", and that he "often paid a sum twice over, for fear of doing wrong". In his financial distress of 1704, he comforted himself with the thought that "there seems to be some sense of Gratitude remaining in them at this day".[2] Printers, especially, whom he described as being "more generous to Debtors than other men", were rewarded in the Life and Errors with flattering portraits. A printer had means of protecting himself, however, and Dunton was willing to forgive the printer such defensive dishonesty as the "working of half an Impression for himself, when the Book-seller hath had his Number he is to pay for; but because the Printer only doth thus to those Book-sellers that he thinks will never pay him, he shall pass ... as an indifferent honest man".[3] For his own part, Dunton asserted that in publishing six-hundred books, he "never swerved from the price agreed on, or made any Printer call twice for money".[4] However oblique his strategy, however devious his tactics, Dunton was scrupulous in fulfilling a commitment once firmly agreed upon. For example, in his will of 1711, twelve years after his retirement from the trade, Dunton directed his executrix to settle outstanding contracts with David Jones, Edmund Hickeringill, Joseph Stevens, Mr. Sadler and Mr. Gidley. He was also concerned in his will for the subscribers to The History of the Famous Edict of Nantes, as well for any author or bookseller to whom he owed money. He directed that his executrix advertise her willingness to discharge any of his outstanding obligations that might be brought forward and proven.[5]

When Dunton first traded, he exchanged works which he published with other booksellers. In so doing, he multiplied the number of titles available at the Black Raven. Co-operation in publishing provided for less individual risk of loss, though with corresponding less individual profit. But Dunton's faith in the success of his own projects was such that he was unwilling to share certain profit with other booksellers. A number of Dunton's most substantial projects were undertaken entirely by himself. Lack of security of investment and copyright led other booksellers into complicated partnerships, but led Dunton to publish periodicals, and other works by subscription. For a few very large works Dunton joined other booksellers, but when he shared the undertaking of a work, it was usually with a friend in the Poultry. His _ad hoc_ partnerships appear to have been handled conscientiously, even to the sharing of the advertisements. For example, William Leybourn's _Panarithmologia_, published by Dunton and John Harris in 1693, had a single page of advertisement, one-half for Dunton, and one-half for Harris; in _A Narrative of the Late Extraordinary Cure_, 1694, they had one and one-half pages each. Again, John Lawrence and Dunton each had five pages of advertisements in the _Works_ of Lord Delamere, which they published jointly in 1694, and Thomas Parkhurst, Jonathan Robinson, and Dunton each had two pages of advertisements in Roger's Practical Discourses, 1691. It seems likely that the advertisements in George Keith's Exact Narrative, 1696, where we find one-third of a page for Brabazon Aylmer, and two-thirds of a page for Dunton, represented their relative shares in the work. Conversely, in The Sense of the United Nonconforming Ministers, published by Dunton and Thomas Cockerill in 1693, Dunton had only one-third of the advertisement page, and Cockerill two-thirds.

When Dunton moved from the Poultry to Jewen Street, he arranged for Edmund Richardson, whose shop was near the Poultry Church, to keep a full stock of his titles. Imprints of this period generally follow the formula cited by R. W. Chapman to indicate a wholesaler or retailer enjoying an agency, "printed for John Dunton, and sold by Edmund Richardson".[6] Richard Baldwin, a bookseller whose interests paralleled Dunton's, was closely associated with Dunton in the 1690's. Unfortunately no specific evidence of the nature of their association survives though Baldwin was often Dunton's partner in this period, and certain works advertised by Dunton as printed for him actually appeared with Baldwin's imprint, and vice versa. To cite another case, George Keith's More Divisions amongst the Quakers, 1693, was advertised in the Term

Catalogues by Dunton, yet it was printed for Baldwin; advertisements in that work for other works printed for Baldwin include another work by Keith which had been printed for John Dunton.[7] In another mixed arrangement Dunton, Baldwin, and John Harris jointly entered Balthazar Bekker's _The World Bewitch'd_, but when the work appeared, it showed only Baldwin's name on the title-page. William Fuller's tracts of 1696, previously described, were "printed for the author"; yet the participation of both Dunton and Baldwin has been demonstrated. No further evidence, however, has been found to clarify their relationship.[8]

3. Pseudonymous Imprints

It is apparent that Dunton on numerous occasions published under a pseudonymous imprint. "P. Smart" published *The Athenian Mercury* until Number 15 of the second volume, when Dunton had grown sufficiently confident of the project to affix his own name to it. The *Mercury* had, of course, been entered and licensed by Dunton, and his participation in it was certainly no secret to the trade. Benjamin Bridgwater's *Religio Bibliopolae* was likewise entered by Dunton. But when it appeared, it bore the imprint of P. Smart, who published only one other known work during his brief career, *The Late King James's Commission to his Privateers*. This broadside has not definitely been attributed to Dunton, although he was, most likely, its sponsor. Similarly, the name of James Dowley appears only once in Wing's *Short-Title Catalogue*, as the publisher of Charles Gildon's *History of the Athenian Society*. Dunton later admitted having commissioned this work, one with which he clearly could not publicly reveal his involvement.

The name of R. Levis appears only on seven works, in 1694-5, all of them short tracts, six by George Keith and one by Robert Hannay, which were advertised variously by John

Gwillim, Richard Baldwin and Dunton. Presumably these three booksellers adopted a fictitious imprint to conceal the fact that they were jointly responsible for the great number of reprinted Quaker tracts that appeared in those years.[1]

Yet another fictitious imprint was that of R. Newcome, which appears only on two of Dunton's works, *A Voyage Round the World* and *The Parable of the Top-Knots*, both printed in 1691. Presumably the imprint of T. Pratt, which appears only on *The Ladies Mercury*, conceals the identity of Dunton as well.

A minor pamphlet controversy of 1691, concerning a tract published by Dunton under a pseudonymous imprint, *The Parable of the Magpies*, appears to have been organized by Dunton precisely in the fashion described in his *Voyage Round the World*, published in the same year. In *A Voyage*, Dunton described a young man gazing in awe at the variety of titles displayed in a bookseller's shopwindow, and his subsequent disillusionment by a more sophisticated passer-by:

> "[among other titles in a shopwindow:] *A full and impartial account of the several contests and disputes among the wits of the last century*. - Heyday, I could not help muttering, cannot your wits agree among themselves! - Not always, young man, cried a subtle fellow, I warrant him, who happened to overhear me: But I'll tell you a secret - this bookseller here has for some time employed two authors to write against each other upon a certain subject, with as much spleen and animosity as the d-v-l or the pope bears against

> *Martin Luther*; and yet once a month they very lovingly settle accounts together, and go snacks in the profits of the controversy."[2]

In this instance, Dunton made use of an astonishing variety of pseudonyms. William Bradshaw, whom Dunton admired as "the best accomplished hackney-author I have met with", wrote *The Parable of the Magpies*.[3] Dunton published *The Parable* under the pseudonym of B. Griffitts (in later issues, W. Griffitts). This pamphlet was answered by *The Parable of the Black Birds*, published by Edward Thompkins,[4] whose imprint is known only on this one tract. Edward Golding (not a fictitious imprint) then published *The Full and Whole Proceedings of the New High-Court of Justice: ... with the Tryal and Examination of the two Late Notorious Criminals, the Magpie and the Black-Bird*;[5] and R. Wallup, whose imprint is known only on this pamphlet, published *The Parable of the Dove: Being a Review of the late Controversie between the Black-Birds, and the Magpies; tending to an Amicable Accomodation of all the Differences which at present Disturb the Feather'd Nations*.[6] Yet another contribution by William Bradshaw, advertised in the first *Parable*, was called *Monsieur in a Mouse-Trap: or, the Parable of the Shark & Herring-Pond*. This tract was printed for Thomas Hinton, presumably still another *ad hoc* imprint, as it is found only on this pamphlet.[7] Dunton also published in 1691 *The Parable of the Top-Knots*, under the pseudonym of R. Newcome (which he had also used for *A Voyage Round the World*), and *The Parable of The Puppies*, under the pseudonyms of W. Griffitts and T. Burdet. These works are all similar in typography and format; but they were not discussed by Dunton in his *Life and Errors* or elsewhere, nor were they advertised by him.

The only evidence linking Dunton with this series of tracts (beyond his statement in *The Life and Errors* that Bradshaw had written the first *Parable* for him) is that which is found in the Stationers' Company Court Books, which confirms that Dunton was indeed the publisher of *The Parable of the Magpies*. The pseudonym under which Dunton published this tract was B. Griffits, a name so close to that of B. Griffin that Griffin was angered and had Dunton summoned before the Court to give an explanation. Dunton's answer was accepted, but he was fined by the Court for not having had the publication entered in the register. The occasion of the hearing was thus recorded in the minutes of the General Court:

> Bennitt Griffin and John Dunton appearing Mr. Griffin complained ag^{t} Mr. Dunton that he had printed a Pamphlett called the Magpie in the name of B: Griffitts wch being soe near his name he Suffered by its reflecting on him, Mr. Dunton affirmed that it was the mistake of the Printer in the printing B: for W: at the first, but it had been since rectifyed and he promised to make good to Mr. Griffen any damage he might sustaine by being soe near his name. But this Court takeing notice that the said Pamphlett was not entred in this Com^{ys} Register before printed and

> published, Whereby the said Mr. Dunton had forfeited 20^{l} to this Company by vertue of their By Law touching Entries, and calling him in & asking him how many of the s^{d} Pamphletts he had printed he owned ab^{t} 1000 in the name of B Griffitts & ab^{t} 1000 more in the name of W: Griffitts, And then ye Court acquainting him wth the s^{d} forfeiture he professed himself wholly ignorant of the By Law, in consideracōn whereof & this being his first fault on his promise never to transgress againe in the like kind The Court mittigated the s^{d} Fine by bringing it to 50 Shillings wch he was ordered to pay to ye Ward^{ns}.[8]

Dunton published one additional work in 1691 under the pseudonym of W. Griffitts, Thomas D'Urfey's *The Triennial Mayor: Or, The New Raparees*.

APPENDICES

4. The Conger

The wholesaling conger developed during a period of uncertainty in the trade. Its purpose was to take the place of regulation and the Stationers' Company in providing security of tenure of copyright and insurance against the risk of loss from piracy and underselling. Ordinary process of the law had proved inadequate; the Stationers' Company lacked effectiveness in dealing with the situation, and the booksellers found it expedient to handle the matter among themselves. Around certain booksellers who enjoyed commanding positions in the trade the smaller men rallied, and in combination they were effective in providing the security against infringement of rights and unfair competition which was wanting in the trade generally, and which they severally were powerless to enforce. Piracy and underselling were not entirely controlled, but they were inhibited, and the booksellers were confident in the power of the group jointly to bring pressure to bear on renegades.

From the wholesaling conger, in which a group of booksellers participated in the sale of a work after it had been printed, and enjoyed an agency for the distribution of the work to the trade generally, it was a short step to the printing conger, in which copyright was shared and publication jointly undertaken. The wholesaling conger was a natural outgrowth of simple sharing and exchanging, the methods by which Dunton first established himself in trade, and the printing conger of the eighteenth century was a natural extension of the functions of the earlier associations. The conger was essentially a practical arrangement; it arose spontaneously from within the trade in the late seventeenth century to meet specific conditions in the trade. When by the middle of the eighteenth century these conditions no longer existed, the conger ceased to be useful and it disappeared.

It is not within the scope of this work to discuss the composition and organisation of the fully mature conger, or to trace its history beyond the earliest years. Rather, it has been my concern to show through the activities of John Dunton, the problems he encountered and the means he chose of dealing with them, the conditions in the trade which favoured the development of these trade associations. The device of the conger, from its beginnings to its death about 1750, has been treated at length by Norma Hodgson and Cyprian Blagden, in their edition of the notebooks of Thomas Bennet and Henry Clements, the only surviving evidence which documents the actual workings of the conger.[1] Dunton's few statements concerning congers which occur in A Voyage Round the World, The

Life and Errors, and in The State Weathercocks, were known to Hodgson and Blagden, who interpreted them in the light of the conger activity evidenced by the Bennet-Clements notebooks. Their explanation of the origin of these trade associations and their early development has been confirmed by the present study.

Although Dunton was the first to apply the designation conger to the wholesaling associations which he observed developing in the trade,[2] he remained an observer on the fringe of their activity. Strong and lasting ties with other booksellers simply did not suit Dunton's temperament, and he was rather more a specialist bookseller than were those who profited from membership in the conger. Furthermore, Dunton had none of the lack of confidence which caused other booksellers to wish to become part of an association. The success of the conger depended largely on confidence in the leadership of a few strong individuals, and Dunton was acquainted with the powerful men who were prominent in the earliest of these groups. He had great admiration for Richard Chiswell, the "Metropolitan Bookseller of England", and the Churchills, Awnsham and John, "Booksellers ... of an universal Wholesale Trade".[3] Although the high cost of paper deterred many booksellers from undertaking large works, Dunton complimented Chiswell, who "has not been known to print either a bad Book, or on bad Paper".[4] Chiswell's name alone on a title-page, wrote Dunton, was sufficient recommendation for a Book.

Characteristically, Dunton greatly admired the confidence and strong position in the trade that enabled these men to undertake the publication of more ambitious works than any bookseller could hope to undertake singlehandedly. He loved a grand design more than almost anything, and in this he perceived the chief benefit that was to be derived from the congers. Dunton saw that the strength derived from their trade associations enabled the Churchills to undertake substantial projects:

> "They are both so well furnished for any great Undertaking, that what they have hitherto proposed they have gone through, with great honour to themselves, and satisfaction to Subscribers; of which their printing 'Camden's Britannia,' and the publication of 'A New Collection of Travels,' lately come abroad, are undeniable instances. 'Sir Richard Blackmore's Poetical Works,' and 'Mr. Locke's Essay,' have received no small advantage by coming abroad through their hands; and, to finish their Characters, they never starve an undertaking, to save charges. In the 'New Collection of Travels' before mentioned, though they make about a Hundred and Fifty Sheets, and Fifty Cuts, more than was promised, yet they ask their Subscribers no advance".[5]

When, after the death of Iris, Dunton considered retiring from the trade in order to have more time for study and meditation, he had the idea of supporting himself by dabbling in the wholesale trade. " ... I could not reconcile myself to live altogether upon the main stock;" he wrote, "and therefore I thought it the most prudent way to keep a Warehouse, which might be managed in privacy, without much hurry".[6] To this end, Dunton took Mr. Shalcrosse's house in Bull Head Court. But his plans for a comfortable life in semi-retirement were thwarted by his second mother-in-law's refusal to pay his debts in the trade, and he took his stock instead to Ireland. Finally in retirement, in 1704, Dunton asserted his belief in the separation of publishing and retail bookselling, and he wrote in his "idea of a new life" that

> "Were I to begin the Trade of Bookselling once again, I would never give myself the trouble to keep *open Shop* .... I would wish no more than a convenient Warehouse, with a good acquaintance among the Booksellers; and a man's honesty in this case would sufficiently recommend him. This method of driving on the Trade by Wholesale, Subscription, &c. would give me leisure to *project* and *write*, for which I have always had a peculiar inclination".[7]

Many years later, in 1719, Dunton complained of the activities of the Castle Conger,[8] which he called the Pyrat-Conger, as they had reprinted copies which belonged to him. After twenty years in retirement, Dunton still retained ownership of many copyrights on which he placed an unrealistically high value. He projected a satirical essay, *The Shop Thief*, in which he promised to publish the characters of the pirate booksellers, in particular those who belonged to the Pyrat-Conger - excepting Daniel Browne, Andrew Bell, John Pemberton, Arthur Bettesworth, and Charles Rivington, the five honest booksellers among the members. Dunton's charge was that the conger had reprinted one of his copies, David Jones's Secret History of Whitehall and "by taking Advantage of his Pinching Necessities [forced] him to refer the Injury he has Receiv'd to an Arbitrator, ... And was my CASE, when (having no Money to go to Law for the Recovery of my whole Right) I was forc'd to take Six Guineas for a Pyrated Edition of The Secret History of Whitehall; that probably wou'd have put One Hundred Guineas into my own Pocket, had I Reprinted this Secret History my self". Dunton asserted that

> "the Highway Thief that crys on the Road, stand, deliver your Purse Sir, (as he fairly gives me warning of my Danger, and says, I may still keep my MONEY if I have COURAGE enough to defend it) is a brave honest Man, if compar'd ... with the Pyrat-Bookseller that first privately (i.e. sneakingly) prints one of my Best Copies, and then (that he might not be call'd a Rogue) gives me what Satisfaction himself pleases".

The five honest booksellers were not to be lampooned in The Shop Thief, because they had been deceived by David Jones, who had led them to believe that he was the owner of the copy. "But I shall stop here;" Dunton concluded, "for I hope I have said enough to convince all the Pyrat Booksellers and Printers of London and Westminster, that as I'll do no Wrong, so I'll receive none if I can help it. And for that Reason I hope all Honest Booksellers will Believe me to be their Most Sincere Friend, and Servant, John Dunton".[9]

INTRODUCTION TO THE CHECKLIST

This checklist has been compiled from personal examination of each item written or published by Dunton. Its primary aim is to epitomize Dunton's career in bookselling, omitting no detail essential to the history of each of the works with which he can be proved to have been concerned. It records the publishing history of many well known works and rescues a few from oblivion. This list should serve not only as a summary of facts but also as an unravelling of Dunton's tangled activities. It thus illumines trade practices and throws occasional rays of light on numerous ancillary problems which can now be understood in the context of their place and time.

Entries in this checklist are presented in the following form:

TITLE Titles of works have been recorded fully, or at least in sufficient length to indicate the nature and contents of the work. Titles of a few works which have not been examined have been recorded as they appeared in the source cited.

IMPRINT Imprints have been recorded fully, as they appeared on the title-pages of the works discussed.

SEPARATE TITLES Separate title-pages and imprints have been noted, with an indication of the relation of the part to the whole work.

FORMAT AND PAGINATION Details of format and pagination have been included primarily to indicate the size and shape of the work discussed. Terminal advertisements have been noted.

NOTES The presence of a signed preface or dedication has been noted only when the signature or date provides significant information; illustrations have not been noted.

LOCATION Wing's *Short-Title Catalogue* location references are cited; the location symbol for the copy which has provided the basic details for the description is italicized. In some instances the National Union Catalogue at the Library of Congress has shown a number of additional copies in American libraries. The number of copies of a work in a library has not been noted.

The checklist has been arranged chronologically, the entries alphabetized by title, with three exceptions: works concerned with the Apprentices' Petition, 1681, have been grouped under that heading, and works published in Dublin in 1698 have also been placed together. Various later editions of *The Athenian Oracle* have been summarized under the entry for the first volume, in 1703. Certain works advertised by Dunton as published by him (particularly in his catalogues of 1694), but of which no edition has been found with his imprint, have been entered under the year of original publication of the work, if an edition of the work has been traced.

The following works have been cited in the checklist in an abbreviated form:

Bradshaw	*Catalogue of the Bradshaw Collection of Irish Books in the University Library, Cambridge*. 3 vols., Cambridge, 1916.
CBEL	*The Cambridge Bibliography of English Literature*, ed. F. W. Bateson, Cambridge, 1940.
C&K	*A Census of British Newspapers and Periodicals 1620-1800*, R. S. Crane and F. B. Kaye, Chapel Hill, 1927.
Dix	*List of Books, Tracts, Broadsides, &c, Printed in Dublin from 1601-1700*, comp. E. R. McC. Dix, Dublin, 1905-12.
DNB	*The Dictionary of National Biography*, ed. Sir Leslie Stephen and Sir Sidney Lee, repr. Oxford, 1949-50.
Dublin Scuffle	*The Dublin Scuffle*, John Dunton, London, 1699.
H&L	*A Dictionary of the Anonymous and Pseudonymous Literature of Great Britain*, Samuel Halkett and John Laing, new and enl. edition, Edinburgh, 1926-62.
Holmes	*Cotton Mather. A Bibliography of his Works*, T. J. Holmes, Cambridge, Mass., 1940; *Increase Mather. A Bibliography of his Works*, T. J. Holmes, Cleveland, Ohio, 1931.
Hope	*Catalogue of a Collection of Early Newspapers and Essayists, Formed by the late John Thomas Hope, Esq. and Presented to the Bodleian Library by the late Rev. Frederick William Hope, M.A., D.C.L.*, J. H. Burn, Oxford, 1865.
LA	*Literary Anecdotes of the Eighteenth Century*, John Nichols, London, 1812-15.
L&E	*The Life and Errors of John Dunton, Citizen of London*, ed. J. B. Nichols, London, 1818. (As the two volumes of this work are paginated continuously, I have omitted citing the volume number in references to this work. In addition to the L&E, this edition contains selections from Dunton's other works which in certain instances it has been convenient to cite in this edition.)
McAlpin	*Catalogue of the McAlpin Collection of British History and Theology in the Union Theological Seminary*, comp. Charles R. Gillet, New York, 1929.

Moore	A Checklist of the Writings of Daniel Defoe, comp. John R. Moore, Bloomington, Indiana, 1960.
Newberry	A Checklist of Courtesy Books in the Newberry Library, Chicago, Illinois, 1942.
Noyes	A Bibliography of Courtesy and Conduct Books in Seventeenth Century England, comp. Gertrude E. Noyes, New Haven, Connecticut, 1937.
NQ	Notes and Queries, 1849-
Plomer	A Dictionary of the Printers and Booksellers who were at work in England, Scotland, and Ireland from 1668 to 1725, comp. Henry R. Plomer, Oxford, 1922.
Rawl.	Rawlinson Manuscripts, Bodleian Library, Oxford.
Rothschild	The Rothschild Library. A Catalogue of the Collection of Eighteenth Century Printed Books and Manuscripts formed by Lord Rothschild, Cambridge, 1954.
Sabin	A Dictionary of Books Relating to America, from its Discovery to the Present Time, Joseph Sabin, New York, 1868-1936.
Stat. Reg.	A Transcript of the Registers of the Worshipful Company of Stationers; from 1640-1708 A.D., ed. G. E. Briscoe Eyre, London, 1914.
T.C.	The Term Catalogues, 1668-1709 A.D.; with a Number for Easter Term, 1711 A.D., ed. Edward Arber, London, 1903.
Wing	A Short-Title Catalogue of Books Printed in England, Scotland, Ireland, Wales, and British America and of English Books Printed in other Countries, 1641-1700, comp. Donald G. Wing, New York, 1945-51.

The Apprentices' Petition, 1681

1. The address of above twenty thousand of the loyal Protestant apprentices of London: humbly presented to the Right Honourable the Lord Mayor, Septemb. 2. 1681, the day appointed by Act of Parliament to be yearly observed in commemoration of the burning that famous Protestant city by Papists, Jesuits, and Tories, Anno 1666 ....
   Colop: London, Printed for William Ingol the Elder. 1681.

   Folio. Pp. [ii].

   Location: Wing A 543 - L; CH, MH.

2. A friendly dialogue between two London-apprentices, the one a Whigg, the other a Tory: concerning the late address to my Lord Mayor ....
   Colop: London: Printed for Richard Janeway, in Queens-Head-Alley in Pater-Noster-Row. 1681.

   Folio. Pp. 1-4.

   Notes: In a catalogue of books printed for Dunton, appended to A New Martyrology, 1689, Dunton advertised: "A Friendly Dialogue between two London Apprentices: Written in the year 82. by J. C. Gent. price 1 d."

   Location: Wing F 2220 - CT; CN, Y. Also, L.

3. A just and modest vindication of the many thousand loyal apprentices that presented an humble address to the Lord Mayor of London ....
   Colop: London, Printed for R. Goodfellow. 1681.

   Folio. Pp. [ii].

   Location: Wing J 1223 - L; CH, MH, NC.

4. A vindication of the Protestant petitioning apprentices, from the scandals cast upon them by a malitious pamphlet

termed A Letter of Advice.
Colop: London: Printed for Richard Janeway in Queens-Head-Ally in Pater-Noster-Row. 1681.

Folio. Pp. [1]-8.

Location: Wing V 528 - O, C; CH, CN, TU, Y. Also, L.

5. True loyalty in its collours: or, a survey of the laudable address of the young men and apprentices of the City of London, to His Majesty. An heroick poem.
Colop: Printed for J. R. And are to be Sold by the Hawkers of London, 1681.

Folio. Pp. 1-2.

Location: Wing T 2757 - O; CH, MH, PU, Y. Also, L.

1682

6. [Drop-head title:]
A CONGRATULATORY POEM to the ministers sons, on their splendid feast, Thursday December 7th, 1682.
Colop: London, Printed by J. A. [James Astwood] for John Dunton at the Black Raven in the Poultrey. 1682.

Folio. Pp. [ii].

Notes: By John Dunton. This poem was reprinted in an appendix to Essay III in Upon this Moment depends Eternity, 1723, p. 33: "for my further thoughts of the Parsons Sons, I refer you to the Congratulatory Poem that was writ in the Year 1682, and publish'd that Day I made one of your Number ... December the 7th, 1682". This poem was also published in Athenianism, 1710.

Location: Wing C 5839 - O, MC; CH, MH, Y.

7. DANIEL IN THE DEN: or, the Lord President's imprisonment, and miraculous deliverance. Represented in a discourse from Heb. XI. v. 33. By S. J. Rector of Chinner in the County of Oxon.

London, Printed by J. A. [James Astwood] for John Dunton at the Sign of the Black Raven in the Poultrey, 1682.

4° Pp. [vi], 1-33, [i].

Notes: By Stephen Jay (L&E 63). This was the second work published by Dunton (L&E 63). T.C. II, 12 (Easter 1683).

Location: Wing J 497 - L, O, CT, DT; CH, NU, Y. Also, C.

8. A FUNERAL SERMON for that faithful and laborious servant of Christ, Mr Richard Fairclough, (who deceased July 4. 1682. in the sixty first year of his age.) BY JOHN HOWE Minister of the Gospel.
London, Printed for John Dunton at the Black Raven in the Poultry, 1682.

8°. Pp. [viii], 1-62.

Notes: T.C. II, 12 (Easter 1683), 123 (Easter 1685).

Location: Wing H 3027 - L, LCL; MH.

9. THE HOUSE OF WEEPING: or, mans last progress to his long home: fully represented in several funeral discourses, with many pertinent ejaculations under each head, to remind us of our mortality and fading state. BY JOHN DUNTON, M.A. late Minister of Aston Clinton near Aylsbury in the County of Bucks. Illustrated with a lively emblem of a funeral solemnity. Recommended as the most proper book yet extant to be given on funeral occasions.
London, Printed for John Dunton at the Black Raven in the Poultrey, 1682.

12°. Pp. [xxiv], 1-198, [vi]. Adv'ts, 2pp., at end.

Notes: Prefixed to this work are poems signed W.S., H.C., S.S., and J.S.; at the end of the work are printed an elegy on the Rev. John Dunton, signed O.O., and an epitaph, signed S.A. This was the fourth work published by Dunton (L&E 63). T.C. II, 12 (Easter 1683).

Location: Wing D 2627 - L. Also, C.

10. THE LORD'S LAST-SUFFERINGS shewed in the Lords-Supper. ... Being a second part to a former treatise of the Lord's Supper. BY THOMAS DOOLITTELL. M.A.
London, Printed for John Dunton, at the Black Raven in the Poultry. 1682.

12°. Pp. [lx], 1-468.

Notes: Epistola dedicatoria signed T.D. Nov. 1681. The first book published by Dunton (L&E 62). A second edition was published by Thomas Parkhurst in 1701 (copy in British Museum). L&E ix, 171. T.C. I, 458 (Michaelmas 1681).

Location: Wing D 1885 - L, LCL, LW; MH.

11. A SERMON PREACHT UPON THE DEATH OF MRS ANNE BARNARDISTON, (daughter of Nathanael Barnardiston Esq; late of Hackney:) who departed this life the 30th day of Decemb. 1681. at the age of seventeen. With a brief account of some remarkable passages of her life and death. Published at the desire of her relations.
London, Printed by J.A. [James Astwood] for Benjamin Alsop at the Angel and Bible, and John Dunton at the Black Raven, in the Poultrey. 1682.

4°. Pp. [xii], 1-38, [ii].

Notes: Epistle dedicatory to Madam Elizabeth Barnardiston signed John Shower. London, Jan. 25. 1681/2. This sermon was reprinted in Shower's Mourner's Companion, 1692. The third work published by Dunton (L&E 63). T.C. II, 12 (Easter 1683).

Location: Wing S 3690 - L, C, LCL, LG, DT; CH, NU. Also, Y.

1683

12. The Arraignment of Mr. Persecution. By Richard Overton.

Notes: On 9 February 1683 Dunton entered "... The famous triall of Mr. Persecution ...." (Stat. Reg. G, 6[127]), and in A New Martyrology, 1689, he advertised: "The Arraignment of Mr. P---on, printed in Quarto .... This Book was never throughly publish'd, 2000 of 'em being burnt by an unhappy accident in the year 83". Wing locates two editions of Richard Overton's Arraignment of Mr. Persecution, 1645; no copy of Dunton's edition has been located.

13. The Blessed Martyrs in Flames, with their Dying Expressions, applied to the present state of Affairs in England. To which is added four Copper Plates. price bound 6 d.

Notes: Dunton advertised the above in A New Martyrology, 1689, and in T.C. II, 12 (Easter 1683). Entered 19 January 1683 (Stat.Reg. F, 648[121]). Dunton also advertised this work in his catalogue of "Books Printed for, and are to be Sold by John Dunton", 1684, and he mentioned the work in A Voyage Round the World, 1691, II, 69. Not located.

14. A CONTINUATION OF MORNING-EXERCISE QUESTIONS and cases of conscience, practically resolved by sundry ministers, in October 1682.
London, Printed by J. A. [James Astwood] for John Dunton at the Sign of the Black Raven in the Poultrey over against the Stocks-Market, 1683.

4°. Pp. [vi], 1-26, ff. 27-32, pp. 33-207, 216-256, 259-322, 385-527, [i], 553-663, [i], 913-935, [i], 939-1038, 905-979, 990-1010.

Notes: To the Reader signed Samuel Annesley, April 9, 1683. Entered 15 December 1682 (Stat.Reg. F, 640 [115]). T.C. II, 12 (Easter 1683). L&E 80.

Location: Wing A 3228 - L, HH, E; MH, NPT, NU.

15. THE DEVILS PATRIARCK, or a full and impartial account of the notorious life of this present Pope of Rome Innocent the 11th .... Written by an eminent pen to revive the remembrance of the almost forgotten plot against the life of his sacred majesty and the protestant religion. Entered according to order.
London, Printed for John Dunton at the Black-Raven in the Poultrey. 1683.

8°. Frontispiece, pp. [xvi], 1-134.

Notes: By Christopher Nesse (H&L II, 49). To the Reader signed T.O. [Titus Oates (H&L II, 48)]. Entered 22 December 1682 (Stat.Reg. F, 645[118]). T.C. II, 15 (Easter 1683). L&E 177.

Location: Wing N 452 - L, O; CH, MH, NU, Y.

16. Directions and Perswasions to a sound Conversion, for prevention of that deceit and damnation of Souls, and of those Scandals, Heresies, and desperate Apostasies, that are the Consequents of a counterfeit or superficial change. By Richard Baxter, Minister of the Gospel.

Notes: Dunton advertised the above in his catalogue of "Books Printed for, and are to be Sold by John Dunton", 1684. Dunton entered on 15 December 1682 his intention to publish this work, "the 4th edition in large 12°" (Stat.Reg. F, 640[115]). Dunton advertised the fourth edition of Directions to the Unconverted in Stephen Jay's Tragedies of Sin, 1689, and in A New Martyrology, 1689. Dunton also advertised "Mr. Baxter's Directions, to prevent Miscarriage in a Sound Conversion" in a list of "Books in the Press, (and design'd for it) Printed for J. Dunton", in his catalogue which was issued with Athenian Mercury, XIII, 4 - 17 February 1694. In his Life and Errors, Dunton stated that this work had been printed for him by Mr. William Bonny (L&E 248). Wing locates numerous editions of Richard Baxter's Directions and Perswasions (Wing B 1243, 1658, to B 1248, third edition, 1673), but none with Dunton's imprint. No copy of Dunton's edition has been located. A. G. Matthews, The Works of Richard Baxter An Annotated List (London, [1933]), No. 33.

17. EARLY RELIGION: or, the way for a young man to remember his creator. Proposed in a sermon preach'd upon the death of Mr. Robert Linager, a young gentleman, who left this world, Octob. 26. 1682. With an account of some passages of his life and death. BY T. ROGERS, M.A.
London, Printed for J. Robinson, at the Golden Lion in St. Paul's Church-yard, and J. Dunton at the Black-Raven

in the Poultrey. M.DC.LXXXIII.

4°. Pp. [xii], 1-51, [i].

Notes: Epistle dedicatory signed Timothy Rogers. London, Nov. 15. 1682. To the Young Reader signed E. Veal. T.C. II, 11 (Easter 1683).

Location: Wing R 1849 - L; NU, Y. Also, C.

18. [Drop-head title:]
AN ELEGY upon that great minister of state Anthony Earl of Shaftsbury.
Colop: London, Printed for John Dunton, at the Black-Raven in the Poultrey, 1683.

Folio. Pp. [ii].

Notes: Entered 29 January 1683 (Stat.Reg. G, 1[124]).

Location: Wing E 458B - CH, MH. Also, O.

19. ENGLAND'S VANITY; or the voice of God against the monstrous sin of pride, in dress and apparel: wherein naked breasts and shoulders, antick and fantastick garbe, patches, and painting, long perriwigs, towers, bulls, shades, curlings, and crispings, with an hundred more fooleries of both sexes, are condemned as notoriously unlawful .... BY A COMPASSIONATE CONFORMIST.
London, Printed for John Dunton, at the Black Raven in the Poultry, 1683.

8°. Pp. [ii], 1-77, 80-144.

Notes: Entered 3 February 1683 (Stat.Reg. G, 3[126]). T.C. II, 12 (Easter 1683).

Location: Wing E 3069 - CN, LC, MH, NPT, Y.

20. THE INFORMER'S DOOM: or, an amazing and seasonable letter from Utopia, directed to the man in the Moon. Giving a full and pleasant account of the arraignment, tryal, and condemnation, of all those grand and bitter enemies, that disturb and molest all kingdoms and states, throughout the

Christian world. To which is added (as a caution to honest Country-men) the arraignment, tryal, and condemnation, of the knavery and cheats, that are used in every particular trade in the City of London. Presented to the consideration of all the tantivy-lads and lasses in Urope, by a true son of the Church of England. Curiously illustrated with about threescore cuts. Entred according to order.

London, Printed for John Dunton, at the Black-Raven, in the Poultrey, over-against Stocks-Market. 1683.

8°. Pp. [iv], [1]-160. Frontispiece, "The Black Raven", signed T: Catlett sc.

Notes: Epistle dedicatory to the Citizens of London signed Philagathus (i.e., John Dunton [H&L III, 152]). Entered 1 March 1683 (Stat.Reg. G, 10[131]). T.C. II, 19 (Easter 1683). L&E 264.

Location: Wing D 2629 - L, LG; MH.

21. A Necessary Companion for a serious Christian, directing him aright through the whole Course of his Life. Written for Publick Good: To which is added, The Death-Bed Counsel of a late Reverend Divine, to his Son an Apprentice in the City of London ... with many things besides of daily Use and Practice.

Notes: Dunton advertised the above in his catalogue of "Books Printed for, and are to be Sold by John Dunton", 1684, in Stephen Jay's Tragedies of Sin, 1689, and in T.C. II, 24 (Trinity 1683). Not located.

22. The swagering damsell, or, severall new curtaine lectures.

Notes: Dunton entered the above, 25 June 1683 (Stat.Reg. G, 44[166]). Not located.

23. The travels of true godliness. By Benjamin Keach.
For John Dunton, 1683. (Wing)

8°

Notes: Entered 12 June 1683 (Stat.Reg. G, 40[162]); second part entered 3 July 1683 (Stat.Reg. G, 48[169]). T.C. II, 24 (Trinity 1683), 52 (Michaelmas 1683). Dunton claimed to have printed ten thousand copies of this work (L&E 177), which he later sold to Nicholas Boddington, who published an edition of it in 1700 (Wing K 100)(L&E 209).

Location: Wing K 97 - L[Copy reported destroyed, 21/XI/1962].

24. -------- Second edition.

Notes: Not located. Four editions of this work were published in 1684.

25. TRUTH WILL OUT: a sermon preached on the 20th. of June, 1683. upon the discovery of the new plot. By a presbyter of the Church of England.
London, Printed for Tho. Manhood, and are to be sold by the Book-Sellers of London, 1683.

4°. Pp. [iv], 1-31, [i].

Notes: Dunton entered this work on 27 June 1683 (Stat. Reg. G, 46[167]), and he advertised it in Dunton's Remains, 1684, and in A New Martyrology, 1689. A note on the title-page of the Harvard copy states that it was transcribed "word for Word" from Jeremiah Burroughes's Irenicum, 1646 (Wing B 6088).

Location: Wing T 3167 - DT; MH. Also, O.

1684

26. THE AMAZEMENT OF FUTURE AGES: or, this swaggering world turn'd up-side down. By which means the astonishing curiosities ... of the world ... are faithfully described, to the satisfaction of every curious palate. Written BY T.R. on purpose to make delightful sport and pastime these winter nights.
London, Printed for John Dunton, at the Black Raven in

the Poultry, over against the Stocks-Market. 1684.

12°. Pp. [iv], 1-144.

Notes: Entered 28 December 1683 (Stat.Reg. G, 116[2191]).

Location: Wing R 78 - L.

27. [Drop-head title:]
BOOKS PRINTED for, and are to be sold by John Dunton at the Black Raven in the Poultrey, over against the Stocks-Market, London. [1684]

8°. Pp. 1-16.

Notes: Dunton advertised 168 works in this list, of which 14 were marked with a pointing hand, indicating that they were his own publications; these works have all been included in this list.

Location: L[bound with The Amazement of Future Ages, 1684], O[two copies, bound with The Travels of True Godliness, third edition, 1684, and Heavenly Pastime, 1685]; NU[bound with The Travels of True Godliness, third edition, 1684].

28. THE COMPLEAT TRADESMAN: or, the exact dealers daily companion. Instructing him throughly in all things absolutely necessary to be known by all those who would thrive in the world, and in the whole art and mystery of trade and traffick, ... Composed BY N. H. Merchant in the City of London.
London, Printed for John Dunton at the Black Raven, over against the Stocks-Market. 1684. Price 1 s.

12°. Pp. [viii], 1-192. Adv'ts, 1 p., at end.

Notes: Entered 25 October 1683 (Stat.Reg. G, 91[203]). This work was continued by The Pleasant Art of Money-Catching, 1684. T.C. II, 48 (Mich. 1683).

Location: O, EN.

29. -------- Second edition.
For John Dunton, 1684. (Wing)

Location: Wing H 97 - MH.

30. -------- Third edition.
London, Printed for John Dunton, at the Black Raven, at the Corner of Princes-street, near the Royal-Exchange. 1684.

12°. Pp. [iv], 1-180, [viii]. Adv'ts, 1p., at end.

Location: Wing H 97A - O, OG.

31. DUNTON'S REMAINS: or, the dying pastour's last legacy to his friends and parishioners .... BY JOHN DUNTON, late rector of Aston Clinton near Aylsbury in the County of Bucks. And author of the House of Weeping. To this work is prefixt the author's holy life and triumphant death. And at the latter end of it is annext his funeral sermon.
London, Printed for John Dunton, at the Black Raven in the Poultrey over against the Stocks-Market. M DC LXXXIV.

[Separate title-page; following the above, at p. 353, with double register:] A funeral sermon for ... Mr. John Dunton .... By N. H. Minister of the Gospel.
London: Printed for John Dunton at the Black Raven in the Poultrey, over against the Stocks-Market. 1684.

8°. Pp.[xvi], 1-387, [v]. Adv'ts, 4p., at end.

Notes: Frontispiece, portrait of John Dunton by F. H. Van Hove, plus 6 engravings by T. Catlett in the text. Epistle dedicatory signed John Dunton. October 12. 1683. Entered 10 October 1683 (Stat. Reg. G, 87[199]). T.C. II, 38 (Michaelmas 1683). This work was printed for Dunton by Francis Clark (L&E 249). One of Dunton's seven repented books (L&E 159). Newberry 491.

Location: Wing D 2633 - L, O, OB; CN, Y.

32. -------- Second edition.
Notes: Advertised in A New Martyrology, 1689

Location: LC.

33. AN IMPARTIAL AND FULL ACCOUNT of the life & death of the late unhappy William Lord Russel, eldest son and heir of the present Earl of Bedford, who was executed for high treason, July 21. 1683. in Lincolns-Inn-Fields.
London, Printed for Caleb Swinock at the Trunck in St. Paul's Church-Yard, and are to be Sold by most Book-Sellers. 1684.

8°. Pp. [iv], 1-96.

Notes: To the Reader signed A.L. In A New Martyrology, 1689, Dunton advertised "The Life and Martyrdom of that pious Nobleman W. L. R. with his Effigies drawn to the Life. Written by Dr. Sland. Price bound 1s."; and in his Life and Errors he wrote: "[Mr. Caleb Swinnock] published for me 'The Life and Death of that great Patriot, William Lord Russell'" (L&E 261).

Location: Wing L 3 - L; CH.

34. A new yeares for the merry cittizen and another for the country bumpkin or the 1600 years travel of old father Xmas.

Notes: Dunton entered the above, 8 January 1684 (Stat. Reg. G, 118[221]). In The Pilgrim's Guide, 1684, Dunton advertised "lately printed for John Dunton ... A New Present for the wary Citizens, another for the Countrey lads". Not located.

35. THE PILGRIMS GUIDE from the cradle to his death-bed: with his glorious passage from thence to the New-Jerusalem ... To which is added the sick-mans passing-bell, with no less than fifty several pleasant treatises besides .... To these are annext, the sighs and groans of a dying man. BY JOHN DUNTON late Rector of Aston Clinton. Illustrated with eight curious copper plates.
London, Printed for John Dunton at the sign of the Black Raven at the Corner of Princes-street, near the Royal Exchange, MDCLXXXIV.

12°. Pp. [xxx], 1-41, 40-220, 213-236, 235-306.
Adv'ts, 2pp., at end.

Notes: Epistle dedicatory to "endeared Relations and Acquaintances" signed John Dunton. Entered 12 June 1684 (Stat.Reg. G, 143[242]). C. A. Moore, in Studies in Philology, XXII (1925), p. 480, wrote that "The mere fact that The Pilgrim's Guide comprises three hundred and six pages of closely-printed matter would lead one to suspect that it was not entirely honest. I am unable to state the full extent of plagiarism, but it is certain that the author borrowed without scruple". CBEL II, 530. NQ 10th Series, VI (1906), 170

Location: Wing D 2632 - L; MH.

36. -------- Second edition.

Notes: Advertised by Dunton in A New Martyrology, 1689. Not located.

37. A PLEA FOR THE NON-CONFORMISTS, giving the true state of the Dissenters case .... BY PHILALETHES.
London, Printed for the Author, 1684.

4°. Pp. [iv], 1-79, [i].

Notes: By Thomas Delaune (H&L IV, 363). In his Life and Errors, Dunton wished Sarah Malthus success in carrying on her late husband's trade (L&E 220); but in his Living Elegy, written two years later, in 1706, Dunton accused Mrs Malthus, among other crimes, of "re-printing a Copy*[Delaune's 'Plea for the Nonconformists.'] I brought her to publish" (L&E 462). An edition of Delaune's Plea was published in 1704, "Printed, & are to be sold by the Booksellers in London & Westminster" (copy in British Museum).

Location: Wing D 893 - L, C, LCL, LW, EN; NPT, NU.

38. THE PLEASANT ART OF MONEY-CATCHING, newly and fully discover'd. Being the second and last part of that very useful book, intituled The Compleat Tradesman ... Composed BY N.H. author of The Compleat Tradesman.
London, Printed For J. Dunton over against the Stocks-Market, 1684.

12°. Pp. [iv], 1-20, 23-46, 49-72, 71-94, 97-120, 119-142.

Notes: Entered 6 December 1685 (Stat.Reg. G, 112[216]). Printed for Dunton by William Bonny (L&E 248). T.C. II, 48 (Michaelmas 1683).

Location: Wing H 100 - MH, NC. Also, L.

39. Poems upon the Death of that great Minister of State, Anthony, Earl of Shaftsbury.

Notes: Dunton advertised the above in his catalogue of "Books Printed for, and are to be Sold by John Dunton", 1684, and in A New Martyrology, 1689. In 1683, Dunton had published An Elegy upon that Great Minister of State Anthony Earl of Shaftsbury; no copy of a collection of poems has been located. Possibly Dunton was advertising his own publication, as well as other separate poems on the death of Shaftsbury.

40. Poems upon the Ministers Sons late Splendid Feast that they made at Merchant-Taylors Hall, Dec. 7.

Notes: Dunton advertised the above in his catalogue of "Books Printed for, and are to be Sold by John Dunton", 1684. In 1682, Dunton had published his own poem, A Congratulatory Poem to the Ministers Sons; no copy of a collection of poems has been located. Possibly Dunton was advertising his own, as well as other separate poems celebrating the feast.

41. THE PROGRESS OF SIN; or the travels of ungodliness: wherein, the pedigree, rise (or original) antiquity, subtilty, evil nature, and prevailing power, of sin, is fully

discovered; in an apt and pleasant allegory: ... BY B. K. author of War with the Devil, and Travels of True Godliness.

London, Printed for John Dunton, at the Sign of the Black Raven, at the corner of Princes Street near the Royal Exchange, 1684.

12°. Pp. [iv], 1-272.

Notes: By Benjamin Keach. Entered 20 February 1684 (Stat. Reg. G, 124[225]). Preface dated April 28. 1684. T. C. II, 81 (Trinity 1684). Later editions were published in 1685.

Location: Wing K 80 - L, LF; MH, NHC, NU.

42. The travels of true godliness. By Benjamin Keach. Third edition.

London, Printed for John Dunton, at the Raven over against the Stocks-Market. MDCLXXXIV.

12°. Pp. [iv], 1-52.

Notes: This work was first published by Dunton in 1683.

Location: Wing K 98 - O; NHC, NU.

43. -------- Fourth edition.

Notes: Not located.

44. -------- Fifth edition.
For John Dunton, 1684. (Wing) 12°.

Location: Wing K 99 - L(Reported missing, 14/ix/1965).

45. -------- Sixth edition.
For John Dunton, 1684. (Wing) 12°.

Location: Wing K 99A - NHC.

1685

46. The Child's Portion, or The unseen Glories of the Children of God, asserted and proved: together with several other choice and excellent Sermons, occasionally preached, and now published. By Samuel Hillard, Minister of the Gospel in New England. Price, bound, 1s. 6d. ....
   ... printed for J. Dunton at the Black Raven, at the corner of Prince's street.

   Notes: Dunton advertised the above in T.C. II, 123 (Easter 1685), and in A New Martyrology, 1689. The Child's Portion, by Samuel Willard, was first published in Boston in 1684 (Wing W 2271). No copy of a London edition has been located.

47. HEAVENLY PASTIME, or, pleasant observations on all the most remarkable passages throughout the Holy Bible, of the Old and New Testament .... BY JOHN DUNTON, author of The Sickmans Passing-Bell.
   London, Printed for John Dunton, at the Black Raven, at the Corner of Princes-street, near the Royal Exchange, 1685.

   12°. Pp. [1]-168, 1-136, [viii]. Adv'ts, 8pp., at end.

   Notes: Entered 7 November 1684 (Stat. Reg. G, 166[259]). One of seven works which Dunton regretted publishing (L&E 159).

   Location: Wing D 2625 - L. Also, O.

48. -------- [another edition]

   Notes: Dunton advertised in T.C. II, 113 (Hillary 1685), "Heaven's Pastimes, or Pleasant Observations on all the most remarkable passages throughout the Holy Bible ... Octavo. Printed for J. Dunton at the Black Raven, over against the Stocks Market". The National Union Catalogue, Washington, D. C., records at the University of Virginia a copy of Heaven's Pastime, London, John Dunton, 1685. Running title: Heavenly Pastime. This edition contains advertisements, 6pp., at end.

49. -------- Second edition.
London, Printed for John Dunton, at the Black Raven, at the Corner of Princes-street, near the Royal Exchange, 1685.

12°. Pp. [1]-168, 1-136, [viii]. Adv'ts, 8pp., at end.

Notes: T.C. II, 131 (Easter 1685).

Location: Wing D 2626 - L, O. Also, C; LC.

50. AN HUE AND CRY AFTER CONSCIENCE: or the pilgrims progress by candle-light, in search after honesty and plain-dealing. Represented under the similitude of a dream .... Written BY JOHN DUNTON, author of The Pilgrims Guide, from the Cradle to his Death-Bed.
London, Printed for John Dunton, at the Black Raven, at the Corner of Princes-street, near the Royal Exchange, in Cornhill, 1685.

12°. Pp. [viii], 1-160.

Notes: Entered 25 May 1685 (Stat. Reg. G, 199[286]). T.C. II, 123 (Easter 1685). One of seven works which Dunton regretted publishing (L&E 159).

Location: Wing D 2628 - L.

51. -------- Second edition

Notes: Advertised by Dunton in A New Martyrology, 1689. No copy has been located.

52. MAGGOTS: or, poems on several subjects, never before handled. BY A SCHOLLAR.
London, Printed for John Dunton, at the Sign of the Black Raven, at the Corner of Princes Street, near the Royal Exchange. 1685.

12°. Pp. [xviii], 1-172.

Notes: By Samuel Wesley (H&L IV, 5). Entered 17 April 1685 (Stat. Reg. G, 191[280]). T.C. II, 126 (Easter 1685). L&E x, 86.

Location: Wing W 1374 - CLC, CN, MH, NN, WF, Y. Also, O.

53. -------- Second edition.
For John Dunton, 1685. (Wing)

Location: Wing W 1375 - O; CH. [Note: O owns only the first edition of this work.]

54. The progress of sin. By Benjamin Keach. Second edition.
For John Dunton, 1685. (Wing)

12°.

Notes: T.C. II, 118 (Hilary 1685). First published by Dunton in 1684.

Location: Wing K 81 - L[L does not own this edition].

55. -------- Third edition.

Notes: Advertised by Dunton in T.C. II, 131 (Easter 1685), and in A New Martyrology, 1689. No copy has been located. Nicholas Boddington (to whom Dunton sold the copyright of Keach's Travels, 1683, q.v.) advertised the third edition of this work in T.C. III, 204 (Trinity 1700) (Wing K 82).

1686

56. A SERMON OCCASIONED BY THE EXECUTION OF A MAN found guilty of murder: preached at Boston in New-England, March 11th 1685/6 .... BY INCREASE MATHER. Teacher of a Church of Christ.
Boston, Printed for John Dunton Book-Seller, lately Arrived from London; and are to be Sold by him, both at his Shop over against the Town-[House an]d his Shop in Salem, 1686. [Holmes 115-A[1]]
Boston, Printed for Joseph Brunni[ng Book-]Seller, & are to be Sold at his Shop [at the Cor-]ner of the Prison Lane next the Town-[House.] Anno 1686. [Holmes 115-A[2]]

8°. Pp. (2), (2), 44 [Holmes].

Notes: "There seems to be no variation in the edition except that of the imprint. Both imprints ... were taken from imperfect examples, and the completion of the text has been supplied" (Holmes II, 480). The sermon by Increase Mather is followed by Cotton Mather's Call of the Gospel, Boston, R.P. [Richard Pierce], [1686] (Holmes 43-A), and Joshua Moodey's Exhortation to a Condemned Malefactor, Boston, [1686], with continuous register and separate pagination (pagination is continuous through Call of the Gospel and Exhortation). Dunton advertised these sermons separately in A New Martyrology, 1689, advising that "These three Discourses (all printed for John Dunton whilst he liv'd in New-England) are usually sold altogether at 12 d. bound". L&E 96.

Location: Wing M 1246 - NHS. Holmes - American Antiquarian Society (Brunning imprint); John Carter Brown Library (lacks title-page); New York Historical Society (Dunton imprint); Yale (imperfect).

1689

57. THE BLOODY ASSIZES: or, a compleat history of the life of George Lord Jefferies, from his birth to this present time ... Faithfully collected by several West-Countrey gentlemen, who were both eye and ear-witnesses to all the matter of fact. With allowance.

London, Printed for J. Dunton at the Black Raven in the Poultrey, over against the Compter, and sold by R. Janeway in Queens-Head-Alley in Pater-noster-row. 1689.

4°. Pp. [1]-70, [ii]. Adv'ts, 1p., and blank, 1p., at end.

Notes: Dedication to Lord Jefferies signed James Bent. The authorship of this work has often been attributed to Dunton; Dunton himself, however, identified John Shirley and Thomas Pitts as the authors (L&E 184-5); see Chapter II for discussion. The Bloody Assizes was later combined with The Dying

Speeches, 1689, and The Second and Last Collection, 1689, and they became A New Martyrology, 1689. See also L&E 201; H&L VI, 296; H&L IX, 32.

Location: Wing B 1905 - L, O, EN; BN, CH, MH, NC, NU, WCL. Also, C.

58. -------- Second edition.

Notes: Advertised by Dunton in A New Martyrology, 1689. Not located.

59. The Character of a Christian Exemplified, in all the Degrees of Perfection attainable on this side Heaven. Written by Drawde Rekoohh [i.e., Edward Hooker] Author of that most excellent Treatise, entituled, Divine Breathings.

Notes: Dunton advertised the above in A New Martyrology, 1689, promising that it "will speedily go to the Press". The British Museum catalogue lists Theologia mystica, by J.P.M.D., 1683, with "The editor's prefatory epistle signed: E. H. Mamp, and the postscript to the epistle signed: E.H. Mamp, alias Drawde Rekooh, pseudonyms of E. Hooker". H&L attribute Divine Breathings to Thomas Sherman (H&L II, 97; Wing S 3388). No copy of The Character of a Christian has been located.

60. A collection of the dying speeches, letters of those ... Protestants who suffered ... under ... Lord Jeffreys. [London,] sold by J. Dunton, 1689.

Notes: Wing C 5202; two copies located, L and YM, and advertisement in T.C. II, 258 (Easter 1689) cited. I have been unable to locate this work at L, and I believe it to be identical with The Dying Speeches, Letters, and Prayers, &c. of those Eminent Protestants who Suffered in the West of England, published by Dunton in 1689; the advertisement in T.C. II, 258, might easily apply to either collection.

61. [Drop-head title:]
A CONTINUATION OF NEWS from that part of His Majesties fleet that now lies at High-Lake near Chester: giving an impartial account of all considerable occurrences since its leaving Harwich, to this present time. Licensed, Aug. 20. 1689. J.F.
Colop: London, Printed for John Dunton at the Black Raven in the Poultrey. 1689.

Folio. Pp. [ii].

Notes: Letter dated: From on Board the Hannibal, Aug. 14. 1689. At upper right corner of recto: Numb. 2. See also News from that part of H.M. Fleet ..., 1689.

Location: Wing C 5958 - CH, MH.

62. THE DYING SPEECHES, letters and prayers, &c. of those eminent protestants who suffered in the West of England, (and elsewhere,) under the cruel sentence of the late Lord Chancellour, then Lord Chief Justice Jefferys: with an account of their undaunted courage at the barr, and afterwards; and the most remarkable circumstances that attended their execution. Never before published.
London, Printed for John Dunton, at the Black Raven in the Poultrey, over against the Compter; and are to be Sold by R. Janeway in Queens-head-Alley in Pater-noster-row. 1689

4°. Pp. [iv], 1-40.

Notes: This work was discussed by J. G. Muddiman, in his edition of The Bloody Assizes (Edinburgh, 1929), in which he attributed it to John Tutchin (p. 7). The Bloody Assizes, 1689, was later combined with this work and the Second and Last Collection of the Dying Speeches, 1689, to become A New Martyrology, 1689. In his Life and Errors, Dunton stated that "Mr. William Rogers, Mr. Harris, and myself, were once Partners with [Mr. Timothy Goodwin] in publishing some 'Dying Speeches'" (L&E 208). T.C. II, 258 (Easter 1689).

Location: Wing D 2956 - L, LG, DC; CH, CN, NU, Y.

63. -------- [another edition]
London, Printed in the Year 1689, and are to be Sold by the Booksellers in London and Westminster.

4°. Pp. [iv], 1-20, 25-40.

Notes: Title-page printed partly from the same setting of type as No. 63.

Location: L, O; NU, Y.

64. -------- Second edition.

Notes: Advertised in A New Martyrology, 1689. Not located.

65. EARLY PIETY, exemplified in the life and death of Mr. Nathanael Mather, who having become at the age of nineteen, an instance of more than common learning and virtue, changed Earth for Heaven, Oct. 17, 1688 .... [BY COTTON MATHER]
London, Printed by J. Astwood for J. Dunton, 1689. [Separate title-page; following the above, with continuous register and separate pagination:] Several sermons concerning walking with God, and that in the dayes of youth: preached at Boston in New-England. By Cotton Mather, Pastor of a church there.
London, Printed by J. Astwood for J. Dunton, at the Black Raven in the Poultrey, over against the Compter. 1689.

8°. Pp. (2), (3), (5), 1-60[pp. 52-3 repeated], (2), 1-86 [Holmes].

Notes: To the Reader signed London February, 5th, 1688/9, Samuel Mather. "Samuel was then with his father [Increase Mather] in London. Cotton compiled the book within twelve days of the death of Nathanael. Rather than send his manuscript directly to a publisher, he sent it most probably to his father [Increase Mather], who was known to publishing circles in London, that he might put it to press. It is Cotton Mather's first book printed in London" (Holmes I, 291). Holmes 100A.

Location: Wing M 1096 - CN, MB, MWA, NN, RPJ, Y[imperfect].

66. -------- Second edition.
London, Printed by J. Astwood for J. Dunton at the Black Raven in the Poultrey, 1689.

8°. Pp. [xiv], 1-53, 52-60, [ii], 1-86.

Notes: To the Reader dated London, June 17. 1689. and signed Matthew Mead. Separate title-page as No. 66. Holmes 100B.

Location: Wing M 1907 - L, O; CN, LC, MB, MH, RPJ.

67. [Drop-head title:]
GREAT NEWS FROM THE DUKE OF SCHOMBERGE'S ARMY: giving an impartial account of the late bloody fight and engagement between the Irish papists and our English forces: with an account of men kill'd and wounded. Together with a journal of the whole siege of Carrickfergus, and an account of the towns retaken since the generals arrival. Written in a letter from Chester, directed to Mr. John Blackhall citizen in London. Licensed September 4. J.F.
Colop: London, Printed for John Dunton at the Black Raven in the Poultrey. 1689.

Folio. Pp. [ii].

Notes: Letter dated: From on Board the Mary Galley at High-Lake, August 31. 1689. Bradshaw 7155.

Location: Wing G 1734 - C.

68. [Drop-head title:]
THE HUMBLE PETITION of the widdows and fatherless children in the West of England, presented to this present convention.

Folio. Pp. [ii].

Notes: This broadside has no imprint, but it contains an advertisement for The Bloody Assizes, to be "Publisht in a few Days .... Sold by John Dunton at the Black Raven in the Poultrey, over against the Compter". Dunton also advertised this broadside in The New Martyrology, 1689.

Location: Wing H 3585A - CH. Also, O; Y.

69. An impartial history of the life and death of George Lord Jeffreys. [By James Bent]
For John Dunton, 1689. (Wing)

Notes: Wing B 1906; two copies located, L and NU. Both copies have been examined and in each case the Impartial History is part of Tutchin's New Martyrology, 1689, with separate title-page and pagination, but with double register.

70. The Joy of Faith, or A Treatise opening the true nature of Faith, its lowest stature and distinction from Assurance: with a preliminary Tract evidencing the Divinity of the Sacred Scriptures. By Samuel Lee, M.A. Price 1s. 6d. ...
... printed for J. Dunton at the Black Raven in the Poultrey.

Notes: Dunton advertised the above in T.C. II, 246 (Easter 1689). Wing locates an edition of this work printed in Boston, 1687, but not a London edition (Wing L 891). The article on Lee in the DNB (by B. Porter, XI, 819) states that in addition to the Boston edition of 1687, an edition appeared in London in 1689. Dunton's edition was advertised as "now published" in The Bloody Assizes, 1689, and in The Dying Speeches, 1689. Dunton continued to advertise this work until 1692. Not located.

71. A new martyrology. [By John Tutchin]
For John Dunton, 1689. (Wing)

Notes: Wing (T 3378) locates three copies of this edition, O, NU and Y. I have been unable to locate the work at O. NU own only the "third" edition, q.v., and the copy at Y is imperfect, lacking the title-page; in other respects, the Y copy of the work is identical with copies of the third edition which have been examined. The advertisement in the Term Catalogue, cited by Wing, refers to a "reprinted" edition (T.C. II, 280 [Trinity 1689]). I believe that the "third" edition was the only edition of this work printed in 1689.

72. A NEW MARTYROLOGY: or, the bloody assizes: now exactly methodized in one volume .... To this treatise is added, the life and death of George Lord Jeffryes. The third edition with large additions.
London, Printed (according to the Original Copies) for John Dunton at the Black Raven in the Poultrey. 1689.

[Separate title-page; following the above, with double register and separate pagination:] An impartial history of the life and death of George Lord Jeffreys late Lord Chancellour of England.
London, Printed for John Dunton at the Black Raven in the Poultrey. 1689. [Dedication to George Lord Jeffreys, signed James Bent.]

8°. Pp. [xii], 1-196, 1-80, [iv], 1-[47], [v]. Adv'ts, 5 pp., at end.

Notes: "Third edition" refers only to the life of Lord Jeffreys, which was originally published as The Bloody Assizes, in two editions, 1689; The Bloody Assizes was combined with The Dying Speeches, 1689, and The Second and Last Collection of the Dying Speeches, 1689, to become A New Martyrology, A later edition of this work was published in 1693. See also entry for The Bloody Assizes, 1689. T.C. II, 280 (Trinity 1689).

Location: Wing T 3379 - L; CN, IU, MHL, NP. Also, NU.

73. News from that part of H.M. Fleet that lies at Harwich.
John Dunton, 1689

Notes: Sold at Sotheby's, 17 October 1961, in a collection of tracts which formerly belonged to Narcissus Luttrell (Lot 990). See A Continuation of news ..., 1689.

Location: Wing O N1004A - SALE

74. POETICAL FRAGMENTS: heart-imployment with God and it self. The concordant discord of a broken-healed heart. Sorrowing-rejoycing, fearing-hoping, dying-living. Written partly for himself, and partly for near friends in sickness, and other deep affliction. BY RICHARD BAXTER .... The Second Edition.
London, Printed for J. Dunton at the Black Raven in the Poultry. 1689.

[Separate title-page; following the above at p. 103 with continuous register:] Additions to the poetical fragments, of Rich. Baxter.
London: Printed for J. Dunton at the Black Raven in the Poultry. 1689.

12°. Pp. [x], 1-158.

Notes: To the Reader signed Rich. Baxter, Aug. 7. 1681. The work is dated at the end of the text Jan. 14, 1682/3. Originally published in 1681 (Wing B 1349). The third edition of this work was published by Thomas Parkhurst in 1699 (Wing B 1351). T.C. II, 294 (Michaelmas 1689). A.G. Matthews, The Works of Richard Baxter An Annotated List (London, [1933]), no. 98.

Location: Wing B 1350 - L; CH, MH, NPT.

75. THE POPISH CHAMPION: or, a compleat history of the life and military actions of Richard Earl of Tyrconnel, Generalissimo of all the Irish forces now in arms .... To this treatise is added the life and memorable actions of Father Petre, &c. Publish'd with allowance.
London, Printed for John Dunton at the Black Raven in the Poultrey, over against the Compter. MDCLXXXIX. Price 1 s.

4°. Pp. [iv], 1-58, [ii]. Adv'ts, 2pp., at end.

Notes: One of the copies of this work in the British Museum (G.14035) is dated on the title-page "March 1689". T.C. II, 250 (Easter 1689).

Location: Wing P 2944 - L, O, DT; CH, IU, MU, NU, Y.

76. The protestant martyrs, or, the bloody assizes.
For J. Bradford, 1689. (Wing P 3838)

Notes: Dunton may have been concerned in the publication of this work (see Chapter II).

77. A RAMBLE ROUND THE WORLD: or, the most pleasant travels, voyages, & adventures of Kainophilus throughout the habitable earth, &c. ... Performed by a single sheet coming out every Friday, to each being added, the Irish courant. Licensed, and entered according to order, 1689. [in upper right corner:] Number I. [Number II.]
Colop: London, Printed for Rich. Janeway, in Queen's-Head-Alley, in Pater-noster-Row, 1689. [dated in ms. on title:] 6. Nov. 1689.

2 nos. published, 6 November & 8 November 1689.

Notes: Entered by R. Janeway 6 November 1689 (Stat. Reg. G, 307[364]). See also A Voyage Round the World, 1691; and The Life ... of Christopher Wagstaff, 1762. CBEL II, 658, 705. C&K 772.

Location: O; CH.

78. REFORMED RELIGION, or, right Christianity described, in its excellency, and usefulness in the whole life of man. BY A PROTESTANT-CHRISTIAN.
London, Printed by J.A. [James Astwood] for John Dunton at the Black Raven in the Poultrey over against the Compter, 1689.

8°. Pp. [viii], 1-126, [ii]. Adv'ts, 2pp., at end.

Notes: T.C. II, 268 (Trinity 1689); in this advertisement, Dunton identified the author as "Mr. [Matthew ?] Barker, Minister of the Gospel".

Location: Wing R 748 - LW.

79. [Drop-head title:]
A RELATION OF A LATE BARBAROUS ASSAULT of the French upon the English, near the Downs, March the 12th. 1688/9. Attested by Captain, Officers, and several of the passengers.

Colop: London, Printed, and sold by R. Janeway in Queens-Head-Alley in Pater-noster-Row, 1689.

Folio. pp. [ii].

Notes: Although Dunton's name is not included in the imprint of this news sheet, at the foot of the sheet are advertisements for the second edition of The Bloody Assizes and other "Western Transactions for the Year 85", "All sold by John Dunton at the Black Raven in the Poultrey, over against the Compter". Dunton also advertised this work in A New Martyrology, 1689.

Location: O.

80. THE SAINTS READINESS for their Lord's coming: a funeral sermon preached upon the death of that faithful and laborious servant of Christ, Mr. John Oakes, Dec. 30. 1688. BY SAMUEL SLATER Minister of the Gospel.
London, Printed by J. Astwood for J. Dunton at the Black Raven in the Poultrey over against the Compter, 1689.

8°. Pp. [x], 1-118, [ii]. Adv'ts, lp., and blank, lp., at end.

Notes: Dedication to Mary Oakes signed Samuel Slater. Jan. 28. 1688/9. T.C. II, 245 (Easter 1689).

Location: Wing S 3970 - L, O, LCL: Y.

81. THE SECOND AND LAST COLLECTION OF THE DYING SPEECHES, letters and prayers, &c. of those eminent protestants who suffered in the West of England, (and elsewhere,) under the cruel sentence of the late Lord Chancellour, then Lord Chief Justice Jefferys: .... With allowance.
London, Printed for John Dunton, at the Black Raven in the Poultrey, over against the Compter; and are to be Sold by R. Janeway in Queens-head-Alley in Pater-noster-row. 1689.

4°. Pp. [1]-30, [ii]. Adv'ts, lp., and blank, lp., at end.

Notes: See Chapter II for discussion of this work.

Location: Wing S 2256 - L, O; NU. Also, C.

82. Sermons on the Prodigal Son. [By Samuel Willard] Price bound 3 s.

Notes: Dunton advertised the above in A New Martyrology, 1689. Wing locates Mercy Magnified on a Penitent Prodigal, or a Brief Discourse, wherein Christs Parable of the lost Son found, is Opened and Applied; as it was Delivered in Sundry Sermons, by Samuel Willard, printed at Boston, 1684 (Wing W 2285). No copy of a London edition has been located.

83. Τὰ καννάκου: The tragedies of sin contemplated, in the [within brackets:] ruine of the angels, fall of man, destruction of the old world, confusion of Babel, conflagration of Sodom, &c. ... Together with remarques on the life of the great Abraham. BY STEPH. JAY, Rector of Chinner in the County of Oxon.
London, Printed by J. Astwood for John Dunton at the Black Raven in the Poultrey, 1689.

[Separate title-page; following the above, with lower-case register and separate pagination:] Remarques on the life of the great Abraham, ... By S. Jay, Rector of Chinner in the County of Oxon.
London, Printed for John Dunton at the Black Raven in the Poultrey, over against the Compter. 1689.

8°. Pp. [xvi], 1-127, [vii], 1-121, 124-234, [ii].
Adv'ts, 2pp., at end.

Notes: T. C. II, 283 (Michaelmas 1689). L&E 152, 267.

Location: Wing J 498 - L, C; BN, NU.

84. ... the Travels of a Person of Quality over most parts of Europe. To which is added a lively Cut. Price bound 6 d.

Notes: Dunton advertised the above in A New Martyrology, 1689. as "A small New-Years Gift in Duodecimo".

Not located.

85. The travels of true godliness. By Benjamin Keach. Seventh edition.

Notes: Advertised by Dunton in <u>A New Martyrology</u>, 1689. Not located. This work was first published in 1683.

86. THE TRUE PROTESTANT MERCURY: or, an impartial history of the times, perform'd by a single sheet, coming out every Friday. To which is added, weekly remarks: or, occasional joco-serious reflections on the distempers of the present age. Written by a true lover of his kind and countrey. Licens'd, and enter'd according to order. Friday, December 6, 1689. [In upper right corner:] Numb. 1.
Colop: London, Printed for Rich. Janeway in Queens Head-Ally, in Pater-noster Row, 1689.

Vol. I. 4 nos. issued, 6 - 27 December 1689.
Vol. II. 6 nos. issued, 3 January - 7 February 1690.

Notes: T. M. Hatfield first identified Dunton as the author of this periodical; Dunton is the sole advertiser in the periodical, and No. 5 includes the anecdote about Mary Gorsam which also appears in Dunton's "Conversation in Ireland" in <u>The Dublin Scuffle</u> and in his will (T. M. Hatfield, <u>The True Secret History of Mr. John Dunton</u>, [unpublished thesis, Harvard University, 1926], pp. 40-1). CBEL II, 705. C&K 2070.

Location: <u>L</u> (No. 1 only), O (Nos. 1 - 4).

87. <u>Useful Observations on the most remarkable Passages of the O. and N. Testament</u>, with the Addition of several Dialogues and Divine Poems. The second Edition; Price bound 2 <u>s</u>. 6 <u>d</u>.

Notes: Dunton advertised the above in <u>A New Martyrology</u>, 1689. Not located.

88. THE YOUNG-MAN'S KINDNESS TO HIS GOD. A sermon preached to young-men, at their desire, Decemb. 25, 1688. at Mr. Oakes's Meeting-Place, in Hand-Alley, by Bishops-Gate-Street. BY SAMUEL SLATER, Minister of the Gospel.
London, Printed for John Dunton, at the Black Raven in the Poultry, over against the Compter, 1689.

8°, Pp. [xvi], 1-88.

Notes: Epistle To Young Men signed Samuel Slater. From my Study, March, 9. 1689. T.C. II, 268 (Trinity 1689).

Location: Wing S 3980 - O, LCL.

1690

89. The abdicated prince: or, the adventures of four years. Price 1s.

Notes: Dunton advertised the above in his first catalogue, of 1694. In Dunton's "Advertisement. To ... Honest Booksellers", printed in The State Weathercocks, 1719, The Abdicated Prince, a Tragedy, is mentioned in a list of copies of which Dunton claimed ownership. Wing located the work, with the imprint: For John Carterson, 1690, but no later editions (Wing A 71); the imprint of John Carterson appears only once in Wing, and it is possibly fictitious. Advertised by Richard Baldwin in T.C. II, 313 (Easter 1690).

90. -------- Second edition.

Notes: Dunton advertised the above in his second catalogue of 1694. Not located.

91. AN ANTIDOTE AGAINST LUST: or, a discourse of uncleanness, shewing [within brackets:] its various kinds, great evil, the temptations to it, and most effectual cure. BY ROBERT CARR, Minister of the Church of England.
London, Printed by J. Astwood for John Dunton, at the Raven in the Poultrey. 1690.

12°. Pp. [x], 1-182.

Notes: T.C. II, 311 (Easter 1690). L&E 186.

Location: Y.

92. The Bloody Duke: Or, The adventures for a Crown. Price 1s.

Notes: Dunton advertised the above in his three catalogues of 1694. Wing locates the work, with the imprint: For W. Bonny, 1690 (Wing B 3233). William Bonny printed a number of works for Dunton (L&E 247-8). Advertised by Richard Baldwin in T.C. II, 313 (Easter 1690).

93. CASUISTICAL MORNING-EXERCISES. The fourth volume. By several ministers in and about London, preached in October 1689.
London, Printed by James Astwood for John Dunton, at the Raven in the Poultrey, over against rhe[sic] Compter. 1690.

4°. Pp. [vi], 1-4, pp. 5-21, 32-40, ff. 41-69, 66-76, 200-261, 300-361, 400-407, 409-440. [frequent misnumbering]

Notes: To the Reader signed Samuel Annesley, Decemb. 4, 1689. The earlier three volumes of Morning-Exercises, collected by Annesley, were published in 1661, 1674 and 1683 (Wing A 3231, A 3239 and A 3228). T.C. II, 283 (Michaelmas 1689); II, 472 (Michaelmas 1693). L&E 152, 742. The McAlpin Catalogue describes two copies, with variant pagination and foliation. See also Adam Clarke, Memoirs of the Wesley Family (London, 1823), pp. 237-8.

Location: Wing A 3225 - L, O, C, E. DT; MH, NF, NPT, NU. Also, Y.

94. The Character of a Jacobite, by a Person of Quality.

Notes: Dunton advertised the above, "lately printed for

John Dunton", in Mather's Wonders of the Invisible World, third edition, 1693, and in Foigny's Terra Incognita, 1693. Also advertised in Dunton's first catalogue of 1694. Wing locates The Character of a Jacobite, printed for the author, 1690 (Wing C 1976), but no later edition.

95. The Character of a Williamite, by a Divine of the Church of England.

Notes: Dunton advertised the above, "lately printed for John Dunton", in Mather's Wonders of the Invisible World, third edition, 1693, and in Foigny's Terra Incognita, 1695. Also advertised in Dunton's first catalogue of 1694. Wing locates The Character of a Williamite, printed for Richard Baldwin, 1690 (Wing C 2002), but no later edition. Advertised by John Harris in T.C. II, 339 (Michaelmas 1690).

96. THE COFFEE-HOUSE MERCURY: containing all the remarkable events that have hapned from Tuesday, November the 4th. to Tuesday, November the 11th. 1690. With reflections thereupon. To be continued weekly. Licensed and entred according to order.
London, Printed by J. Astwood.

Three weekly numbers were issued, 11 - 25 November 1690.

Notes: Advertised by Dunton in T.C. II, 333 (Michaelmas 1690). CBEL II, 705. C&K 1129a.

Location: O.

97. GOOD NEWS FROM IRELAND. [BY JAMES CRYSLY]
Colop: For John Dunton, 1690. (Wing)

brs.

Location: Wing C 7453 - MC; CH.

98. The Key of the Holy Bible, unlocking the Richest Treasury of the Holy Scriptures, ... The Fourth Edition diligently revised. Written by Francis Roberts, D.D. Printed in

Folio. Price Bound 16 s.

Notes: Dunton advertised the above in his catalogue of "Books Printed for John Dunton", at the end of Lukin's Practice of Godliness, 1690, and in Rogers's Practical Discourses, 1691. Wing (R 1588) locates Clavis Biblorum. The Key of the Bible. Fourth edition. By J. R. for Peter Parker and Thomas Guy, 1675. This edition is in folio, and it was advertised in T.C. I, 200 (Hilary 1675). No edition of this work with Dunton's imprint has been located.

99. The late revolution: or, the happy change. Written by a person of quality. Price 1s.

Notes: Dunton advertised the above in his first and second catalogues of 1694. In Dunton's "Advertisement. To ... Honest Booksellers", printed in The State Weathercocks, 1719, The Late Revolution, a Comedy, is mentioned in a list of copies of which Dunton claimed ownership. Wing locates the work, with the imprint: Printed, and are to be sold by Richard Baldwin, 1690 (Wing L 558), but no later edition. Advertised by Baldwin in T.C. II, 313 (Easter 1690).

100. A NARRATIVE OF THE SIEGE OF LONDON-DERRY: or, the late memorable transations of that city .... BY JOHN MACKENZIE, chaplain to a regiment there during the siege .... with allowance.
London, Printed for the Author, and are to be Sold by Richard Baldwin, in the Old Baily. 1690.

4°. Pp. [viii], 1-64.

Notes: In his Life and Errors, Dunton included this work in a list of projects that he had engaged in, during his years in the trade (L&E 152), and in his portrait of John Lawrence, Dunton wrote that "We were neighbours some years, and Partners in printing ... 'Mackenzie's Narrative of the Siege of Londonderry'" (L&E 205). Although only Baldwin's name appears in the imprint, the single advertisement in Mackenzie's work, on p. viii, is for Boyse's Vindication of Mr. Alexander Osborn,

"Sold by J. Lawrence, and J. Dunton, in the Poultry". T.C. II, 333 (Michaelmas 1690).

Location: Wing M 216 - L, O, C, EN, DT; CH, CN, IU, MH, NC, Y.

101. News from New-England in a letter written to a person of quality wherein is a true account of the present state of that country, with respect to the late revolution and the present war with the Indians there together with a relation of a late and bloody fight between the English and the Indians.
John Dunton, 1690.

Notes: Sold at Sotheby's, 17 October 1961, in a collection of tracts which formerly belonged to Narcissus Luttrell: "Appears to be completely unrecorded. Not in Sabin, Church catalogue, or Wing. No auction record in England. An earlier, very rare, piece under the same title was published in 1676; but this text is quite a new one, the letters from Boston printed here being dated April and October 1689. Luttrell's acquisition date is March 1689/90 (the day of the month is not readable). The date of licensing is February 27, 1689" (Lot 990).

Location: Wing O N983A - SALE

102. News from the Fleet being a full account of a victory by Admiral Killegrew over the French Thoulon fleet [signed N. R. at end]
J. Dunton, 1690.

Notes: Sold at Sotheby's, 17 October 1961, in a collection of tracts which formerly belonged to Narcissus Luttrell (Lot 990).

Location: Wing O R55A - SALE

.03. THE PRACTICE OF GODLINESS: or brief rules directing Christians how to keep their hearts in a constant holy frame, and how to order their conversation aright .... The third edition revised and corrected. BY HENRY LUKIN

Minister of the Gospel.
London, Printed for John Dunton at the Black Raven in the Poultrey. 1690.

12°. Pp. [xii], 1-116, [iv]. Adv'ts, 3pp., at end.

Notes: Epistle dedicatory signed H. L. May 30. 1659. The first two editions of this work were published in 1659. Dunton claimed to have printed 10,000 copies of this edition (L&E 175). T.C. II, 307 (Hilary 1690).

Location: Wing L 3480 - LW.

104. THE PRESENT STATE OF EUROPE; or, the historical and political monthly mercury. [By John Phillips] [Title-page for Volume I reads:] THE GENERAL HISTORY OF EUROPE, contained in the historical and political monthly mercuries, from the late happy revolution in November, 1688, to July, 1690, where the translation was begun, and is continued to this Time ....
London, Printed by W. and J. Wilde, for Henry Rhodes near Bride-lane in Fleet-street, and John Harris at the Harrow in the Poultry: MDCXCII. [The work began with the second volume in 1690; Volume I was added in 1692; all other titles are: The Present State of Europe.]

Monthly, July 1690 - December 1736.

Notes: Dedication to Viscount Sydney signed J. Phillips. Dunton was concerned in the publication of this work for the first five months that it was issued, but his name did not appear in the imprint, and the earliest entries in the Stationers' Register were made by Henry Rhodes (Stat. Reg. G, 323 [375], 15 September 1690; and Stat. Reg. G, 324 [376], 15 October 1690). In his Life and Errors, Dunton wrote that he brought "[Mr. Wild] to be concerned in printing 'The Present State of Europe'", and that "Mr. Harris and myself brought Mr. Rhodes into this 'Monthly Mercury;' but we lost by it five months successively, which made me a little apprehensive of that design, and I thereupon threw up my interest in it for five pounds" (L&E 252, 208). See also L&E 181, 223; and Cyprian Blagden, "Henry Rhodes and the

'Monthly Mercury'", The Book Collector, Winter 1956, pp. 343-53. CBEL II, 705. C&K 745.

Location: C.

105. The Royal Voyage: Or, the Irish Expedition. Price 1s.

Notes: Dunton advertised the above in his three catalogues of 1694; in his Life and Errors, Dunton wrote that Mr. Fraser had licensed the work for him (L&E 266). Wing locates this title, with the imprint: For Richard Baldwin, 1690 (Wing R 2157), and Baldwin advertised the work in T.C. II, 322 (Trinity 1690).

106. A SECOND MODEST ENQUIRY into the causes of the present disasters in England. And who they are that brought the French fleet into the English Channel, described. Being a farther discovery of the Jacobite plot. Together with a list of those noble-men, gentlemen, and others now in custody.
London, Printed for John Dunton at the Raven, and John Harris at the Harrow, in the Poultry. M DC XC.

4°. Pp. [1]-31, [i]. Adv'ts, 2/3p., at end, 1/3 Dunton and 1/3 Harris.

Notes: A Modest Enquiry into the Causes of the Present Disasters was printed for Richard Baldwin, 1690 (Wing M 2367).

Location: Wing S 2292 - O, C, AU; CH, CLC, CN, NU, Y. Also, MB.

107. THE SOULS RETURN TO ITS GOD, in life, and at death. A funeral sermon, preached upon occasion of the death of Mr. John Kent, late of Crouched Friars, who departed this life Decem. 16. 1689. BY SAMUEL SLATER, Minister of the Gospel.
London, Printed for John Dunton at the Black Raven in the Poultry. 1690.

4°. Pp. [iv], [28](Copy badly cropped).

Notes: Dedication to Mary Kent signed Samuel Slater. From my Study, Jan. 24. 1690. T.C. II, 297 (Hilary 1690).

Location: Wing S 3976 - L; WES.

108. A TREATISE OF FORNICATION: shewing [within brackets:] What the sin is. How to flee it. Motives and directions to shun it. Upon I Cor. VI. XVIII. Also, a penetentiary sermon upon John viii. II. BY W.B. M.A.
London, Printed for John Dunton at the Raven in the Poultrey. 1690.

[Separate title-page; following the above, with continuous register and pagination:] A penitentiary sermon, upon John viii. II. - Go, and sin no more.
London, Printed for John Dunton at the Raven in the Poultrey. 1691.

8°. Pp. [viii], 1-80, [ii], 85-110, [iv]. Adv'ts, 3pp., and blank, 1p., at end.

Notes: By William Barlow (L&E 160, 267). Reviewed in Compleat Library, September 1692. T.C. II, 330 (Michaelmas 1690); II, 471 (Michaelmas 1693).

Location: Wing B 848 - L, O, OB.

109. THE VANITY AND IMPIETY OF JUDICIAL ASTROLOGY .... BY FRANCIS CROW, M.A. Minister of the Gospel.
London, Printed for John Dunton, at the Raven in the Poultrey. MDCXC. Price Stitcht [erased]

12°. Pp. [x], 1-25, [i]. Adv'ts, 1p., at end.

Notes: T.C. II, 338 (Michaelmas 1690).

Location: Wing C 7366 - L, O, LCL.

110. A VINDICATION OF THE REVEREND MR. ALEXANDER OSBORN, in reference to the affairs of the North of Ireland: in which some mistakes concerning him (in the printed account of the siege of Derry; the observations on it, and Mr. Walker's vindication of it) are rectified ....

Written at Mr. Osborn's request by his friend MR. J. BOYSE. Licens'd Nov. 22. 1689. And entred according to order.
London, Printed for Tho. Parkhurst, Tho. Cockerill, John Lawrence, and John Dunton, in Cheapside and the Poultry. 1690.

4°. Pp. [ii], 1-28, [ii].

Notes: Licensed and entered 22 November 1689 (Stat. Reg. G, 310[336]).

Location: Wing B 4082 - L, O, C, LVF, EN; MH, NC, Y.

111. THE WEEKLY PACQUET OF ADVICE FROM IRELAND. To which is added, the Irish courant. Licens'd, April the 2d. 1690. J. F. Friday, April the 4th. 1690. [at upper right corner:] Numb. I.

2 nos. published, 4 & 11 April 1690.

Notes: Both numbers of this periodical in the Bodleian Library are defective, lacking the imprint; on the verso of the second number, however, there survives a fragment of an advertisement for the fourth volume of Casuistical Morning-Exercises, which was published by Dunton in 1690. T. M. Hatfield suggested that Dunton was the author of this periodical (The True Secret History of Mr. John Dunton, unpublished thesis, Harvard University, 1926, p. 42). CBEL II, 705.

Location: O.

112. THE WONDERS OF FREE-GRACE: or, a compleat history of all the remarkable penitents that have been executed at Tyburn, and elsewhere, for these last thirty years. To which is added, a sermon preached in the hearing of a condemn'd malefactor immediately before his execution.
London, Printed for John Dunton at the Raven in the Poultry. 1690.

12°. Pp. [viii], 1-180, [1]-32. Adv'ts, 4pp., at end, required by Holmes but lacking in the copies examined.

Notes: Bound following this work, with continuous register and separate pagination, is Increase Mather's Sermon Occasioned by the Execution of a Man, 1691, q.v. The Wonders of Free-Grace is attributed to Increase Mather by Wing, but not by Holmes (II, 482). T.C. II, 330 (Michaelmas 1690); II, 472 (Michaelmas 1693).

Location: Wing M 1262 - L, O, C; V.

1691

113. The Antiweesils -, a Poem; giving an Account of some Historical and Argumental Passages happening in the Lyonss-Court. Price 6d.

Notes: Dunton advertised the above in his second and third catalogues of 1694. Wing locates this title, with the imprint: Printed, and are to be sold by Randall Taylor, 1691 (Wing A 3516).

114. [General title-page, Volume I:]
THE ATHENIAN GAZETTE: or casuistical mercury, resolving all the most nice and curious questions proposed by the ingenious: from Tuesday March 17th, to Saturday May 30th, 1691. The first volume, treating on the several subjects mentioned in the contents at the beginning of the book.
London, Printed for John Dunton, at the Raven in the Poultry, MDCXCI.

Volume I, No. 1, has the drop-head title: THE ATHENIAN GAZETTE, resolving weekly all the most nice and curious questions propos'd by the ingenious. From No. 2 the title of individual numbers was changed to THE ATHENIAN MERCURY, although the former title continued to appear on the general title-pages issued with each complete volume. Individual numbers had the imprint (with minor variations): London, Printed for P. Smart, 1691, until Volume II, No. 16; thereafter, the imprint (with minor variations) was: London: Printed for John Dunton at the Raven in the Poultrey. 1691.

Volumes I-XIX, 17 March 1691 - 8 February 1696, 30 nos. per volume. Volume XX, 14 May - 14 June 1697, 10 nos.

A folio half-sheet, The Athenian Mercury was published weekly until I, 3; from I, 4, twice weekly. From VI, 9 to VI, 12, the Mercury was issued four times weekly, thereafter twice weekly, except for the period 26 July - 17 September 1692, when the Mercury was not published. Supplements were issued to accompany Volumes I-V. Occasional numbers include an extra half-sheet of proposals or advertisements, and from time to time several numbers were issued together. 18 numbers were issued serially, in Volumes I-VI, the remaining 12 being issued with the general title-page, preface and index to complete the volume; from Volume VII, the entire volume of thirty numbers was issued serially.

Notes: Athenian Gazette entered 17 March 1691 (Stat. Reg. G, 336[383]); Athenian Mercury entered 18 April 1691 (Stat. Reg. G, 338[383]). Supplement I entered 17 July 1691 (Stat. Reg. G, 346[390]), and the Mercury in five volumes, with supplements, and an index to the whole was entered 22 February 1692 (Stat. Reg. G, 358[398]). CBEL II, 497, 658. Rothschild 825, 1990. Teerink 467. C&K 32. Hope 50. Noyes 160. L&E xvii, 187ff., 266. T.C. II, *passim*.

Location: L(Vols. I-X), C(Vols. I-V, XI, No. 2 - XIX), EN(Vols. I-XX); MH(Vols. I-V), Y(Vols. I-XX).

115. THE COUNTRY'S CONCURRENCE with the London united ministers in their late heads of agreement: shewing the nature and advantages of a general union among Protestants .... BY SAMUEL CHANDLER, author of The Excellency of the Christian Religion.
London, Printed for John Dunton at the Raven in the Poultry, and John Salusbury at the Rising-Sun over against the Royal Exchange in Cornhil, 1691.

12°. Pp. [viii], 1-98, [ii]. Adv'ts, 2pp., at end, 1p. for Dunton and 1p. for Salusbury.

Notes: Published 5 October 1691 (adv't, Athenian Mercury, IV, 2-3 October 1691). T.C. II, 407 (Trinity 1692).

Location: Wing C 1930 - L, O, LW.

116. Early Religion. By Timothy Rogers. Second edition.

Notes: Published 10 August 1691 (adv't, Athenian Mercury, III, 4 - 8 August 1691). Advertised as "newly published" in Barker's Flores Intellectuales, 1691; and advertised in Dunton's three catalogues of 1694. Not located.

117. FLORES INTELLECTUALES: or, select notions, sentences and observations, collected out of several authors, and made publick, especially for the use of young scholars, entring into the ministry. BY MATTHEW BARKER, Minister of the Gospel in London.
London, Printed[sic] by J. Astwood for John Dunton at the Raven in the Poultrey. 1691.

8°. Pp. [vi], 1-145, [i]. Adv'ts, 1p., at end.

Notes: Part II was published in 1692.

Location: Wing B 774 - L, LCL; CU.

118. HEADS OF AGREEMENT ASSENTED TO BY THE UNITED MINISTERS in and about London: formerly called Presbyterian and Congregational. Licensed and entred according to order.
London: Printed by R.R. for Tho. Cockerill, at the Three Legs, and John Dunton at the Raven, in the Poultrey. MDCXCI.

4°. Pp. [vi], 1-16, [ii].

Notes: Entered 11 March 1691 (Stat. Reg. G, 335[382]). T.C. II, 355 (Easter 1691). L&E 152. This work was mainly drawn up by John Howe (McAlpin IV, 417). The McAlpin catalogue describes one copy as above, and another, identical except for the addition of "Black Raven" in the imprint.

Location: Wing H 1282A - L, O, E; CH, LC, MH, NU, Y. Also, EN, LV.

119. The History of the Royal Congress at the Hague, with the Names, Characters, and Equipage of the Soveraign Princes that composed that most August Assembly, together with an Account of the glorious Canopy and Chair of State .... Translated from the Dutch Copy, printed at Lyden.

Notes: Dunton advertised the above in his second and third catalogues of 1694. Wing locates this title, with the imprint: Reprinted at London, for Thomas Axe, 1691 (Wing H 2178).

120. THE LIFE AND DEATH OF THE RENOWN'D MR. JOHN ELIOT, who was the first preacher of the Gospel to the Indians in America. With an account of the wonderful success which the Gospel has had amongst the heathen in that part of the world: and of the many strange customes of the pagan Indians, in New-England. Written BY COTTON MATHER. THE SECOND EDITION carefully corrected.
London: Printed for John Dunton, at the Raven in the Poultrey. M DC XC I.

8°. Pp. [vi], [1]-138.

Notes: This work was first published in Boston in 1691, as The Triumphs of the Reformed Religion in America. This edition, the first London edition, was published 3 August 1691 (adv't, Athenian Mercury, III, 2 - 1 August 1691). Holmes 409C. L&E 152. T.C. II, 474 (Michaelmas 1693). Dunton published the third edition in 1694.

Location: Wing M 1120 - L, O, EN; CH, CN, LC, MH, MU, MWA, NN, RPJ, Y.

121. MONSIEUR IN A MOUSE-TRAP: or, the parable of the shark & herring-pond. By the author of the Magpies.
London, Printed for Tho. Hinton. 1691.

4°. Pp. 1-4.

Notes: By William Bradshaw. Published 6 February 1691 (adv't, The Parable of the Magpies, p. 4). The name of Thomas Hinton, which appears on this work alone in Wing's Short-Title Catalogue, is presumably a pseudonym of John Dunton.

Location: Wing M 2458 - L, O; CH, CN, MH, Y.

122. Of mourning for the dead. By John Shower.
For J. Dunton and A. Chandler, 1691. (Wing)

Notes: Wing S 3678, locating one copy, at Yale. This listing is a duplication, as the sermon Of Mourning is one of four sermons in Shower's Mourner's Companion, 1692. Each of the sermons in this collection has a separate title-page, and imprint as above.

123. [Drop-head title:]
THE PARABLE OF THE BLACK-BIRDS. And the magpies vindicated.
London, Printed for Edward Thompkins, a Lover of the Magpies, 1691.

4°. Pp. 1-4.

Notes: Edward Thompkins may have been a pseudonym of John Dunton (see Appendix IV).

Location: Wing T 997 - L, MR, HH; CH, MH. Also, EN, O.

124. [Drop-head title:]
THE PARABLE OF THE DOVE: being a review of the late controversie between the black-birds, and the magpies; tending to an amicable accommodation of all the differences which at present disturb the feather'd nations.
Colop: London, Printed for R. Wallup, 1691.

4°. Pp. 1-4.

Notes: R. Wallup may have been a pseudonym of John Dunton (see Appendix IV).

Location: Wing P 322 - L; CN, MH, Y. Also, O.

125. [Drop-head title:]
THE PARABLE OF THE MAGPIES.
Colop: London, Printed for B. Griffitts, 1691.

4°. Pp. 1-7, [i]. Adv'ts, p. 7, for 9 works published by Dunton.

Notes: By William Bradshaw (L&E 182). Published by Dunton under the pseudonym of B. Griffitts (see Appendix IV)

Location: Wing P 321 - L, LL, HH; Y. Also, O, CT.

126. -------- [anr edn]
For B. Griffiths, 1669[sic]. (Wing)

Location: Wing P 323 - CT; CH, MH. [Note: CT owns only Wing P 321]

127. -------- [anr edn]
Colop: London, Printed for W. Griffitts, 1691.

4°. Pp. 104. Adv'ts, for several works published by Dunton, on p. 4.

128. -------- [another edition]
For B. Griffitts, 1691. (Wing)

Notes: Wing locates three copies of this edition in England, and they are identical with his locations of the first edition, P 321; the British Museum, in fact, owns only one copy, as described above, no. 121.

Location: Wing P 332B - L, LL, HH.

129. [Drop-head title:]
THE PARABLE OF THE PUPPIES: or the top-knots vindicated. Licensed and entred according to order.
Colop: For W. Griffitts, 1691. (Wing)

4°. Pp. 1-4.

Notes: W. Griffitts was a fictitious imprint used by Dunton.

Location: Wing P 324 - L[Copy trimmed, imp. lacking]; Y.

130. -------- [anr edn]
Colop: For T. Burdet, 1691. (Wing)

Notes: Advertised in The Parable of the Top-Knots, 1691, as to be "publish'd next Wednesday: Printed for T. Burdet". Presumably another fictitious imprint used by Dunton.

Location: Wing P 325 - MH, WF.

131. [Drop-head title:]
THE PARABLE OF THE TOP-KNOTS. Licensed according to order.
Colop: London, Printed for R. Newcome. 1691.

4°. Pp. 1-3, [i]. Adv'ts, 1p., at end, for 11 books published by Dunton.

Notes: Entered by Dunton 13 February 1691 (Stat. Reg. G, 332[381]). Published 11 February 1691 (adv't, Monsieur in a Mouse-Trap, p. 4.)

Location: Wing D 2631 - CH. Also, L; Y.

132. PRACTICAL DISCOURSES on sickness & recovery, in several sermons, as they were lately preached in a congregation in London. BY TIMOTHY ROGERS, M.A. after his recovery from a sickness of near two years continuance.
London, Printed for Thomas Parkhurst at the Bible and Three Crowns at the lower End of Cheapside, Jonathan Robinson at the Golden Lion in St. Paul's Church-yard, and John Dunton at the Raven in the Poultrey. MDCXCI.

8°. Pp. [i]-xxxii, 1-104, 113-277, [xi]. Adv'ts, 6pp., at end, 2pp. each for Parkhurst, Robinson and Dunton.

Notes: Epistle dedicatory to Sir William Ashurst and Sir Thomas Lane signed Timothy Rogers. London, Sept. 22. 1690. T.C. II, 329 (Michaelmas 1690). L&E 152.

Location: Wing R 1852 - L, C, LCL, LW; IU, MH, Y.

133. PROPOSALS for printing a book, entituled the Young Students Library.
Colop: For John Dunton, 1691. (Wing)

brs.

Notes: Also printed in the preface to Volume III of Athenian Mercury, which was published about 24 October 1691 (adv't, Athenian Mercury, IV, 8 - 24 October 1691), and issued as an extra half-sheet with Athenian Mercury, IV, 11 - 3 November 1691.

Location: Wing P 3730 - OP.

134. RELIGIO BIBLIOPOLAE. In imitation of Dr. Browns Religio Medici. With a supplement to it. BY BENJ. BRIDGWATER, Gent.
London, Printed for P. Smart, and are to be sold at the Raven in the Poultry. 1691.

12°. Pp. [vi], 1-104.

Notes: Entered 13 March 1691 (Stat. Reg. G, 335[383]). Written only in part by Bridgwater (L&E 177). William Bradshaw may also have been involved in the writing of this work (see Chapter II), as well as Dunton. See also, "To the Reader" in Religio Bibliopolae. "Stated by Crossley [Wilkin II, xix] to have been largely plagiarized from other authors" (Keynes, Bibl. Sir Thomas Browne [Cambridge, 1924], No. 407). Reprinted 1694, 1702, 1728, 1742, 1750, 1780 (see Keynes, op. cit.); translated into German and printed in 1737. Portions of this work were included in The New Practice of Piety, 1704. H&L V, 58. L&E xxv. T.C. II, 370 (Trinity 1691).

Location: Wing B 4486 - L, O, GK; BN, CLC, CN, MH, MMO, WF, Y. Also, C.

135. A SERMON OCCASIONED BY THE EXECUTION OF A MAN FOUND GUILTY OF MURDER: Preached at Boston in New-England, March 11th 1686 .... BY INCREASE MATHER, Teacher of a Church of Christ.
Boston, Printed for John Dunton and Reprinted at London,

in the Year 1691.

12°. Pp. [1]-32.

Notes: This work is bound following The Wonders of Free-Grace, q.v., with continuous register and separate pagination. "Increase Mather's Sermon is mentioned in the title-page and the table of Contents of Wonders of Free-Grace. The difference of the dates of the title-page of Wonders of Free-Grace and of Sermon Occasioned might be explained by the first work being printed towards the end of 1690, and the second work being printed at the beginning of 1691 (Holmes, II, 482). Neither Cotton Mather's Call of the Gospel nor Joshua Moodey's Exhortation is printed with this edition. Holmes 115-C.

Location: Wing M 1249 - L, O; MB, MWA.

136. THE TRIENNIAL MAYOR: or, the new Raparees. A poem. London, Printed for Will. Griffits. 1691.

4°. Pp. [1]-7, 14-38.

Notes: By Thomas D'Urfey (L&E 86). Dunton advertised this poem in his second and third catalogues of 1694. W. Griffitts was a pseudonym used by Dunton in the publication of several works in 1691 (see Chapter II).

Location: Wing T 2273 - O; CH, IU, MH, Y.

137. THE VANITY OF CHILDHOOD & YOUTH, wherein the depraved nature of young people is represented, and means for their reformation proposed. Being some sermons preached in Hand-Alley, at the request of several young men. To which is added a catechism for youth. BY DANIEL WILLIAMS. London, Printed for John Dunton at the Black Raven in the Poultrey. MDCXCI.

8°. Pp. [x], 1-136. Adv'ts, 1/2p., at end.

Notes: Entered 6 March 1691 (Stat. Reg. G, 334[382]). T.C. II, 366 (Trinity 1691).

Location: Wing W 2657 - O.

138. A VOYAGE ROUND THE WORLD: or, a pocket-library, divided into several volumes. The first of which contains the rare adventures of Don Kainophilus, from his cradle to his 15th. year ....
London, Printed for Richard Newcome. Price Bound 1 s. 6 d.

-------- Volume II. Containing the rare adventures of Don Kainophilus during his seven years prenticeship.
London, Printed for Richard Newcome. 1691. Price Bound 1 s. 6 d.

-------- Vol. III. Containing a further account of the juvenile rambles of Don Kainophilus, with his first project of girdling the world, &c. ....
London, Printed for Richard Newcome. 1691. Price Bound 1 s. 6 d.

8°. Vol. I. Pp. [xxviii], 1-67, 96-158, [ii]. Adv'ts, 2pp., at end.
Vol. II. Pp. [xvi], 1-115, [v]. Adv'ts, 5pp., at end.
Vol. III. Pp. [viii], 1-68, 353-416.

Notes: By John Dunton; panegyric verses in Volume I include "The Authors Name When Anagramatized is Hid unto None", by A.Y. Batchelor of Arts. H&L VI, 200. Text signed Kainophilus Evander. One of seven works repented of by Dunton (L&E 159). LA V, 696; IX, 631. See also J. M. Stedmond, "Another Possible Analogue for Swift's Tale of a Tub", Modern Language Notes, LXXII (1957), 13-18. T.C. II, 338 (Michaelmas 1690).

Location: Wing V 742 - L; CN, LC. Also, O(Vol. I), LG(Vol. I); MB.

139. THE WORKS OF THE LEARNED, or an historical account and impartial judgment of books newly printed, both foreign and domestick., to be published monthly. August, 1691. BY J. DE LA CROSE, a late author of the Universal and Historical Bibliotheque.
London, Printed for Tho. Bennet, at the Half-Moon in

St. Paul's Church-Yard, and are to be sold by Randal Taylor near Stationers-Hall. MDCXCI.

4°. Eight monthly numbers were published, August 1691 - March/April 1692.

Notes: Entered by Bennet 8 October 1691 (Stat. Reg. G, 349[392]). Dunton became concerned in the publication of this work in January 1692 and one copy of the January number has been located with Dunton's imprint and advertisements for books published by him on f. ff_4r (S.R. Parks copy); two copies have been located of the number for September 1691 with the bookseller's advertisement on the verso of the title-page which la Crose disapproved of and had left out of "those Copies that were for his own Use" (DU and SRP copies); see Athenian Mercury, IV, 4 - 10 October 1691. C&K 965. L&E 180, 198, 207.

Location: L(Nov., Dec., 1691, & Feb., 1692 with Dunton imprint), C (Jan., Feb., March/April, 1692, with Bennet imprints), CT (Aug. 1691 - March/April, 1692, lacking adv't for September, and with Bennet imprints), DU (Aug. 1691 - March/April 1692, with adv't for September, and Bennet imprints and adv'ts for January 1692), S. R. Parks (Aug. 1691 - March/April 1692, lacking October 1691, with adv't on verso of title-page for September 1691, and with Dunton's imprint and adv'ts for January 1692).

140. THE YOUNG MAN'S CLAIM unto the holy sacrament of the Lords Supper. Entred by him into a Church of Christ, received and accepted by the pastor, and its other officers. BY JOHN QUICK, Minister of the Gospel.
London, Printed for John Dunton, at the Black Raven in the Poultrey, 1691.

4°. Pp. [xii], 1-19, [i]. Adv'ts, 1p., at end.

Notes: T.C. II, 366 (Trinity 1691).

Location: Wing Q 212 - O, LCL.

141. An Account of the Divisions amongst the Quakers in Pensilvania. [By George Keith]

Notes: Advertised by Dunton in his three catalogues of 1694. Wing locates this title, attributed to George Keith, with the imprint: Printed for, to be sold, by John Gwillim, and Rich. Baldwin, 1692 (Wing K 136). See A Farther Account, 1693.

142. AN ALPHABETICAL TABLE, comprehending the contents of [within brackets:] The five first volumes of the Athenian Gazette. The five Supplements to 'em. The Young Student's Library; and of the History of the Athenian Society ... Which several volumes compleat the entire sett for the year 1691.

Folio. Pp. [xvi].

Notes: Published 6 June 1692 (adv't, Athenian Mercury, VII, 20 - 4 June 1692). In Athenian Mercury, II, 4 - 6 June 1691, Dunton advertised the publication of 12 numbers of the Mercury to complete the first volume, and he added that: "We design to add a general Title, Preface and Index to every Volume, (as we have to this first) and at the end of every twelve Months to draw an Alphabetical Table for the whole Year". Only this first index was published.

Location: EN; MH.

143. THE CELESTIAL RACE. A discourse perswading to the practice of celerity, constancy, & sincerity in the ways of God. Preached at the funeral of Mrs. Elizabeth Knock, daughter of Mr. Thomas Knock, of Edgerton in Kent, who died January 2. Anno Dom. 1692. in the eleventh year of her age. BY WILLIAM BUSH Minister of the Gospel. London: Printed for John Dunton at the Raven in the Poultry. MDCLXCII [sic; i.e., MDCXCII].

8°. Pp. [viii], 1-64.

Notes: T.C. II, 390 (Hilary 1692).

Location: Wing B 6232 - L, C.

144. THE COMPLEAT LIBRARY: or, news for the ingenious. Containing [within a bracket:] several original-pieces. An historical account of the choicest books printed in England, and in the forreign journals. Notes on the memorable passages happening in May. As also, the state of learning in the world. To be published monthly. May, 1692. By a London divine, &c.
London, Printed for John Dunton at the Raven in the Poultrey, 1692.

Vol. I, May - November 1692.
Vol. II, December 1692 - December 1693. [From February 1693: By R.W. M.A.]
Vol. III, January - June 1694.

Notes: Edited for Dunton by Richard Wolley (L&E 163). "... the Compleat Library, is a Continuation of the Young Students Library, and a perfecting of that undertaking" (Compleat Library, Nov. 1692). See also W.L. Graham, Beginnings of English Literary Periodicals (New York, 1926), pp. 29-30. T.C. II, 466 (Trinity 1693), 483 (Michaelmas 1693). L&E 163, 180, 198. CBEL II, 675. C&K 116.

Location: L[copy reported destroyed], O[entire], LL [Dec. 1692 - Dec. 1693], CT[May 1692 - Dec. 1693].

145. THE DOUBLE DESCENT. A poem.
London, Printed for John Dunton at the Raven in the Poultrey. 1692.

4°. Pp. [1]-28.

Notes: By Richard Ames (L&E 186). Published 10 May 1692 (adv't, Athenian Mercury, VII, 13 - 10 May 1692).

Location: Wing A 2976 - L, DT; Y. [Note: L owns only Wing A 2976A]

146. -------- [variant imprint]
London, Printed for D. Kean. 1692.

4°. Pp. [1]-28.

Location: Wing A 2976A - MH. Also, L.

147. FALL NOT OUT BY THE WAY: or, a perswasion to a friendly correspondence between the conformists & non-conformists. In a funeral discourse on Gen. 45. 24. Occasioned by the desire of Mr. Anthony Dunwell, in his last will. BY TIMOTHY ROGERS, M.A.
London: Printed, for John Dunton, at the Raven in the Poultery, 1692.

8°. Pp. [xvi], 1-108, [iv]. Adv'ts, 4pp., at end.

Notes: Epistle dedicatory signed T. Rogers, London, Decemb. 12th 1691. T.C. II, 390 (Hilary 1692); II, 472 (Mich. 1693).

Location: Wing R 1850 - L, O, C, LCL, E; NF, NU.

148. FLORES INTELLECTUALES: THE SECOND PART. Containing three centuries more, of [within brackets:] select notions, sentences, and observations. Collected out of several authors, &c. BY MATTHEW BARKER Minister of the Gospel in London.
London, Printed by Tho. Snowden for John Dunton at the Raven in the Poultrey, 1692.

8°. Pp. [viii], 1-102.

Notes: Published June 1692 (adv't, Athenian Mercury, VII, 26 & 27 & 28 June 1692). The first part was published in 1691.

Location: Wing B 775 - L, LCL.

149. THE GOOD OLD CAUSE: or, the divine captain character-iz'd. In a sermon (not preach'd, nor needful to be preach'd, in any place so properly as in a camp.) BY EDM. HICKERINGILL, Rector of the Rectory of All-Saints in Colchester. Licens'd according to order, Feb. 1. 1691/2.

London, Printed for John Dunton, at the Raven in the Poultry, 1692.

4°. Pp. [iv], 1-32.

Notes: Published February 1692 (adv't, *Athenian Mercury*, VI, 6 - 20 February 1692). T.C. II, 390 (Hilary 1692). L&E 161.

Location: Wing H 1807 - L, C; NC, NU.

150. GOSPEL-TRUTH STATED AND VINDICATED. Wherein some of Dr. Crisp's opinions are considered; and the opposite truths are plainly stated and confirmed. BY DANIEL WILLIAMS. London, Printed for John Dunton, at the Raven in the Poultrey, 1692.

12°. Pp. [xii], 1-250, [ii].

Notes: *To the Reader* signed D. Williams, London, May 4. 1692. Published 18 May 1692 (adv't, *Athenian Mercury*, VII, 15 - 17 May 1692. A list of errata for this work was printed in *Athenian Mercury*, VII, 17 - 24 May 1692, and questions about the work were answered in VII, 25 - 21 June 1692. *Gospel-Truth* was reviewed in *The Compleat Library*, March, 1693. Isaac Chauncy replied to Williams in *Neonomianism Unmask'd*, 1692 (Wing C 3754), and Williams's further reply, published by Dunton, was *A defence of Gospel-Truth*, 1693. L&E 152, 167.

Location: Wing W 2649 - C, OM, E; NU, Y. Also, EN.

151. -------- Second edition London: Printed for John Dunton, at the Raven in the Poultrey, 1692.

12°. Pp. [xii], 1-214, [ii].

Notes: Published September 1692 (adv't, *Athenian Mercury*, VIII, 9 - 27 September 1692).

Location: Wing W 2650 - L, O, EN.

152. THE HISTORY OF THE ATHENIAN SOCIETY, for the resolving all nice and curious questions. By a gentleman, who got secret intelligence of their whole proceedings. To which are prefix'd several poems, written by Mr. Tate, Mr. Motteux, Mr. Richardson, and others.
London: Printed for James Dowley, and are to be Sold by the Booksellers of London and Westminster. Price 1 s.

Folio. Pp. [iv], 1-36.

Notes: By Charles Gildon (L&E 181, 191-2). Epistle dedicatory to the Gentlemen of the Athenian Society signed R.L. Six poems prefixed to this work signed N. Tate, P. Motteux(2), D.F.[Daniel Defoe], D.T., and Charles Richardson. The History was published in the spring of 1692, and the Athenian Society at first claimed to know nothing of it (adv't, Athenian Mercury, VII, 10 - 30 April 1692); ten days later, the Mercury advertised that the History was printed in the same size as the Mercury, that they might be bound up together (VII, 13 - 10 May 1692). Later in the year, Dunton advertised the History as printed for himself (Compleat Library, September 1692), and in his Life and Errors he confessed that he had had James Dowley publish it for him (L&E 261). T.C. II, 476 (Michaelmas 1693).

Location: Wing G 730 - L, O, C, HH, DT; MH, MU, WF, Y. Also, EN.

153. The late King James's commission to his privateers.
For P. Smart, 1692. (Wing)

brs.

Notes: This broadside, the early numbers of Athenian Mercury, and Religio Bibliopolae, 1691, are the only works published with the imprint of P. Smart, which may have been a pseudonym of John Dunton.

Location: Wing J 155A - MH.

154. THE LIFE AND FUNERAL SERMON of the Reverend Mr. Thomas Brand. BY DR. SAMUEL ANNESLEY.
London: Printed for John Dunton, at the Raven in the Poultrey, 1692.

8°. Pp. [viii], 1-135, [ix].

Notes: Published 23 June 1692 (adv't, Athenian Mercury, VII, 25 - 21 June 1692). Reviewed in Compleat Library, June 1692. Of the elegies printed at the end of this work, signed A., S.W., J.O., and J.E., that signed J.O. is identified in a contemporary hand in the LCL copy as by J. Oldfield. L&E 152. LA V, 64. T.C. II, 472 (Michaelmas 1693).

Location: Wing A 3230 - L, O, C, LCL, LW; BN.

155. THE MOURNERS COMPANION: or, funeral discourses on several texts. BY JOHN SHOWER.
London, Printed by J.A. [James Astwood] for J. Dunton at the Raven in the Poultrey, and A. Chandler at the Chyrurgeons Arms at the Entrance into Bartholomews-Close in Aldersgate-street, 1692.

Separate title-pages: This work contains four sermons, Of Mourning for the Dead, followed by, with continuous register and pagination, Prepare to Follow, followed by A Sermon Preacht upon the Death of Mrs. Anne Barnardiston, The Second Edition, with double register and separate pagination (this sermon was originally published by Dunton in 1682), followed by Sickness and Death for the Glory of Christ, by John Spademan, with continuous register and pagination. All the sermons have the imprint: London, Printed for J. Dunton and A. Chandler. 1691.

8°. Pp. [viii], [1]-125, [xxiii], 1-84.

Notes: Published 2 November 1691 (adv't, Athenian Mercury, IV, 10 - 31 October 1691). L&E 152.

Location: Wing S 3673 - L, LG; MH, Y.

156. A MOURNING-RING, in memory of your departed friend, [blank space provided for insertion of friend's name] Containing. [within brackets:] The house of weeping. The sick man's passing-bell. Death-bed-thoughts. The fatal moment. The treatment of the dead, in order to their burial. The funeral solemnity. A conference between the mourners. The history of those that have died suddainly, &c. Observations on the bills of mortality. A walk among the tombs. The pilgrim's guide from his cradle to his grave. The author's tears, or meditations on his own sickness, death and funeral. &c. The second edition. Recommended as proper to be given at funerals.

London, Printed for John Dunton, at the Raven, in the Poultrey, 1692.

12°. Pp. [xxii], 1-266, 81-296, 161-256.

Notes: By John Dunton, Rector of Aston Clinton (H&L IV, 124). C.A. Moore, in _Studies in Philology_, XXII (1925), p. 485n, wrote that this work was called the second edition with reference only to _The House of Weeping_; "The two other so-called second editions of _A Mourning Ring_ [in British Museum] show that cheaper copies were issued without the illustrations, the separate title-page for 'The House of Weeping,' and the three sermons inserted after p. 266". T.C. II, 463 (Trinity 1693), 472 (Michaelmas 1693). Reviewed in _Compleat Library_, August 1692.

Location: Wing D 2630 - L, O, _C_; CH. Also, LC.

157. NEW ROME UNMASK'D, and her foundation shaken; by a farther discovery of the grand errors, deep hypocrisies, Popish practices, and pernitious principles of the teachers and leaders of the people, call'd Quakers; .... BY FRANCIS BUGG. Licensed, May 4. 1692.

London, Printed for the Author, 1692. And are to be sold by John Gwillim, Bookseller in Bishopsgate-street, over against the Royal-James, and John Dunton, at the Raven, in the Poultry, and Sam. Manship, at the Black-Bull in Cornhill.

4°. Pp. [xxxiv], 1-90.

Notes: Epistle dedicatory to the Honourable Sir H. N. signed Fran. Bugg, MildenHall, September the 3d. 1692; Epistle to the Noble Bereans signed Francis Bugg, Sept. the 7th. 1692. Text dated June 15th. 1692.

Location: Wing B 5378 - L, O, C, LF; NPT, PH, PSC, Y.

158. Ode to the Athenian Society. By Jonathan Swift.

Notes: In Athenian Mercury, VI, 16 - 19 March 1692, Dunton announced that "The Ode to the Athenian Society, written by a Countrey Gentleman, (it being his Request) will be prefixt to the Supplement to our 5th. Volume, which is now in the Press"; and the Ode was first printed in the Supplement, which was published on 1 April 1692 (adv't, Athenian Mercury VII, 1 & 2 - 29 March & 2 April 1692). The Ode was later reprinted in A Supplement to the Athenian Oracle, 1710. The Ode was also published separately. Advertised as "newly published for John Dunton" in Compleat Library, September 1692, and as "lately printed for John Dunton" in the third edition of Mather's Wonders of the Invisible World, 1693. Advertised as well in Dunton's three catalogues of 1694. No copy has been located. Teerink 467. Rothschild 1990. The Ode was also separately printed in Dublin in 1724 (Teerink 468).

159. THE POST-BOY ROB'D OF HIS MAIL: or, the pacquet broke open. Consisting of five hundred letters, to persons of several qualities and conditions. With observations upon each letter. Publish'd by a gentleman concern'd in the frolick. Licens'd and entred, according to order.
London, Printed for John Dunton, at the Raven in the Poultry, 1692.

12°. Pp. [xii], 1-396, [xxiv]. Adv'ts, 4pp., at end.

Notes: Epistle dedicatory to George Porter, Esq., signed C.G. [i.e., Charles Gildon (H&L IV, 400)]. Licensed 1 September and entered 28 September 1692, by John Taylor (Stat. Reg. G, 370[408]). Published 29 September 1692 (adv't, Athenian Mercury, VIII, 9 - 27 September 1692). Discussed

Mercury, VIII, 9 - 27 September 1692). Discussed in Compleat Library, July 1692. One of seven works which Dunton later regretted publishing (L&E 159, 201). A second volume was published in 1693.

Location: Wing G 735A - MH. Also, L, LV.

160. A PRACTICAL DISCOURSE ON THE LATE EARTHQUAKES: with an historical account of prodigies and their various effects BY A REVEREND DIVINE.
London, Printed for J. Dunton at the Raven in the Poultry. 1692.

4°. Pp. [iv], 1-35, [i].

Notes: Published 8 October 1692 (adv't, Athenian Mercury VIII, 12 - 8 October 1692).

Location: Wing P 3152 - L, O, EN.

161. A scheme of Enquiries, proposed to all Ingenious Gentlemen, and other inquisitive Persons, containing Instructions in order to form a Body of the Natural, Artificial, and Civil History of England and Wales, Scotland and Ireland, with the foreign Plantations thereunto belonging. By the Athenian Society; given gratis by their Bookseller.

Notes: Dunton advertised the above in The Compleat Library, September 1692, as "newly printed for John Dunton", and in Foigny's A New Discovery, 1693, and in his third catalogue of 1694. A Scheme of Enquiries was also printed in Athenian Mercury, VII, 3 - 5 April 1692. Not located.

162. THE VISIONS OF THE SOUL, before it comes into the body. In several dialogues. Written BY A MEMBER OF THE ATHENIAN SOCIETY.
London, Printed for John Dunton, at the Raven in the Poultrey, 1692.

8°. Pp. [viii], 1-151, [i].

Notes: Usually attributed to John Dunton (H&L VI, 192), however in the first dialogue, between the Secretary of Fate and the Author's Soul, the author is told that he will 'commence Temporality' in June 1664; Dunton was born in 1659. Published 18 November 1691 (adv't, Athenian Mercury, IV, 15 - 17 November 1691). T.C. II, 390 (Hilary 1692), 472 (Michaelmas 1693).

Location: Wing D 2634 - L, O; CH, CN, MH, Y.

163. THE YOUNG-STUDENTS-LIBRARY, containing, extracts and abridgments of the most valuable books printed in England, and in the forreign journals, from the year sixty five, to this time. To which is added, a new essay upon all sorts of learning; wherein the use of the sciences is distinctly treated on. BY THE ATHENIAN SOCIETY. Also, a large alphabetical table, comprehending the contents of this volume. And of all the Athenian Mercuries and Supplements, &c. printed in the year 1691.
London, Printed for John Dunton, at the Raven in the Poultry. Where is to be had the Intire Sett of Athenian Gazettes, and the Supplements to 'em for the Year, 1691. bound up all together, (with the Alphabetical Table to the Whole Year) or else in Separate Volumes, (Or single Mercuries to this Time.) 1692.

[Separate title-page; following the above, with quadruple register and continuous pagination:] [a line in Hebrew, then:] seu, de punctorum origine, antiquitate & authoritate: or, a discourse concerning the antiquity, divine original and authority of the points, vowels, and accents, that are placed to the Hebrew Bible. In two parts. By a member of the Athenian Society.
London, Printed for John Dunton, at the Raven in the Poultrey, M DC XCII.

Folio. Pp. [vi], i-xviii, 1-240, [ii], 241-289, 288-316, 321-479, [xvii]. Frontispiece by F. H. Van Hove, 'An Emblem of Ye Athenian Society'.

Notes: Entered 12 October 1691 (Stat. Reg. G, 350[393]). Published 6 June 1692 (adv't, Athenian Mercury, VII, 19 & 20 - 31 May & 4 June 1692). T.C. II, 483 (Michaelmas 1693). H&L VI, 268. See also Proposals for ... the Young Students Library,

1691. An Alphabetical Table, 1692, has been entered separately, q.v.

Location: Wing D 2635 - O, C, LW, HH, EN; CH, LC, MH, NU, Y. Also, LCL, GM.

1693

164. AN ACCOUNT OF THE CONVERSION OF THEODORE JOHN, a late teacher among the Jews, together with his confession of the Christian faith, which he delivered immediately before he was baptized in the presence of the Lutheran congregation in the German Church in Little Trinity-Lane, London, on the 23d. Sunday after Trinity, being the 31st. of October, in the year of our Lord God 1692. Translated out of High Dutch into English.
London: Printed for John Dunton, at the Raven in the Poultrey. 1693. Price 6d.

12°. Pp. [xii], 1-54, [vi]. Adv'ts, 6pp., at end.

Notes: Preface signed Theodore ... Puddle-Dack, March 16. 1692-3. Licensed 9 March 1693 and entered 15 March 1693 (Stat. Reg. G, 382[417]). Published 22 March 1693 (adv't, Athenian Mercury, IX, 29 - 21 March 1693). Reviewed in Compleat Library, March 1693. T.C. II, 463 (Trinity 1693).

Location: Wing J 762 - L, O, C.

165. THE AGREEMENT IN DOCTRINE among the dissenting ministers in London, Subscribed Decemb. 16. 1692.
London, Printed for Thomas Cockerill at the Three Leggs over against Stocks-Market; And John Dunton at the Raven in the Poultrey. 1693.

4°. Pp. [ii], 1-16, [ii]. Adv'ts, 2pp., at end, 1p for Dunton and 1p. for Cockerill.

Notes: Published March 1693 (adv't, Athenian Mercury, IX, 24 - 4 March 1693).

Location: Wing A 771 - EN; NU.

166. An apology for atheisme by the methodizer of the second Spira.

Notes: Licensed 14 March and entered 15 March 1693 (Stat. Reg. G, 382[417]). See A Conference Betwixt a Modern Atheist and his Friend, 1693.

167. An Appendix to [A Further Account of the Tryals of the New-England Witches, by Increase Mather], giving an Account of the late Dispossessing of a Person in England by Fasting and Prayer. Printed by the Consent of the Minister chiefly concern'd. With a Preface to it by a Reverend Divine living in London. Printed for John Dunton, at the Raven in the Poultrey.

Notes: Dunton advertised the above, "now preparing for the Press", on the verso of the title-page of Increase Mather's A Further Account, 1693.

168. The Celestial Pair, by Mr. Buck.

Notes: Dunton advertised the above in the first edition of The Second Spira, 1693. No copy has been located (but cf. The Celestial Race, by William Bush, 1692).

169. COMFORT FOR PARENTS, mourning over their hopeful children, that dye young. In a funeral discourse upon Jer. 31. xvii. .... BY THOMAS WHITAKER, Minister of the Gospel at Leeds, in York-shire.
London: Printed for John Dunton, at the Raven, in the Poultrey, 1693.

8°. Pp. [xvi], 1-109, [iii]. Adv'ts, 3pp., at end.

Notes: Published 31 July 1693 (adv't, Athenian Mercury, XI, 6 - 29 July 1693). T.C. II, 472 (Michaelmas 1693). Contains a preface by Timothy Rogers.

Location: Wing W 1713 - LCL. Also, C.

170. A CONFERENCE betwixt a modern atheist, and his friend. By the methodizer of The Second Spira. [RICHARD SAULT]
London, Printed for John Dunton at the Raven in the Poultry. 1693.

12°. Pp. [xii], 1-56, [iv]. Adv'ts. 4pp., at end.

Notes: Published 18 March 1693 (adv't, Athenian Mercury, IX, 28 - 18 March 1693). Imprimatur, on verso of title-page, signed Char. Heron. March the 14th. 1692/3. Reviewed in Compleat Library, March 1693. T.C. II, 472 (Mich. 1693). Two issues of this work have been located. The first begins on page 1: An Apology for Atheism. Dialogue I. Copies of this issue at L and NU have (or formerly have had) a slip of paper pasted over the top half of the page, cancelling the words An Apology for Atheism. Another issue, without the heading An Apology for Atheism, has been located at C and LC. Dunton had licensed on 14 March and entered on 15 March 1693, An Apology for Atheisme by the Methodizer of the second Spira (Stat. Reg. G, 382[417]).

Location: Wing S 732 - L, O; LC, NU. Also, C.

171. The Day of Jubilee; or, a plain and a practical Discourse of the Saints gathering together, and of their meeting the Lord in Glory at his second coming, on 1 Thess. 4. 17. by J. Brandon Rector of Winchamstead in Berks.

Notes: Dunton advertised the above in Foigny's New Discovery, 1693, and in his three catalogues of 1694. Not located.

172. A DEFENCE OF GOSPEL-TRUTH. Being a reply to Mr. Chancy's first part. And as an explication of the points in debate, may serve for a reply to all other answers .... BY DANIEL WILLIAMS.
London: Printed for John Dunton at the Raven in the Poultrey, 1693.

4°. Pp. [viii], 1-48.

Notes: Published 3 November 1692 (adv't, Athenian Mercury, VIII, 19 - 1 November 1692). Isaac Chauncy replied in A Rejoynder to Mr. Daniel Williams His Reply to the First Part of Neonomianism Unmaskt (Wing C 3757), Neonomianism Unmask'd ... The Second Part (Wing C 3754A), Neonomianism Unmask'd ... the Continuation of the Second Part (copy in British Museum), and Neonomianism Unmask'd ... Part III (Wing C 3755), all printed in 1693. T.C. II, 463 (Trinity 1693).

Location: Wing W 2646 - L, O, C, EN; LC, MH, NU.

173. A DIRECTORY FOR YOUTH through all the difficulties attending that state of life. Or a discourse of youthful lusts. In which the nature and kinds of them are described, and remedies against them laid down. First preached to young people, and now published at their request. BY SAMUEL POMFRET, Minister of the Gospel.
London, Printed for John Dunton at the Black-Raven in the Poultry. 1693.

8°. Pp. [viii], 1-238, [ii].

Notes: Published 10 August 1693 (adv't, Athenian Mercury, XI, 9 - 8 August 1693). T.C. II, 472 (Michaelmas 1693).

Location: Wing P 2798 - LCL; MH.

174. AN EARNEST CALL to family-catechising, and reformation. BY A REVEREND DIVINE.
London, Printed by J.W. for John Dunton, at the Raven in the Poultrey. 1693.

12°. Pp. [ii], i-xix, [i], 1-50.

Notes: Published 14 March 1693 (adv't, Athenian Mercury, IX, 27 - 14 March 1693). T.C. II, 463 (Trinity 1693).

Location: Wing E 95 - L, O.

175. ENGLAND'S ALARUM: being an account of God's most considerable dispensations of mercy and judgment towards these kingdoms for fourteen years last past. And also, of the several sorts of sins and sinners therein; especially the murmurers against the present government. With an earnest call to speedy humiliation, supplication and reformation, as the chief means of prospering their majesties counsels and preparations. Dedicated to the King and Queen.
London: Printed for Thomas Parkhurst, at the Bible and Three Crowns in Cheap-side, near Mercers-Chappel. 1693.

4°. Pp. [vi], 1-29, [i]. Adv'ts, 1 1/2pp., at end.

Notes: Dedication signed J.D. [i.e., John Dunton (H&L II, 463 (Trinity 1693).

Location: Wing D 2623 - L, O, C, CT, EN; CLC. Also, Y.

176. A FARTHER ACCOUNT OF THE GREAT DIVISIONS among the Quakers in Pensilvania .... With an apology for the present publication of these things. [BY GEORGE KEITH]
London, Printed for J. Dunton, at the Raven in the Poultrey, 1693.

4°. Pp. [1]-23, [i].

Notes: Page 23: "A Quantity of the foregoing, with another of their Books, Intituled, The Plea of the Innocent, &c. Being sent over for Sale, which the chief Quakers here having notice of, bought them all up, in order to stifle them, which occasions their Re-printing here in England, this 9th. of January, 1692/3."

"Books concerning the Quakers" -- Under this heading, Dunton advertised in his third catalogue of 1694 nine works; eight of these had been advertised in his second catalogue of 1694 (with the ninth, advertised as "in the press"); and six of them had been advertised in his first catalogue of 1694. Dunton advertised that imported copies of these works had been bought up by the chief Quakers, "designing to stifle them, which occasions their being Re-printed". Three of these works were advertised by Dunton in the Term

Catalogues; but only A Farther Account bears Dunton's imprint. Each of these works is entered separately in this checklist.

Location: Wing K 166 - L, O, C, LF, GU; CH, LC, MU, PH.

177. THE FRAILTY AND UNCERTAINTY OF THE LIFE OF MAN. Delivered in a sermon at the funeral of a person that dyed suddainly. BY WILLIAM BUSH, Minister of the Gospel.
London, Printed for John Dunton, at the Sign of the Black Raven in the Poultry, MDCXCIII.

8°. Pp. [viii], 1-62, [ii].

Location: Wing B 6233 - O.

178. A FURTHER ACCOUNT OF THE TRYALS OF THE NEW-ENGLAND WITCHES. With the observations of a person who was upon the place several days when the suspected witches were first taken into examination. To which is added, cases of conscience concerning witchcrafts and evil spirits personating men. .... BY INCREASE MATHER, President of Harvard Colledge. Licensed and entred according to order.
London: Printed for J. Dunton, at the Raven in the Poultrey. 1693. Of whom may be had the Third edition of Mr. Cotton Mather's First Account of the Tryals of the New-England Witches, Printed on the same size with this Last Account, that they may bind up together.

[Separate title-page; following the above, with lower-case register and separate pagination:] Cases of conscience concerning evil spirits personating men; .... By Increase Mather, President of Harvard Colledge at Cambridge, and Teacher of a Church at Boston in New England.
Printed at Boston, and Re-printed at London, for John Dunton, at the Raven in the Poultrey. 1693.

4°. Pp. [ii], 1-10, [iv], 1-[44], [iv]. Adv'ts, 4pp., at end.

Notes: Licensed and entered 1 June 1693 (Stat. Reg. G, 388[422]). Published 15 June 1693 (adv't, Athenian Mercury, X, 22 - 10 June 1693). Reviewed in Compleat Library, June 1693. T.C. II,

476 (Mich. 1693). L&E 248. Holmes 22B. W.G. Hiscock (The Christ Church Supplement to Wing's Short-Title Catalogue 1641-1700, Oxford, 1956) locates an edition of Cases of Conscience, Reprinted at London for John Dunton, 1693, supplementary to Wing M 1193; most probably the Christ Church copy is not a separate edition, but simply Cases of Conscience, as above (Christ Church copy not examined). Hiscock also locates, supplementary to Wing M 1213, "The tryals of several witches lately executed in New-England. 3rd ed. [Lond., 1693], 4°. [Anr. ed. of M 1213]".

Location: Wing M 1213 - L, O, C, LSC, EN; CH, LC, MH, MWA, NN, RPJ, Y. Note also Wing F 2546, entered under the title (L; CH, MH, VUL) which appears to be identical with M 1213.

179. THE GENUINE REMAINS OF THAT LEARNED PRELATE DR. THOMAS BARLOW, late Lord Bishop of Lincoln. Containing divers discourses theological, philosophical, historical, &c. ... Published from his Lordship's. original papers.
London, Printed for John Dunton, at the Raven in the Poultery, 1693.

8°. Pp. [xxiv], [1]-643, [v]. Adv'ts, 5pp., at end.

Notes: Entered 4 July 1693 (Stat. Reg. G, 391[424]). Published 23 October 1693 (adv't, Athenian Mercury, XI, 30 - October 1693). Reviewed in Compleat Library, July - November 1693. Epistle to the Reader signed P. Pett. In 1694 was published Reflections to ... the Genuine Remains of Dr. Tho. Barlow ... Falsly Pretended to be Published from His Lordship's Original Papers (By Henry Brougham, Wing B 4996). The dedication of this work was signed by William Ofley, who wrote to Dr. Fuller, Chancellor of Lincoln Cathedral, that "When I was with you at Lincoln in May last, you were pleased to enquire about the late Bishop of Lincoln's Original MSS, which were entrusted with my Brother Chaplain and my self; .... I did then assure you, that we that had the Bishop's MSS had taken all imaginable Care of them, having never parted with any of them, nor gave consent that any part or parcel of them should be Printed; and that what had happen'd was altogether without our knowledge .... I then satisfied you both [i.e. the Chancellor and the Sub-Dean], that one Sir P.P. and the late Vicar of Bugden, were the confederate Pedlars, that have endeavour'd to impose upon the World so much varnish'd Ware, for the sake of Twenty Guineas gave for the Copy; as his Wife inform'd a Reverend Friend of Mind." In 1694, Dunton advertised A Vindication of Bishop Barlows Remains, q.v. L&E 152, 742. T.C. II, 483 (Michaelmas 1693).

Location: Wing B 832 - L, O, C, EN, DT; CN, CU, MH, NU.

180. THE LADIES MERCURY. Vol. I. Numb. 1. Monday, February 27. 1693.
Colop: London, Printed for T. Pratt. 1693.

4 nos. published 27 February 1693 - 17 March 1693.

Notes: See Bertha-Monica Stearns, "The First English Periodical for Women", Modern Philology, XXVIII (1930-31), 45-59: "Dunton was obviously not eager to acknowledge so pitiful an enterprise, for he made no mention of it either in his Life and Errors (1705) or in Athenianism (1710). But he did not, which is much more important, boast of driving an interloper from the field, as he certainly would have done had the periodical been launched by anyone else" (p. 57). No. 3 of The Ladies Mercury contains questions about the forthcoming Ladies Dictionary; and The Athenian Mercury for 18 March contains questions identical to those in The Ladies Mercury, No. 1. T. Pratt is presumably a fictitious imprint used by Dunton. Noyes 163. C&K 1490. CBEL II, 658.

Location: L(Nos. 1 & e), O(Nos. 1-4).

181. LITURGIA TIGURINA: or, the book of common prayers, and administration of the sacraments. And other ecclesiastical rites and ceremonies, usually practised and solemnly performed in all the churches and chappels of the city and canton of Zurick in Switzerland; .... Faithfully

translated out of the Helvetian into the English tongue, BY JOHN CONRAD WERNDLY, formerly Minister of the French and Dutch congregation of Santoff in the Isle of Axholme in the County of Lindoln: and now Minister of Wraisbury cum Langley in the County of Bucks.
London: Printed for D. Newman, R. Baldwin, J. Dunton. 1693.

12°. Pp. [xl], 1-152, 145-320, [xvi].

Notes: Published 10 April 1693 (adv't, Athenian Mercury, X, 4 - 8 April 1693). T.C. II, 450 (Easter 1693). L&E 152, 252, 256.

Location: Wing L 2589 - O, OB, NPL, MR, ENC; MH, NU.

182. MEMOIRS OF THE RIGHT HONOURABLE ARTHUR EARL OF ANGLESEY, late Lord Privy Seal. Intermixt, with moral, political and historical observations, by way of discourse in a letter. To which is prefixt a letter written by his lordship during his retirement from court in the year 1683. Published by Sir Peter Pett Knight, Advocate General for the Kingdom of Ireland.
London, Printed for John Dunton, at the Raven in the Poultry, 1693.

8°. Pp. [xxxii], 1-351, [i]. Adv'ts, 1/2p., at end.

Notes: Epistle dedicatory to Lord Altham signed P. Pett. July 17. 1693. Licensed 30 June and entered 4 July 1693 (Stat. Reg. G, 391[424]). T.C. II, 476 (Michaelmas 1693). L&E 570.

Location: Wing A 3175 - L, O, MR, EN, DT; BN, CN, LC, MH, NU, Y.

183. MENSALIA SACRA: or, meditations on the Lord's Supper ... BY THE REVEREND MR. FRANCIS CROW, late Minister of the Gospel at Clare in Suffolk. To which is prefixt a brief account of the author's life and death.
London, Printed for John Dunton, at the Raven in the Poultry, 1693.

8°. Pp. [ii], 1-142.

Notes: The account of the author's life is written by Henry Cuts. Published September 1693 (adv't, Athenian Mercury, XI, 17 - 5 September 1693). T.C. II, 471 (Michaelmas 1693).

Location: Wing C 7365 - L, O, LCL, LW.

184. Monthly Letters concerning Education.

Notes: Advertised as printed for John Dunton, to be published "about the 10th of July next", in Lord Delamere's Works, 1694; see also Athenian Mercury, XIII, 28 - 12 May 1694. The letters were published in a volume, in October 1694, called The Knowledge of the World, q.v.

185. More Divisions among the Quakers .... By George Keith.

Notes: Advertised by Dunton in T.C. II, 474 (Michaelmas 1693), and in his three catalogues of 1694. Wing locates this title, with the imprint: First printed beyond sea, and now re-printed, and are to be sold by Richard Baldwin, 1693 (Wing K 182). See A Farther Account, 1693.

186. A NEW DISCOVERY OF TERRA INCOGNITA AUSTRALIS, or the southern world. BY JAMES SADEUR a Frenchman [pseud., Gabriel de Foigny] .... Translated from the French copy, printed at Paris, by publick authority. April 8, 1693. Imprimatur, Char. Heron.
London, Printed for John Dunton, at the Raven in the Poultry. 1693.

12°. Pp. [viii], 1-88, 97-186, [vi]. Adv'ts, 6pp., at end.

Notes: Licensed 9 April 1693 and entered 15 April 1693 (Stat. Reg. G, 384[419]). Published 24 April 1693 (adv't, Athenian Mercury, X, 8 - 22 April 1693). T.C. II, 464 (Trinity 1693).

Location: Wing F 1395 - L, O, E; CLC, CN, MH.

187. A NEW MARTYROLOGY: or, the bloody assizes: now exactly methodized in one volume .... To this treatise is added the life & death of George L. Geffreys. The fourth edition .... Written BY THOMAS PITTS Gent.
London, Printed (according to the Original Copies) for John Dunton at the Raven in the Poultrey. 1693.

[Separate title-page: following the above, with continuous register and separate pagination:] An impartial history of the life and death of George Lord Jeffreys. Late Lord Chancellour of England. The fourth edition with large additions. [Dedication signed James Bent]
London, Printed for John Dunton at the Raven in the Poultry, 1693.

8°. Pp. [xii], 1-203, 368-432, 417-533, [v]-70, [viii].

Notes: By John Tutchin (H&L IV, 176). Thomas Pitts, a pseudonym of John Tutchin, appeared for the first time on the title page of this edition. This edition published 3 December 1692 (adv't, Athenian Mercury, VIII, 28 - 3 December 1692), and advertised by Dunton in T.C. II, 486 (Michaelmas 1693). This work was first published by Dunton in 1689.

Location: Wing T 3380 - L, O, C, LL, DT; LC, NR.

188. New Proposals for Leybourn's Pleasure with Profit ....

Notes: Advertised as above by the undertakers, the author, Dorman Newman, R. Baldwin, and John Dunton, in the third edition of Mather's Wonders of the Invisible World, 1693, and in Athenian Mercury, X, 9 - 25 April 1693. Pleasure with Profit was published in 1694. See also Proposals for ... Pleasure with Profit, 1693. Not located.

189. NEW ROME ARRAIGNED, and out of her own mouth condemned: containing a farther discovery of the dangerous errours and pernitious principles of the teachers and leaders of the people called Quakers, which tend to overthrow the Christian faith: in answer to George Whitehead's charitable essay, &c. .... By one who was more than five and twenty years a member of their society, being carried away with their dissimulation, FRANCIS BUGG.

London: Printed for the Author, and are to be sold by J. Dunton at the Raven in the Poultry, R. Baldwin in Warwick-lane, and J. Guillim in Bishopsgate-street over against the Great James. 1693.

4°. Pp. [xvi], 1-68.

Notes: Epistle dedicatory to Henry Goldwell, Esq., signed Fra. Bugg. Sept. 6. 1693; prefatory letter To the Noble Bereans signed F.B. Sept. 24. 1693; An Apologitical Introduction signed Francis Bugg. July the 25th, 1693; and the text signed Fra. Bugg. Mildenhall, Sept. 20. 1693.

Location: Wing B 5376 - L, C, CK, LF; MH, PH, PSC.

190. PAEDOBAPTISMUS VINDICATUS: or, infant-baptism stated. In an essay to evidence its lawfulness from the testimony of holy scripture; .... With an account of a conference publickly held with an Antipaedobaptist of no small fame. BY J.R.A.M. A Presbyter of the Church of England.
London, Printed for John Dunton at the Raven in the Poultrey, M DC XCIII.

8°. Pp. [xii], [1]-LXII, [vi], 1-148, [ii].

Notes: By John Rothwell. Epistle dedicatory to William Strong, Esq., signed J.R.; preface dated July, 26. 1692, and imprimatur on verso of leaf preceding title-page dated Octob. 8. 1692. Dunton identified John Rothwell as the author of this work in his three catalogues of 1694, and Benjamin Keach addressed his reply directly to Rothwell: The Ax laid to the Root: Containing an Exposition of that Metaphorical Text of Holy Scripture, Mat. 3. 10. Part II .... Also a brief Reply to Mr. Rothwell's late Treatise, Intituled, Paedo-Baptismus Vindicatus, 1693 (Wing K 48). Reviewed in Compleat Library, January 1693. T.C. II, 437 (Hilary 1693).

Location: Wing R 2005 - C; NHC.

191. PANARITHMOLOGIA, being a [within brackets:] Mirror Breviate Treasure Mate for [within brackets:] Merchants, Bankers, Tradesmen, Mechanicks, and a sure guide for purchasers, sellers, or mortgagers of land, leases, annuities, rents, pensions, &c. In present possession or reversion. And a constant concomitant fitted for all mens occasions .... Calculated and published BY W. LEYBOURN. To which is added a necessary appendix, containing heads of daily use to all traders.
London, Printed by T.J. for John Dunton at the Raven, and John Harris at the Harrow, in the Poultrey. 1693.

[Separate titlepage; following the above, with triple register and separate pagination:] An appendix, containing heads of daily use to all traders.
London: Printed for John Dunton, and John Harris, in the Poultry. 1693.

8°. Pp. [1]-16, [cccxxii], [1]-144. Adv'ts, lp., at end. half for Dunton and half for Harris.

Notes: T.C. II, 479 (Michaelmas 1693). L&E 231.

Location: Wing L 1926 - L, O, C; Y.

192. A PEACEABLE ENQUIRY into the nature of the present controversie among our united brethren about justification. Part I [all published]. BY STEPHEN LOBB, a lover of peace and truth.
London, Printed for John Dunton at the Raven in the Poultrey. 1693.

8°. Pp. [viii], 1-159, [i].

Notes: To the Reader signed S.L. .... Hampstead, July 26. --93. T.C. II, 472 (Michaelmas 1693).

Location: Wing L 2728 - L, O, C, LCL; MH.

193. The Principles, Doctrines, Laws and Orders of the Quakers. [By Francis Bugg]

Notes: Dunton advertised the above in his first catalogue of 1694 and later in his second and third catalogues of 1694. Wing locates this title, attributed to Francis Bugg, with the imprint: For John Gwillim, [and Richard Baldwin,] 1693 (Wing B 5395). See A Farther Account, 1693.

194. Proposals for Printing a Book of Will. Leybourn's, Author of the late Cursus Mathematicus, etc., to be Entituled, Pleasure with Profit. It consisting of Recreations of divers kinds .... Published for Ingenious Spirits to make further scrutiny into these, and the like sublime Sciences; and to divert them from following such Vices as Youth in this Age are too much inclin'd. The Proposals at large are to be had of the Undertakers, Dorman Newman at the King's Arms in the Poultrey; R. Baldwin in Warwick lane; and John Dunton at the Raven in the Poultrey.

Notes: Dunton advertised the above in T.C. II, 469 (Trinity 1693). These proposals were also issued with Athenian Mercury, IX, 26 - 11 March 1695. Pleasure with Profit was published in 1694. Not located.

195. Proposals for printing by subscription, The Second, Third, and Fourth volume of the French book of Martyrs, or History of the famous Edicts of Nants: which Three Volumes, with the First already published, contain an account of all the persecutions that have been in France, from the beginning of the Reformation to this present time; .... Printed first in French, by the Authority of the States of Holland: now translated into English, with Her Majesties Royal Priviledg. These proposals are to be had of the Undertaker, J. Dunton, at the Raven in the Poultrey; and of most booksellers in London and the Countrey.

Notes: Dunton advertised the above in T.C. II, 489 (Michaelmas 1693). These proposals were also issued with Athenian Mercury, XII, 3 - 31 October 1693. The first two volumes of the History were published in 1694; no more were published. Not located.

196. Proposals [for printing The Ladies Dictionary] may be had at Mr. John Duntons at the Raven in the Poultry, and of most other Booksellers in both the Town and Country.

Notes: Advertised in Compleat Library, December 1693, p. 458. Not located.

197. THE SECOND SPIRA: being a fearful example of an atheist, who had apostatized from the Christian religion, and dyed in despair at Westminster, Decemb. 8. 1692 .... BY J.S. a Minister of the Church of England, a frequent visitor of him during his whole sickness.
London, Printed for John Dunton at the Raven in the Poultry. 1693.

12°. Pp. [xiv], 1-56, [ii]. Adv'ts, 2pp., at end.

Notes: Preface signed J.S. This work was written by Richard Sault (L&E 157), although the memoir was originally given to Dunton by Sault (L&E 154) with the explanation that it had come to him from the Rev. J. Sanders (L&E 157). The statement in H&L (V, 208) that the initials J.S. are those of the Rev. J. Sault is incorrect. Published 9 January 1693 (adv't, Athenian Mercury, IX, 8 - 7 January 1693). Entered 13 January 1693 (Stat. Reg. G, 378[414]). Reviewed in Compleat Library, January 1693. See also C.A. Moore, in Studies in Philology, XXII (1925), pp. 486-9; and L&E xii, 159, 268, 436.

Location: Wing S 733 - L, C, LV, EN; LC, NU.

198. -------- Second edition.
London, Printed for John Dunton at the Raven in the Poultry. 1693.

12°. Pp. [xiv], 1-56, [ii]. Adv'ts, 2pp., at end.

Notes: Published 17 January 1693 (adv't, Athenian Mercury, IX, 11 - 17 January 1693).

Location: C, LV.

199. -------- Third edition.

Notes: Published 24 January 1693 (adv't, Athenian Mercury, IX, 13 - 24 January 1693). Not located.

200. -------- Fourth edition.
London, Printed for John Dunton at the Raven in the Poultry. 1693.

12°. Pp. [xiv], 1-56, [ii]. Adv'ts, 2 1/2pp., at end.

Notes: Published early February, 1693 (adv't, Athenian Mercury, IX, 16 - 4 February 1693).

Location: Wing S 733B - MH.

201. -------- Fifth edition.

Notes: Advertised in Theodore John's Account of the Conversion, which was published 22 March 1693, and in Foigny's New Discovery, which was published in April 1693. Not located.

202. -------- Sixth edition.
London, Printed for John Dunton at the Raven in the Poultry. 1693.

12°. Pp. [xiv], 1-56, [ii]. Adv'ts, 2 1/2pp., at end.

Location: Wing S 733C - LC. Also, C, EN; NU.

203. THE SECOND VOLUME OF THE POST-BOY ROBB'D OF HIS MAIL: or, the pacquet broke-open. To which are added several ingenious letters lately sent to the gentlemen concern'd in this frollick. As also copies of those private letters which lately past between ------ With observations upon each letter.
London, Printed by J. Wilde, for John Dunton, at the Raven in the Poultrey, 1693.

12°. Pp. [xvi], 1-311, [i], 529-600, [viii]. Adv'ts, 5pp., and blank, 1p., at end.

Notes: Epistle dedicatory signed C.G. [Charles Gildon]. Published 1 March 1693 (adv't, Athenian Mercury, IX, 23 - 28 February 1693). The first volume of this work was published in 1692. T.C. II, 466 (Trinity 1693).

Location: Wing G 4 - O. Also, LV.

204. [Drop-head title:]
THE SENSE OF THE UNITED NONCONFORMING MINISTERS, in and about London, concerning some of the erroneous doctrines, and irregular practices, of Mr. Richard Davis, of Rothwell in Northamptonshire.
Colop: London: Printed for Thomas Cockerill, at the Three Legs over-against the Stocks-Market: And John Dunton, at the Raven in the Poultrey. 1693.

4°. Pp. 1-7, [i]. Adv'ts, lp., at end, 2/3 for Cockerill and 1/3 for Dunton.

Notes: Text dated Decemb. 26. 1692. Published December 1692 (adv't, Athenian Mercury, IX, 6 - 31 December 1692).

Location: Wing S 2553 - ENC; MH, NU.

205. The Translation of the Prince Royal of Denmark's Voyage into Germany, Italy and France, to which will be added his Continuation of it thro' Flanders and Holland 'till he arrive back unto the King his Father's Dominions ..... The Undertakers are J. Dunton, H. Rhodes, T. Goodwin, R. Baldwin, J. Harris, and R. Parker.

Notes: Advertised as "now undertaken" in Athenian Mercury, X, 1 - 28 March 1693.

206. The Tryals of Peter Boss, George Keith, Thomas Budd, and William Bradford, Quakers, for several great Misdemeanours, before a Court of Quakers, at a Sessions held at Philadelphia in Pensylvania, the 9, 10, 12, of December, 1692 ....

Notes: Dunton advertised the above in T.C. II, 476 (Michaelmas 1693), and in his three catalogues of 1694. Wing locates this title, with the imprint: Printed first beyond-sea, and now reprinted in London, for Richard Baldwin, 1693 (Wing T 2254). See A Farther Account, 1693.

207. THE WONDERS OF THE INVISIBLE WORLD: being an account of the tryals of several witches, lately excuted in New-England: and of several remarkable curiosities therein occurring .... BY COTTON MATHER. Published by the special command of his excellency the Govenour of the Province of the Massachusetts-Bay in New-England.

Printed first, at Bostun in New-England; and reprinted at London, for John Dunton, at the Raven in the Poultry. 1693.

4°. Pp. [iv], [1]-16, [i], 2-16, 33-80, 41-56, 89-98, [ii]. Adv'ts, 2pp., at end.

Notes: Licensed and entered 24 December 1692 (Stat. Reg. G, 377[413]). Published 29 December 1692 (adv't, Athenian Mercury, IX, 4 - 24 December 1692. T.C. II, 472 (Michaelmas 1693). Reviewed in Compleat Library, December 1692. L&E 248. Holmes 454B.

Location: Wing M 1174 - L, C, MR, GU; CH, LC, MH, MU, MWA, NN, RPJ, WCL, Y. Also, O.

208. -------- Second edition.

Printed first, at Boston in New-England, and reprinted at London, for John Dunton, at the Raven in the Poultrey. 1693.

4°. Pp. [1]-24, 43-50, 41-46, 46, 48-56, 47-62.

Notes: Holmes 454C.

Location: Wing M 1175 - O; CN, MB, MH, NN, WCL. Also, C.

209. -------- Third edition.

Printed first at Boston in New England, and reprinted at London, for John Dunton, at the Raven in the Poultrey. 1693.

4°. Pp. [1]-64, [iv]. Adv'ts, 4pp., at end.

Notes: Holmes 454D.

Location: Wing M 1176 - L, O, C, EN; CH, MH, NN, V.

210. ADVERTISEMENT, concerning some mistakes in the late proposals for printing a pretended compleat history of England, &c.
[Signed:] Henry Rhodes, John Dunton, John Salusbury, John Harris. [1694]

Folio. Pp. [ii].

Notes: James Tyrrell's General History of England, planned for several years, was published in 1696; this advertisement criticises proposals which had been published for a rival work.

Location: Y.

211. ANIMADVERSIONS ON GEORGE WHITEHEAD'S BOOK, falsly stiled [Innocency Triumphant.] Wherein he, and his abettors, are proved guilty of contempt of the person of our blessed Saviour, the Holy Scriptures, and governours, perverseness and falshood ....
London, Printed for John Dunton, at the Raven in the Poultrey, 1694.

4°. Pp. [2], [iv], 3-40.

Notes: Introduction signed T.C. [Thomas Crisp]. Published 17 March 1694 (adv't, Athenian Mercury, XIII, 12 - 17 March 1694).

Location: Wing C 6947 - O, C, LF, BBN, PSC.

212. The Arraignment of Worldly Philosophy; or the False Wisdom: Its being a great hindrance to the Christian Faith, and a great Enemy to the true Divine Wisdom. By George Keith.

Notes: Dunton advertised the above as "in the press" in his second and third catalogues of 1694. Wing locates this title, with the imprint: For R. Levis, 1694 (Wing K 143). See A Farther Account, 1693.

213. The benefit of a well ordered conversation, as it was delivered in a Sermon on a day of publick Humiliation; as also a Funeral Discourse, occasion'd by the Death of the Worshipful Major General Denison, by Mr. William Hubbard. To which is annexed an Irenicon, or a Salve for New England's sore, penned by the said Major General, and left behind him as his Farewel, and last advice to his Friends of the Massachusetts.

Notes: Dunton advertised the above in his second and third catalogues of 1694. This work was first printed at Boston, in 1684 (Wing H 3208; Evans 362). No copy of a London edition has been located.

214. [Drop-head title:]
A CATALOGUE of new books printed for John Dunton, who is remov'd from the Poultry, to the Raven in Jewen-Street ....

4°. Pp. [xii].

Notes: Published 19 November 1694 (adv't, Athenian Mercury, XV, 23 - 20 November 1694). Only one copy of this catalogue has been located, bound with Some Remarkable Passages in the Life and Death of Mr. John Mason, 1694, signed I-L^2 to follow the text of that work.

Location: NU.

215. The causeless ground of Surmises, Jealousies and unjust Offences removed .... By George Keith.

Notes: Dunton advertised the above in his second and third catalogues of 1694. Wing locates this title, with the colophon: For R. Levis, 1694 (Wing K 149). See A Farther Account, 1693.

216. A continuation of morning-exercise questions and cases of conscience. The second edition.

Notes: Dunton advertised the above as "in the press" in his first catalogue of 1694.

217. A DETECTION OF THE COURT AND STATE OF ENGLAND during the four last reigns, and the inter-regnum. Consisting of private memoirs, &c. with observations and reflections. Also an appendix discovering the present state of the nation. In two volumes. [Vol. II] BY ROGER COKE, Esquire.
London, Printed in the Year, MDCXCIV.

8°. Vol. I: Pp. [lvi], 1-423, [i].
Vol. II: Pp. [ii], 1-128, 113-527, [i].

Notes: Reviewed in Athenian Mercury, XV, 6 - 22 September 1694, where it is described as "printed privately". "The following Books, among many more, may serve to give the Reader a taste of what I engaged in: .... Mr. Coke's 'Detection of the Court and State of England'" (L&E 152). "Mr. Jones ... brought me acquainted with Esquire Coke, whose 'Detection of the Court and State of England' met with very good success" (L&E 182). "Mr. Harris and I were Partners in 'Coke's Detection'" (L&E 231). The work was advertised as "lately printed for John Dunton" in Athenian Mercury, XVII, 6 - 20 April 1695, and in XVII, 28 - 6 July 1695, Dunton announced that a new edition, in one volume, octavo, of Coke's Detection was "reprinting ... seeing the Additions to this New Impression will be very considerable, a Number of them shall be printed singly, for the sakes of those Gentlemen that bought the first Impression". The second edition was published in 1696.

Location: Wing C 4973 - L, C, OM, LVF, DT; CH, MBP, Y.

218. A Discourse shewing what Repentance of National Sins God requires, if ever we expect National Mercies .... by Daniel Williams.

Notes: Dunton advertised the above in his three catalogues of 1694. Daniel Williams's sermon, "What Repentance of National Sins doth God require, as ever we expect National Mercies?" was printed in the fourth volume of Casuistical Morning-Exercises, 1690. No copy of a separate printing has been located.

219. A Discovery of the horrid Association and Conspiracy of the Papists in Lancashire, about the year 1692 In a Letter of Instruction from a Roman Catholick of great Quality in London, to a Papist Mutineer in Lancashire. Price 6d.

Notes: Dunton advertised the above in his second and third catalogues of 1694. Not located.

220. Early piety. [By Cotton Mather] The third edition.

Notes: Dunton advertised the above as "in the press" in his first catalogue of 1694. Early Piety was first published by Dunton in 1689.

221. AN ESSAY UPON REASON, and the nature of spirits. BY RICHARD BURTHOGGE, M.D.
London: Printed for John Dunton at the Raven in the Poultrey. 1694.

8°. Pp. [viii], 1-280.

Notes: Published 30 April 1694 (adv't, Athenian Mercury, XIII, 25 - 1 May 1694). Dedication to John Lock signed Rich. Burthogge. L&E 152, 182.

Location: Wing B 6150 - L, C, OME, E, DT; BN, CN, LC, MH, WCL, Y.

222. The Great Historical Dictionary.

Notes: In his Life and Errors, Dunton included this title in a list of works printed for him by Mrs. Elizabeth Harris (L&E 223). The Great Historicall, Geographicall and Poeticall Dictionary was licensed 28 January 1692, and entered 20 March 1695, by Henry Rhodes, Luke Meredith, John Harris and Thomas Newborough (Stat. Reg. G, 427[453]). The work when published in 1694 was printed for Rhodes, Meredith, Harris and Newborough; and the same four booksellers advertised the work in T.C. II, 481 (Michaelmas 1693). Dunton's name appears in the work only in the list of subscribers. Wing M 2725.

223. THE HISTORY OF THE FAMOUS EDICT OF NANTES: containing an account of all the persecutions, that have been in France from its first publication to this present time. Faithfully extracted from all the public and private memoirs, that cou'd possibly be procured. Vol. I[II]. Printed first in French, by the authority of the States of Holland and West-Friezland. And now translated into English. With Her Majesties Royal Priviledge. [BY ELIE BENOIST]

London, Printed for John Dunton, at the Raven in the Poultry. MDCXCIV.

4°. Vol. I: Pp. [xx], i-lxxxviii, 1-80, 101-187, 200-482, 401-567, [xvii].
Vol. II: Pp. [iv], i-xxxv, [i], 1-168, ff. 169-184, pp. 201-424, 301-540, 401-561, [xv]

Notes: Epistle dedicatory to the Queen signed by the translator, --- Cooke. Licensed 5 June 1693 and entered 12 June 1693 (Stat. Reg. G, 389[423]). Vol. I published October 1693 (adv't, Athenian Mercury, XI, 28 - 14 October 1693), and reviewed in Athenian Mercury, XI, 27 - 10 October 1693. Dunton was proud that this work "was a wonderful pleasure to Queen Mary, ... and was the only Book to which she ever granted her Royal Licence" (L&E 153); the original license survives in Ms. Rawl. Letters, 44 (Bodleian Library). Dunton issued proposals for the second, third and fourth volumes of this work in October 1693, but only the second volume was published, in June 1694 (adv't, Athenian Mercury, XIV, 8 - 16 June 1694); a quantity of sheets were eventually sold to Mr. Tyson, "the **Waste**-paper Stationer of London .... **of whom I never bought**, but sold many hundred reams of ... 'Edict of Nantes,' and other books that my Friends had forgot to ask for" (L&E 256). L&E xvii, 742.

Location: Wing B 1898 - OM, LIL, ENC, DT; CN, MH, NPT, NU. Also, C.

224. The Judgment given forth by 28 Quakers against George Keith and his Friends: with an Answer to it, declaring those 28 Quakers to be no Christians ....

Notes: Dunton advertised the above in T.C. II, 471 (Michaelmas 1693) and in his three catalogues of 1694. Wing locates this title, with the imprint: Printed at Pensilvania; and now re-printed at London, for Richard Baldwin, 1694 (Wing J 1173). See A Farther Account, 1693.

225. THE KNOWLEDGE OF THE WORLD: or, the art of well-educating youth, through the various conditions of life. By way of letters. Vol. I. To be continued in that method till the whole design is finisht. Printed first at Paris, afterwards Re-printed at Amsterdam, and now done into English.
London, Printed for John Dunton, who is remov'd from the Poultry, to the Raven in Jewen-Street.

4°. Pp. [xii], 1-20, 23-190.

Notes: By Jean Baptiste de Chevremont (Newberry 352). Licensed 8 May, and entered 9 May 1694 (Stat. Reg. G, 413[440]). Published 9 October 1694 (adv't, Athenian Mercury, XV, 10 - 6 October 1694). Dunton's original intention was to publish this work in the form of monthly letters, but only this first volume appeared (see adv't, Athenian Mercury, XIII, 28 - 12 May 1694).

Location: Wing K 728A - CN. Also, L.

226. THE LADIES DICTIONARY; being a general entertainment for the fair-sex: a work never attempted before in English. Licens'd and enter'd according to order.
London: Printed for John Dunton at the Raven in the Poultrey, 1694. Price Bound Six Shillings.

8°. Pp. [viii], 1-240, 161-352, 301-484, 401-528.

Notes: Dedication to the Fair Sex signed N.H. Licensed 23 February 1694 and entered 24 February 1694 (Stat. Reg. G, 408[436]). Published 19 March 1694 (adv't, Athenian Mercury, XIII, 13 - 20 March 1694). Noyes 162. Newberry 842.

Location: Wing H 99 - L, O, C; CH, CN, LC, MH, NC, Y. Also, NN.

227. THE LIFE AND DEATH OF THE REVEREND MR. JOHN ELIOT, who was the first preacher of the Gospel to the Indians in America .... Written BY COTTON MATHER. The third edition carefully corrected.
London: Printed for John Dunton, at the Raven in the Poultrey. M DC XC IV.

12°. Pp [viii], 1-168, [iv]. Adv'ts, 4pp., at end.

Notes: Published November 1693 (adv't, Athenian Mercury, XII, 11 - 28 November 1693). The second edition of this work, the first London edition, was published by Dunton in 1691. Reviewed in Compleat Library, December 1693. Holmes 409D.

Location: Wing M 1121 - L, O; CN, LC, MH, MWA, NN, RPJ, WCL.

228. MALEBRANCH'S SEARCH AFTER TRUTH. Or a treatise of the nature of the humane mind, and of its management for avoiding error in the sciences. Vol. I. Done out of French from the last edition.
London, Printed for J. Dunton at the Raven in the Poultrey, and S. Manship at the Ship in Cornhil, 1694.

8°. Pp. [xxxii], 1-168, 161-271, [i], 1-95, [i], 1-96.

Notes: Epistle dedicatory to the Marquess of Normanby signed by the translator, Richard Sault. Licensed 5 May and entered 7 May 1694 (Stat. Reg. G, 413 [440]). Published 26 July 1694 (adv't, Athenian Mercury, XIV, 19 - 24 July 1694). On 19 May and 22 May 1694, Thomas Bennet licensed and entered a translation of the same work by T. Taylor, of Magdalen College, Oxford. T.C. II, 556 (Trinity 1695) contains rival announcements for the work by Dunton and Manship, and by Bennet. Taylor's translation was published in Oxford in 1694, printed by L. Lichfield (Wing M 317), and finally in London in 1700, printed by W. Bowyer for Thomas Bennet (Wing M 318). For discussion of Bennet's edition, and its trade in the wholesaling conger, see Hodgson & Blagden, Notebook of Thomas Bennet and Henry Clements (Oxford, 1956), pp. 101, 160, 205. Vol. II of Sault's translation was published in 1695. L&E 152.

Location: Wing M 315 - L, O, C, CK, LL, E; MBC, MH, TU. Also, Y.

229. MAN MADE RIGHTEOUS by Christ's obedience. Being two sermons at Pinners-Hall. With enlargements, &c. also some remarks on Mr. Mather's Postscript, &c. BY DANIEL WILLIAMS.
London, Printed for J. Dunton at the Raven in the Poultry, 1694.

12°. Pp. [xii], 1-238, [ii]. Adv'ts, 2pp., at end.

Notes: Published 11 June 1694 (adv't, Athenian Mercury, XIV, 7 - 12 June 1694).

Location: Wing W 2653 - L, LCL, ENC; NU, Y.

230. A NARRATIVE OF THE CONVERSION OF THOMAS MACKERNESSE late of March in the Isle of Ely. Who was condemn'd for robbery, &c. and executed at Wisbech, Aug. 19. 1694. With an account of his penitential behaviour, and discourses with the ministers who came to visit him. Publish'd BY THE REVEREND MR. J. BURROUGHS Minister at Wisbech.
London, Printed for John Dunton at the Raven in the Poultrey, 1694.

4°. Pp. [viii], 1-30, [ii]. Adv'ts, 2 1/2pp., at end.

Location: Wing B 6128 - L.

231. A Narrative of the Dissenters Plot in the Year 1690. with a large and exact Relation of all their old ones .... By one who was deeply concerned therein. This peice was Licensed, and is a Witty Irony, clearing the Dissenters from those ill designs against the Government, and of subverting the Church of England, which the Tories charged them with in the Year 1690. But by being misunderstood by them, it made a great noise in the World in the year 1690. which was the time when 'twas first Publisht.

Notes: Dunton advertised the above in his second and third catalogues of 1694. Not located.

232. A NARRATIVE OF THE LATE EXTRAORDINARY CURE wrought in an instant upon Mrs. Eliz. Savage, (lame from her birth) without the using of any natural means. With the affidavits which were made before the Right Honorable the Lord Mayor; and the certificates of several credible persons, who knew her both before and since her cure ....
London: Printed for John Dunton at the Raven, and John Harris at the Harrow in the Poultry. MD CX CIV. Price 6d.

8°. Pp. [1]-46, [ii]. Adv'ts, 3pp., at end, half for Dunton and half for Harris.

Notes: Published 12 February 1694 (adv't, Athenian Mercury, XIII, 3 - 13 February 1694). License on verso of leaf preceding title: "This may be Printed. Edw. Cooke. Feb. 7. 1693/4. Advertisement. The Original Affidavits and Certificates, inserted in the following Narrative, are in the Hands of John Dunton, and John Harris; where any, who please, may peruse them."

Location: Wing N 193 - O, GH; CH. Also, C.

233. PLEASURE WITH PROFIT: consisting of recreations of divers kinds, ... Published to recreate ingenious spirits; and to induce them to make farther scrutiny into these (and the like) sublime sciences. And to divert them from following such vices, to which youth (in this age) are so much inclin'd. BY WILLIAM LEYBOURN, Philomathes. To this work is also annext, a treatise of algebra, according to the late improvements, ... BY R. SAULT, Master of the Mathematick School in Adam's-Court, in Broadstreet, near the Royal Exchange, London.
London: Printed for Richard Baldwin, and John Dunton; near the Oxford-Arms in Warwick-Lane: And at the Raven in the Poultrey. 1694.

[Note: Sault's Treatise of Algebra, which follows the above, has a separate title-page without imprint. Register and pagination are confused.]

Folio. Pp. [ii], I-VI, [vi], 1-52, 1-56, 1-68, 1-31, [i], 1-24, [1]-63, [i], 1-28, 1-13, 2-10, 1-[10], 1-[12], 1-26, [ii]. Adv'ts, 1p., at end.

Notes: Proposals for this work were issued in 1693.

Location: Wing L 1931 - L, O, C, EO, DT; MU, NAI, NC.

234. PROPOSALS FOR A NATIONAL REFORMATION, of manners, humbly offered to the consideration of our magistrates & clergy. To which is added, I. The instrument for reformation. II. An account of several murders, &c. and particularly a bloody slaughter-house discover'd in Rosemary-lane .... As also the black roll, containing the names and crimes of several hundreds persons, who have been prosecuted by the Society, for whoring, drunkenness, sabbath-breaking, &c. Published by the Society for Reformation. Licensed, Feb. 12th. 1693/4. D. Poplar.
London, Printed for John Dunton, at the Raven in the Poultry. MDCXCIV.

8°. Pp. [iv], 1-24, 29-35, [i]. Adv'ts, lp., at end.

Notes: Published February 1694 (adv't, Athenian Mercury, XIII, 4 - 17 February 1694).

Location: Wing P 3725 - C; CH, MH, Y.

235. PROPOSALS FOR PRINTING A GENERAL HISTORY OF ENGLAND from the flood, according to the best traditional account, ... down to the reign of their present majesties .... Written BY JAMES TYRRELL of Okely in the County of Bucks, Esquire, author of Bibliotheca Politica .... The undertakers are Henry Rhodes, John Dunton, John Salisbury, John Harris.

Folio. Pp. [ii].

Notes: Published 21 November 1694 (adv't, Athenian Mercury, XV, 23 - 20 November 1694). The first volume of Tyrrell's History was published in 1696; further volumes in 1700 and 1704.

Location: MH.

236. QUAKERISM WITHERING, and Christianity reviving or, a brief reply to the Quakers pretended vindication. In answer to a printed sheet deliver'd to the Parliament. Wherein their errors, both in fundamentals and circumstantials, are further detected, and G. Whitehead further unmask'd. By an earnest contender for the Christian

faith, FRANCIS BUGG. Licens'd, March 3. 1693/4.
London: Printed for the Author, and sold by J. Dunton at the Raven in the Poultry, and J. Guillam Bookseller in Bishopsgate-street, 1694.

8°. Pp. [viii], 1-72.

Notes: Published 17 March 1694 (adv't, Athenian Mercury, XIII, 12 - 17 March 1694).

Location: Wing B 5386 - L, O, C, LF, OM; MH, NU, PH, PSC, Y.

237. Religio Bibliopolae. By Benjamin Bridgwater. [reprinted] London, 1694.

Notes: Sir Geoffrey Keynes, Bibl. Sir Thomas Browne (Cambridge, 1924), no. 410: "This edition is recorded by Wilkin [Sir Thomas Browne's Works ... edited by Simon Wilkin (London, 1836)], II, xix. I have not seen a copy". Not located.

238. The remaines of the famous Monsieur de Valois, Councellor and Historiographer to the French King, consisting of crititcall historicall and morall reflections &c., together with remarkes on the lives of certaine persons, published by his son. The author ordering these papers should be kept secrett till after his death. To this worke is prefixt an accot of the author's life written by the President Cousin; as alsoe a catalogue of all his writeings. These Remaines were printed first in Paris and afterwards reprinted in Amsterdam and now translated into English.

Notes: Licensed 5 May 1694, and entered as above by Dunton 7 May 1694 (Stat. Reg. G, 412[440]). Not located.

239. REMARKS ON A LATE DISCOURSE OF WILLIAM LORD BISHOP OF DERRY: concerning the inventions of men in the worship of God. BY J. BOYSE.
London: Printed for J. Lawrence, at the Angel, and J. Dunton at the Raven in the Poultry. 1694.

8°. Pp. [viii], 1-192.

Notes: Licensed 5 June 1694 and entered 6 June 1694 (Stat. Reg. G, 414[441]). Published 18 June 1694 (adv't, Athenian Mercury, XIV, 9 - 19 June 1694). This work was written in reply to Dr. King's Discourse Concerning the Inventions of Men in the Worship of God (Wing K 526); and Dr. King replied to Boyse in An Admonition to the Dissenting Inhabitants of the Diocese of Derry, 1694 (Wing K 520, K 521), and A Second Admonition, 1696 (Wing K 533, K 534). Boyse's Remarks were also published in Dublin in 1694, Printed for Eliphal Dobson, Matthew Gun, and Patrick Campbel, Booksellers in Dublin (Wing B 4073, Dix 262). T.C. II, 508 (Trinity, 1694). L&E 152, 168.

Location: Wing B 4072 - L, O, C, OB, EN; NU, Y.

240. Remarks on the Tryals of the Lord Preston and Mr. Ashton. By a Gentleman who was present at those Tryals.

Notes: Dunton advertised the above in his second and third catalogues of 1694. Not located.

241. Remarks upon the Life, Tryal, and Acquitment of Arthur Earl of Torrington.

Notes: Dunton advertised the above in his second and third catalogues of 1694. Not located.

242. SOME REMARKABLE PASSAGES in the life and death of Mr. John Mason, late minister of Water-Stratford, in the County of Bucks .... Drawn up BY A REVEREND DIVINE, &c. .... To which is added the letters Mr. Mason sent to several of his friends, ... As also many poems which he writ on special occasions. Never printed before.
London, Printed for John Dunton, who is removed from the Poultry to the Raven in Jewen-street. 1694. Price 1 s.

4°. Pp. [iv], 1-52, [xii]. Adv'ts, 12pp., at end.

Notes: Licensed 7 June 1694, and entered 8 June 1694, by John Lawrence, John Dunton, and William Lindsey (Stat. Reg. G, 414[441]).

Location: Wing S 4596 - L, DT; MH, NU. Also, O.

243. The Soldiers Manual, or Directions, Prayers, and Ejaculations for such as lead a military life. By a member of the Athenian Society: Price 2d. or an hundred of 'em for 14 s. stitch up in Blew Paper to those Gentlemen (or Officers in his Majesties Army) that buy 'em to disperse.

Notes: Dunton advertised the above in his second and third catalogues of 1694. Published 25 April 1694 (adv't, Athenian Mercury, XIII, 23 - 24 April 1694). Not located.

244. Spectral Thoughts, &c.

Notes: Dunton advertised the above title in a list of "Books now in the Press, and going to it", in his second and third catalogues of 1694.

245. TRI-UNITY: or the doctrin of the Holy Trinity, asserted, in a discourse on 2 Cor. XIII. xiv. BY ISAAC MAUDUIT, Minister of the Gospel.
London, Printed by Hannah Clark, for John Dunton, at the Raven in the Poultrey. 1694.

8°. Pp. [viii], 1-43, [v]. Adv'ts, 5pp., at end.

Notes: Preface signed I.M. Feb. 5. 1693/4. Published 17 March 1694 (adv't, Athenian Mercury, XIII, 12 - 17 March 1694).

Location: Wing M 1334 - NU. Also, O.

246. A True Account of the Proceedings. Sence and Advice of the People called Quakers ...... [By Robert Hannay]

Notes: Dunton advertised the above in his second and third catalogues of 1694. Wing locates this title, attributed to Robert Hannay, with the imprint: For R. Levis, 1694 (Wing H 656). See A Farther Account, 1693.

247. A Vindication of Bishop Barlows Remains, proving them to be all Genuine, and many of 'em to be Published upon the Bishops own desire.

Notes: Dunton advertised the above in a list of "Books now in the Press, and going to it" in his second catalogue of 1694; and in his third catalogue of that year, in a list of "Books now in the Press, and going to it", he advertised "An Appendix to Bishop Barlow's Remains, to which will be annext a Vindication of those lately Publish'd, Proving them to be all Genuine, and many of 'em to be Published upon the Bishops own desire". The Genuine Remains of Thomas Barlow was published by Dunton in 1693. No copy of A Vindication has been located.

248. THE WORKS OF THE RIGHT HONOURABLE HENRY LATE L. DELAMER, and Earl of Warrington: containing his lordships advice to his children, several speeches in Parliament, &c. with many other occasional discourses on the affairs of the two last reigns: being original manuscripts written with his lordships own hand. Never before printed.
London, Printed for John Lawrence at the Angel, and John Dunton at the Raven in the Poultrey. 1694.

8°. Pp. [xvi], 1-144, 353-399, [i], 399-[414], ff. 409-416, pp. 421-468, 467-513, [i], 541-668, 679-684, [x].

Adv'ts, 10pp., at end, 5pp. for Dunton and 5pp. for Lawrence.

Notes: Epistle dedicatory to the Earl of Warrington signed J. De la Heuze. Published 15 August 1694 (adv't, Athenian Mercury, XIV, 25 - 14 August 1694). L&E 152, 178, 205, 742.

Location: Wing D 873 - L, O, LL, EN, DT; CH, NC, Y.

249. A COLLECTION OF THE FUNERAL ORATIONS, pronounc'd by publick authority in Holland upon the death of the most serene and potent princess, Mary II. Queen of Great Britain, &c. by [within brackets:] DR. JAMES PERIZONIUS, Professor ... in Leiden. DR. GEORGE GREVIUS, Professor ... in Utrecht. P. FRANCIUS, of Amsterdam. MR. ORTWINIUS of Delph. And, the learned author of the collection of new and curious pieces. To which is added, the invitation of the Chancellor of the Electoral University of Wittenberg, in Saxony, to George Wilhain Kirchmais ... Done into English from the Latin originals.
London, Printed for John Dunton at the Raven in Jewen-street, and are also to be Sold by Edmund Richardson near the Poultry-Church, 1695.

[Separate title-pages; following the above, with multiple register and separate pagination:] A funeral oration of J. G. Grevius, upon the death of Mary II. ...
London. Printed for John Dunton at the Raven in Jewen-street, and are also to be Sold by Edm. Richardson near the Poultry-Church. MD C XCV.

An oration of Peter Francius, upon the funeral of the most august princess Mary II. ...
London. Printed for John Dunton at the Raven in Jewen-street, and are also to be Sold by Edm. Richardson near the Poultry-Church. MD C XCV.

A funeral oration upon the death of the most serene and potent princess, Mary Stuart, ... By John Ortwinius. ...
London: Printed for John Dunton, at the Raven in Jewen-street: And are also to be Sold by Edm. Richardson, in the Upper Court in Scalding-Alley, near the Poultry-Church, 1695.

A funeral oration on the most high, most excellent, and most potent princess, Marie Stuart, ...
London, Printed for J. Dunton at the Raven in Jewen-street; and Sold by Edmund Richardson near the Poultry-Church, 1695.

[Following the preceeding sermon, with continuous register and separate pagination:] An invitation to hear a panegyrical oration in remembrance of Mary. ...

London. Printed for John Dunton at the Raven in Jewen-street, and are also to be Sold by Edm. Richardson near the Poultry-Church. MD C XCV.

4°. Pp. [1]-54, [ii], 1-37, [iii], 1-24, [iv], I-16, [1]-16, 22, 21, [1]-4, [i], 26-28, [iv]. Adv'ts, 4pp., at end.

Notes: Published 31 July 1695 (adv't, <u>Athenian Mercury</u>, XVIII, 5 - 30 July 1695).

Location: Wing C 5203 - OB; LC, <u>Y</u>.

250. AN ESSAY UPON THE WORKS OF CREATION and providence: being an introductory discourse to the history of remarkable providences, now preparing for the press. To which is added a further specimen of the said work: as also meditations upon the beauty of holiness. BY WILLIAM TURNER M.A. and Vicar of Walberton in Sussex.
London, Printed for John Dunton, at the Raven in Jewen-street, and are also sold by Edm. Richardson near the Poultry Church. 1695.

[Separate title-page; following the above, with continuous register and pagination:] Medications upon the beauty of holiness. By William Turner, M.A. and Vicar of Walberton in Sussex.
London, Printed by J. Astwood for John Dunton, at the Raven in Jewen-street, and are also to be Sold by Ed. Richardson, near the Poultrey-Church. 1695.

8°. Pp. [xiv], 1-74, 97-160, [xl]. Adv'ts, 6pp., at end.

Notes: Published 8 July 1695 (adv't, <u>Athenian Mercury</u>, XVII, 29 - 9 July 1695).

Location: Wing T 3346 - <u>L</u>.

251. A FUNERAL ORATION to the sacred memory of the most serene and potent Mary II. Queen of Great Britain, France and Ireland. BY FRANCIS SPANHEIMIUS, F.F. Chief Professor of the Academy of Leyden. .....
London. Printed for John Dunton at the Raven in Jewen-street, and are to be Sold by Edm. Richardson near the

Poultry-Church. MD C XCV.

4°. Pp. [ii], 1-51, [iii]. Adv'ts, 3pp., at end.

Location: Wing S 4800 - L, O; CH, CLC, MH, Y.

252. THE HISTORY OF ALL RELIGIONS IN THE WORLD: from the creation down to this present time. ..... To which is added, a table of heresies: as also a geographical map ..... BY WILLIAM TURNER, M.A. and Vicar of Walberton in Sussex.
London, Printed for John Dunton, at the Raven in Jewen-street; And are also to be sold by Edm. Richardson, in the Upper Court in Scalding-Alley, near the Poultrey-Church. 1695.

8°. Pp. [xvi], 1-307, [i], 305-684. Adv'ts, 3pp., at end.

Notes: Wing locates two editions of this work in 1695, with identical imprints; I have examined one copy of each edition and they appear to be identical. L&E 161, 760.

Location: Wing T 3347 - L, O, OB, CK; CU, IU, MH, MU, Y.
Wing T 3348 - MY; NU.

253. LACHRYMAE SACERDOTIS. A pindarick poem occasion'd by the death of that most excellent princess, our late gracious sovereign lady, Mary the Second, of glorious memory. BY HENRY PARK, Curate of Wentworth in Yorkshire.
London: Printed for John Dunton, at the Raven in Jewen-street, and are also to be Sold by Edm. Richardson, in the upper Court in Scalding-Alley, near the Poultry-Church, 1695.

4°. Pp. [ii], 1-8, [ii]. Adv'ts, 2pp., at end.

Notes: Published 2 April 1695 (adv't, Athenian Mercury, XVII, 1 - 2 April 1695).

Location: Wing P 362 - L, O; CH, CU, MH.

254. THE LAY-CLERGY: or, the lay-elder. In a short essay in answer to this query; whether it be lawful for persons in holy orders to exercise temporal offices, honours, jurisdictions and authorities. With arguments and objections on both sides, poyz'd, and indifferently weigh'd. BY EDM. HICKERINGIL, Rector of the Rectory of All-Saints in Colchester.
London, Printed for John Dunton, at the Raven in Jewen-Street, 1695.

4°. Pp. [1]-36.

Location: Wing H 1818 - L, O, EN; CH, NU.

255. MALEBRANCH'S SEARCH AFTER TRUTH: or, a treatise of the nature of the humane mind, and of its management, for avoiding error in the sciences. .... Vol. II. Done out of French from the last edition.
London, Printed for J. Dunton at the Raven in Jewen-street. 1695.

[Separate title-page; following the above, with continuous register and separate pagination:] A defence of the author of the Search after Truth: against the accusation of Monsieur de la Ville. .....
London, Printed in the Year, MDCXCV.

8°. Pp. [xvi], 1-104, 129-312, 353-488, 737-820, [ii], 1-23, [iii]. Adv'ts, for S. Manship, 3pp., at end.

Notes: Volume I was published, by Dunton and Manship, in 1694. The second volume was also issued with the imprint: London, Printed for S. Manship at the Ship in Cornhil. 1695. (Wing M 316).

Location: Y.

256. A Practical Discourse upon Col. 3. 5. by R. Carr, Vicar of Sutton.

Notes: Dunton advertised the above, "lately printed for J. Dunton", in Athenian Mercury, XVII, 6 - 20 April 1695. Not located.

257. Dr. Singleton's Practical Discourses upon I John 12. 28.

Notes: Dunton advertised the above, "lately printed for J. Dunton", in Athenian Mercury, XVII, 6 - 20 April 1695. John Singleton's sermon on John 12. 28. was printed in A Continuation of Morning-Exercise Questions, 1683. No separate printing of this sermon has been located.

258. The present State of the Empire of Morocco. Written in French by Monsieur St. Olon, the French King's Ambassador. Lately Publish'd at Paris, and Re-printed in Holland.

Notes: Dunton advertised the above in a list of "Books now in the Press, and going to it", in his second and third catalogues of 1694. Wing locates this title, with the imprint: For R. Bentley: W. Freeman: and S. Manship, 1695 (Wing S 347).

259. Proposals for Printing by Subscription -- An History of all the Remarkable Providences which have happened in this present Age, ... By W. Turner, M.A. ... Proposals and Specimens ... may then [on 17 May] be had of the Undertaker, John Dunton, at the Raven in Jewen-street, and of Edm. Richardson, near the Poultrey Church, and of most Booksellers in London, and the Country.

Notes: Published 17 May 1695 (adv't, Athenian Mercury, XVII, 13 - 15 May 1695). Also advertised in Spanheim's Funeral Oration, 1695, and in Williams's Excellency of a Public Spirit, 1697. These proposals were not identical to An Essay, 1695, q.v.; see advertisements in Athenian Mercury, XVII, 29 - 9 July 1695. Turner's Compleat History of the Most Remarkable Providences was published by Dunton in 1697. No copy of these proposals has been located.

260. Proposals for Printing the Life of the Reverend Mr. Richard Baxter; ... 'Tis proposed to Subscribers at 17s. and 6d. per Book in Quires (7 paying for 6) but to all others not under 20s each Book in Quires. Proposals, giving a fuller Account of this Work, are to be had of the Undertakers, Thomas Parkhurst, Jonathan Robinson,

John Lawrence, and John Dunton.

Notes: Dunton advertised the above in Athenian Mercury, XIX, 1 - 29 October 1695. Reliquiae Baxterianae was published by Parkhurst, Robinson, Lawrence and Dunton in 1696. No copy of these proposals has been located.

261. A SERMON UPON THE DEATH OF THE QUEEN OF ENGLAND preach'd in the Walloon Church at the Hague, Feb. 6. 1695. ..... BY ISAAC CLAUDE, Minister of the Walloon-Church. Done into English from the second edition printed in French. London. Printed for John Dunton at the Raven in Jewen-street, and are to be Sold by Edm. Richardson near the Poultry-Church. MD C XCV.

4°. Pp. [iv], 1-20.

Notes: Published May, 1695 (adv't, Athenian Mercury, XVII, 14 - 19 May 1695).

Location: Wing C 4587 - L, O; MH, Y.

262. THE WORLD BEWITCH'D: or, an examination of the common opinions concerning spirits: their nature, power, administration, and operations. As also, the effects men are able to produce by their communication. Divided into IV parts. BY BALTHAZAR BEKKER, D.D. and Pastor at Amsterdam. Vol. I.[all published] Translated from a French copy, approved of and subscribed by the author's own hand. Printed for R. Baldwin in Warwick-Lane, 1695.

12°. Pp. [lxxxiv], 1-264.

Notes: This work was entered jointly by Richard Baldwin, John Dunton, and John Harris, on 17 August 1694, and licensed 19 August 1694 (Stat. Reg. G, 417 [445]). Dedication, from the original edition, to Feyo John Winter, Doctor of Physick, signed B. Bekker. Amsterdam, July 18, 1693. T.C. II, 527 (Michaelmas 1694).

Location: Wing B 1781 - L, C, EN, AU; CH, LC, MH.

263. A BRIEF DISCOVERY of the true mother of the pretended Prince of Wales known by the name of Mary Grey. .... BY WILLIAM FULLER, Gent. sometime page of honour to the late Queen in France.
London, Printed for the Author, Anno Dom. 1696.

8°. Pp. [iv], [1]-42, [vi].

Notes: In The Whole Life of Mr. William Fuller ... Impartially writ, by Himself (London, 1703), Fuller wrote: "as to what I writ and published concerning the pretended Prince of Wales, and of one Mrs. Mary Grey, I must own, That all my Assertions did not amount to any Proof of the Matter; but it is no Secret, nor would I have it be so, that the Affair was much improved by Mr. Richard Baldwin, John Dunton, and others Booksellers, who were zealous for the Cause, and as fond of the Gain they reap'd thereby" (p. 132). Dunton replied in his Life and Errors that "[Mr. Fuller] has told the World, in his 'History of his Life,' that Mr. Baldwin and I did improve his 'Narrative of the sham Prince of Wales,' on purpose to make it sell; which is the most formal lie I have met with, in regard the Copy was printed off before we saw it" (p. 181). See also A Further Confirmation and Mr. William Fuller's Third Narrative, 1696.

Location: Wing F 2479 - L, O, C, LG, EN; BN, CH, CN, LC, MH, NU, Y.

264. A DETECTION OF THE COURT AND STATE OF ENGLAND during the four last reigns, and the inter-regnum. .... The second edition corrected. ... In two volumes. [Vol. II.] BY ROGER COKE, Esquire.
London, Printed in the Year, MDCXCVI.

8°. Vol. I: Pp. [xli], 1-134, 1-200.
Vol. II: Pp. [ii], 1-88, 1-208, 1-77, [i].

Notes: First published in 1694. Dunton and John Harris sold the copyright of this work in 1696 to

Andrew Bell for £30; the third edition was published by Bell in 1697 (Wing C 4975).

Location: Wing C 4974 - L, C, MR, E; BN, MH, MU, NC, Y.

265. ELISHA'S CRY after Elijah's God consider'd and apply'd, with reference to the decease of the late Reverend Mr. Richard Baxter. Who left this life Decemb. 8th, 1691. And preach'd in part on Decemb. 18th, An. Dod. being the Lord's-Day, at Rutland-House in Charter-house-Yard, London. BY MATTHEW SYLVESTER, his unworthy fellow-labourer in the gospel there, for near four of the last years of his life and labours.
London, Printed for T. Parkhurst, J. Robinson, J. Lawrence, and J. Dunton. 1696.

Folio. Pp. [ii], 1-18.

Notes: Generally bound with Reliquiae Baxterianae, q.v., but with separate register and pagination.

Location: Wing S 6330 - L, O; CH, CN, LC, NU, TY, Y. Also, C, EN.

266. AN EXACT NARRATIVE of the proceedings at Turners-Hall, the 11th of the month called June, 1696. Together with the disputes and speeches there, between G. Keith and other Quakers, differing from him in some religious principles. The whole published and revised, BY GEORGE KEITH.
London, Printed for B. Aylmer at the Three Pigeons in Cornhill, and J. Dunton at the Raven in Jewen-street, 1696.

4°. Pp. [1]-62, [ii]. Adv'ts, 1p., and blank, 1p., at end; 1/3p adv't for Aylmer and 2/3p. for Dunton.

Notes: T.C. II, 587 (Trinity 1696). L&E 206.

Location: Wing K 161 - L, O, C, LF, BBN, AU; LC, MH, RDH, PH, Y.

267. A FURTHER CONFIRMATION, that Mary Grey was the true mother of the pretended Prince of Wales. .... Published BY

WILLIAM FULLER, who was privy to the whole management. To which is added, the author's vindication of himself, from the male-contents of this kingdom.
London, Printed for the Author, 1696.

8°. Pp. [1]-46, [ii]. Adv'ts, 1p., and blank, 1p., at end.

Notes: See entry for A Brief Discovery, 1696.

Location: Wing F 2482 - L, C, EN; CH, CN, LC, MH, Y.

268. THE GENERAL HISTORY OF ENGLAND, as well ecclesiastical as civil, from the earliest accounts of time, to the reign of his present majesty King William. Taken from the most antient records, manuscripts, and historians. Containing the lives of the kings, and memorials of the most eminent persons both in church and state: with the foundations of the noted monasteries, and both the universities. Vol. I. BY JAMES TYRRELL, Esq;
London, Printed for Henry Rhodes in Fleetstreet, John Dunton in Jewenstreet, John Salusbury in Cornhil, and John Harris in Little-Britain. MDCXCVI.

Folio. Pp [iv], i-cxxxvi, 1-355, [i], 1-116, [x], i-xci, [i].

Frontispiece, 3 fold-out tables, and 2 royal pedigree charts.

Notes: Entered 27 December 1694, by Henry Rhodes, John Dunton, John Salusbury, and John Harris (Stat. Reg. G, 423[450]). Proposals for this work were issued in 1694, q.v. Apparently Rhodes, Dunton and Salusbury sold their shares in this work, as it was advertised in T.C. Hilary 1697, by W. Rogers, J. Harris, J. Knapton, A. Bell, and T. Cockerill. Volume II appeared in 1700, printed for W. Rogers, R. Knaplock, A. Bell, and T. Cockerill; John Harris had died in 1698 (Plomer). Volume III appeared in 1704, printed for W. Rogers, J. Taylor, J. Nicholson, and A. Bell. The History was later traded in the wholesaling conger (see Hodgson and Blagden, Notebook of Thomas Bennet and Henry Clements [Oxford, 1956], p. 188). L&E 178.

Location: Wing T 3585 - L, LG, CE, EN.

269. THE GENERAL HISTORY OF THE QUAKERS: containing the lives, tenents, sufferings, tryals, speeches, and letters of all the most eminent Quakers, both men and women; from the first rise of that sect, down to this present time. Collected from Manuscripts, &c. A work never attempted before in English. Being written originally in Latin BY GERARD CROESE. To which is added, a letter writ by George Keith, and sent by him to the author of this book: containing a vindication of himself, and several remarks on this history.
London, Printed for John Dunton, at the Raven in Jewen-street. 1696.

[Separate title-page; following the above, with continuous register and pagination:] Our antient testimony ....
London, Printed and Sold by T. Sowle, in White-Hart-Court in Gracious-Street. 1695. [Note: Wing records this work separately (Wing O 591); catchword, register and pagination indicate that it was here reprinted as a part of the General History.]

8°. Pp. [xvi], 1-189, [iii], 1-80, 85-196, 167-181, 180, 213-276, 1-40.

Notes: Epistle dedicatory to Nicholas Witsen, signed Gerard Croese.

Location: Wing C 6965 - L, O, LF, EN, DT; CN, IE, MH, NU, PH, PSC, Y.

270. MR. WILLIAM FULLER'S THIRD NARRATIVE, containing new matters of fact, proving the pretended Prince of Wales to be a grand cheat upon the nation with an answer to some reflections cast upon him. The whole written with his own hand.
London, Printed in the Year 1696.

8°. Pp. [vi], 1-10, 17-45, [iii]. Adv'ts, 2pp., and blank, 1p., at end.

Notes: Preface dated Tunbridge-Wells August 30 96. See entry for A Brief Discovery, 1696.

Location: Wing F 2486 - L, C, CT, EN; CH, LC, MH, NU. Also, Y.

271. A NARRATIVE OF THE EXTRAORDINARY PENITENCE OF ROB. MAYNARD, who was condemn'd for the murder of John Stockton, late victualler in Grub-street. And executed at Tyburn May the 4th .... BY JOSEPH STEVENS Lecturer of Cripplegate on Sunday mornings.
London, Printed for John Dunton at the Raven in Jewen-Street. 1696. - Price 6d.

4°. Pp. [ii], 1-46, 31-36, [ii]. Adv'ts, 2pp., at end.

Location: Wing S 5498 - L.

272. THE NIGHT-WALKER: or, evening rambles in search after lewd women, with the conferences held with them &c. To be publish'd monthly, 'till a discovery be made of all the chief prostitutes in England, from the pensionary miss, down to the common strumpet. This for September, 1696. Dedicated to the whore-masters of London and Westminster.
London, Printed for James Orme, in St. Bartholomew's-Hospital, 1696. Price 6 d.

Eight monthly numbers were issued, September 1696 - April 1697.

Notes: By John Dunton. "My Eighth Project was a design to expose Vice, intituled 'The Night-Walker; or, Evening Rambles in search after Lewd Women, with the various Conferences held with them'" (L&E 201). An article called "Six Nights Rambles" had appeared in The Ladies' Dictionary in 1694. Dunton probably got the idea for this periodical from a pamphlet called The Wandering Whore, 1660, for which see Walter Graham, Beginnings of English Literary Periodicals (New York, 1926), p. 55.

Location: L(6 nos.), LG(8 nos.), EN(2 nos.), DT(8 nos.); MH(5 nos.)

273. [General title-page:]
PEGASUS: being an history of the most remarkable events, which have happened in Europe, but more especially in England. From Monday June 15. to Friday August 21. With observations thereupon. To be continued every Monday, Wednesday and Friday. The first volume. Treating on the several subjects mentioned in the contents at the beginning of this book.
London, Printed for John Dunton, at the Raven in Jewen-street, 1697. And are to be sold by Richard Baldwin, at the Oxford-Arms-Inn in Warwick-lane, and by Edm. Richardson near the Poultry-Church Price 2 s. 6 d.

General title-page and contents, pp. [iv].

[Drop-head title:]
PEGASUS, with news, an observator, and a Jacobite courant. Monday June the 15th. 1696.
[colop:] London, Printed for John Dunton, at the Raven in Jewen-Street. [From Vol. II, No. 1:] Pegasus, with an observator on publick occurrences.

Folio, a half-sheet, issued three times weekly.

Volume I. 30 nos., 15 June - 21 August 1696.
Volume II. 10 nos., 24 August - 14 September 1696.

Notes: General title-page and contents of Volume I published 5 September 1696 (adv't, Pegasus, II, 6 - 4 September 1696). Remarks made in Pegasus on 6 July 1696 about the Quakers were replied to, anonymously, in A Curb for Pegasus, or Observations on the Observator, Number 10 .... In Relation to the People called Quakers (Wing C 7619). CBEL II, 706.

Location: L; IU.

274. POEMS on several occasions. Written BY PHILOMELA.
London: Printed for John Dunton at the Raven in Jewen-street. 1696

8°. Pp. [xxiv], 1-72, 1-69, [xi]. Adv'ts, 10pp., and blank, 1p., at end.

Notes: Preface signed Elizabeth Johnson. Harding-Rents, May 10th 1696. By Elizabeth Singer, the Pindarick Lady of The Athenian Mercury, later Mrs. Elizabeth Singer Rowe (L&E 153). Published 19 August 1696 (adv't, Pegasus, I, 29 - 19 August 1696). L&E 185, 408.

Location: Wing R 2062 - O; CH, MH, NU, WF, Y.

275. RELIQUIAE BAXTERIANAE: or, Mr. Richard Baxter's narrative of the most memorable passages of his life and times. Faithfully publish'd from his own original manuscript, BY MATTHEW SYLVESTER.
London: Printed for T. Parkhurst, J. Robinson, J. Lawrence, and J. Dunton. M DC XC VI.

Folio. Pp. [xxviii], 1-448, 1-200, 1-132, [viii].

Notes: Preface signed M.S. London, May 13. 1696. Entered 23 June 1696 (Stat. Reg. Entries of Copies 1695-1708, 6[470]). See also Proposals ... Reliquiae Baxterianae, 1695, and Elisha's Cry, 1696. A. G. Matthews, The Works of Richard Baxter An Annotated List (London, [1933]), No. 140.

Location: Wing B 1370 - L, O, C, MR, EN: BN, CH, CU, LC, MH, NP, Y.

276. The Lord Faulklands Works, Secretary of State to King Charles the I. collected all together into one Volume; to which will be prefix'd Memoirs of his Lordships Life and Death. Never Printed before. Written by a Person of Honour.

Notes: Dunton advertised the above, in a list of "Books in the Press (and design'd for it) Printed for J. Dunton", in his first catalogue of 1694; this work was also advertised as "in the press" in Barlow's Genuine Remaines, 1693, and in Philomela's Poems on Several Occasions, 1696. Wing records various works by two Viscounts Falkland, but no collected edition.

277. Advice to those who never receiv'd the sacrament: or, the true penitent instructed, before, at, and after the receiving the Lord's Supper. With meditations suited to the several parts of that solemn ordinance, particularly with respect to Easter, Whitsuntide and Christmass. The whole written in a different method from any thing published on this subject. By a person of honour.
London, Printed, Sold by E. Whitlock near Stationers-Hall, 1697.

8°. Pp. [xxiv], 1-216.

Notes: In Athenian Mercury, XX, 3 - 21 May 1697, Dunton advertised this work as printed for himself and also sold by E. Whitlock. It was also advertised by T. Speed in T.C. III, 72 (Trinity 1698).

Location: O.

278. THE CHALLENGE, sent by a young lady to Sir Thomas ---- &c. Or, the female war. Wherein the present dresses and humours, &c. of the fair sex are vigorously attackt by men of quality, and as bravely defended by Madam Godfrey, and other ingenious ladies, who set their names to every challenge. The whole encounter consists of six hundred letters, pro and con, on all the disputable points relating to women. And is the first battle of this nature that was ever fought in England.
London, Printed, and Sold by E. Whitlock, near Stationers-Hall. 1697.

12°. Pp. [viii], 1-264, 257-260, 1-110, [xxii].
Adv'ts, 6pp., at end.

Notes: Preface signed Philaret [i.e., John Dunton]. "My Sixth Project was, 'The Challenge' .... In this Challenge (or Female War) there was an absolute freedom of speech allowed by both Sexes, which was given and taken without the least offence. The whole encounter consists of several Challenges, in which the Ladies attack the Men with such strength of reason, and wit, and gaiety, that they generally come off with victory"

(L&E 200). This work was advertised in Philomela's Poems on Several Occasions, 1696, and discussed in The Athenian Mercury, XV, 20 - 10 November 1694, and XV, 28 - 8 December 1694. C.A. Moore, in Studies in Philology, XXII (1925), p. 468, wrote that "Those diverting epistles [in The Challenge]represent an important stage of transition between the brief 'answers' in the Mercury and the completed essay-form of the Spectator". Although a list of subjects for the second battle is given, no further volumes were published. LA V, 73. Noyes 161.

Location: Wing C 1796 - L, O, C; OCI.

279. THE CHARACTER OF THE LATE DR. SAMUEL ANNESLEY, by way of elegy: with a preface. Written by one of his hearers. London: Printed for E. Whitlock, near Stationers-Hall, 1697.

4°. Pp. [vi], 1-16.

Notes: Preface signed D.F. [Daniel Defoe]. "Mr. De Foe wrote for me the 'Character of Dr. Annesley'" (L&E 180). "After [Dr. Annesley's] decease, Mr. Williams preached his Funeral Sermon, and Mr. De Foe drew his Character, which I published" (L&E 166). Defoe reprinted this elegy in A True Collection, 1703, without Dunton's permission, and Dunton complained angrily, in his Life and Errors, p. 180, and in Dunton's Whipping-Post, 1706, p. 89. Moore 14.

Location: LW.

280. The Church-History of New England, is now almost finished, ... by Mr. Cotton Mather, ... from whom I shall receive the Manuscript Copy as soon as compleated; and being a large Work, 'twill be printed in Folio, by way of subscription.

Notes: Dunton announced the above in Turner's Compleat History of the Most Remarkable Providences, 1697. Publication was delayed and Magnalia Christi Americana finally appeared in 1702, printed for

Thomas Parkhurst. For discussion of the delays, see Holmes, II, 583-8, and C. N. Greenough, "A Letter Relating to the Publication of Cotton Mather's Magnalia", in Pub. Col. Soc. Mass., XXVI (1926), 296-312, and Chapter II. Holmes 213A.

281. A Compendious History in Folio, of the lives, and Deaths of all the most eminent Persons, from the Crucifixion of our Blessed Saviour to this time. By a Learned Hand, who will add a Collection of several 100 modern Lives omitted in all other works of this Nature.

Notes: Dunton advertised the above, in a list of "Books now in the Press, and designed for it", in Turner's Compleat History, 1697. No copy has been located; but see The History of Living Men, 1702.

282. A COMPLEAT HISTORY OF THE MOST REMARKABLE PROVIDENCES, both of judgment and mercy, which have hapned in this present age. Extracted from the best writers, the author's own observations, and the numerous relations sent him from divers parts of the three kingdoms. To which is added, whatever is curious in the works of nature and art. The whole digested into one volume, under proper heads; being a work set on foot thirty years ago, by the Reverend Mr. Pool, author of the Synopsis Criticorum: and since undertaken and finish'd, BY WILLIAM TURNER, M.A. Vicar of Walberton, in Sussex. ...
London: Printed for John Dunton, at the Raven, in Jewen-Street. M DC XC VII.

[Separate title-pages; Parts II and III follow the above, with multiple register and separate pagination:]
The Wonders of nature. Part II. ...
London: Printed for John Dunton, at the Raven, in Jewen-Street. M DC XC VII.

The curiosities of Art. Part III. ...
London: Printed for John Dunton, at the Raven in Jewen-street, M DC XC VII.

Folio. Pp. [vi], 1-26, [iv], 1-140, 1-152, 1-144, [iv], 145-172, 1-24, [iv], 1-82, [iv], 1-31, [i].
Adv'ts, 1p., at end.

Notes: Published 15 April 1697 (adv't, Flying Post, 15 April 1697). Proposals for this work were published in 1695. L&E 161, 278, 283, 496. Sabin 97495.

Location: Wing T 3345 - L, O, C, EN, DT; CH, CN, MH, NU, V, Y.

283. Conferences about the ill Practices of some vile Persons.

Notes: Dunton advertised the above, in a list of "Books now in the Press, and designed for it", in Turner's Compleat History, 1697.

284. A CONTINUATION OF THE SECRET HISTORY OF WHITE-HALL; from the abdication of the late K. James, in 1688. to the year 1696. .... Published from the original papers. .... BY D. JONES, Gent.
London, Printed, and are to be Sold by R. Baldwin, in Warwick-lane, MDCXCVII. Of whom is to be had the First Part of the Secret History of White-Hall, from the Restoration of King Charles II. to the Abdication of the late King James.

[Separate title-page; following the above, with double register and separate pagination:] The tragical history of the Stuarts. .... By D. Jones, Gent.
London: Printed in the Year, 1697.

8°. Pp. [xix], 1-80, [1]-48, 45-156, 161-392.

Notes: See entry for The Secret History of White-Hall, 1697. Advertised by Baldwin in T. C. III, 13 (Easter 1697). Advertised in Dunton's list of books "now in the Press, and designed for it", in Turner's Compleat History, 1697.

Location: Wing J 929 - L, O, C, E, DT; CLC, LC, MH, NF, NU, Y.

285. Debates upon several Nice and Curious Points. Price 2 s. 6 d.

Notes: Dunton advertised the above, in a list of "Books now in the Press, and designed for it", in Turner's Compleat History, 1697.

286. THE DYING PASTOR'S LAST FAREWEL to his friends in Froome, Selwood, Shepton-Mallet, Brewton, Wincalton, and the adjacent parts. Being several sermons on I Joh. 2. 15. preached by that learned, and pious divine, MR. HENRY ALBIN, and prepared for the press with his own hand a little before his death. To which is added by another hand, an elegy on Mrs. Mary Hamlen, late of Froome, in Somersetshire.
London, Printed for J. Dunton, at the Raven in Jewen-street, 1697.

8°. Pp. [viii], 1-113, [vii].

Notes: L&E 177.

Location: Wing A 879 - LW. Also, EN.

287. THE EXCELLENCY OF A PUBLICK SPIRIT: set forth in a sermon preach'd (since much enlarged) at the funeral of that late reverend divine Dr. Samuel Annesley: who departed this life Dec 31. 1696. In the 77th year of his age. With a brief account of his life and death. BY DANIEL WILLIAMS, Minister of the Gospel.
London, Printed for John Dunton, at the Raven in Jewen-street, 1697.

8°. Pp. [iv], 1-147, [i]. Adv'ts, 1p., at end.

Notes: L&E 166.

Location: Wing W 2648 - L, C, LCL; IU, NU, Y.

288. Reformed religion, or right Christianity described. [By Matthew Barker] Second edition.

Notes: Dunton advertised the above, in a list of "Books now in the Press, and designed for it", in Turner's Compleat History, 1697. Reformed Religion was first published by Dunton in 1689.

289. THE SECRET HISTORY OF WHITE-HALL, from the restoration of Charles II. down to the abdication of the late K. James. .... Publish'd from the original papers. BY D. JONES, Gent.

London, Printed, and are to be Sold by R. Baldwin near the Oxford-Arms Inn in Warwick-Lane, MDCXCVII.

8°. Pp. [xix], 1-80, 10-80, 1-80, 1-64, 1-80, 1-110, [ii].

Notes: *Preface* signed D. Jones., Clerkenwell, Nov. 9th. 1696. In his *Life and Errors* Dunton wrote that Richard Wolley "took the *private* Minutes that composed 'The Secret History of Whithall'", and that "Mr. Harris and I were Partners in ... 'The Secret History of Whitehall'" (L&E 163, 231). In his "Advertisement. To ... Honest Booksellers", printed in *The State Weathercocks*, 1719, Dunton wrote: "I was forc'd to take *Six Guineas* for a Pyrated Edition of, *The Secret History of* White-hall; that probably wou'd have put *One Hundred* Guineas into my own Pocket, had I reprinted this *Secret History* my self (which owes its *Projection* and *Title to my Pen*, and was compos'd of *Memoirs* that I purchast my self from the *Secretary*, *Interpreter* to the Marquis of *Louvois*) .... [the honest booksellers belonging to the Conger] would not have Reprinted my *Secret History of Whitehall*, had not that *Welsh Knaw Post* D--- J--- meerly trickt 'em into this *Pyracy*, by affirming the Copy was his, tho' he own'd afterwards ... that he receiv'd *the Secret Memoirs* that compos'd it from my Hands; and the Truly Honest Mr. *George Ridpath* declar'd upon his Reading that Receipt which J---s gave me in full for his *Methodizing* this *Secret History of Whitehall*, that he never saw a *fairer or clearer Title* than I had to that Copy". Advertised by Richard Baldwin in T.C. III, 5 (Hilary 1697).

Location: Wing J 934 - L, O, C, E, DT; CLC, LC, MH, NC, NF, NU, Y.

290. THE WHOLE PARABLE OF DIVES AND LAZARUS, explain'd and apply'd: being several sermons preached in Cripplegate and Lothbury Churches. BY JOSEPH STEVENS, Lecturer at

both. Publish'd at the request of the hearers. And recommended as proper to be given at funerals.
London, Printed for John Dunton, at the Raven in Jewen-street, 1697.

8°. Pp. [1]-197, [xi]. Adv'ts, 11pp., at end.

Notes: T.C. III, 72 (Trinity 1698). L&E 152.

Location: Wing S 5499 - L; NU.

1698

291. AN ESSAY, PROVING, WE SHALL KNOW OUR FRIENDS IN HEAVEN. Writ by a disconsolate widower, on the death of his wife, and dedicated to her dear memory. Being a subject never handled before in a distinct treatise. Sent in a letter to a reverend divine.
London: Printed, and are to be Sold by E. Whitlock, near Stationers Hall, 1698.

8°. Pp. [1]-56, 1-95, [1].

Notes: Dedication To the Memory of Dear Eliza signed Philaret. From Eliza's Grave, July 10th. 1697. By John Dunton (H&L II, 203).

Location: Wing D 2624 - LCL; CU. Also, L.

292. Dunton's Irish Ramble, 1698.

During the eight months Dunton lived in Dublin in 1698, he published a number of advertisements, open letters, and auction sale catalogues; no surviving copy of any of these has been located, nor has any copy been located of the Dublin reprinted Flying Post, in which both Dunton and Patrick Campbel printed advertisements.

In his published account of The Dublin Scuffle, which Dunton published early in 1699, after his return to London, Dunton reprinted several of his Dublin letters and advertisements and alluded to others. The following list of Dunton's publications in Dublin has been compiled from The Dublin Scuffle.

I. Dunton's letters.

(1) An Account of the _Three Auctions_ to be held in the City of _Dublin_: In a Letter to the Wise, Learned, and Studious Gentlemen in the Kingdom of _Ireland_, but more especially to those in the City of _Dublin_.

Dublin June 24. 1698. (_Dublin Scuffle_, pp. 1-7)

(2) An Account of my Third Auction in _Dublin_, to be held at _Patt's_ Coffee-House, over against _St. Michael's_ Church in _High-street_, on _Monday November_ 7th, 1698, with my _Reasons_ for removing thither. In a second Letter to those Gentlemen, who have bought Books at my two former _Auctions_.

Dublin, Nov. 5th. 1698. (_Dublin Scuffle_, pp. 19-32)

(3) The Farewel-Sale at _Patt's_ Coffee-House.

Dublin, Nov. 23, 1698. (_Dublin Scuffle_, pp. 58-62)

(4) The Packing Penny.

Dublin, Decem. 12th. 1698. (_Dublin Scuffle_, pp. 67-70)

(5) My _Last Farewel_ To my Acquaintance in Dublin Whether Friends, or Enemies.

Dublin, Dec. 26. 1698. (_Dublin Scuffle_, pp. 108-51)

II. Dunton's advertisements.

It is not clearly stated, in _The Dublin Scuffle_, whether these advertisements were published as broadsides or printed in the Dublin reprinted _Flying Post_.

(1) [Begins:] _Gentlemen_, The Reasons for Removing my Third Auction to _Patt's_ Coffee-House ....

[Dublin, 2 November 1698] (_Dublin Scuffle_, pp. 41-2)

(2) [Begins:] A Brief Answer to some Lying and Scandalous Reflections, Published by _Richard Pue_, in the Reprinted _Flying Post_, _November_ 7. 1698.

[Dublin, 7 November 1698] (*Dublin Scuffle*, pp. 43-5)

III. Dunton's catalogues

The Dublin Scuffle, p. 5: "There will be a *Distinct Catalogue* for every *Auction*, and when Printed ... will be delivered *Gratis* at *Dick's Coffee-House*".

(1) Auction I, 7 July 1698. (*Dublin Scuffle*, p. 5)

(2) Auction II, date not known.

(3) Auction III, 7 November 1698. (*Dublin Scuffle*, p. 17)

IV. Richard Wilde's advertisements.

It is not clearly stated, in *The Dublin Scuffle*, whether these advertisements were published as broadsides or printed in the Dublin reprinted *Flying Post*.

(1) [Begins:] Whereas *R. Pue* hath Yesterday, by the Instigation of his Neighbour Mr. *Campbel*, Published in the Re-printed *Flying Post*, a Notorious False Advertisement ....

[Dublin, 8 November 1698] (*Dublin Scuffle*, pp. 45-6)

(2) [Begins:] My Friend Mr. *Dunton's Three* Auctions, *Farewel Sale*, and *Packing Penny*, ending this Night, I thought fit to give *Notice* to all the *Lovers* of *Learning*, That I *design* (God willing) within a few Days after Mr. Dunton's departure, to *Expose* by *Auction* a *considerable* Parcel of good Books of my own ....

[Dublin, 13 December 1698] (*Dublin Scuffle*, p. 71)

1699

293. THE DUBLIN SCUFFLE: being a challenge sent BY JOHN DUNTON, citizen of London, to Patrick Campbel, bookseller in Dublin. Together with the small skirmishes of bills and advertisements. To which is added, the billet doux, sent him by a citizens wife in Dublin, tempting him to lewdness. With his answers to her. Also some account of

his conversation in Ireland, intermixt with particular characters of the most eminent persons he convers'd with in that kingdom; but more especially in the city of Dublin. In several letters to the spectators of this scuffle; with a poem on the whole encounter.
London, (Printed for the Author) and are to be Sold by A Baldwin, near the Oxford-Arms in Warwick-Lane, and by the Booksellers in Dublin. 1699.

[Separate title-pages; following the above, with multiple register and continuous pagination:]
The billet doux, sent by a citizens-wife in Dublin tempting me to leudness: with my answers to her.
London: Printed by George Larkin, Jun. (for the Author) and are to be Sold by A. Baldwin near the Oxford-Arms in Warwick-Lane, and by the Booksellers in Dublin, 1699.

Some account of my conversation in Ireland. In a letter to an honourable lady. With her answer to it.
London: Printed (for the Author,) and are to be Sold by A. Baldwin, near the Oxford-Arms in Warwick-Lane, and by the Booksellers in Dublin. 1699.

Remarks on my conversation in Ireland. By an honourable lady.
London: Printed, and are to be Sold by A. Baldwin, near the Oxford-Arms in Warwick-lane, and by the Booksellers in Dublin. 1699.

8°. Pp. [viii], 1-16, 1-160, [ii], 201-246, [ii], 303-443, [iii], 503-544, [iv].

Notes: Dedication to Col. Butler signed John Dunton. London, February 20. 1698/9. There may also have been a Dublin edition of this work; see E.R.McC. Dix, List of Books ... Printed in Dublin from 1601-1700 (Dublin, 1905), citing Lowndes, I, 698 and Bibliotheca Hibernica; no copy has been located. CBEL II, 159. L&E xix, 491-647.

Location: Wing D 2622 - L, O, C, EN, DT; CH, CLC, LC, MH, WF, Y.

294. THE ART OF LIVING INCOGNITO, being a thousand letters on as many uncommon subjects. Written by John Dunton, during his retreat from the world. And sent to that honourable lady to whom he address'd his conversation in Ireland: with her answer to each letter. Part I. To be continued till the whole correspondence is finished.
London, Printed (for the Author) and are to be Sold by A Baldwin, near the Oxford Arms in Warwick-Lane. 1700. Price Stitcht 1s.

4°. Pp. [iv], [1]-72.

Notes: Dunton announced in the preface that "this whole Correspondence will be contained in about 200 parts (at 12d. each) , but only the second part was published.

Location: L, LCL; BN, CLC, CN, MH, Y. Wing D 2620.

295. THE SECOND PART of the art of living incognito, or, Dunton represented as dead and buried, in an essay upon his own funeral. To which is added, his essay upon every thing. .... To be continued 'till the whole correspondence is finish'd.
London, Printed (for the Author) and are to be sold by A. Baldwin near the Oxford Arms in Warwick-Lane; of whom is to be had the First and Second Part. Price of each 1s.

4°. Pp. [ii], 73-126, 201-224.

Location: Y, MH.

296. THE CASE OF JOHN DUNTON, Citizen of London: with respect to his mother-in-law, Madam Jane Nicholas, of St. Albans; and her only child, Sarah Dunton. With the just reasons for her husband's leaving her. In a letter to his worthy friend, Mr. George Larkin, Senior. To which is added, his letter to his wife.
London Printed, and are to be sold by A. Baldwin, near the Oxford Arms in Warwick-Lane. MDCC. Price Three Pence.

4°. Pp. [ii], 1-10.

Location: Wing D 2621 - MHL, Y. Also, MB.

297. A description of Mr. Dunton's Funeral Poem. [1700]

Notes: Not located.

298. -------- Second edition.

Notes: Advertised in The Post Man, 29 June 1700. Not located.

299. -------- Third edition.

Notes: Advertised in The Post Man, 10 August 1700. Not located.

300. An essay, proving, we shall know our friends in heaven. [By John Dunton] Second edition.

Notes: Advertised in The Art of Living Incognito, 1700, p. 71. First published in 1698. Not located.

301. [Drop-head title:]
REFLECTIONS on Mr. Dunton's leaving his wife. In a letter to himself.
[Unsigned, without imprint]

4°. Pp. 1-4.

Notes: Advertised in The Art of Living Incognito, p. 71: "... Price 1d. ... sold by A. Baldwin, near the Oxford Arms in Warwick Lane".

Location: MB.

302. A STEP TO OXFORD: or, a mad essay on the Reverend Mr. Tho. Creech's hanging himself, (as 'tis said) for love. With the character of his mistress. In a letter to a person of quality.

London: Printed in the Year, MDCC.

4°. Pp. [1]-23, [o].

Notes: L&E 252: "[Mr. Mead] .... printed for me, a while ago, 'A Step to Oxford'".

Location: Wing S 5410 - L, O; CU, Y.

1701

303. THE CASE IS ALTER"D: or, Dunton's re-marriage to the same wife. Being the first instance of that nature that has been in England. To which is added, the tender letters that pass'd between this new bride and bridegroom; the history of their courtship, &c. As also the articles agreed on for the ruling a wife, &c. With a poem on the re-marriage.
London, Printed; and Sold by A. Baldwin in Warwick-lane. 1701. Price Six Pence.

4°. Pp. [xx], 1-56.

Notes: Dedication to Madam Jane Nicholas signed John Dunton and dated London, Nov. 5. 1701. Dunton's poem on his re-marriage is "The Conjugal Amour". LA V, 80.

Location: L, O, DT; CLC.

304. THE MERCIFUL ASSIZES: or, a panegyric on the late Lord Jeffreys hanging so many in the West. With the lives, characters, and dying speeches of the many hundreds that were converted by his Lordship's sentence. As also some secret memoirs relating to the West, never publish'd till now. In a letter to Madam H--- who had a brother drawn, hang'd and quarter'd at Taunton.
London: Printed for Eliz. Harris at the Harrow in Little Britain; and are to be Sold by Thomas Wall in Bristol, Philip Bishop in Exeter, Henry Chalklin in Taunton, and by most other Booksellers in the West of England. An. Dom. 1701.

[Separate title-page; following the above, with

continuous register and separate pagination:] An answer to the panegyric on the late Lord Jeffreys. By a friend of the lady's, to whom 'twas directed.

London: Printed for Eliz. Harris at the Harrow in Little-Britain; and are to be Sold by Tho. Wall in Bristol, Philip Bishop in Exeter, Henry Chalklin in Taunton, and by most other Booksellers in the West of England. Anno Dom. 1701.

8°. Pp. [ii], [1]-238, 201-[365], [iii], [1]-24.
Adv'ts, 3pp., following p. 365.

Notes: Contains "To my Friend the Author, Upon his Surprising Book", signed G.L.S. [George Larkin, Senior]. By John Dunton. "My last Project ... was intituled 'The Merciful Assizes; or, A Panegyrick on the late Lord Jeffreys' hanging so many in the West'" (L&E 201). L&E 223. H&L IV, 66.

Location: L, O, E, LW, CE; Y, NN, CLC.

305. THE POST-ANGEL: in five distinct parts. Viz. I. The remarkable providences (of judgment and mercy) that hap'ned in January, &c. II. The lives and deaths of the most eminent persons that died in that month, &c. III. A new Athenian Mercury; resolving the most nice and curious questions proposed by the ingenious of either sex. IV. The publick news at home and abroad. V. An account of the books lately publish'd, and now going to the press. With a spiritual observator upon each head. To be continued monthly. This for January.

London: Printed and are to be sold by A. Baldwin, near the Oxford-Arms in Warwick-Lane. 1701. Price 1s.

[Imprint, from August, 1702:] London, Printed; And are to be sold by A. Baldwin, near the Oxford-Arms in Warwick-Lane; and Eliphal Faye, at the Golden-Candlestick, near Mercers-Hall, in Cheapside. 1702.

4°. Volume I, January - June, 1701.
Volume II, July - December, 1701.
Volume III, January - June, 1702.
Volume IV, July - September, 1702.

Notes: Continuous register and pagination in each volume. L&E 199, 252, 376. CBEL II, 676. C&K 740.

Location: L(entire); Y(Vols. I-III).

1702

306. The Daily Courant. Numb. 1. Wednesday, March 11. 1702.
Colop: London. Sold by E. Mallet, next Door to the King's Arms Tavern at Fleet-Bridge.
[From 22 April 1702:] London Printed, and Sold by Sam. Buckley at the Dolphin in Little-Britain.

No. 1, 11 March 1702 - No. 6002, 28 June 1735.

Notes: W. T. Morgan, A Bibliography of British History (1700-1715) (Bloomington, Indiana, 1934-42), V47. Morgan states that "This paper was at first edited by John Dunton and printed and sold by Mallet next door to the Kings' Arms Tavern at Fleet Bridge, London. By April 22, 1702, it was both edited and printed by Samuel Buckley at the sign of the Dolphin in Little Britain". In 1702, Elizabeth Mallet published for Dunton Petticoat-Government, The New Quevedo, The Secret Mercury, and The History of Living Men; but I have found no evidence that Dunton was concerned in the writing of The Daily Courant.

307. THE HISTORY OF LIVING MEN: or, characters of the royal family, the ministers of state, and the principal natives of the three kingdoms. Being an essay on a thousand persons that are now living. With a poem upon each life. Dedicated to His Royal Highness, Prince George of Denmark.
London, Printed and are to be Sold by E. Mallet near Fleet-Bridge, 1702.

8°. Pp. [xviii], 1-118.

Notes: Published 15 August 1702 (adv't, The Post Man, 15 August 1702). Dedication signed John Dunton. "For want of room", Dunton reserved many characters "for The Second part of the Living History;

which will be publish'd in a few Weeks, if this _First Part_ meets with Encouragement" (p. 118). Many of the characters in this work were later used in Dunton's _Life and Errors_, 1705. L&E 260, 272.

Location: _EN_; Y.

308. _The New Quevedo_; or a Vision of Charon's Passengers from the Creation of the World down to this present Year 1702, with their Names, Qualities, and particular Crimes. Written by the Author of _The Post-Angel_. Price 1 _s_.

Notes: Dunton advertised the above in _Petticoat-Government_, 1702, where he also advertised, as in the press, the second part of _The New Quevedo_, to be "Sold by _E. Mallet_ near _Fleetstreet-Bridge_: Of whom is to be had the First Part, already Publish'd". Part I was advertised in _The Post Man_, 19 May 1702; and according to an advertisement in _The Post Man_ on 28 July, the second part was published on 28 July 1702. Part I was reviewed in _The Post Angel_, March 1702. _The New Quevedo_ was one of seven works which Dunton later regretted publishing (L&E 159).

Location: IU.

309. PETTICOAT-GOVERNMENT. In a letter to the court ladies. By the author of The Post-Angel.
London, Printed and are to be Sold by E. Mallet near Fleet-Bridge, 1702. Price 1 s.

8°. Pp. [viii], 1-111, [i]. Adv'ts, 1p., at end.

Notes: Published 2 July 1702 (adv't, _The Post Man_, 2 July 1702). See also _The Prerogative of the Breeches_, 1702.

Location: _O_.

310. THE PREROGATIVE OF THE BREECHES, in a letter to the sons of men: being an answer to Petticoat-Government. Written by a true-born English man.

London: Printed, and are to be Sold by A. Baldwin, at the Oxford-Arms in Warwick-Lane. MDCCII. Price Six Pence.

8°. Pp. [viii], 1-40.

Notes: Published 14 July 1702 (adv't, The Post Man, 14 July 1702).

Location: O.

311. Religio bibliopolae. [Reprinted, 1702?]
London: Printed for C. Corbett, opposite St. Dunstan's Church, Fleet-Street. [Price 1s. 6d.]

8°. Pp. [ii], 1-2, [1]-84.

Notes: Religio Bibliopolae was first published in 1691. This edition has a new preface. Keynes, Bibl. of Sir Thomas Browne (Cambridge, 1924), No. 416.

Location: L, GK, GM, A.N.L.Munby.

312. THE SECRET MERCURY. Or the adventure of seven days. To be continued weekly. From Wednesday Sept. 2. to Wednesday Sept. 9. 1702. [From No. 2:] The Secret Mercury. Or the adventures of seven days
London Printed for Eliz. Mallet, near Fleet-Bridge. 1702.

No. 1, 9 September 1702 - No. 4, 30 September 1702.

Notes: Attributed to Dunton by T. M. Hatfield (The True Secret History of Mr. John Dunton, unpublished thesis, Harvard University, 1926, pp. 164-5), who had seen only an announcement for the paper in The Post Man, 15 September 1702; "the tone of the announcement is perfectly [Dunton's]". The tone of the paper itself ("The main design of this Paper is to expose the Vanity and secret lewdness of the Town") is as well perfectly Dunton's, and it may be attributed to him without question.

Location: O.

313. THE ATHENIAN ORACLE: being an entire collection of all the valuable questions and answers in the old Athenian Mercuries. Intermix'd with many cases in divinity, history, philosophy, mathematics, love, poetry, never before published. To which is added, an alphabetical table for the speedy finding of any questions. By a member of the Athenian Society.
London, Printed, for Andrew Bell, at the Cross-Keys and Bible, in Cornhil, near Stocks Market, 1703.

8°. 3 volumes: Vols. I, II, 1703; Vol. III, 1704.

Notes: Volume I published 4 March 1703 (adv't, The Post Man, 4 March 1703). Dunton sold to Andrew Bell the copyright of the old questions and answers from The Athenian Mercury, and Bell intended to publish four volumes, if the project met with success; Dunton reserved the right to continue the project with fresh material (their agreement is in the Bodleian Library, Ms. Rawlinson D 72, no. 67). Volume II was published 2 May 1703 (adv't, The Post Man, 2 May 1703). CBEL II, 186, 187, 199.

Location: C, CS(Vol. III); BN(Vols. I, II).

The Athenian Oracle. Later editions. 1703 - 1728.

Notes: To the three volumes of the Oracle was added a fourth, A Supplement, first published in 1710. The Athenian Oracle was a popular work, and several editions were printed to 1728; most sets of the Oracle consist of four volumes, of varying editions. Later editions of the work were as follows, all with the imprint of Andrew Bell, except where noted:

Vol. I. The Second Edition more Correct, 1704.
The Third Edition Corrected, 1706.
The Third edition. London, Printed for J. and J. Knapton, A. Bettesworth, W. Mears, F. Fayram, J. Osborn and T. Longman, W. Innys and C. Rivington. M.DCC.XXVIII.

Vol. II. The Second Edition Corrected, 1704.
The Third Edition Corrected, 1708.
The Third Edition. London, Printed for J. and J. Knapton, A. Bettesworth, W. Mears, F. Fayram, J. Osborn and T. Longman, W. Innys, and C. Rivington. M.DCC.XXVIII.

Vol. III. The Second Edition, 1706.
The Third edition, 1716.
The Third Edition. London, Printed for J. and J. Knapton, A. Bettesworth, W. Mears, F. Fayram, J. Osborn and T. Longman, W. Innys, and C. Rivington. M.DCC.XXVIII.

Vol. IV. [First published as _A Supplement to the Athenian Oracle_, 1710]
The Third Edition. London, Printed for J. and J. Knapton, A. Bettesworth, W. Mears, F. Fayram, J. Osborn and T. Longman, W. Innys, and C. Rivington. M.DCC.XXVIII.

314. A SATYR UPON KING WILLIAM; being the secret history of his life and reign. Written by a gentleman that was near his person for many years.
London, Printed in the Year, 1703.

8°. Pp. [xxvi], 1-84, [ii].

Location: _O_; LC.

315. -------- Second edition.

Location: MB.

316. -------- Third edition.
London, Printed in the Year, 1703.

8°. Pp. [xxvi], 1-84, [ii].

Notes: The fourth edition was printed in _Athenianism_, 1710.

Location: _O_.

317. The Secret History of the Calves Head Club. 1703.

Notes: Often attributed, incorrectly, to Dunton. The problem was discussed by R.J. Allen, in The Clubs of Augustan London (Cambridge, Mass., 1933), pp. 58-61; Allen attributed The Secret History to Edward Ward. Ward stated that the "anthems" included in The Secret History were composed by Benjamin Bridgwater (see entry for Religio Bibliopolae, 1691), and Edward Arber, in his edition of the Term Catalogues, erroneously assumed this to be a pseudonym of John Dunton.

318. THE SHORTEST-WAY WITH WHORES AND ROGUES: or, a new project for reformation. Dedicated to Mr. Daniel de Foe, author of The Shortest Way with Dissenters.
London, Printed in the Year 1703.

8°. Pp. [xii], 1-106, [ii].

Notes: By John Dunton; attributed to Dunton in an advertisement for the second edition in The Post Man, 15 April 1703; the first edition was advertised anonymously in The Post Man, 9 April 1703.

Location: LV; MB, Y.

319. -------- Second edition.

Notes: Advertised in The Post Man, 15 April 1703.

1704

320. ATHENAE REDIVIVAE: or the new Athenian Oracle, under three general heads, viz. I. The divine oracle .... II. The philosophick and miscellaneous oracle .... III. The secret (or ladies) oracle .... Vol. I Part I [-VI]. To be continued in this method, till the question-project is compleated.
London: Printed by Geo: Larkin, for S. Malthus, in London-House-Yard, at the West End of St. Pauls. 1704.

8°. Six parts, with continuous register and pagination,

complete Volume I.

Notes: Narcissus Luttrell's copies of parts I-V, at Yale, are dated: I, 2 June; II, 1. July 1704; III, 12 August 1704; IV, 4. September. 1704; V, 5. October 1704. In Part VI, to which Dunton added an index to the volume, Dunton announced that "_The Second Volume of the New Athenian Oracle_ ... will be publish'd Compleat at _Lady Day_ - The Third Volume at _Midsummer_; and so 'twill be continued to be publish'd (_Quarterly_) in Volumes ..... Querists may continue to send .... to _Smith's Coffee-House_, in _Stocks-Market_". L&E 195-6.

Location: _L_(Parts I-VI), C(Part IV); _Y_(Parts I-V).

321. The Athenian Catechism. Volume I, nos. 1-20, 1704.

Notes: In _Athenae Redivivae_, 1704 (Part V, p. 198), Dunton advertised that "On the Tenth of _October_ we shall publish a weekly Paper, Entituled, _The Athenian Catechism_ (_or Universal Instructor_) To which we shall add, _Pegasus; Or, News for the Ingenious_ and hope to make it a Pleasant Entertainment for the Lovers of Novelty .... Thirty numbers shall compleat a Volume, to which we'll add, _A General Title_, _Preface_, and _Contents_. This Athenian Catechism, will be sold at _A Penny each Numb._ that the poorer Sort may be able to buy it, and will be publish'd twice every week, (_viz._ _Tuesday_ and _Friday_). [sgd:] _New Athens_". Volume I, containing 20 numbers, was advertised in _Dunton's Whipping-Post_, 1706; the contents of the volume were listed in this advertisement. No. 17 of _The Athenian Catechism_ was referred to in _The Observator_, 23 December 1704, and _The Rehearsal_, No. 21. L&E 332. LA V, 77. _Not located._

322. THE ATHENIAN SPY: discovering the secret letters which were sent to the Athenian Society by the most ingenious ladies of the three kingdoms .... Intermix'd with great variety of poems. Being an intire collection of love-secrets communicated from time to time to the Athenian

Society.
London, Printed for R. Halsey, at the Bible in the Poultrey, at the corner of the Old Jewry. 1704.

12°. Pp. [xxii], [1]-242, *1-*36, 219-326.

Notes: Published 23 February 1704 (adv't, The Observator, 23 February 1704). A second edition of this work was published in 1709. Dunton published a periodical of the same title in 1720.

Location: O; LC, MH, CU.

323. THE NEW PRACTICE OF PIETY; writ in imitation of Dr. Browne's Religio Medici: or the Christian virtuoso: discovering the right way to heaven between all extreams. To which is added, a satyr on the House of Lords ....
London: [Print]ed in the Year MDCCIV. [Title-page mutilated]

8°. Pp. [xxvi], 1-5, 8-64, 51-70.

Notes: Dedication to John Lock signed H.N. The New Practice of Piety is an expanded version of Religio Bibliopolae, 1691. Printed by Edward Brewster (L&E 207). Advertised by S. Malthus in T.C. III, 397 (Easter 1704). Keynes, Bibl. of of Sir Thomas Browne (Cambridge, 1924), no. 418. L&E 200, 478. H&L IV, 178.

Location: O.

324. -------- Second edition.
London: Printed for S. Malthus, in London-House-Yard, at the West-End of St. Pauls. 1704.

8°. Pp. [xxvi], 1-5, 8-64, 51-70.

Notes: Published 3 July 1704 (adv't, The Observator, 1 July 1704). Advertised by J. Marshall in T.C. III, 444 (Hilary 1705). A third edition was published by Marshall in 1705. Keynes, Bibl. of Sir Thomas Browne (Cambridge, 1924), no. 419.

Location: L.

325. The Picture of a High-Flyer. 1704.

Notes: Included, with doubts, by T. M. Hatfield in his checklist of Dunton's works (T. M. Hatfield, The True Secret History of Mr. John Dunton, unpublished thesis [Harvard University, 1926], p. 425). Advertised with other tracts by Dunton in The Observator, 15 July 1704. Not located.

326. A Poetick Chronicle, Or History of the Times in Verse, To be publish'd in Parts, 12d. each .... If this Historical Poem meets with Encouragement, we shall continue to publish it every Quarter ....

Notes: Dunton advertised the above in Athenae Redivivae, Part V, September 1704, p. 198b, as preparing for the press. See also L&E 352.

327. THE ROYAL DIARY: or, King William's interiour portraicture. Containing I. His secret devotion .... II. His practice of self-examination .... III. His conscientious performance .... IV. His serious inquiry .... V. His religious conferences .... VI. His table-talk .... VII. His occasional speeches .... VIII. The private minutes relating to his last sickness. Part of this diary was written by King William and found amongst his papers since his death.
London: Printed for S. Malthus, in London-House-Yard at the West-End of St. Pauls.

8°. Pp. [vi], [1]-90.

Notes: Advertised as "newly published" in Athenae Redivivae, part I, June 1704. Advertised by Malthus in T.C. III, 397 (Easter 1704).

Location: O.

328. -------- The second edition. To which is prefixt, the character of his royal consort, Queen Mary II. With her memorable speeches and sayings, from her childhood to the time of her death.
London: Printed for S. Malthus in London-House-Yard, at the West-End of St. Pauls, Price 1 s.

8°. Pp. [iv], 1-11, [i], [1]-90.

Notes: Advertised by J. Marshall in T.C. III, 444 (Hilary 1705). Marshall published the third edition in 1705. Three works written by Dunton, and another work of which he owned the copyright, are advertised on f. A_8v, "Printed for S. Malthus".

Location: EN.

329. Yet Plainer English, or the Shortest-Way to convert the Atheist, Murderer, Thief, Whore-master, Strumpet, Drunkard, Swearer, Lyar, Sabbath-breaker, Slanderer, Persecutor, Coward, Gamester, Ungrateful, Scold; and other Scandalous Livers, Dedicated to the Reverend Mr. William Bissett Author of the Reformation-Sermons, entituled, Plain English, and more Plain English. Price 1 s.

Noted: Advertised as above in The Royal Diary, second edition, 1704. Published 15 July 1704 (adv't, The Observator, 15 July 1704). L&E 369. Not located.

1705

330. A CAT MAY LOOK ON A QUEEN: or, a satyr on her present majesty.
London: Printed in the Year 1705.

8°. Pp. [xii], 1-75, [i]. Adv'ts, 1p., at end.

Notes: Dedication to the Queen, signed J.N. [O copy is signed J.N., the N being altered to D in ink; Y copy is unaltered.] Advertised in Dunton's catalogue printed in Athenian News: Or, Dunton's Oracle, Vol. I, No. 1, 7 March 1710.

Location: O; CN, MB, Y.

331. THE LIFE AND ERRORS OF JOHN DUNTON late citizen of London; written by himself in solitude. With an idea of a new life; wherein is shewn how he'd think, speak, and act,

might he live over his days again: intermix'd with the new discoveries the author has made in his travels abroad, and in his private conversation at home. Together with the lives and characters of a thousand persons now living in London, &c. Digested into seven stages, with their respective ideas.
London: Printed for S. Malthus, 1705.

8°. Pp. [xx], 1-368, 353-463, 200-251, [i]. Adv'ts, 1p., at end.

Notes: Dunton was at work on his autobiography as early as 1702, when it was announced as "preparing for the Press" in The History of Living Men, 1702, p. 118.

Location: L, O, C, LCL, LV.

332. The new practice of piety. Third edition.
London: Printed for John Marshall at the Bible in Gracechurch-street. MDCCV.

8°. A-O^4.

Notes: The above description from Keynes, Bibl. of Sir Thomas Browne (Cambridge, 1924), no. 421; Keynes states that this edition contains a portrait of Dunton, and he cites one copy, in the collection of Cosmo Gordon. Advertised by Marshall in T.C. III, 474 (Trinity 1705), 598 (Easter/Trinity 1708). First published in 1704.

Location: Cosmo Gordon.

333. PLAIN FRENCH: or, a satyr upon the Tackers. To which is added the character of a true patriot. Written to caution and direct English free-holders in the choice of a new Parliament; and particularly the electors in Bucks. By John Dunton, a free-holder of the same county. The fourth edition, corrected and enlarged.
London: Printed in the Year MDCCV.

8°. Pp. [ii], 1-38, 23-30.

Notes: No other editions of this work have been located.

Location: O, LV.

334. A Ramble through Six Kingdoms, By John Dunton, late Citizen of London. Wherein he relates, 1. His Juvenile Travels. 2. The History of his Sea Voyages. 3. His Conversation in Foreign Parts. With Characters of Men and Women, and almost ev'ry thing he Saw or Convers'd with. The like Discoveries (in such a Method) never made by any Traveller before. Illustrated with Fourty Cuts, representing the most pleasant Passages in the whole Adventure. With Recommendatory Poems, written by the chief Wits in both Universities.

Notes: Dunton advertised the above in his Life and Errors, 1705, as preparing for the press; although the work was not published, Dunton's manuscript, called A Summer's Ramble, survives in the Bodleian Library, Ms. Rawlinson D 71.

335. The royal diary. Third edition.
London, Printed for John Marshall, at the Bible in Gracechurch-street. MDCCV.

8°. Pp. [iv], 1-11, [i], [1]-90.

Notes: Frontispiece, a portrait of King William III, signed T.B. Sc. First published in 1704.

Location: O.

336. THE WESTERN MARTYROLOGY: or, bloody assizes .... Together with the life and death of George L. Jeffreys. The fifth edition ....
London: Printed for John Marshall at the Bible in Grace-Church-Street. M DCC V.

[Separate title-page; following the above, with continuous register and pagination:] An impartial history of the life and death of George Lord Jeffreys .... The fifth edition, with large additions.
London: Printed for John Marshall at the Bible in Grace-Church Street. M DCC V.

8°. Pp. [xvi], 1-231, 228-279, [i]. Adv'ts, 1p., at end.

Notes: Dunton first published A New Martyrology in 1689. In Athenae Redivivae, 1704 (Part IV, pp. 156-7), it was advertised that "The Book Intituled, The New Martyrology .... having bin out of Print, for several Years, and now much wanted, A West-Country Gentleman .... is now preparing a Fifth Edition of the said Book, for the Press, which he Entitles, The Western Martyrology .... 'Tis desired, That all Gentlemen that have any WESTERN MEMOIRS, proper to be inserted in this Work .... that they'd send .... to Mrs. Malthus in London-House-Yard ...."

Location: O.

1706

337. DUNTON'S WHIPPING-POST: or, a satyr upon every body. To which is added, a panegyrick on the most deserving gentlemen and ladies in the three kingdoms. With the whoring-pacquet: or, news of the st--ns and kept m---s's. Vol. I. To which is added, the living elegy: or, Dunton's letter to his few creditors. With the character of a summer-friend. Also, the secret history of the weekly writers, in a distinct challenge to each of them.
London: Printed, and are to be Sold by B. Bragg, at the Black Raven in Pater-noster-Rowe. 1706.

[Separate title-page; following the above, with double register and separate pagination:] The living elegy: or, Dunton's letter (being a word of comfort) to his few creditors: with the character of a summer-friend. To which is added, the lives, religion, and honesty of the Moderator, Wandering Spy, Rehearsal, London C--D (alias Post) Interloping Whipster, and the other attachers of my person and goods.
London: Printed in the year 1706.

8°. Pp. [vi], [1]-28, 27-120, [1]-63, [i]. Adv'ts, 1p. at end.

Notes: Dunton has often been identified as the author of The Whipping-Post, At a New Session of Oyer and Terminer, which began publication in 1705; in fact, Dunton in 1705 had projected a journal called *The Whipping Post*, although it did not appear until 1706. Meanwhile, the "interloping Whipster" had begun publication. The interloper was William Pittis; for a discussion of the two works, see Theodore Newton, "William Pittis and Queen Anne Journalism" in *Modern Philology*, XXXIII (1935-6), 169-86, 279-302. This work includes *The Living Elegy*, which is dated April the 10th, 1706.

Location: L, O, LV; Y.

338. An Essay upon Dead Men's Shoes, &c.

Notes: First announced in Part I of *The Art of Living Incognito*, 1700, p. 71, to be included in Part II, this essay was described as "now ready for the Press" in *Dunton's Whipping-Post*, 1706 (L&E 465).

1707

339. ATHENIAN SPORT: or, two thousand paradoxes merrily argued, to amuse and divert the age: .... By a member of the Athenian Society.
London, Printed for B. Bragg in Pater-noster-Row. 1707.

8°. Pp. [i]-xxxii, 1-544.

Notes: *Preface* signed Philaret, a Member of Athens. Eight of the paradoxes in this work were reprinted from John Donne's *Paradoxes and Problems*; see G.R. Potter, "Donne's Paradoxes in 1707", *Modern Language Notes*, LV(1940), p. 53; and Sir Geoffrey Keynes, *Bibl. of John Donne* (London, 1958), p. 75. CBEL II, 187. H&L I, 156.

Location: L, O, C, CE, CS, LLL, DT, E, GK.

340. BUMOGRAPHY: or, a touch at the Lady's tails, being a lampoon (privately) dispers'd at Tunbridge-Wells, in the year 1707. By a water-drinker. With the names and characters of the most noted water-drinkers. Also, a merry elegy upon Mother Jefferies, the antient water-dipper. London: Printed in the Year MDCCVII.

8°. Pp. [ii], i-vi, v-xviii, [ii], 1-56.

Notes: Narcissus Luttrell's copy, at the British Museum, is dated 29 November. In Stinking Fish, 1708, p. 18, Dunton mentioned "my Tunbridge Lampoon, entitled A Touch at the Lady's Tails: To which is annexed A Merry Elegy on Mother Jeffries, the Antient Water-Dipper". A second edition, called The Rump, or a Touch at the Ladies Tails, was published in 1708.

Location: L.

341. Heaven, Or, The Celestial Court; An Heroick Poem. Attempted by the Author of The Pulpit Fool.

Notes: Advertised as preparing for the press in The Pulpit-Fool, 1707, p. 40.

342. The He-Strumpets: A Satyr on the Sodomite-Club.

Notes: In Bumography, 1707, p. ii, Dunton referred to the "He-Strumpets .... A title given to the Sodomite-Club, in my Satyr Entituled the He-Strumpets. Sold by B. Bragge in Pater-noster-Rowe"; and in Athenianism, 1710, Dunton printed the "fourth edition" of The He-Strumpets: A Satyr on the Sodomite-Club. No copy of a separate printing has been located. In 1725, Dunton planned to revive the title, and he announced in The Athenian Library that future numbers were to contain a variety of essays, including The He-Strumpets (p. viii).

343. THE PHENIX: or, a revival of scarce and valuable pieces from the remotest antiquity down to the present times. Being a collection of manuscripts and printed tracts, no

where to be found but in the closets of the curious. By a gentleman who has made it his business to search after such pieces for twenty years past.
London, Printed for J. Morphew near Stationers Hall. M.DCC.VII.

8°. Pp. [i]-vi, 1-570.

Notes: Published 10 April 1707 (adv't, Daily Courant No. 1605, 7 April 1707). Remarks and Collections of Thomas Hearne (Oxford, 1885-1921), II, 5: "April 13, 1707. Quaere about a Book, newly publish'd in 8vo, call'd the Phoenix, which pretends to give an Account of Fragments from MSSts, in which the Author says he has been conversant for about 20 years .... The Publisher sd to be Mr. Collins who had a Hand in the Rights of the Church". The second volume of The Phenix appeared in 1708. H&L IV, 332.

Location: L, LW, CE, DU, EN.

344. THE PULPIT-FOOL. A satyr.
London: Printed in the Year M DCC VII.

THE SECOND PART OF THE PULPIT-FOOL. A satyr. Containing, a distinct character of the most noted clergy-men in the Queens dominions, both Church-men and Dissenters.
London: Printed for B. Bragge at the Raven in Paternoster-Row, of whom is to be had the First Part of the Pulpit-Fool, a Satyr, which (together with the Second Part) comprehends a general History of the Clergy in Verse; but more especially of such as are Heterodox, Leud, and Noted for Railing at Protestant Dissenters. 1707.

4°. Part I: Pp. [vi], 1-66. Part II: Pp. [1]-36, 33-40.

Notes: The British Museum owns Narcissus Luttrell's copies, dated in his hand 22 May and 15 July. Thomas Hearne wrote of The Pulpit-Fool: "July 17, 1707. There is just publish'd the IId Part of The Pulpit Fool, by John Dunton a poor craz'd silly Fellow. In it he gives Characters of ye chief & most Learned (as he calls 'em) of ye Low

Clergy Dissenters as well as others" (Remarks and Collections of Thomas Hearne [Oxford, 1885-1921], II, 26). H&L IV, 460.

Location: L(Parts I, II), O(I); CH(I), MH(I, II), MB(II), WF(I), Y(I, II).

1708

345. A cat may look on a Queen: or, a satyr on her present majesty. Attempted by John Dunton, author of the Satyr on King William. The Second Edition. To which is added, a distinct account of the several jewels in the crown of England.
London: Printed, and are to be Sold by John Morphew, near Stationer's Hall. M DCC VIII.

8°. Pp. [xii], 1-75, [i], 1-2.

Notes: Dedication signed J.N. L copy dated in ms. on title-page: 2 August. Advertised by John Morphew in T.C. III, 623 (Michaelmas/Hilary 1708/9). First published in 1705.

Location: L; BN, MH.

346. THE HAZARD OF A DEATH-BED-REPENTANCE, fairly argued, from the late remorse of W--- late D--- of D--- .... To which is added, conjugal perjury, or an essay upon whoredom; address'd to the husbands of quality that keep misses.
London: Printed in the Year M DCC VIII.

8°. Pp. [1]-56.

Notes: "Conjugal Perjury" is not present in this edition; it was first printed in The Hazard of a Death-Bed-Repentance, further argued, 1708, and it was also printed with the tenth edition of The Hazard .... fairly argued, 1728. LA IV, 88; V, 59-83. H&L III, 16.

Location: L, O, C, CT.

347. -------- [anr edn] [Double-rule border surrounding title]
London: Printed in the Year M DCC VIII.

8°. Pp. [ii], i-vi, 1-63, [i]. Adv'ts, 1p., at end.

Location: L, O, C, CS.

348. -------- Second edition. [Double-rule border surrounding title]
London: Printed by R. Tookey, and are to be Sold by J. Morphew, near Stationer's Hall. 1708.

8°. Pp. [ii], i-vi, 1-63, [i]. Adv'ts, 1p., at end.

Location: L, O, C; MB.

349. -------- Third edition.

Notes: Advertised by John Morphew in T.C. III, 623 (Michaelmas/Hilary 1708/9). Not located.

350. -------- [other editions]

Notes: In The Bull-Baiting, 1709, p. 1, Dunton wrote of The Hazard: "... six Times Printed in London,* [*With the Three Editions the Pyratical Printers robb'd me of] several Times at Oxford, Dublin Holland and Edinburgh"; the Oxford edition is also referred to in William Egerton's Faithful Memoirs of the Life ... of Mrs. Anne Oldfield, 1731, p. 119.

351. THE HAZARD OF A DEATH-BED-REPENTANCE, further argued, from the late remorse of W--- late D--- of D--- with serious reflections on his adulterous life. Being a second answer to Dr. K---'s sermon preach'd at the D---'s. Funeral .... To which is added, conjugal perjury, or an essay upon whoredom; address'd to the husbands of quality that keep misses. With the secret history of the author's failings, or D--- at confession.
London: Printed in the Year M DCC VIII.

8°. Pp. [1]-56.

Notes: Published September 1708 (adv't, The Supplement, 1 October 1708). "Conjugal Perjury" is present in this work, but the author's secret history of his failings was reserved for a future edition. Advertised by John Morphew in T.C. III, 623 (Michaelmas/Hilary 1708/9).

352. The Rump, or a Touch at the Ladies Tails, being a Lampoon privately dispers'd at Tunbridge-Wells in the Year 1707. by a Water-drinker; with the Names and Characters of the most noted Water-drinkers: Also a Merry Elegy upon Mother Jeff'ries, the antient water-dipper; the Second Edition. To which is added, The Lady's Dressing-room, or the Morning Conference between the Beauish Mistress and her Tire-woman, whilst they equip for Tunbridge-Wells. Price 1s.

Notes: Dunton advertised the above in his catalogue which was published with the index to Athenian News, Volume I, 1710. Published 12 July 1708 (adv't, The Supplement, 12 July 1708). Advertised by John Morphew in T.C. III, 623 (Mich./Hilary 1708/09). First published in 1707, as Bumography.

353. THE SECOND VOLUME OF THE PHENIX: or, a revival of scarce and valuable pieces no where to be found but in the closets of the curious. With a preface giving some account of the pieces in this volume.
London, Printed for J. Morphew near Stationers Hall. M.DCC.VIII. Where may be had the First Volume.

8°. Pp. [i]-[xvi], 1-552.

Notes: The first volume of The Phenix was published in 1707. Remarks and Collections of Thomas Hearne (Oxford, 1885-1921), II, 94: "Feb. 15, 1708. A Second Vol. of ye Phoenix, containing divers scarce Papers, &c. was lately publish'd. The Publisher Mr. Collins, who is of Deistical Republican Principles, & 'tis sd had a very great Hand in ye Rights of ye Church"; also II, 102, 194. Dunton announced a third volume of The Phenix, in Neck or Nothing, 1713; but it was not published (p. 55). Dunton later used the title for one of the departments of his Athenian Spy, 1720.

Location: L, LW, CE, DU, EN.

354. Sir Courtley, or a Touch at the Beaus, however dignify'd or distinguished. Sold by John Morphew near Stationer's Hall.

Notes: Advertised as preparing for the press in Stinking Fish, 1708, p. 79; also in Stinking Fish, p. 90, Dunton announced that "In December next will be publish'd Sir Courtley .... Being a Tunbridge Lampoon for the Year 1708".

355. STINKING FISH: or, a foolish poem, attempted by John the hermit. Part I. To be continu'd 'till the hermit has cry'd all his stinking fish. i.e. publish'd a secret, as well as publick history, of all the fools and knaves in the world.
London: Printed by R. Tookey, and are to be Sold by John Morphew, near Stationer's Hall. M DCC VIII. Of whom also is to be had the Tunbridge Lampoon, entitl'd The Rump, or a Touch at the Ladies Tails. The Second Edition; written by the same Author.

8°. Pp. [ii], i-ix, [i], 1-44, 49-89, [i]. Adv'ts, 1 1/2pp., at end.

Notes: Published 16 July 1708 (adv't, The Supplement, 16 July 1708). Advertised by Morphew in T.C. III, 623 (Michaelmas/Hilary 1708/9). Part II was advertised in The Works of the Learned, July 1708; no copy has been located.

Location: L, O.

1709

356. THE ATHENIAN SPY: .... The Second Edition, Enlarg'd.
London: Printed for R.H. and Sold by Samuel Ballard, at the Blue-Ball in Little-britain, 1709. Price 2s.

12°. Pp. [xxii], [1]-194, 219-242, *1-*36, 219-326.

Notes: Dedication to Mrs. Singer, the Pindaric Lady, signed New Athens. First published in 1704.

Location: L.

357. THE BULL-BAITING: or, Sach--ll dress'd up in fire-works. Lately brought over from the bear-garden in Southwark; and expos'd for the diversion of the citizens of London, at six pence a-piece. By John Dunton, author of the answer to Dr. K--net, entitl'd The Hazard of a Death-Bed-Repentance. ....
London, Printed for the Author, and are to be Sold by John Morphew near Stationers-Hall; and take notice whatever of these Books are Publish'd, not having Mr. Morphew's Name to 'em (or that are Sold at a Lower Price than 6 d.) are a wrong to the Author and a Cheat to the Buyers; All such Stol'n and Imperfect Books, not containing the Fourth Part of Mr. Dunton's Original Copies. 1709.

8°. Pp. [iv], [1]-44, 37-44. Adv'ts, pp. 37-44.

Notes: F. Madan, Bibliography of Dr. Henry Sacheverell (Oxford, 1884), No. 194.

Location: L, O, DT, E, EN, CT, CS; CN, IU, MH, Y, InU.

358. -------- [anr edn]

Notes: In The Preaching Weathercock, 1712, Dunton wrote that a pirated edition of this work had been published at 3d. (p. 112).

359. [Title-page in black and red:]
THE CHRISTIANS'S GAZETTE: or, news chiefly respecting the invisible world. Being a pacquet for the pious virtuosi, on subjects never started before.
London: Printed by R. Tookey, and are to be Sold by John Morphew, near Stationer's Hall. M DCC IX.

8°. Pp. [ii], i-xvii, [i], 1-80.

Notes: Published 14 February 1709 (adv't, The Supplement, 14 February 1709). Dunton intended The Christians's Gazette "to be continued occasionally, as the Author's Time and Health will admit", but no further numbers appeared; the title, however, was revived in 1713. T.C. III, 623 (Michaelmas/Hilary 1708/9).

Location: EN, O; Y, InU.

360. The Second Bull-Baiting: Or, Sach--ll dress'd up again in Fire-works. By John Dunton, ... Being further Remarks on the Scandalous Sermon bellow'd out at St. Paul's before the Right Honourable the Lord Major and Court of Aldermen, by Dr. Sach--ll: To which is added Dunton's Religion, or his Reason's for conforming to the Rites and Ceremonies of the Church of England, with the Character of a True (not high or low) Church-man, as con-tradistinguish'd from Dr. Sach--ll, and his Tacking Brethren, the High-Flyers; also Dunton's Mite, or the Healing Project, being an Expedient for a General Conformity; address'd to the Protestant Dissenters of all Perswasions. To be sold by John Morphew, near Stationers Hall. Price 6 d.

Notes: Advertised as to be published "in a few days" in The Bull-Baiting, 1709, p. 44.

361. Vox Populi, vox Dei, being true maxims of government.... London, T. Harrison, 1709. [From the second edition, 1710:] The judgment of whole kingdoms and nations....

Notes: The University of Indiana Library owns Professor W. P. Trent's copy of this work, with his note: "This has been attributed to Lord Somers, John Dunton, Defoe, Charles Povey, and T. Harrison (the publisher). Harrison is the most likely". For discussion, see Sir Egerton Brydges, Censura Litteraria (second edition, London, 1815), VII, 5; T. M. Hatfield, The True Secret History of Mr. John Dunton, unpublished thesis (Harvard University, 1926), pp. 221-3; and H&L III, 206.

362. ATHENIANISM: or, the new projects of Mr. John Dunton, author of the essay entitl'd, The Hazard of a Death-Bed-Repentance. Being, six hundred distinct treatises .... To which is added, Dunton's farewel to printing .... Vol. I. ....

London: Printed by Tho. Darrack, in Peterborough-Court, in Little-Britain, and are to be Sold by John Morphew, near Stationers-Hall, and by most booksellers in London, and the Country. 1710. Price Bound 6s.

8°. Pp. [ii], i-[xxx], 1-224, i-[ix], [i], 11-360.

Notes: Published 12 January 1710 (adv't, The Bull-Baiting, 1709). Frontispiece, a portrait of Dunton engraved by Vandergucht. This volume contains 24 of the 600 essays promised on the title-page; in the dedication, Dunton lists 35 projects intended for the second volume, which was not published, although several of the essays were published separately. Dunton later gave the title Athenianism to one of the departments of The Athenian Spy, 1720. LA V, 78. CBEL II, 189.

Location: L, O, C; MH.

363. ATHENIAN NEWS: OR, DUNTON'S ORACLE. In three thousand several posts. To which is added, the casuistical-post, or Athenian mercury, resolving the most nice and curious questions propos'd by the ingenious of either sex .... Enter'd into the hall-book of the Company of Stationers, pursuant to Act of Parliament.

London, Printed by T. Darrack, in Peterborough-Court in Little-Britain, and Sold by J. Morphew near Stationers Hall, and at most Booksellers Shops in Town and Country. Price 2s. 6d. stitch'd in blue Paper.

Volume I. No. 1, Tuesday, 7 March 1710 to No. 30, Saturday, 17 June 1710 (issued Tuesday and Saturday).
Volume II. No. 1, Tuesday, 20 June 1710 to No. 26, Saturday, 16 September 1710 (no more published; publication suspended after No. 26 because of ill-health; "Numb. 26 .... compleats the Second Volume").

Notes: Stationers' Register, Entry Book of Copies, 4 July 1710, Dunton, as sole proprietor, entered Volume I; Volume II entered 20 October 1710. C&K 1034. CBEL II, 660.

Location: L(Vol. I), C(Vols. I-II).

364. A SUPPLEMENT TO THE ATHENIAN ORACLE: being a collection of the remaining questions and answers in the old Athenian Mercuries. Intermixt with many cases in divinity, history, philosophy, mathematicks, love, poetry, never before publish'd. To which is prefix'd the history of the Athenian Society, and an essay upon learning. By a member of the Athenian Society.
London: Printed for Andrew Bell, at the Cross-Keys and Bible in Cornaill, near Stocks-Market, 1710.

8°. Pp. [ii], 1-487, [xv]. Adv'ts, 1 1/2 pp., at end.

Notes: Advertised by Bell in T.C. III, 677 (Easter 1711). H&L V, 395. Frontispiece: a reproduction of the engraving of the Athenian Society which had first appeared in The Young Students Library, 1692. Reprinted in 1728, as Volume IV of The Athenian Oracle.

Location: C, CS, G, E, LL; BN, Y.

1712

365. HIGH-CHURCH: or a vindication of the Reverend Mr. William Richardson, from near an hundred aspersions that are cast upon him, by Mr. John Dunton, in his paradox intituled The Preaching Weather-Cock.... In a letter to Doctor Calamy a dissenting minister. To which is added, killing no sin, or a panegyrick upon Mr. William Richardson, for attempting to murder his wife and mother ....
London. Printed by R. Tookey (for the Author) and Sold by J. Baker in Pater-noster-Row. 1712. Price 6d.

8°. Pp. [ii], [i]-ii, [1]-31, [i]. Adv'ts, 1p., at end.

Notes: Published 20 September 1712 (adv't, The Flying Post, 20 September 1712). Text signed J.H. Attributed by T.M. Hatfield to John Dunton (The True Secret History of Mr. John Dunton, unpublished thesis [Harvard University, 1926], pp. 254-9). Includes "To his most Ingenious and Reverend Friend, Mr. J.H.", by G.L.D. "Killing No Sin" is not present.

Location: L, LW, EN.

366. THE PREACHING-WEATHERCOCK: a paradox, proving Mr. W---R---dson (lately a dissenting minister, and now a Presbiter of the Church of England) will cant, recant, and re-recant, ... Written by John Dunton, a true and constant son of the Church of England, without respect to parties, and author of those two answers to Dean Kennet, and Dr. Sacheverel, intituled - The Bull-Baiting, - and Hazard of a Death-Bed-Repentance.

London, Printed by R. Tookey, for the Author, and Sold by the Booksellers of London and Westminster. Price One Shilling.

8°. Pp. [ii], i-vi, 1-112.

Notes: Published 14 May 1712 (adv't, The British Mercury, 14 May 1712). Entered by Dunton, Stationers' Register, Entry Book of Copies, 21 April 1712, stating that the copy was wholly owned by him. Dunton intended to publish this work in three parts, but only this first part was published (p. 112). LA V, 696.

Location: L, E, EN.

1713

367. THE CHRISTIANS GAZETTE: or nice and curious speculations chiefly respecting the invisible world. Being a pacquet for the pious virtuosi, ... To which is added, the lame-post, ... also the court-spy, ... The second edition, corrected and greatly enlarg'd.

London. Printed for the Author, and sold by J. Baker, in Pater-Noster-Row, and by most Booksellers in London and Westminster.

8°.   Pp. [i], i-ii, [i], 1-108.

Notes: Published 31 July 1713 (adv't, The Flying Post, 31 July 1713). Dunton first used the title The Christian's Gazette in 1709. The running title in this edition is "The Christian's Gazette, for January, February, March and April", but there is no evidence that this work was issued serially; presumably this issue, covering four months, was intended to be Part I (as it was advertised in The Impeachment, 1714). A second edition of The Court Spy was advertised in 1714. CBEL II, 660. C&K 107, 1169b.

Location: L, O, EN; MB, Y, InU.

368. -------- Third edition.

Notes: Mentioned by Dunton in several advertisements; see entry for Neck-Intelligence, 1715.

369. A Hue and Cry after Dr. Sacheverell By the author of the Hazard of a Death Bed Repentance.

Notes: Forthcoming publication announced in The Flying Post, 8 August 1713.

370. **NECK OR NOTHING:** in a letter to the Right Honourable the Lord ----- Being a supplement to The Short History of the Parliament. Also the new scheme (mention'd in the aforesaid history) which the English and Scotch Jacobites have concerted for bringing in the Pretender, popery and slavery. With the true character or secret history of the present ministry. Written by His Grace John Duke of ----.

London, Printed by T. Warner near Ludgate. 1713. Price 6 d.

8°.   Pp. [1]-60.

Notes: A Short History of the Parliament, by Sir Robert Walpole, had been published earlier in 1713. Narcissus Luttrell's copy of Neck or Nothing was dated 3 November (Pickering & Chatto, Booksellers, Catalogue 351, no. 320). Queen Robin, the second part of this work, was published in 1714; the third part, The Shortest Way with the King, in 1715. Later editions were advertised in 1715 and 1716; the "twentieth" edition was printed in The State Weathercocks, 1719. Two parts of the work were reprinted in Dublin, 1714. H&L IV, 161.

1714

371\. THE CONVENTICLE: or, a narrative of the dissenters new plot against the present constitution in church and state. With the names of the plotters, and their places of meeting. Humbly address'd to her most excellent majesty, by one of the conspirators, and ready to be depos'd upon oath before her principal secretary of state. To which is added, the reasons for disabling all dissenters for ever voting more for Parliament-men, and for wholly repealing the act of toleration ....

London: Printed for the Author, and are to be Sold by John Oldsworth near the Change, 1714. (Price 1 s.)

8°. Pp. [1]-100.

Notes: Introduction signed Philaret. Published 4 September 1714 (adv't, The Flying Post, 4 September 1714). Includes an introductory essay, "High-Church Loyalty". Later editions were published in 1715. H&L VI, 320.

Location: L; NN.

372\. The court-spy. Second edition. [1714]

Notes: Advertised in The Flying Post, 6 February 1714. The Court-Spy first appeared as a department of The Christian's Gazette, of which the first part, for the months of January to April 1713, was issued in July 1713; The Court-Spy was also included in The State Weathercocks, 1719. See also Neck Intelligence, 1715.

373. DUNTON'S GHOST: or, a speech to the most remarkable persons in church and state; but more especially to a very great lord now at the helm of public affairs. By the unknown author of Neck or Nothing, since he was number'd among the dead. To be continued weekly, or as often as the ghost thinks fit to appear. Being the Hanover courant: or, merry observator ....
London, Printed in the Year 1714. [page 1:] Numb. I.

4°. 2 nos. published, 4 March and 20 March 1714.

Notes: No. 1 published 4 March 1714 (adv't, The Flying Post, 4 March 1714); No. 2 published 20 March 1714 (adv't, The Flying Post, 20 March 1714). No. 3 was announced for 30 April 1714 (in The Impeachment, 1714), but no copy has been located. CBEL II, 660.

Location: O(no. 1); Y(no. 1).

374. -------- [anr edn] To which is added, The Impeachment, ... Also a letter of thanks to the loyal author of The Flying-Post ....
London. Printed for the Author, and sold by J. Baker in Pater-Noster-Row, J. Harrison by the Royal Exchange, A. Boulter without Temple-Bar, R. Bond near Charing-cross, and at the Hanover Coffee-House in Fleet-lane (where may be had all the Books, Pamphlets, and single Sheets, written by John Dunton.)

4°. Pp. [x], 1-9, [i]. Adv'ts, 1p., at end.

Notes: The Impeachment is not present.

Location: LC, Y.

375. THE GOLDEN AGE: exemplified in the glorious life and reign of his present majesty King George, and his numerous issue: or a vision of the future happiness of Great Britain, under truly protestant kings and queens to the world's end. To which is prefix'd the Hanoverian

martyrology, or a distinct essay upon the lives, sufferings, and characters of all those illustrious patriots, that have distinguish'd themselves by their eminent zeal and loyalty for the Hanover succession. Part I. Being a necessary introduction to that glorious vision of the golden age, which the world may expect in Part II. The whole humbly inscrib'd to his most excellent majesty by Mr. John Dunton, author of Neck or Nothing, and will be continued monthly to remind us of our miraculous deliverance from the Pretender, Popery, and slavery.
London: Printed by S. Keimer, and are to be sold by J. Harrison near the Royal Exchange, S. Popping in Pater-Noster-Row, A. Dod, and A. Boulter without Temple-Bar, 1714. (price 1 s.)

8°. Pp. [cxliv].

Notes: Published 30 December 1714 (adv't, The Flying Post, 30 December 1714). Dunton intended to continue The Golden Age in monthly parts (f. A_4^r), and in The Hereditary Bastard he announced that "The First Part of this Undertaking having met with an extraordinary kind Reception ... 'twill be continu'd in Parts at Twelve Pence each .... Part II ... now preparing for the press". A second edition was advertised in 1716.

Location: L, O, EN, DT; CLC.

376. The High-Church Revolution, or Passive-Obedience and Non-Resistance in Arms. A Trage-Comedy; as it was acted (with great Applause) throughout the English Dominions, in the Year 1688, by the Rt. Rev. Henry late Lord Bishop of London, and other Church-men of great Quality. With a Dedication to all true Englishmen, detecting the present deplorable State of the British Nation. Written by Mr. John Dunton, Author of The Court-Spy.

Notes: Dunton advertised the above, to be published in a "few days", in Whigg Loyalty, 1714, p. 28.

377. THE IMPEACHMENT, or Great Britain's charge against the present m---y, Sir Roger Bold, the L--- C---ly, and Dr. S---ll. With the names of those credible persons, that are able to prove (before her majesty, or either of her

two houses of Parliament) the whole impeachment, consisting of sixty articles. Dedicated to the most illustrious and ever victorious prince John Duke of Marlborough. By the unknown author of Neck or Nothing, who being buried alive (i.e. forc'd to abscond) for daring to call a spade a spade, does here appear (as a ghost) to do justice to himself and witnesses.
London. Printed for T. Warner, near Ludgate.

4°. Pp. [xii], [1]-32.

Notes: Published 13 May 1714 (adv't, The Flying Post, 13 May 1714). Includes "The Sacheverellite-Plot, Or The Church's Real Danger Detected", at p. 17. H&L III, 137 (incorrect date, or possibly confusion with an earlier work; see below). F. Madan, Bibl. of Dr. Henry Sacheverell (Oxford, 1884), no. 207. A work with a similar title may have been published in 1710: The Impeachment, or the Nation Mad, occasioned by the late Tryal of Dr. Sacheverell (see Remarks and Collections of Thomas Hearne, ed. C. E. Doble [Oxford, 1885-1921], II, 372; and Stationers' Register, Entry Book of Copies, 25 July 1710). Also H&L V, 157. A second edition was advertised in 1715.

Location: O.

378. Neck or nothing; or, the history of Queen Robin; detecting the secret reign of the four last years. In a familiar dialogue between Mr. Truman and his friend, meeting accidentally at the proclaiming K. George.
Dublin [reprinted], 1714. 2 parts.

Notes: The above description from the printed catalogue of the library of Trinity College, Dublin. The two parts of this work, Neck or Nothing and Queen Robin, were originally published in London in 1713 and 1714.

379. QUEEN ROBIN: or the second part of Neck or Nothing, detecting the secret reign of the four last years. In a familiar dialogue between Mr. Truman (alias Mr. John Dunton) and his friend, meeting accidentaly at the proclaiming King George. ....

London: Printed for M. Brudenell, and are to be sold by J. Harrison near the Royal Exchange, S. Popping in Pater Noster Row, A. Dod and A. Boulter without Temple-Bar; at which four Places are to be had, Mr. Duntons First Part of Neck or Nothing, and all the other Books he has publish'd lately.

8°. Pp. [ii], i-vi, 1-66, [ii]. Adv'ts, 2pp., at end.

Notes: Published 21 October 1714 (adv't, The Flying Post, 21 October 1714). Neck or Nothing was published in 1713.

Location: L, EN; MB, Y.

380. -------- Second edition.
London: Printed for M. Brudenell, and are to be sold by J. Harrison near the Royal Exchange, S. Popping in Pater Noster Row, A. Dod and A. Boulter without Temple-Bar; at which four Places are to be had, Mr. Duntons First Park of Neck or Nothing, and all the other Books he has publish'd lately.

8°. Pp. [ii], i-vi, 1-66, [ii]. Adv'ts, 2pp., at end.

Notes: Published 26 October 1714 (adv't, The Flying Post, 26 October 1714).

Location: O.

381. -------- Third edition.

Notes: Published 2 November 1714 (adv't, The Flying Post, 2 November 1714).

Location: MB.

382. WHIGG LOYALTY, or an humble address to her majesty. By Mr. John Dunton, author of The Court-Spy. In which he offers to appear and prove all his discoveries, and several others of great moment, to the Queen and Kingdom, if her majesty will be pleased to grant her royal protection to himself and witnesses.
London. Printed by T. Warner near Ludgate. 1714.

8°. Pp. [iv], 1-28.

Notes: Published 22 December 1713 (adv't, The Flying Post, 22 December 1713). Contains "The Fiery-Tryal: or the Case of the Protestants of Great-Britain, if the Pretender shou'd ever Usurp Her Majesty's Throne, and be Crown'd King", at p. 19. The second edition of this work was printed in The State Weathercocks, 1719.

Location: L, O, C, CT, DU, EN; BN, MB.

1715

383. [Drop-head title:]
BOOKS LATELY WRIT BY MR. JOHN DUNTON, author of Neck or Nothing. [1715]

8°. Pp. [viii].

Notes: Fifteen works are advertised in this list, all "sold by S. Popping, in Pater-Noster-Row, J. Harrison, near the Royal-Exchange, A. Dod, and A. Boulter without Temple-Bar; and whatever Books are written by Mr. John Dunton, if not publish'd with these Four Names, are imperfect Copies, and consequently a wrong to the Author, as well as the Publick".

Location: L[bound with King Abigail, 1715(in the catalogue, King Abigail is advertised as "lately published")], G[bound with King Abigail, 1715].

384. BUNGEY: or the false brother, prov'd his own executioner, in a sermon, upon these words, and went and hang'd himselself[sic], Matth. xxvii. 5. In which, the secret vices, lewd principles, and (suppos'd) shameful death of that tool Dr. S---rel (alias Bungey) is set in a new light; and the black charge exhibited against him, offer'd to be attested in any court of justice (or even in St. Andrews pulpit) when ever the Dr. will appoint the time. By Mr. John Dunton, author of Neck or Nothing, and the three late sermons intitled, The Hereditary Bastard, Ox--- and Bull--- and King Abigail.

London: Printed for the Author, and are to be Sold by S. Popping in Pater-Noster-Row, J. Harrison, near the Royal Exchange, A. Dod, and A. Boulter without Temple-Bar, 1715. (Price 6d.)

8°. Pp. [ii], [i]-ii, [1]-26, [ii]. Adv'ts, 2pp., at end.

Notes: Published 28 May 1715 (adv't, The Flying Post, 28 May 1715).

Location: L.

385. -------- Second edition.

Notes: Advertised in Dunton's Recantation, 1716.

386. -------- Third edition.

London: Printed for the Author, and are to be Sold by S. Popping in Pater-Noster-Row, J. Harrison, near the Royal-Exchange, A. Dod, and A. Boulter without Temple-Bar, 1715. (Price 6d.)

8°. Pp. [ii], [i]-ii, [1]-26, [ii]. Adv'ts, 2pp. at end.

Location: L.

387. The Committee of Secrecy; or the glorious Peace (as the late Ministry call'd it) most justly expos'd, in a Sermon upon these Words, We looked for Peace, but no good came: and for a Time of Health, and behold Trouble, Jer. 8. 15.

Notes: Advertised as "now in the Press" in Books lately writ by Mr. John Dunton, 1715.

388. The conventicle. Second edition.

London: Printed for the Author and are to be Sold by J. Harrison, at the Corner of Castle-Alley, near the Royal Exchange in Cornhill, 1715 (Price 1s.)

8°. Pp. [1]-100.

Notes: Published 12 October 1714 (adv't, The Flying Post, 12 October 1714). First published in 1714.

Location: L.

389. -------- Third edition.

Notes: Advertised in King Abigail, 1715. A fourth edition was advertised in 1716.

390. A Glorious Vision of the New Parliament, with other surprizing Visions of the Future Happiness of Great-Britain in the Illustrious House of Hanover to the World's End. Most humbly inscrib'd to his Royal Highness, George, Prince of Wales. Price 1 s.

Notes: Advertised as in the press in The Medal, 1715. Intended to be the second part of The Golden Age, 1714.

391. The Hanover-Packet.

Notes: Advertised as "a weekly paper, soon to be published", in King George for Ever, 1715.

392. THE HEREDITARY-BASTARD: or, the royal-intreague of the warming-pan: fully detected, in a sermon upon these words, and a bastard shall dwell in Ashdod, Zech. 9. 6. ....

London: Printed for the Author, and sold by S. Keymer at the Printing Press in Pater-Noster-Row, J. Harrison near the Royal-Exchange, and A. Dod, without Temple-Bar. 1715. (Price 6 d.)

8°. Pp. [1]-37, [iii]. Adv'ts, 3pp., at end.

Notes: Published 10 February 1715 (adv't, The Flying Post, 10 February 1715). Advertised in Royal Gratitude, 1716, An Appeal, 1723, etc., as written by Dunton.

Location: Y, MB.

393. -------- Third edition.
London: Printed for the Author, and sold by S. Keymer at the Printing Press in Pater-Noster-Row, J. Harrison near the Royal-Exchange, and A. Dod, without Temple-Bar. 1715. (Price 6 d.)

8°. Pp. [1]-37, [iii]. Adv'ts, 3pp., at end.

Location: LV.

394. The impeachment. Second edition.

Notes: Advertised in The Medal, Books lately Writ by Mr. John Dunton and The Manifesto of K. John, 1715; and Royal Gratitude and Dunton's Recantation, 1716. First published in 1714.

395. KING-ABIGAIL: or, the secret reign of the she-favourite, detected and applied; in a sermon upon these words, and women rule over them, Isa. 3. 12. Deliver'd (I can't say preach'd) by Mr. John Dunton, author of Queen-Robin, and the late sermon, intitl'd, Ox--- and Bull---.
London: Printed for the Author, and are to be sold by S. Popping in Pater-Noster-Row; J. Harrison near the Royal-Exchange; A. Dodd, and A. Boulter without Temple-Bar. 1715. (Price 6 d.)

8°. Pp. [iv], 1-20.

Notes: A fourth edition was advertised in 1716.

Location: L, O, G; MB.

396. KING GEORGE FOR EVER: or, Dunton's speech to the Protestant associators of Great-Britain: .... To which is added, the neck-adventure; or, the case and sufferings of Mr. John Dunton, for daring to detect the treason and villany of Oxford and Bolingbroke, whilst they were reigning favourites, in his four essays, intituled, The Court-Spy, Neck or Nothing, Queen Robin, and The Impeachment ....
London: Printed for the Author, and are to be sold by S. Popping in Pater-noster-Row, and by most Booksellers in Great-Britain and Ireland. (Price 6d.)

[Separate title-page; following the above, with lower-case register and lower-case Roman pagination:] The neck-adventure: or the case and sufferings of Mr. John Dunton, author of those early discoveries, intitled, The Court-Spy, Neck or Nothing, Queen Robin, and, The Impeachment ....
London: Printed in the Year, 1715.

8°. Pp. [i]-xii, 1-40, [i]-xxiv. Adv'ts, "Twelve Books lately written by Mr. John Dunton", at pp. 37-40.

Notes: Published 8 December 1715 (adv't, The Flying Post, 8 December 1715). Later editions were advertised in 1716.

Location: L; Y, MB.

397. THE MEDAL: or, a loyal essay upon King George's picture, as 'twas presented to Mr. John Dunton, (author of The Golden Age) by His Majesty's order. Most humbly inscrib'd to His Excellency the Baron de Bothmer.
London: Printed for the Author, and are to be sold by S. Popping in Pater-noster-Row; where is to be had The First Part of the Golden Age, printed on the same Size with this Essay, intitl'd, The Medal, that they may bind together when The Golden Age is compleated.

8°. Pp. [xii], 1-65, [vii]. Adv'ts, 7pp., at end.

Notes: Published 12 April 1715 (adv't, The Flying Post, 12 April 1715).

Location: L, O, DT; Y, MB.

398. -------- Second edition.

Notes: Published 21 April 1715 (adv't, The Flying Post, 21 April 1715). A third edition was advertised in 1716.

399. THE MOB-WAR: or a detection of the present state of the Brittish Nation: but more especially with respect to that wou'd-be-King (or little Popish work of darkness)

that threatens us with a speedy invasion. In sixteen letters. Containing such discoveries (in Church and State) as were never publish'd before .... To these letters is added, a trip to the Pope, or the Papists farewel to Great Britain, spoke in the person of a Roman Catholick. Also, the neck-adventure, or the case and sufferings of Mr. John Dunton, for early detecting the secret steps taken by Oxford and Bolingbroke, to restore the Pretender.

London: Printed for the Author, and are to be Sold by S. Popping in Pater-Noster-Row, J. Harrison near the Royal Exchange, A. Dodd and A. Boulter without Temple-Barr. (Price 1s.)

8°. Pp. [i]-xvi, 1-86, [ii]. Adv'ts, 2pp., at end.

Notes: Published 6 October 1715 (adv't, The Flying Post, 6 October 1715). Eight letters were printed in this volume, and eight letters were promised in a second volume; the second volume was not published, but several of the letters were later published separately (p. xvi). "The Neck-Adventure" and "A Trip to the Pope" were not included in this volume, but "The Neck-Adventure" was published with King George for Ever, 1715.

Location: L, O, LW; MB.

400. Neck Intelligence, or a Detection of such secret, odd and uncommon transactions in Church and State, as other Authors have not dar'd to publish; to be continu'd Monthly, this for January containing, (1.) The Christian's Gazette .... (2.) The Lame-Post .... (3.) The Court-Spy .... (4.) Dunton's Ghost again embody'd .... (5.) Mercurius Clericus .... (6.) King William's Legacy .... (7.) Dunton's Mad-House .... Neck-Intelligence for January, to be publish'd the first Tuesday in March. Sold by S. Popping in Pater-Noster-Row. Price 1s.

Notes: Advertised in The Hereditary Bastard, which was published in February 1715. Dunton intended Neck-Intelligence to be a continuation of The Christian's Gazette: "This is to give Notice to all Lovers of Novelty, that the first Essay of the Christian's Gazette and Court-Spy, tho' sold for

18*d*. having met with such a kind Reception as to come to a third Edition in a short Time, the same *Athenian Project* will be now continu'd monthly at 12*d*. price, and with this Title, *viz*. *Neck Intelligence* .... "

401. Neck or nothing. Tenth edition.

Notes: Advertised in *The Mob-War*, 1715. First published in 1715.

402. -------- Twelfth edition.

Notes: Advertised in *The Medal*, 1715, *Books lately Writ by Mr. John Dunton*, 1715, and *The Manifesto of K. John*, 1716. Later editions were advertised in 1716.

403. OX--- AND BULL--- Or, a funeral sermon for the two beasts that are to be slaughter'd upon Tower-Hill, next session of Parliament .... Also, an elegy upon their untimely end, to be sung the same day they are quarter'd .... By Mr. John Dunton, (author of Neck or Nothing, and the sermon, intituled, The Hereditary-Bastard) and is his second attempt to reform the pulpit.
London: Printed for the Author, and are to be sold by S. Popping in Pater-Noster-Row, J. Harrison near the Royal-Exchange, A. Dodd, and A. Boulter without Temple-Bar, 1715. (Price 6d.)

8°. Pp. [i]-viii, vii-x, [1]-31, [i]. Adv'ts, 1 3/4 pp., at end.

Notes: Published 24 February 1715 (adv't, *The Flying Post*, 24 February 1715).

Location: L, *O*; BN, CLC.

404. -------- Second edition.
London: Printed for the Author, and are to be sold by S. Popping in Pater-Noster-Row, J. Harrison near the Royal-Exchange, A. Dodd, and A. Boulter without Temple-Bar, 1715. (Price 6 d.)

8°. Pp. [i]-viii, vii-x, 1-31, [i]. Adv'ts, 1 3/4pp., at end.

Location: <u>L</u>, LV, DT.

405. -------- Third edition;
London: Printed for the Author, and are to be sold by S. Popping in Pater-Noster-Row, J. Harrison near the Royal Exchange, A. Dodd, and A. Boulter without Temple-Bar, 1715. (Price 6d.)

8°. Pp. [i]-viii, vii-x, 1-31, [i]. Adv'ts, 1 3/4 pp., at end.

Notes: Later editions were advertised in 1716.

Location: <u>L</u>; Y.

406. THE SHORTEST WAY WITH THE KING: or, plain English spoke to his majesty. Being the third part of Neck or Nothing; containing, the secret history of King George's reign, ... By Mr. John Dunton, author of the first and second part of Neck or Nothing.
London: Printed for the Author, and are to be sold by S. Popping in Pater-Noster-Row, J. Harrison near the Royal-Exchange, A. Dod, and A. Boulter without Temple- [imprint cropped]

8°. Pp. [i]-xvi, 1-78.

Notes: Published 8 September 1715 (adv't, <u>The Flying Post</u>, 8 September 1715).

Location: <u>O</u>, DT; CLC, MB.

407. -------- Third edition.

Notes: Advertised in <u>The Mob-War</u>, 1715, and <u>Frank Scammony</u>, 1716. Later editions were advertised in 1716.

408. Athenian News, or, Dunton's Packet for the Virtuosi of Great Britain; ....

Notes: Advertised as to be published "about a Month hence" in Dunton's Recantation, 1716; the quarto paper was to be published on Monday and Friday at 2d., 30 numbers to the volume, to which Dunton promised to add a general title-page, preface and index. Also announced, to be published "on 1st September", in Royal Gratitude, 1716. An earlier work with a similar title was published by Dunton in 1710.

409. The British Maecenus; or, The Character of A Generous Patron. An Heroick Poem. Written by Mr. John Dunton, Author of Neck or Nothing; and Inscrib'd, to his Grace Holles Duke of Newcastle, and the rest of those Noble Patriots, to whom he dedicated his late Essays.

Notes: Dunton advertised the above, as preparing for the press, in The Devil's Martyrs, 1716.

410. The conventicle. Fourth edition.

Notes: Advertised in Dunton's Recantation, 1716. First published in 1714.

411. THE DEVIL'S MARTYRS: or, plain dealing, in answer to the Jacobite speeches of those two perjur'd rebels, William Paul a clergyman, and John Hall a Justice of Peace .... To which is added, the high-church martyrology: or, a funeral oration, spoke at the interment of this Tory-priest and mob-justice .... Written by Mr. John Dunton, author of those early discoveries of Oxford's and Bolingbroke's treason, intitl'd, Neck or Nothing: -- and inscrib'd, to that truly noble, and most accomplisht General William Lord Cadogan, Baron of Reading.
London, Printed for the Author, and are to be sold by S. Poping in Pater-Noster-Row, and most Booksellers in Great Brittain and Ireland, 1716. -- Price 6 d.

8°. Pp. [ii], i-v, [i], 1-34.

Notes: Published 2 August 1716 (adv't, The Post Man, 2 August 1716). Copy offered for sale by Percy Dobell and Son, Cat. 178 (1967), contained advertisement leaf at end.

Location: L, DT; LC.

412. -------- Third edition.

Notes: Published 7 August 1716 (adv't, The Post Man, 7 August 1716). Advertised in Dunton's Recantation, 1716.

413. Dunton's Kingdoms.

Notes: Advertised in The Manifesto of K. John, 1716, "to be finished in a month, and published at Trinity Term" (p. 23).

414. DUNTON'S RECANTATION; or, his reasons for deserting his Whiggish principles and turning Jacobite, at this time when a new rebellion is so much talk'd off. With the cause of his disaffection to King George, and the present ministry ....
London, Printed for the Author, and are to be sold by S. Poping in Pater-Noster-Row, and most Booksellers in Great-Brittain and Ireland, 1716. -- Price 1 s.

8°. Pp. [i]-xiii, [iii], 1-35, [v]. Adv'ts, 3pp., following dedication, and 5pp., at end.

Location: L, O; LC, Y.

415. Feeling's the Truth; or a Satyrical Answer to a Treasonable Pamphlet intitled, Seeing's Believing, ...

Notes: Forthcoming publication announced in The Flying Post, No. 3795, 1 May 1716, "There will be publish'd in few Days, ... Sold by S. Popping in Pater-Noster-Row, and most Booksellers in London and Westminster".

416. FRANK SCAMMONY: or, the restoring clergy detected, in their names, haunts, plots, heresies, and lewd conversation, in a sermon, upon these words, her priests have violated my law - and I am profaned among them, Ezek. 22. 26. Occasion'd by a certain B---p's swearing, We'll have the Pretender by G-d. To which is added, the pulpit trumpeter; or the substance of all the treasonable sermons that have been preach'd at Whitechappel, by that passive rebel, that drinks a health to the fatherless child and the widdow. Attested by two of his constant hearers. The sermon (with all the discoveries) dedicated to that pious, loyal, and healing prelate, Francis, Lord Bishop of Rochester. By Mr. John Dunton, author of Neck or Nothing; and of those four sermous[sic], intitled, - The Hereditary Bastard, Ox--- and Bull--- Bungey - and King Abigail.
London: Printed for the Author; and are to be sold by S. Popping in Pater-Noster-Row. J. Harrison near the Royal-Exchange, A. Dod, and A. Boulter, without Temple-Bar. - Price 1 s.

8°. Pp. [i]-x, [1]-70. Adv'ts, 2/3p., at end.

Notes: Published 14 February 1716 (adv't, The Flying Post, 14 February 1716).

Location: L, O, CS, DU.

417. -------- Fourth edition.

Notes: Advertised in Royal Gratitude, 1716.

418. -------- Sixth edition.

Notes: Advertised in Dunton's Recantation, 1716.

419. The golden age. Second edition.

Notes: Advertised in Royal Gratitude, 1716, and in Dunton's Recantation, 1716. First published in 1714.

420. The Hanover Catechism, (or, The Bite of the Church being in Danger, plainly detected in a Dialogue between a High-Churchman, a bold Asserter of Hereditary Right, and a Loyal Dissenter of Revolution-Principles.

Notes: Commented on, "[Mr. Dunton] has just finish'd a Piece, intitled: The Hanover Catechism, ..." in Mordecai's Memorial, 1716, p. 25.

421. The Hanoverian Patriots: or, An Heroick Poem ....

Notes: Advertised as preparing for the press, in Royal Gratitude, 1716.

422. The High Church Gudgeons; or, A Day's Ramble to catch the Foolish Jacks with their own Treason: Being A Key to that Loyal Irony, intitled, Seeing's Believing; or, King George Prov'd a Us--per; for writing whereof, Mr. Dunton was Three Times carry'd before a Magistrate the same Day, and as often Acquitted, for a Loyal Subject and Honest Man.

Notes: No. 15 in Dunton's list of "Forty Political Tracts" printed in An Appeal, 1723. Although The High Church Gudgeons was printed in Royal Gratitude, 1716 (pp. 33-54), it was apparently also published separately, as the third edition was advertised in The Post Man, 17 July 1716.

423. King Abigail. Fourth edition.

Notes: Advertised in Dunton's Recantation, 1716. First published in 1715.

424. King George for ever. Fourth edition.

Notes: Advertised in Dunton's Recantation, 1716. First published in 1715.

425. -------- Fifth edition.

Notes: Advertised in Frank Scammony, 1716, and Manifesto

of *K. John*, 1715.

426\. *King William's Legacy*; An Heroick Poem. In two Parts. Containing - (1.) The Celestial Coronation; or, The Joyful Acclamations of the Blessed in Heaven, on the same Day on which our Glorious *George* was Crowned Monarch of *Great Britain*. (2.) *No Pretender*; or, The General Thanksgiving on Earth: Being a Comment in Prose and Verse upon all the rejoycing Sermons that were Preached June the 7th, upon the Total Defeat of the *English* and *Scotch* Jacobites.

Notes: No. 22 in Dunton's list of "Forty Political Tracts" printed in *An Appeal*, 1723. Advertised as preparing for the press in *Royal Gratitude*, 1716.

427\. THE MANIFESTO OF K. JOHN THE SECOND; and of those noblemen, gentlemen, and others, now arming in defence of his indefeasible and hereditary right to the Imperial Crown of Great Brittain and Ireland: declaring he has fairer pretentions to be sole monarch of these kingdoms, then that Popish imposter that styles himself James the Third. With a satyr upon royalty, writ by King John the Second, on purpose to quiet his own mind, in case he should not succeed in his royal claim, but (like his hereditary rival) be forc'd to continue a common subject ....
This Manifesto is sold by S. Poping in Pater-noster-Row, and most Booksellers in Great-Brittain and Ireland. -- Price 6d.

8°. Pp. [i]-xx. 1-23, [i]. Adv'ts, 1p., at end.

Notes: *Dedication* and *Preface* signed John Dunton.

Location: L, O, *EN*, LV; LC.

428\. -------- Second edition.

Notes: Advertised in *Dunton's Recantation* and *Royal Gratitude*, 1716.

429. -------- Third edition.

Notes: Advertised in Frank Scammony, 1716.

430. The medal. Third edition

Notes: Advertised in Dunton's Recantation and Royal Gratitude, 1716. First published in 1715.

431. MORDECAI'S MEMORIAL: or, there's nothing done for him. Being a satyr upon some-body, but I name no-body: (or, in plainer English, a just and generous representation of unrewarded services, by which the Protestant succession has been sav'd out of danger.) Written by an unknown and disinterested clergy-man, and most humbly inscrib'd to his royal highness the Prince of Wales, guardian of these realms. Esther VI. 2, 3. .... There is nothing done for him.

London: Printed for S. Popping; and are to be Sold by J. Harrison, near the Royal Exchange, and A. Dodd without Temple-Bar. 1716. (Price One Shilling.)

8°. Pp. [ii], i-x, 1-44, 37-51, [i].

Notes: Dedication signed Philo-Patris. Published 16 October 1716 (adv't, The Post Man, 16 October 1716). Possibly written in part by Maria Jones and the Rev. William Clark (see T. M. Hatfield, The True Secret History of Mr. John Dunton, unpublished thesis [Harvard University, 1926], pp. 322-8). The second edition formed a part of The State Weathercocks, 1719. H&L IV, 114. LA V, 696.

Location: L, LV; LC.

432. -------- Fifth edition.

Notes: Advertised in the St. James Post, 10 December 1716.

433. Neck or nothing. Sixteenth edition

Notes: Advertised in Royal Gratitude, 1716. First published in 1713.

434. -------- Eighteenth edition.

Notes: Advertised in Dunton's Recantation, 1716. The twentieth edition was printed in The State Weathercocks, 1719.

435. Newcastle; or, The Immortal Hero; an Heroick Poem ....

Notes: Advertised as preparing for the press in Royal Gratitude, 1716.

436. Ox--- and Bull---. Sixth edition.

Notes: Advertised in The Manifesto of K. John, 1716. First published in 1715.

437. -------- Eighth edition.

Notes: Advertised in Dunton's Recantation, 1716.

438. Pope on the Stool of Repentance; or the Purge given to Sir Alexander Knaw-Post, to prepare his body for the new Madhouse, erected for the cure of Atheists, Blasphemers, Libertines, Punsters, Jacobites, and other Prophane Lunaticks; to which is added A Challenge sent to this Rhiming Knight upon several nice and curious Points in Philosophy, Poetry and Conversation, which if he refuses to answer he'll be posted for a B--d .... The whole Satyr written by Dr. Dunton, Physician to the New Madhouse ....

Notes: Announced by Dunton, as preparing for the press, in The St. James Post, 10 December 1716.

439. Queen Robin. Fifth edition.

Notes: Advertised in The Manifesto of K. John, 1716.

First published in 1714.

440. -------- Tenth edition.

Notes: Advertised in Dunton's Recantation, 1716.

441. ROYAL GRATITUDE; (or King George's promise never to forget his obligations to those who have distinguish'd themselves in his service) critically consider'd. In a letter to the Right Honourable Robert Walpole, Esq; the First Lord of the Treasury, occasion'd by a general report that Mr. John Dunton, (author of Neck or Nothing) will speedily be rewarded with a considerable place or pension. Written by that person of honour that sent Mr. Dunton those early discoveries of Oxford's and Bolingbroke's treason, which no man durst publish but himself, and which he therefore call'd Neck or Nothing. To which is added, the high-church gudgeons: or, a day's ramble to catch the foolish Jacks with their own treason, with Mr. Dunton's speech to the Lord-Mayor of London upon this occasion. Also, a trip to the loyal Mug-House at night, to drink a health to King George and the Royal Family.
London: Printed by R. Tookey, and are to be sold by S. Popping in Pater Noster Row, and most Booksellers in Great Britain and Ireland. Price 1 s. Where is also to be had The Fifth Edition of Seeing's Believing; or, King George prov'd a Us--per. Price 1 s. 1716.

8°. Pp. [ii], [1]-54, [viii]. Adv'ts, 8pp., at end.

Notes: Text signed Philo-Patris (p. 32).

Location: L.

442. -------- Fourth edition.

Notes: Advertised in Dunton's Recantation, 1716.

443. SEEING'S BELIEVING: or, K-ng G--rge prov'd a us--per; and his whole reign one continu'd act of cr---ty and op--n, and other notorious fail--ngs. Written by a subject to the lawful king. And inscrib'd to a noble Earl, who lately fought in defence of the right title to the

British Crown.

London; Printed for S. Keimer (now a close Prisoner in the Fleet); and are to be Sold (Privately) by most Booksellers in Great-Britain and Ireland. - Price 1s.

8°. $A^4a\text{-}b^4c^2B\text{-}G^4H^2$.

Notes: Dunton identified himself as author in Mordecai's Memorial, 1716, p. 25, and in Royal Gratitude, 1716, p. 24. See also Feeling's the Truth, 1716.

Location: LC, MH, MB.

444. -------- Third edition.

Notes: Published 5 May 1716 (adv't, The Flying Post, 5 May 1716).

445. -------- Fifth edition.

Notes: Advertised in Dunton's Recantation, 1716.

446. The shortest way with the King. Fourth edition.

Notes: Advertised in Royal Gratitude, 1716, and The Manifesto of K. John, 1716. First published in 1715.

447. -------- Fifth edition.

Notes: Advertised in Dunton's Recantation, 1716.

448. A Trip to the Mug House At Night to Drink a Health to King George. 1716.

Notes: Printed in Royal Gratitude, 1716; also published separately. Advertised in The Post Man, 3 July 1716.

449. -------- Third edition.

Notes: Published 17 July 1716 (adv't, The Post Man,

17 July 1716).

1717

450. Mordecai's dying groans from the Fleet-Prison: or, the case and sufferings of Mr. John Dunton ....
London: Printed for S. Popping, in Pater-Noster Row. 1717.

8°. Pp. [i]-x, 1-42.

Notes: Copies of this pamphlet remaining unsold in 1719 were bound as part of Neck for Nothing, q.v.

Location: Y.

451. MORDECAI'S LAST SHIFT. Or a most humble address to the nobility, gentry, and clergy .... being proposals for printing by subscription new and surprizing thoughts upon all manner of subjects, to be intituled, The Athenian Library ....
Printed for the Author, in the Year, 1717.

Folio. A-C^2

Notes: Published 30 April 1717 (adv't The Post Man, 30 April 1717). The Athenian Library was published in 1725.

Location: The above description from Peter Murray Hill, Booksellers, Catalogue 70.

452. THE PULPIT-LUNATICKS: or, a mad answer to the mad report, made by a committee of mad priests, against Benjamin, Lord Bishop of Bangor. Being a mad venture of neck or nothing to save the Church, by that mad author, who ran the same hazard to save the State ....
London: Printed, and Sold by S. Popping, in Pater-noster-row. Price 6d.

8°. Pp. [1]-32.

Notes: Published 23 July 1717 (adv't, The Flying Post,

23 July 1717). H&L VI, 427.

Location: <u>L</u>; MB.

453. -------- Sixth edition.

Notes: Published 6 August 1717 (adv't, <u>The Flying Post</u>, 6 August 1717).

<u>1718</u>

454. THE HANOVER-SPY: or, secret history of St. James's. From the reign of Queen Robin, down to the late misunderstanding in the royal palace. .... By Mr. John Dunton, (Author of Neck or Nothing) ....
London: Printed for the Author, and are to be sold by S. Popping in Pater-Noster Row, and most Booksellers in Great Britain and Ireland. 1718. (Price One Shilling.)

8°. Pp. [i]-xii, 1-60.

Notes: <u>Dedication</u> to Benj. Childe, Esq., signed John Dunton. Consists of two essays, "The Secret History of Whiggish Ingratitude: Or, the Case and Sufferings of Mr. John Dunton", and "The Hanover Spy".

Location: <u>Y</u>, CLC.

455. -------- Third edition.

Notes: Advertised in <u>The Flying Post</u>, 18 March 1718.

456. -------- Fourth edition.

Notes: Advertised in <u>The Flying Post</u>, 18 March 1718.

457. -------- Fifth edition.

Notes: Advertised in The Flying Post, 25 March 1718.

458. NECK FOR NOTHING: or, satyr upon two great little men now in the ministry .... To which is added, Mordecai's dying groans from the Fleet-Prison: or, Mr. John Dunton's humble appeal .... The whole written by Mr. John Dunton, author of Neck or Nothing, and will be presented to the King at his return to London, by Mr. Dunton himself, that his distinguish'd services to his majesty's sacred person and government might be no longer conceal'd from the royal family, by those Whigg-favourites, who (tho' they know that Mordecai has ruin'd himself to save his Country) han't yet inform'd the King that nothing is done for him.

London: Printed for the Author (Mr. John Dunton) and are to be Sold by S. Popping at the Black-Raven in Pater noster-Row, and most Booksellers in Great-Britain and Ireland. - Price 1 s.

[Separate title-page; following the above, with separate register and pagination:] Mordecai's dying groans from the Fleet-Prison: or, the case and sufferings of Mr. John Dunton ....

London: Printed for S. Popping, in Pater-Noster Row. 1717.

8°. Pp. [1]-10, [ii], [i]-x, 1-42.

Notes: Published 6 July 1719 (adv't, The Post Boy, 6 July 1719).

Location: Y.

459. Neck or Nothing, in verse; or, a collection of all the treasonable poems that have been privately dispers'd throughout the British dominions in favour of the pretender; with answers to 'em in rhime .... Part I. [and] fair warning to the whigs, or an essay upon the fiery-tryal.

Notes: The above title from the printed catalogue of the library of Trinity College, Dublin. Published 25 May 1719 (adv't, St. James Post, 25 May 1719). Attributed to Dunton in Neck for Nothing, 1719, p. 10.

Location: DT.

460. The second Spira: .... By J.S. .... The thirtieth edition. To which is added, (1.) A Key to the Second Spira, (never published in any former edition of that narrative) .... (2.) Impenitent sinners read and tremble; or, a dialogue betwixt a modern Atheist and his friend. Written by Mr. Richard Sault, (the second Spira) .... (3.) Double hell, or an essay on despair; occasion'd by Mr. Richard Sault (the second Spira) crying out in Mr. Dunton's hearing, I am damn'd! .... (4.) A conference between the famous Mr. John Dod and Mr. Throgmorton .... being an original manuscript never printed before. (5.) A wounded spirit who can bear; or a narrative of five desperate sinners .... The whole address'd to all the harden'd sinners (or practical Atheists) in the King's dominions. By Mr. John Dunton, - the first publisher of The Second Spira - a member of the Athenian Society, - and - author of the essay entitled, The Hazard of a Death Bed Repentance.

London: Printed for S. Popping in Paternoster Row, and are to be Sold by Most Booksellers. -- Price One Shilling.

8°. Pp. [iv], 1-76. Adv'ts, 1p., at end.

Notes: Published 3 September 1719 (adv't., The Flying Post, 3 September 1719). The Second Spira was first published in 1693.

Location: L, EN.

461. THE STATE-WEATHERCOCKS: or, a new secret history of the most distinguished favourites, both of the late and present reign. Intermixt with strange discoveries in the Royal Palace. - A detection of the pride, avarice and ingratitude of some pretended Whigs, now in the ministry. - The pulpit bite: or, the cant of the Church being in danger, under a protestant king, prov'd a meer trick (or Jacobite plot to restore the Pretender, by the confession of a Jesuit that lately preached in Whitechappel Church, in a canonical habit. - The secret loyalty of the dissenting ministers, or a discovery in what manner they pray for the King, and the Royal Family, in their private houses. - A discovery of the masqueradings at Court. - The names, lewd conversation, and characters of some of

the kept-misses. - The parable of the late Marquess of Wh--ton's puppies. - The Earl of S--'s revenge: or, a specimen of the satyr intitled Neck for Nothing. With other discoveries both in Church and State. Writ by that person of honour, that sent to Mr. John Dunton all those Jacobite secrets that composed Neck or Nothing, and is now published as a key to that narrative. To these new discoveries is added, the twentieth edition of Neck or Nothing .... Also Mordecai kneeling at the King's gate: or, Mr. John Dunton's humble petition to his majesty's royal honour ....

London: Printed for the Author, and are to be sold by S. Poping.

[Separate title-page; following the above, after p. 110, with lower-case register:] Mordecai's memorial: .... The second edition corrected.

London: Printed for S. Popping; and are to be Sold by the Booksellers of London and Westminster, 1719.

8°. Pp. [i]-xxiv, 1-79, 88-110, [ii], i-iii, 1-3, 3-26, 21-22, 19-20, 25-26, 23-34.

Notes: Published 2 June 1719 (adv't, The Flying Post, 2 1719). Contents: Earl of S---'s Revenge; Neck or Nothing, 20th edition; Queen Robin; State Weathercocks; Court Spy, or a Detection; Pulpit Bite; Whig Loyalty, 2nd edition; Mordecai's Ramble to Court; Mordecai Kneeling at the King's Gate; Mordecai's Memorial; National Thanks, list of 40 political tracts written by Dunton; and Dunton's Advertisement. To ... Honest Booksellers.

Location: L, O, LV; MH.

1720

462. THE ATHENIAN SPY: or, a packet for the virtuosi of Great-Britain; containing, (1) The lame post; .... (2) Athenianism; .... (3) The phaenix; .... (4) Intellectual sport; .... To which is added, a mad-house, for the cure of spiritual lunaticks: .... By the whole Athenian Society, the several members of it being all engag'd in this curious search after rarities. Note, this Athenian spy will

be publish'd every month .... at one shilling price. - six parts to compleat a volume. Part I.
London: Printed for S. Popping, at the Black-Raven in Pater noster-Row; and are to be Sold by most Booksellers in London and Westminster. Price One Shilling.

8°. Pp. [1]-104. Adv'ts, 3pp., at end.

Notes: Published January 1720 (adv't, The Flying Post, 2 January 1720). Narcissus Luttrell's copy, at Yale, dated Januar. 1719.20. Part II announced as forthcoming in The Flying Post, 16 January 1720, and advertised as in the press in A Word without Doors, 1720; no copy has been located.

Location: Y, InU.

463. A WORD WITHOUT DOORS: or, a paradox, proving the honour of deserving a knighthood exceeds the title. In two letters: (that lately pass'd betwixt a clergyman of the Church of England, and Mr. John Dunton, the unrewarded author of Neck or Nothing.) ....
London: Printed for S. Poping in Pater-Noster-Row. 1720. -- Price 6 d.

8°. Pp. [1]-22, [ii]. Adv'ts, 1p., at end.

Notes: Published 11 March 1720 (adv't, The Flying Post, 11 March 1720). T. M. Hatfield proved this tract to have been written by Maria Jones (T. M. Hatfield, The True Secret History of Mr. John Dunton, unpublished thesis [Harvard University, 1926], pp. 348-9, 381).

Location: Y.

1721

464. A COLLECTION of choice, scarce, and valuable tracts, ... By a gentleman who has search'd after them for above twenty years.
London, Printed for D. Browne at the Black Swan without Temple-Bar, and G. Strahan at the Golden Ball in Cornhill. 1721.

8°. Pp. [iv], 1-[12], v-vi, 1-570.

Notes: A re-issue of the first volume of The Phenix, 1707, with a new title-page and one additional tract added at the beginning of the volume.

Location: L, G, S. R. Parks; Y.

1723

465. AN APPEAL to his majesty's most gracious promise of never forgetting those that have distinguished themselves in his service; or, the humble petition of John Dunton, Gent. (to his lawful and ever glorious sovereign King George) that he might not be left to starve in a jail, after his early, bold, and successful venturing his life and fortune in detecting his majesty's enemies, when plotting in the royal palace, and other parts of Great Britain and Ireland, to restore the Pretender .... To which is added, some impartial remarks upon Mr. Dunton's petition to his majesty; writ by that reverend clergyman that published the narrative, intitled, Mordecai's Memorial, or there's nothing done for him; proving 'tis now a national complaint, that the author of Neck or Nothing has gone nine years unrewarded for his distinguished services to his king and country ....
[without imprint]

4°. Pp. [1]-16.

Notes: Reprints Dunton's list of "Forty Political Tracts". L&E xxxi, 735-6. LA V, 82.

Location: L.

466. UPON THIS MOMENT DEPENDS ETERNITY: or, Mr. John Dunton's serious thoughts upon the present and future state, in a fit of sickness that was judg'd mortal, ... Being, a new directory for holy living and dying; compos'd of the author's own experience in religion, politicks, and morals, from his childhood to his sixty third year .... To which is added, the sick-man's passing-bell .... submitted to the impartial censure of the Right Reverend Father in God William Lord Bishop of Ely. By Mr. John Dunton, a

member of the Athenian Society, and author of the essay intitled - The Hazard of a Death-bed Repentance.
Printed for S. Popping in Pater-noster-Row. --Price 1 s. 6 d.

[Separate title-page; following the above, with double register and separate pagination:] An appeal to his majesty's most gracious promise .... [without imprint]

8°. Pp. [vi], 1-23, 16-48, 47-48, [1]-16. Adv'ts, 4pp., at end.

Notes: Published 15 August 1723 (adv't, The Flying Post, 15 August 1723). This work consists of three essays: "Labour in Vain"; "Every Man his own Parson, or Dunton Preaching to Himself"; and "Upon this Moment"; as well as An Appeal.

Location: L.

1725

467. An Angel in Flesh; or, The Heavenly Life and Character of .... Mrs. Elizabeth Dunton.

Notes: Advertised as preparing for the press in The State-Weathercocks, 1719, and The Athenian Library, 1725.

468. THE ATHENIAN LIBRARY, or a universal entertainment for the lovers of novelty .... Part I. Written by Mr. John Dunton .... Sold by S. Popping in Pater-Noster-Row. Price 1s. 6d.

8°. Pp. [viii], 1-70, [ii]. Adv'ts, 2pp., at end.

Notes: Published 9 March 1725 (adv't, The Post Man, 9 March 1725). Consists of five essays: "The Lost Rib Restored"; "Knowledge of the Saints in Heaven"; "Female Courtship"; "In Praise of Poverty"; and "The Wedding Night .... or a Satyr on Brutish Husbands". Proposals for this work, called Mordecai's Last Shift, were published in 1717. In The Athenian Spy, 1720, Dunton announced this work as preparing for the press, to be published quarterly in parts, four parts to complete each volume.

Location: O.

469. The Contemporary Brethren and Sisters, or a most Friendly Exhortation to all such Gentlemen and Ladies that were born in the Year 1659 ....

Notes: Advertised as preparing for the press in The State-Weathercocks, 1719, and The Athenian Library, 1725.

470. Heaven upon Earth; or, A Critical Essay upon the Life ... of .... Dr. Samuel Annesley .... Written by his Son-in-Law, Mr. John Dunton ....

Notes: Advertised as preparing for the press in The State-Weathercocks, 1719, and The Athenian Library, 1725.

471. Kainographia, or the History of Dunton's Projects; being a Catalogue of Three Hundred Books, Pamphlets and single Sheets written with his own Hand, with a Paraphrase on each. To which is added The Author's Farewel to Printing, ... This HISTORY will be continu'd in Parts .... And then Proposals will be made .... for Printing the whole Work (or Three Hundred Projects) in One Volume in Folio; with an Alphabetical Table, and the Author's Effigies.

Notes: Advertised as preparing for the press in Mr. John Dunton's Dying Groans, 1725.

472. The Moderate Clergyman, Or A True Son of the Church of England. Exemplify'd in the Holy Life and Triumphant Death of .... Mr. John Dunton, late Rector of Aston Clinton in Bucks. Written by his Eldest Son Mr. John Dunton ....

Notes: Advertised as preparing for the press in The State-Weathercocks, 1719, and The Athenian

Library, 1725.

473. MR. JOHN DUNTON'S DYING GROANS from the Fleet-Prison: or the national complaint, that the author of Neck or Nothing has gone twelve years unrewarded, for his early, bold, and successful venture of life and fortune, in detecting his majesty's enemies ....
London: Printed for the Author, (Mr. John Dunton) and are to be Sold by most Booksellers in Great-Britain and Ireland.

8°. Pp. [i], 1-15. Adv'ts, 2pp., at end.

Notes: Referred to in *The Athenian Library*, 1725, as "just published".

Location: *L*.

474. Mr. John Dunton's Legacy to his Native Country, or, A Dying Farewell to this Life and World ....

Notes: Advertised as preparing for the press in *Mr. John Dunton's Dying Groans*, 1725; *Dunton's Legacy* was to contain six-hundred essays, including: "Prepare to Follow John Dunton", "God Save the King, or, a Dying Farewell", "Royal Intrigue of the Warming Pan", "A Short History of Sir Robert Walpole", "A Second Judge Hales", "The Real Pindarick Lady", and "The Nonsuch-Water Drinker".

475. *The Parson's Son*; Or, An Essay upon the Honour of descending from the Tribe of Levi: Being a Congratulatory Poem .... The Third Edition.....

Notes: Advertised as preparing for the press in *The State-Weathercocks*, 1719, and *The Athenian Library*, 1725. Dunton's first published work, *A Congratulatory Poem to the Ministers Sons*, was first published in 1682; the second edition of *The Parson's Son, or a Congratulatory Poem* was published in *Athenianism*, 1710. *The Parson's Son* was also printed in *Upon this Moment depends Eternity*, 1723.

476. The Seventh Son; or a Legacy Left by Mr. John Dunton to his Godson Mr. John Dunton Dove, the 7th Male Child of Mr. John and Mrs. Eleanor Dove.

Notes: Advertised as preparing for the press in The State-Weathercocks, 1719, and The Athenian Library, 1725.

1728

477. AN ESSAY ON DEATH-BED-CHARITY, exemplify'd in the life of Mr. Thomas Guy, late bookseller in Lombard-Street, Madam Jane Nicholas, of St. Albans. And Mr. Francis Bancroft, late of London draper: proving that great misers giving large donatives to the poor in their last wills is no charity, to which is added the last will of Mr. Francis Bancroft. Now publish'd as a necessary appendix to the Hazards of a Death-Bed-Repentance, of which the tenth edition was lately published.
London: Printed by D. L. and Sold by J Roberts near the Oxford Arms, in Warwick Lane. Where may be had, The Hazard of a Death-Bed-Repentance 1728.

8°. Pp. [ii], 1-38.

Notes: CBEL II, 100.

Location: L.

478. The hazard of a death-bed-repentance .... To which is added conjugal perjury .... The tenth edition.
Printed for J. Roberts, near the Oxford-Arms in Warwick-Lane. Price 1 s. 6 d. M.DCC.XXVIII,[sic]

8°. Pp. [i]-xiv, [ii], 1-100.

Notes: "Conjugal Perjury' is present in this edition, pp. 90-100. The Hazard was first published in 1708.

Location: L.

479. Religio Bibliopolae. [Reprinted, 1728]
London: Printed, and sold by T. Warner at the Black Boy in Pater-noster-row, MDCCXXVIII. Price One Shilling and Sixpence.

8°. Pp. [viii], [1]-111, [i].

Notes: Religio Bibliopolae was first published in 1691. Sir Geoffrey Keynes, Bibl. of Sir Thomas Browne (Cambridge, 1924), No. 429.

Location: L, O, A.N.L.Munby; MU.

WORKS OF UNCERTAIN DATE

All's at State; or, The only Way to Retrieve the Lost Glory, Honour, Piety, Morals, and Unanimity of Great-Britain, is by the Choice of a Good Parliament.

Notes: No. 40 in Dunton's list of "Forty Political Tracts", printed in An Appeal, 1723.

The best of Wives exemplifyed in the Holy Life and triumphant Death of Mrs Elizabeth Dunton, Dr. Annesley's beloved Daughter.

Notes: Advertised by Dunton in a list of works written since the publication of Neck or Nothing, 1713, in Mr. John Dunton's Dying Groans, 1725, p. 11.

Black Bartholomew; or the Dissenting Doctors. A Poem ....

Notes: The "second edition" of Dunton's poem, "The Dissenting Doctors", was printed in Athenianism, 1710, but Dunton apparently planned to bring it up to date, for he advertised the above in The State-Weathercocks, 1719; and in The Athenian Library, 1725, he advertised Black Bartholomew ... to this present year 1725.

Burnet and Wharton; or, The Two Immortal Patriots; An Heroick Poem. Inscribed to all true Lovers of their King and Country; but more especially those that had the Honour to be Personally known either to the late Bishop of Salisbury, or the Marquis of Wharton.

Notes: No. 23 in Dunton's list of "Forty Political Tracts", printed in An Appeal, 1723.

"... discovery of a Jacobite-plot in Southwark to defeat the Protestant Succession [by "Mr. William Clark, a Dissenting Minister, living in Shadwell"], which Mr. Dunton published at the hazard of his life, and for which Mr. Clark was actually shot at by three men".

Notes: The above description from an extract of Dunton's _Mordecai's Memorial_, 1716, printed in _Life and Errors_, p. 732. This work has not been identified. Several sermons by William Clark are listed in the British Museum catalogue.

George _the Second_; or, The True Prince of _Wales_: An Heroick Poem. Dedicated to that Truly, Loyal, and Thoughtful Patriot, who was the first Proposer of that _Blessed Legacy_, the Protestant Succession in the _Illustrious House_ of Hannover.

Notes: No. 36 in Dunton's list of "Forty Political Tracts" printed in _An Appeal_, 1723.

God Save the King; or, A speech to our Rightful and ever Glorious Sovereign upon his first Landing at _Greenwich_: Giving him a hearty Welcome to his New Dominions.

Notes: No. 34 in Dunton's list of "Forty Political Tracts" printed in _An Appeal_, 1723.

The Ideal Kingdom; or, A Description of what Court _John_ the _Second_ resolves to keep, and in what Manner he intends to _Reign_, in Case (after the Death of _King_ George, _and the several Branches of his Illustrious House_) he should Defeat his _Popish Rival_ for the British Crown, and be chose _Sole Monarch_ of Great-Britain.

Notes: No. 20 in Dunton's list of "Forty Political Tracts" printed in _An Appeal_, 1723.

The Passive Rebels; or, A Satyr upon the High Church Impudence of wearing Oaken Boughs on the Restoration Day, Rue and Thyme on the Thanksgiving-Day, and White Roses on the Pretender's Birth-Day.

Notes: No. 29 in Dunton's list of "Forty Political Tracts" printed in An Appeal, 1723.

The Pretender; or, Sham King: A Trage-Comedy. As it was Acted upon the Theatre of Great-Britain during the late Cursed Rebellion.

Notes: No. 33 in Dunton's list of "Forty Political Tracts" printed in An Appeal, 1723.

The Protestant Nosegay; or, A Panegyrick upon the Royal Orange, and upon all Things dignify'd with an Orange-Colour, as it is to King William we owe the invaluable Blessing of the Protestant Succession in the Illustrious House of Hannover.

Notes: No. 35 in Dunton's list of "Forty Political Tracts" printed in An Appeal, 1723.

The Queen by Merit; A Paradox fully proved in the Illustrious Character of her Royal Highness the Princess of Wales.

Notes: No. 37 in Dunton's list of "Forty Political Tracts" printed in An Appeal, 1723.

The Royal Pair; or, A Panegyrick upon Conjugal Love: Inscrib'd to (that Matchless Instance of It) the Prince and Princess of Wales.

Notes: No. 38 in Dunton's list of "Forty Political Tracts" printed in An Appeal, 1723.

The Unborn Princes; An Heroick Poem: Inscribed to the Royal Issue of the *Illustrious House* of Hannover, not yet in Being; but is most Particularly Address'd to Prince *Frederick George*, and the Two Young Princesses, more lately arrived at the *Port of Life*.

Notes: No. 39 in Dunton's list of "Forty Political Tracts" printed in *An Appeal*, 1723.

POSTHUMOUS EDITIONS

Religio bibliopolae: oder die religion eines buch-handlers, ...
Frankfurt und Leipzig, ben Johann Christian Martini, Anno 1737.

8°. Pp. [viii], [1]-157, [i].

Notes: *Religio Bibliopolae* was first published in 1691.

Location: *L*.

The danger of living in a known sin, and the hazard of a death-bed repentance, fairly argued from the late remorse of W--- D--- of D--- .... The second edition.
Printed for R. Cater, and sold by the Booksellers of London and Westminster, 1738. [Price 1s.]

8°. Pp. [ii], i-ii, 1-56.

Notes: *Reasons for Reprinting* signed The Editor. Walthamstow, Aug. 7. 1738. *The Hazard* was first published in 1708.

Location: *L*.

Religio bibliopolae. [Reprinted, 1742]
London: Printed for W. Warren; and sold at the Three-Flower de Luces in the Old-Baily. MDCCXLII. (Price One Shilling.)

8°. Pp. [vi], [1]-111, [i].

Notes: Religio Bibliopolae was first published in 1691. Sir Geoffrey Keynes, Bibl. of Sir Thomas Browne (Cambridge, 1924), No. 434: "The same sheets as the issue of 1728 with a new title-page".

Location: L; BJ.

Religio bibliopolae. [Reprinted, 1750]

Notes: Sir Geoffrey Keynes, Bibl. of Sir Thomas Browne (Cambridge, 1924), No. 436. Not located.

[A Voyage Round the World, 1691, repr. 1762:] The life, travels, and adventures, of Christopher Wagstaff, Gentleman, grandfather to Tristram Shandy. Originally published in the latter end of the last century. Interspersed with a suitable variety of matter, by the editor. The whole being intended as a full and final answer to every thing that has been, or shall be, written in the out-of-the-way way. Vol. I. [Vol. II]
London: Printed for J. Hinxman, in Pater-noster Row. M.DCC.LXII.

8°. Vol. I: Pp. [i]-[xx], [1]-150, [ii].
Vol. II: Pp. [1]-203, [i].

Notes: Volumes I-VI of Tristram Shandy has been published in 1760-62; the editor of Wagstaff writes that he reprints the work "as a proof that Shandeism had an existence in this kingdom long before a late well-known publication". See Chapter II. H&L III. 366.

Location: C.

[A Voyage Round the World, 1691, repr. 1763:] The humorous life, travels, and adventures, of Christopher Wagstaff, Gentleman, grandfather to Tristram Shandy .... Vol. I. [Vol. II] The second edition.
London: Printed for Hawes, Clarke, and Collins, in Pater-Noster-Row. M.DCC.LXIII.

8°. Vol. I: Pp. [i]-xix, [i], [1]-150.
Vol. II: Pp. [1]-203, [i].

Location: O.

Religio bibliopolae. [Reprinted, 1780?]
London: Printed for C. Corbett, opposite St. Dunstan's Church, Fleet-Street. [Price 1 s. 6 d.]

8°. Pp. [ii], 1-2, [1]-84.

Notes: Religio Bibliopolae was first published in 1691.

Location: L; MU, CU.

Extracts from the Life and Errors of John Dunton, Late Citizen of London; Written by Himself in Solitude, 1705.
Massachusetts Historical Society Collections, Second Series, Volume I. Boston, 1814.

The life and errors of John Dunton, Citizen of London; with the lives and characters of more than a thousand contemporary divines, and other persons of literary eminence. To which are added, Dunton's Conversation in Ireland; selections from his other genuine works; and a faithful portrait of the author. Vol. I. [Vol. II]
Printed By And For J. Nichols, Son, And Bentley, At The Printing-Office Of The Votes Of The House Of Commons, 25, Parliament Street, Westminster: Sold Also At Their Old Office In Red Lion Passage, Fleet Street, London. 1818.

The Athenian Oracle abridged; containing the most valuable questions and answers, in the original work; on history, philosophy, divinity, love and marriage.
London: Printed By and For John Nichols and Son, 25, Parliament-street, Westminster. 1820.

Letters written from New England, A.D. 1686 .... Now first published from the original manuscript .... with notes and an appendix, by W. H. Whitmore.
Boston, 1867. (Publications of the Prince Society, Vol. IV)

"The Athenian Oracle." A selection, edited by John Underhill. With a prefatory letter from Walter Besant.
London: Walter Scott, 24 Warwick Lane, Paternoster Row. [1893]

[The Life and Errors of John Dunton, extracts:] The tribute of a London publisher to his printers.
Cambridge: Printed at the University Press by W. Lewis, University Printer, for his Friends in Printing & Publishing Christmas 1930.

NOTES

Chapter I. Early Life, Apprenticeship, and Beginnings in the Trade (1659-1688)

1. Remarks and Collections of Thomas Hearne, ed. C. E. Doble et al. (Oxford, 1885-1921) II, 26; Alexander Pope, The Dunciad, ed. Sutherland (London, 1943), p. 117; Edward Harley, Earl of Oxford, "Notes on Biographies", Harl. Ms. 7544, in Notes and Queries, Second Series, IX (1860), 418-9.

2. H. Lemoine, in a letter to The Gentleman's Magazine, LV(1785), 287; Life and Errors, p.v.

3. Isaac Disraeli, in a letter to John Nichols, printed in Nichols' Literary Anecdotes of the Eighteenth Century (London, 1812-15) IX, 631-2.

4. C. A. Moore, in Studies in Philology XXII (1925), 469.

5. T. M. Hatfield, The True Secret History of Mr. John Dunton, unpublished dissertation (Harvard University, 1926), p. ii.

6. See Donald A. Stauffer, The Art of Biography in Eighteenth Century England (Princeton, 1941), pp. 269-74.

7. George Lipscomb, History and Antiquities of the County of Buckingham (London, 1847) II, 397; W.P.W. Phillimore and F. W. Ragg, eds., Buckinghamshire Parish Registers (London, 1902-23) VII, 104-Little Missenden Parish.

8. John Dunton, Dunton's Remains (London, 1684), pp. 1-3.

9. Ibid., p. 4.

10. J. and J. A. Venn, eds., Alumni Cantabrigienses, Part I. (London, 1922-27) II, 76. Although his son often spoke of him as a fellow of Trinity, there exists no record of this fellowship, and none of his having taken the M.A. degree.

NOTES

11. A. C. Matthews, _Walker Revised_ (Oxford, 1948), p. 66: after deprivation of Giles Thorn from the living of St. Mary's, Bedford, John Dunton was rector in 1652, R. Fish in 1658.

12. F.G. Emmison, ed., _Bedfordshire Parish Registers_ (Bedford, 1931-), St. Mary's, Bedford.

13. John Dunton, _Dunton's Remains_ (London, 1684), p. 19.

14. _Life and Errors_, pp. 23, 568.

15. George Lipscomb, _History and Antiquities of the County of Buckingham_ (London, 1847) II, 89.

16. _Life and Errors_, pp. 23-24.

17. John Dunton, _A Voyage Round the World_ (London, 1691) I, 60, 103.

18. _Life and Errors_, pp. 27-8.

19. _Ibid._, p. 28.

20. _Ibid._, p. 38.

21. _Ibid._, p. 39.

22. _Ibid._, p. 42.

23. Stationers' Company, Apprentices' Register Book 1666-1727.

24. _Life and Errors_, p. 43.

25. _Ibid._, p. 43.

26. _Ibid._, p. 47.

27. John Dunton, _Dunton's Remains_ (London, 1648), p. 63.

28. _Life and Errors_, pp. 50-1.

29. John Dunton, Will, PRO, Price fol. 82, p. 10.

30. _Ibid._, pp. 8-9.

NOTES

31. Reverend John Dunton, Will (dated 15 March 1675), unpublished ms. at Buckinghamshire County Record Office, Aylesbury, Bucks., p. 2.

32. *The Address of above Twenty Thousand of the Loyal Protestant Apprentices of London: Humbly presented to the Right Honourable the Lord Mayor, Septemb. 2, 1681* (Wing A 543).

33. John Dunton, *The Neck Adventure*, 1715, p. vi.

34. *Life and Errors*, p. 49.

35. *Ibid.*, p. 49.

36. Stationers' Company, Register of Freemen 1605-1751.

37. *Life and Errors*, p. 61.

38. [William Roberts], "Bookselling in the Poultry", *The City Press*, Vol. XXXIV, No. 2386 (London, 16 August 1890), p. 7. See also Henry R. Plomer, "The Long Shop in the Poultry", *Bibliographica* (London, 1895-7) II, 61-80.

39. *Life and Errors*, p. 86.

40. *Ibid.*, p. 61.

41. *Ibid.*, p. 62.

42. *Ibid.*, p. 63.

43. *Ibid.*, p. 64.

44. *Ibid.*, pp. 64-65.

45. Iris to Philaret, 9 July 1682, printed in *Life and Errors*, pp. 67-8.

46. *Life and Errors*, pp. 62, 77-8. Dunton had first met Wesley before 1680, when Wesley was a pupil at Veal's academy in Wapping (see Irene Parker, *Dissenting Academies in England* [Cambridge, 1914], p. 139.

47. Ibid., p. 79.

NOTES

48. *Ibid;*, pp. 68-9.

49. Daniel Defoe was apparently not, as has often been stated, a son-in-law of Dr. Annesley. William Lee wrote that: "Dunton was married to a daughter of the Rev. Dr. Annesley, and Mr. Wilson [*Life and Times of Defoe*, 1830] inclines to the opinion that Defoe married another daughter, and that thus he and Dunton were brothers-in-law. Many minute circumstances - which, however, would occupy too much space, and still leave the matter doubtful - induce me to agree with Mr. Wilson, as to the probability that Defoe's first wife was the daughter of Dr. Annesley" (*Daniel Defoe: His Life and Recently Discovered Writings*, [London, 1869] I, 33-4. J. R. Moore, the most recent biographer of Defoe, stated simply that other writers have confused Defoe with Dunton, in stating that he married a daughter of Dr. Annesley, but Moore cites no further evidence (*Daniel Defoe Citizen of the Modern World* [Chicago, 1958], p. 18). Had Dunton and Defoe been brothers-in-law, it is highly improbable that the fact would have escaped mention in the *Life and Errors*, which contains a lengthy character of Defoe, and extensive information about various members of the Annesley family.

50. See Adam Clarke, *Memoirs of the Wesley Family* (London, 1823), pp. 243-362. See also Mabel R. Brailsford, *Susanna Wesley, the Mother of Methodism* (London, 1938); and John Kirk, *The Mother of the Wesleys* (2nd edn., London, 1864).

51. John Dunton's half-sister Sarah Dunton married Richard Sault about 1686 (see *Life and Errors*, p. 139; Bodleian Library, Ms. Rawlinson D 71, Letter VII, f. 204; and, for discussion, T. M. Hatfield, *The True Secret History of Mr. John Dunton*, unpublished thesis [Harvard University, 1926], pp. 27-31.)

52. *Life and Errors*, p. 79.

53. Bound 5 February 1683 (Stationers' Company, Apprentices' Register Book 1666-1727).

54. S. P. Dom. Car. II 427, No. 135.

55. S. P. Dom. Car. II 428, No. 31.

NOTES

56. When published, Truth Will Out bore the imprint (presumably fictitious) of Thomas Manhood. See Appendix, Part 4, on pseudonymous imprints.

57. Life and Errors, p. 79.

58. Ibid., p. 214.

59. John Dunton to Samuel Annesley, 7 August 1685, printed in Life and Errors, p. 80.

60. Life and Errors, p. 81. In his Voyage Round the World, 1691, Dunton wrote with less restraint in his characterisation of the rambling temperament: "... a Dutch Post ravshes him [i.e., a rambler], and the meer Superscription of a Letter ... from Boston, Italy, or France, sets him up like a Top, Colen or Germany makes spin ... and at seeing the world Universe, America, Flanders, or the Holy Land, tho but on the Title of a Book, he's ready to break Doublet, let fall Breeches, (in a civil way) and overflow the room with all those Wonderments have surpriz'd him in these flourishing Contreys" (I.10).

61. Life and Errors, p. 82. £50 was only a small part of the debt of £1200 which Dunton claimed to have contracted for Iris's sister (Life and Errors, p. 81). See also The case of John Dunton, 1700, passim, and The Living Elegy, 1706, passim.

62. The debt to Nevet of £50 was paid by Iris while Dunton was in New England.

63. Life and Errors, p. 86. Some writers have conjectured that Dunton may himself have left England for political reasons. Dunton travelled with a ship-load of fugitives, his apprentice chose to remain in New England after Dunton returned to England ("he had not the courage to see Old England again, for he had been dabbling in Monmouth's Adventure" [Life and Errors, p. 130]) and Dunton on his return remained in concealment. He visited Holland in 1687-8, where he encountered many fugitives from the Monmouth fiasco, and returned to his shop only after the Prince of Orange had come to London. On the other hand, even though some Whigs may have been reticent in later years about their activities in 1683-5, it is inconceivable

that Dunton would have remained silent about his political activities. Dunton, in fact, wrote tracts boasting of his work for the Whig interests, and nowhere in his writings did Dunton suggest that anything but financial motives precipitated his flight in 1685. Dunton was certainly a fugitive in 1685, but it was his creditors he fled, not political arrest.

64. Life and Errors, p. 87.

65. Ibid., p. 88.

66. Although Dunton himself claimed to have been four months at sea (Bodleian Library Ms. Rawlinson D 71, f. 235), C. N. Greenough noted that an entry in Samuel Sewall's Diary establishes the date of the arrival of the Susannah and Thomas in Boston as 27 January 1686 (Diary, Massachusetts Historical Society Collections, Series 5, V-VII [Boston, Mass., 1878-82], I, 119).

67. Life and Errors, p. 90.

68. Ibid., pp. 135-6. There is no evidence, beyond Dunton's own statement, that he was given the freedom of Boston. C. N. Greenough, who searched the archives of Boston, found only a bond for £40 given by Francis Burroughs on 16 February 1686, as a surety that "John Dunton, booke seller or any of his Familie shall not be chargable to this town during his or any their abode therein" (see T.M. Hatfield, op. cit., pp. 32-3).

69. Bodleian Library, Ms. Rawlinson D 71, f. 82. Dunton's letters from New England were prepared for publication in Ireland in 1698 (Dublin Scuffle, 1699, p. 369), and the eight letters, with a general title-page (A Summer Ramble through Ten Kingdoms) survive in Ms. Rawlinson D 71. John Dunton's Letters from New-England were printed in Boston for the Prince Society in 1867, edited by W. H. Whitmore, who identified the sources of many of Dunton's unacknowledged borrowings from other authors. C. N. Greenough has since further demonstrated the lack of originality of the letters in two papers read before the Colonial Society of Massachusetts ("John Dunton's Letters from New-England", Pub. Col. Soc. Mass. XIV [1912], 213-57; and "John Dunton

Again", Pub. Col. Soc. Mass. XXI [1919], 232-51). The New-England letters will not be quoted extensively here; they chiefly are concerned with Dunton's rambles in New England and the characters of his friends there.

70. Iris to Philaret, 14 May 1686, printed in Life and Errors, pp. 92-3.

71. Life and Errors, pp. 92, 112.

72. Ibid., p. 112.

73. Ibid., pp. 114-22.

74. A Sermon Occasioned by the Execution of a Man found Guilty of Murder, Boston, 1686 (Wing M 1246).

74a. Life and Errors, pp. 109-110.

75. Ibid., p. 124.

76. Ibid., p. 124.

77. Bodleian Library, Ms. Rawlinson D 71, f. 196.

78. Life and Errors, p. 127.

79. Ibid., p. 137.

80. Bodleian Library, Ms. Rawlinson D 71, f. 235.

81. Life and Errors, p. 138.

82. Ibid., p. 139.

83. Ibid., p. 140.

84. Of the English ministers in Holland, Mr. Spademan was Dunton's particular friend, and he later sent Dunton valuable copies to publish. The publication of the History of the Edict of Nantes was made possible by Spademan's sending the copy to Dunton before other London booksellers were able to obtain it. See Life and Errors, pp. 140-1; and below, Chapter II.

85. Life and Errors, pp. 143-4.

86. Ibid., p. 148.

87. Ibid., p. 149.

88. Ibid., pp. 150-1.

Chapter II. Maturity in the Trade (1688-98)

1. Life and Errors, p. 151.
2. John Evelyn, Diary (ed. De Beer, Oxford, 1955) IV, 611-2.
3. Life and Errors, pp. 151-2.
4. Ibid., p. 214.
5. 24 March 1680 (Stationers' Company, Register of Freemen 1605-1751).
6. T. C. I, 457, 503, 509; II, 24, 40, 55.
7. T. C. II, 114 (Wing T 3382). This work contains two pages of advertisements of "Books Printed for Jonathan Greenwood, at the Black Raven in the Poultry, near the Old Jury"; none of the eight works advertised, however, was published by Dunton, or advertised by him.
8. Life and Errors, p. 228.
9. Ibid., p. 228.
10. Ibid., pp. 92-3.
11. John Dunton, An Essay, Proving we shall Know our Friends in Heaven, 1697, p. 32.
12. In A New Martyrology, 1689, Dunton advertised: "Courteous Reader, Understanding that many of these Books now recited have been much enquired for during my late Travels into America and the Low Countries, &c. these are therefore to

acquaint thee, that several of them that are now out of Print will speedily go to the Press; and as for the Rest, they are now to be bought At the Black Raven in the Poultry, over-against the Compter: Where you may be very kindly used for all manner of Bibles, Bible-Cases, Histories, School-Books, new Pamphlets, and all sorts of Practical Books".

13. Quoted by J. G. Muddiman, The Bloody Assizes (Edinburgh, 1929), p. 5.

14. Wing P 3838.

15. The Protestant Martyrs was not advertised by Dunton in the many advertisements he printed concerning the various components of his New Martyrology. S. Schofield (Jeffreys of 'The Bloody Assizes' [London, 1937], p. 308) believed Dunton responsible for the work, whereas J. G. Muddiman (The Bloody Assizes [Edinburgh, 1929], p. 8) suggested Dunton or John Tutchin. However, The Protestant Martyrs may have been a piracy, printed after the publication of Dunton's two collections of dying speeches, and The Bloody Assizes, which appeared in that order. In an advertisement printed at the end of The Bloody Assizes, Dunton described his three publications and cautioned his readers not to accept false copies.

16. Life and Errors, p. 208.

17. J. G. Muddiman, The Bloody Assizes (Edinburgh, 1929), pp. 5-10.

18. Life and Errors, pp. 184-5. See also Barbara Louise Magaw, "The Work of John Shirley, an Early Hack Writer", in the Papers of the Bibliographical Society of America, LVI (1962), 332-43.

19. Ibid., pp. 184-5.

20. Ibid., pp. 184-5.

21. Ibid., p. 243.

22. 5 March 1689 (Stationers' Company, Apprentices' Register Book 1666-1727); also Life and Errors, p. 574.

NOTES

23. Life and Errors, pp. 154, 503, 512.

24. In fact, 111; five are repeated.

25. Marjorie Plant, The English Book Trade (London, 1939), p. 90.

26. Life and Errors, p. 205.

27. Dr. Annesley was active in securing trade for Dunton. Dunton wrote of Dr. Horneck that "I cannot say I actually printed any thing for this eminent Divine; yet I may truly call him my Author; for whilst he was preaching on the Parable of Dives and Lazarus, the present Bishop of Gloucester (at the request of Dr. Annesley, his Predecessor at Cripplegate) did me the honour to engage Dr. Horneck's promise that I should print the Sermons he preached upon that subject; and Dr. Horneck sent me a letter, ... wherein he tells me ... that no other person should print them but me" (Life and Errors, p. 162). The letters survive in the Bodleian Library, Ms. Rawlinson D 72, Nos. 70-71.

28. T. J. Holmes, Increase Mather A Bibliography of His Works (Cleveland, 1931), No. 42. "The first edition, no copy of which has come to our notice, very likely appeared in Boston in 1695 or 1696" (I, 197).

29. T. J. Holmes, Cotton Mather A Bibliography of His Works (Cambridge, Mass., 1940), No. 213-A. Completed in 1697, the Magnalia was not published until 1702, because of bickering with Parkhurst.

30. Life and Errors, p. 186.

31. Ibid., p. 175.

32. Sir Geoffrey Keynes, A Bibliography of Sir Thomas Browne, Kt, M. D. (Cambridge, 1924), No. 407. A. C. Howell intended to publish a second part to his article "John Dunton and an Imitation of the Religio Medici" (Studies in Philology XXIX [1932], 442-62), discussing in detail the sources for the work, but it did not appear.

NOTES

33. *Life and Errors*, p. 177. See also J. and J. A. Venn, *Alumni Cantabrigienses, Part I* (Cambridge, 1922-27), I, 216. Bridgwater was admitted sizar, aged 16, to Trinity College on March 6, 1678/9, from St. Paul's School. He took his B. A. in 1682/3 and was admitted to the Middle Temple, November 1687. E. Arber, in editing the *Term Catalogues*, was the first to mistake Bridgwater for Dunton; the British Museum catalogue followed his example, and the error has since turned up frequently.

34. Offered for sale by H. W. Edwards Booksellers, Ltd., Ashmore Green, Newbury, Berks., Catalogue 110 [January 1964], No. 43.

35. *Life and Errors*, p. 182. But see article on Robert Midgeley in DNB (XIII, 366-7) for a discussion of the authorship of *The Turkish Spy*.

36. H. J. Reesink, *L'Angleterre et la Litterature Anglaise dans les Trois Plus Anciens Periodiques Francais de Hollande* (Zutphen, 1931), Number 911.

37. *Religio Bibliopolae: Oder die Religion Eines Buchhandlers*, Frankfurt und Leipzig, ben Johann Christian Martini, Anno 1737.

38. *Life and Errors*, p. 159.

39. J. M. Stedmond, "Another Possible Analogue for Swift's *Tale of a Tub*", in *Modern Language Notes*, LXXII (1957), 13-18.

40. *The Life, Travels, and Adventures, of Christopher Wagstaff, Gentleman, Grandfather to Tristram Shandy* (London, 1762), I, xii.

41. W. L. Cross, *Life and Times of Laurence Sterne*, (New Edition, New Haven, 1925), I, 132-3. T. M. Hatfield (*The True Secret History of Mr. John Dunton*, unpublished thesis [Harvard University, 1926], p. 91n, corresponded with Prof. Cross: "This letter has been lost but Dean Cross who writes me that his search for it has been vain believes that the statement 'should be taken at its face value'".

NOTES

42. *Life and Errors*, p. 203.

43. John Dunton, Will, PRO, Price fol. 82, p. 8. Also *Life and Errors*, pp. 202-3.

44. *Life and Errors*, p. 203. At a General Court of the Stationers' Company held on 12 September 1692, John Dunton, among others, was ordered to show cause at the next General Court why he should not be elected to the Livery of the Company; on 3 October 1692, the Court ordered that John Dunton be summoned to take the clothing at the next Court; and on 7 November 1692, Dunton accepted the Livery and promised payment of £20 Livery fine (Stationers' Company, Court Book F, ff. 178v-179r, 180v, 181v). Dunton's payment of his livery fine is recorded in the Stationers' Company Calls on Livery 1606-1736, call begun 5 May 1690.

45. *Ibid.*, p. 203.

46. John Dunton, Will, PRO, Price fol. 82, p. 1.

47. *Athenian Mercury* IV, 15 - 17 November 1691.

48. *Life and Errors*, p. 159.

49. *Compleat Library*, July 1692, p. 206

50. R. J. Allen, *Clubs of Augustan London* (Cambridge, Mass., 1933), p. 155.

51. *Life and Errors*, pp. 256-7.

52. *Ibid.*, p. 153. Warrant issued 30 June 1693, see PRO, S. P. Dom. Warrant Book 38, p. 307; the original licence issued to Dunton survives in the Bodleian Library, Ms. Rawlinson, Letters 44, f. 23.

53. *Ibid.*, p. 256.

54. C. E. Kenney, "William Leybourn, 1626-1716", in *The Library*, 5th Series, V (1950), 159-171.

55. STC 1178-9; Wing B 357-B 366.

NOTES

56. C. A. Moore, "John Dunton: Pietist and Impostor" in *Studies in Philology*, XXII (1925), 467-99.

57. *Life and Errors*, p. 157.

58. *Ibid.*, pp. 206, 436.

59. *Athenian Mercury* IX, 17 - 7 February 1693.

60. *Life and Errors*, p. 155.

61. *Ibid.*, p. 157.

62. Bennet, in London, was a fortnight behind Dunton in licensing and entering his translation (See below, checklist). Taylor's edition was printed by L. Lichfield in Oxford in 1694, and not in London for Bennet until 1700. Sault's translation sold well, however, and Dunton advertised (in Burroughs' *Narrative*, 1694) that "*Several Gentlemen* of the Universities ... have so highly approved Mr. Sault's Translation of *Malebranches Search after Truth*, ... *as that it has greatly encouraged the Sale* at *Oxford* and *Cambridge*, and occasioned the Undertakers to send great Numbers thither a *Second Time*, and to expedite the Publication of the *Second Volume*".

63. Moorpark, 9 November 1694. Osborn Collection, Yale University Library. See also T. P. Courtenay, *Memoirs ... of Sir William Temple, Bart*. (London, 1836), II, 221-3.

64. Gertrude E. Noyes, "John Dunton's *Ladies Dictionary*, 1694", in *Philological quarterly*, XXI (1942), 129-145.

65. *Life and Errors*, pp. 274-5, 404.

66. *Ibid.*, p. 231.

67. *Ibid.*, pp. 257-8.

68. Athenian Mercury XVI, 10 - 19 January 1695; *Life and Errors*, p. 198. Dunton visited Bristol Fair only in 1695 and in one other year (*Life and Errors*, p. 236). Dunton also sold books at Sturbridge Fair, where he was kindly treated by the booksellers of Cambridge (*Life and*

Errors, pp. 221-2, 237). Special techniques, apparently, were necessary for successful merchandising at a fair, for Dunton commented that Mr Shrowsbury of Cambridge, "a constant frequenter of Sturbridge Fair, ... perhaps is the only Bookseller that understands Fair-keeping to any advantage" (Life and Errors, p. 221).

69. William Fuller, The Whole Life of Mr. William Fuller (London, 1703), pp. 70-1.

70. Ibid., p. 132.

71. Life and Errors, p. 181. Fuller did not, however, repeat his charge against Dunton in The Sincere and Hearty Confession of Mr. William Fuller, which was published in 1704, although in that work he named others who had been involved with him in the tracts of 1696. George Campbell, Impostor at the Bar (London, 1961), pp. 219 et passim. In a still later version of his autobiography, of which the autograph manuscript, dated 1732, is in the Osborn Collection, Yale University Library (MS. f.c. 66), Fuller wrote that "the rebellion in the north gave me an Occasion to renew my former pretendent proofs that Mrs Mary Grey was the true mother of the prince of Wales, which I write out by the assistance of Mr John Dunton" (p. 75).

72. Adam Clarke, Memoirs of the Wesley Family (London, 1823), p. 240.

73. Life and Errors, pp. 284-5.

74. Ibid., p. 285.

75. Ibid., p. 181.

76. Remarks made about the Quakers in I, 10 elicited a reply: A Curb for Pegasus, or Observations on the Observator, Number 10 ... In relation to the People called Quakers (London, 1696). Wing C 7619.

77. Walter Graham, English Literary Periodicals (New York, 1930), p. 376.

78. Stanley Morison, The English Newspaper (Cambridge, 1932), p. 87n.

79. R. M. Wiles, Serial Publication in England before 1750 (Cambridge, 1957), p. 77.

Chapter III. The Athenian Society (1691-1697)

1. Life and Errors, p. 187.

2. Ibid., p. 188. Dunton called his project The Athenian Gazette, citing Acts xvii, 21, "For all the Athenians and strangers which were there spent their time in nothing else, but either to tell, or to hear some new thing". W. L. Graham (Beginnings of English Literary Periodicals [New York, 1926], p. 16) quoted Mercurius Bifrons, No. I, 1681, "People of late have all turned Athenians, and there is much inquiry after news". He observed that the word was used in that sense in 1643, in A Letter Sent from London, by John Taylor. When a reader of The Athenian Mercury asked why the name had been altered from Gazette to Mercury, the Athenian Society replied, in Vol. I, No. 12, for 2 May 1691, that "Gaza signifies a Treasury, and therefore we reserve it for the general Title of our Volumes, designing to entitle 'em the Athenian Gazette, or Casuistical Mercury: And Mercurius signifying a Messenger, 'tis the more proper Title for the single Papers, which run about to Coffee houses and elsewhere, to seek out Athenians".

3. R. J. Allen, Clubs of Augustan London (Cambridge, Mass., 1933), p. 229.

4. Miriam K. Starkman, in Swift's Satire on Learning in A Tale of a Tub (Princeton, 1950), and Mabel Phillips (Mrs. William C. DeVane), in her dissertation on Jonathan Swift's Relations to Science (Yale University, 1925), have examined the range of queries dealt with in the Mercury, particularly in connection with Swift's changing attitude towards the Athenian Society. See also The Oracle of the Coffee House, by Gilbert D. McEwen (The Huntington Library, 1972).

5. Adam Clarke, Memoirs of the Wesley Family (London, 1823), p. 75.

NOTES

6. Alexandre Beljame, *Men of Letters and the English Public in the Eighteenth Century* (ed. B. Dobree, London, 1948), p. 256.

7. *Athenian Mercury*, I, 2 - 24 March 1691.

8. *Ibid.*, I, 3 - 31 March 1691.

9. *Ibid.*, I, 18 - 23 May 1691.

10. *Life and Errors*, p. 190; the completed volumes however were called *The Athenian Gazette*.

11. *Ibid.*, p. 189.

12. *Ibid.*, pp. 189-90.

13. Bodleian Library, Ms. Rawlinson D 72, No. 65.

14. J. R. Moore, *Daniel Defoe Citizen of the Modern World* (Chicago, 1958), p. 232.

15. *Life and Errors*, pp. 180-1; Daniel Defoe, *A True Collection*, 1702.

16. John Dunton, *The Whipping Post*, 1706, in *Life and Errors*, p. 423.

17. *Athenian Mercury*, I, 13 - 5 May 1691.

18. Elkanah Settle, *The New Athenian Comedy* (London, 1693), p. [vi].

19. *Athenian Mercury*, II, 6 - 13 June 1691.

20. *Ibid.*, I, 15 - 11 May 1691; I, 23 - Out of series; II, 5 - 9 June 1691.

21. *Ibid.*, II, 3 - 3 June 1691.

22. *Ibid.*, IV, 14 - 14 November 1691, and IV, 18 - 28 November 1691.

23. London, 1691. Wing C 5360.

NOTES

24. [London, 1692]. Wing C 5358A.

25. London, 1692. Copy in British Museum.

26. London, 1691. Wing K 78, K 79.

27. London, 1692. Wing K 84.

28. T. W. Davids, Annals of Evangelical Nonconformity in the County of Essex (London, 1863), No. 16, p. 461; no copy has been located.

29. Life and Errors, pp. 191-5.

30. 3 May 1692. Jonathan Swift, Correspondence (ed. H. Williams, Oxford, 1963-65), I, 8.

31. Jonathan Swift, Correspondence (ed. H. Williams, Oxford, 1963-65), I, 5-6. Printed in the supplement to Volume V of The Athenian Gazette.

32. Teerink No. 467. No copy of a separate London printing has been located, although Dunton advertised the ode for several years.

33. 3 May 1692. Jonathan Swift, Correspondence (ed. H. Williams, Oxford, 1963-65), I, 8. Rothschild 2277.

34. Samuel Johnson, Lives of the Poets (ed. G. Birkbeck Hill, Oxford, 1950), III, 7.

35. Sir Henry Craik, Life of Jonathan Swift (London, 1882), p. 35.

36. Ricardo Quintana, Mind and Art of Jonathan Swift (London, 1936); the ode is discussed in detail, pp. 33-35.

37. Mabel Phillips (Mrs. William C. DeVane), Jonathan Swift's Relations to Science, unpublished thesis, Yale University, 1925.

38. London, 1692. Copy in British Museum.

39. Ibid., Wing P 1325, P 1362, P 1382.

NOTES

40. [London,] 1692. Wing B 106A.

41. Athenian Mercury, VII, 22 & 23 - 11 & 14 June 1692.

42. London, 1692. Wing B 1133A.

43. London (Lacedemonian) Mercury, I, 1 - 1 February 1692.

44. Ibid.

45. Athenian Mercury, VI, 1 - 2 February 1692.

46. London (Lacedemonian) Mercury, I, 2 - 5 February 1692.

47. Ibid., I, 5 - 22 February 1692.

48. Benjamin Boyce, Tom Brown of Facetious Memory (Cambridge Mass., 1939), p. 37.

49. Athenian Mercury, VII, 18 - 28 May 1692.

50. Ibid., VII, 19 - 31 May 1692.

51. Life and Errors, pp. 190-1.

52. Benjamin Boyce has noted that Dunton stated in his Living Elegy, 1706, that the undertaker of The Lacedemonian Mercury "undermined my 'Question project,' till he lost about twenty pounds, and flung up his 'Lacedemonian Mercury'" (Benjamin Boyce, Tom Brown of Facetious Memory [Cambridge, Mass., 1939], p. 39n.).

53. Athenian Mercury, VII, 19 - 31 May 1692.

54. Life and Errors, pp. 191-2.

55. Athenian Mercury, VII, 10 - 30 April 1692.

56. Ibid., VII, 13 - 10 May 1692.

57. Compleat Library, September, 1692; Life and Errors, p. 261.

58. [Charles Gildon,] The History of the Athenian Society, [London, 1692], p. 3.

59. *Ibid.*, pp. 6, 7.

60. John Norris, *Christian Blessedness*, 1692, Wing N 1247; *Practical Discourses*, 1693, Wing N 1258-64.

61. Wing C 3754.

62. *Life and Errors*, p. 191; the question referred to was printed in *Athenian Mercury*, VII, 29 - 5 July 1692 (Question 18).

63. London, 1693. Wing S 2701.

64. Frank C. Brown, *Elkanah Settle His Life and Works* (Chicago 1910), p. 98.

65. *Jovial Mercury*, C. & K. 1476; *Ladies Mercury*, C. & K. 1490; CBEL II, 658.

66. Moderator, C. & K. 1701; Benjamin Boyce, *Tom Brown of Facetious Memory* (Cambridge, Mass., 1939), p. 43; CBEL II, 658.

67. *Athenianism*, 1710, p. 113.

68. *Athenian Mercury*, XIII, 23 - 24 April 1694.

69. *Ibid.*, XIX, 30 - 8 February 1696.

Chapter IV. Dunton and La Crose

1. Bodleian Library, MS. Rawlinson D 72, No. 65.

2. Stat. Reg. G, 338 (385).

3. *Weekly Memorials for the Ingenious*, 16 January 1682, preface.

4. According to James Crossley, *Notes and Queries*, I, vi (1852), 435-6.

5. *Universal Historical Bibliotheque*, January 1687.

NOTES

6. Advertisement, Athenian Mercury, ii, 4 - 6 June 1691; ii, 11 - 30 June 1691.

7. "Proposals for Printing a Book, Entituled, The Young Students Library", printed in the preface to Volume iii of The Athenian Mercury.

8. E. and E. Haag, La France Protestante (Paris, 1846-58), IV, 63-4; Ferdinand Hoefer, ed., Nouvelle Biographie Generale (Paris, 1855-66), XXVIII, 610; Rev. David C. A. Agnew, Protestant Exiles from France in the Reign of Louis XIV [Edinburgh,] 1866), p. 300; J. Balteau, et al., eds., Dictionnaire de Biographie Francaise (Paris, 1933-), IX, 667.

9. Walter Graham believed La Crose to have been the author of the English Universal Historical Bibliotheque, and he cited an advertisement which appeared in The Athenian Mercury for 15 Feb. 1692, which referred to his authorship (English Literary Periodicals, New York, 1930, p. 30). To have written the Universal Historical Bibliotheque, La Crose would have had to be in England in 1687, although he might have begun to translate the work while yet engaged in the writing of it in Holland. La Crose's statement in his note 'To The Reader' in the August 1691 number of The Works of the Learned, not noted by Graham, rules out any possibility of his participation in the English periodical: 'If you judge of this sort of Writings, by some late Translations of Foreign Journals, or by the History of Learning, printed with my Name, you will have perhaps a mean opinion of it: For, not to speak of the first wherein I am not concern'd, in the latter I was unluckily ingaged with a Bookseller, who thought himself wiser than I, and would over-rule in every thing'. Wing L 137.

10. The History of Learning, 1691, preface. The History of Learning was published in July 1691 (Graham, English Literary Periodicals, p. 39).

11. Life and Errors, pp. 180, 198.

12. Athenian Mercury, iii, 13 - 8 September 1691.

13. Ibid., iv, 3 - 6 October 1691.

NOTES

14. Ibid., iv, 4 - 10 October 1691. Apparently La Crose was paid at least in part for his writing by the gift of a number of copies of the periodical for his own disposal.

15. Bennet's advertisement, on the reverse of the title-page, survives in this writer's copy of the September 1691 number of The Works of the Learned, but not in the copy at Trinity College, Cambridge.

16. Advertised as 'just now publish'd' in Athenian Mercury, iv, 8 - 24 October 1691.

17. "Proposals for Printing a Book, Entituled, The Young Students Library", printed in the preface to Volume iii of The Athenian Mercury.

18. The Works of the Learned was published on the first Monday in the month (Works of the Learned, August 1691, 'To The Reader').

19. Athenian Mercury, iv, 13 - 10 November 1691.

20. Works of the Learned, November 1691, p. 149.

21. Ibid., p. 154.

22. Athenian Mercury, v, 3 - 8 December 1691.

23. Ibid., v, 10 - 2 January 1692.

24. Ibid., vi. 2 - 6 February 1692.

25. TC ii, 395 (Hilary 1692).

26. The Young Students' Library was published in June 1692 (advertisement, Athenian Mercury, vii, 19 & 20 - 31 May & 4 June 1692).

27. Universal Historical Bibliotheque, February 1687, "To the Reader". Dunton experienced this difficulty as well, and in The Athenian Mercury, iii, 13 - 8 September 1691, Dunton advertised for review copies of newly published works: "All those Learned Gentlemen that send us in their Books when newly Printed, or Abstracts of their Books ready drawn, or any remarkable Observations that may be

useful to the Publick, if they send 'em to the Raven in the Poultry, they shall be inserted in our next Supplement".

28. Bennet retained the right to publish The Works of the Learned, having sold to Dunton the right to a monthly journal of books. Cyprian Blagden (TLS, 3 Dec. 1954) discussed The History of the Works of the Learned: or, An Impartial Account of Books Lately Printed in all Parts of Europe. With a Particular Relation of the State of Learning in each Country ... Done by several Hands. This serial was published for a dozen years, from 1699, by Bennet, with Henry Rhodes, John Harris, Andrew Bell, Daniel Midwinter, and Thomas Leigh. Blagden stated that The Works of the Learned had been entered on 8 October 1691, but he was unaware of the appearance of a work of that name before one appeared in 1695, printed for H. Rhodes and W. Lindsey, which lasted only a very short time. There is no information available concerning the further career of Jean de la Crose, except that he compiled Memoirs for the Ingenious from January to December 1693, and that he wrote An Historical and Geographical Description of France, which was published in 1694 (not located by Wing; offered for sale by H. W. Edwards, Booksellers, Catalogue 110, 1964, no. 195). La Crose was not concerned with the later periodical called The Works of the Learned. Although Walter Graham believed so (Beginnings of English Literary Periodicals, New York, 1926, p. 32), he failed to note Dunton's statement that "Lecrose dying, it [The Works of the Learned] was discontinued, though the same design, under the same title, is yet on foot, and managed by several hands, one of which is the ingenious Mr. Ridpath" (Life and Errors, p. 199). La Crose's death, therefore, must be the explanation for the short life of the periodical of 1695.

29. Memoirs for the Ingenious ... By J. de la Crose, i, 1, January 1693.

30. Athenian Mercury, vii, 13 - 10 May 1692.

31. Compleat Library, July - November 1693, preface.

32. Athenian Mercury, xiv, 18 - 21 July 1694.

NOTES

Chapter V. The Dublin Scuffle (1698)

1. Life and Errors, p. 277.

2. Wesley to Dunton, 24 July 1697, printed in Life and Errors, p. 164.

3. Life and Errors, p. 357. In his will, Dunton gave a legacy of £10 to Elizabeth Goodall, "to reward her kind Intentions in helping me to a good wife" (p. 3).

4. John Dunton, The Case is Alter'd, 1701, p. 46.

5. Letter V in The Art of Living Incognito, part I, 1700.

6. Volume I of Tyrrell's General History was advertised in the Term Catalogue as early as February 1697, by Rogers, Harris, Knapton, Bell and Cockerill (T. C. III, 4 [Hilary 1697]). See also Wing T 3586.

7. See Dunton's "Advertisement. To ... Honest Booksellers", in The State Weathercocks, 1719.

8. Wing B 1351, S 3674, W 2651.

9. See Dunton's "Advertisement. To ... Honest Booksellers", in The State Weathercocks, 1719.

10. 29 November 1680. A. W. Pollard, List of Catalogues of English Book Sales 1676-1900 (London, 1915), p. 2.

11. Dublin Scuffle, p. 142.

12. Ibid., pp. 22, 324.

13. This is not surprising; in fact only 3 surviving Dublin catalogues prior to 1700 have been located by A. N. L. Munby, two of which were for sales at Dick's Coffee-House in 1698 and 1699. One of them bears the imprint: Dublin, Printed at the Back of Dick's Coffee-House, 1699.

14. Dublin Scuffle, p. 324.

15. Ibid., p. 325.

16. *Ibid.*, pp. 324-5.

17. *Ibid.*, pp. 316-7.

18. *Ibid.*, p. 340.

19. *Ibid.*, p. 325.

20. *Ibid.*, p. 327.

21. *Ibid.*, pp. 328, 359.

22. *Ibid.*, pp. 359-63. "I give to my Dear and adopted Child Mrs Isabella Edwards Widdow late of Dean Street in Holbourn Parish three hundred pounds Sterlin (for the tender and matchless Friendship She Shewed both to my Soul and body from our first Acquaintance in Ireland to the day of my death)" (Will, p. 1, *et passim*).

23. *Ibid.*, p. 363.

24. *Life and Errors*, p. 238; *Dublin Scuffle*, pp. 342-3.

25. *Dublin Scuffle*, p. 343.

26. *Ibid.*, p. 21.

27. *Ibid.*, p. 22.

28. *Ibid.*, p. 357.

29. *Ibid.*, p. 337.

30. Dunton's Will, p. 3.

31. *Dublin Scuffle*, p. 317.

32. *Ibid.*, p. 364.

33. *Ibid.*, pp. 369, 384-5. Bodleian Library, Ms. Rawlinson D 71, include the New England letters, *A Summer Ramble*, and letters from Dublin. Ms. Rawlinson D 1211, *Essay in Praise of an Owl*.

34. Ibid., pp. 7, 138-9, 368.

35. Ibid., pp. 1-7.

36. Ibid., pp. 20-1.

37. Ibid., p. 385.

38. Ibid., p. 380.

39. Ibid., p. 368.

40. Ibid., p. 321.

41. Ibid., pp. 321-2.

42. Ibid., p. 416.

43. Ibid., pp. 19, 358.

44. Ibid., p. 20.

45. Ibid., p. 29.

46. Ibid., pp. 58-9.

47. Ibid., pp. 67-70.

48. Ibid., p. 128.

49. Ibid., pp. 141-2.

Chapter VI. The Abusive Scribbler (1700-1732)

1. Indicated by various addresses on letters to Dunton of that year. See Bodleian Library, Ms. Rawlinson D 72, Nos. 3, 37, 41, 45, 54.

2. John Dunton, A Voyage Round the World, 1691, III, 2.

3. Theodore M. Hatfield, in The True Secret History of Mr. John Dunton (unpublished thesis, Harvard University, 1926), was very much interested in the curious history of Dunton's last years; Dunton's complicated relationships

with his female friends, his tracts and their public reception, were the chief concern of Hatfield's study.

4. John Dunton, The Art of Living Incognito, Part II, 1700, "Dunton Represented as Dead and Buried".

5. George Larkin to Dunton, 6 July 1700. Bodleian Library, Ms. Rawlinson D 72, No. 42.

6. Life and Errors, p. 159.

7. See Dunton's "Advertisement. To ... Honest Booksellers", in The State Weathercocks, 1719.

8. John Marshall reprinted A New Martyrology, called The Western Martyrology, in 1705 (advertised in T.C. III, 446 [Hilary 1705], et passim); and John Sprint published the second edition of The Post-Boy Robb'd in 1705 (advertised in T.C. III, 483 [Michaelmas 1705] [dated 1706]).

9. Copy in British Museum.

10. Bodleian Library, Ms. Rawlinson D 72, No. 67.

11. The receipt is in Luttrell's hand, but signed by Dunton. Osborn Collection, Yale University Library; see James M. Osborn, "Reflections on Narcissus Luttrell", The Book Collector, VI (1957), 15-27.

12. John Dunton, Dunton's Whipping-Post, 1706, in Life and Errors, p. 423.

13. Bodleian Library, Ms. Rawlinson D 72, No. 1.

14. John Dunton, Dunton's Whipping-Post, 1706, p. 1.

15. See Theodore F. M. Newton, "William Pittis and Queen Anne Journalism", Modern Philology, XXXIII (1955-6), 169-86, 279-302.

16. John Dunton, The Living Elegy, in Life and Errors, p. 461

17. Ibid., pp. 447, 475.

18. Ibid., p. 448.

NOTES

19. Ibid., p. 479.

20. John Nichols, Literary Anecdotes of the Eighteenth Century (London, 1812-15), IV, 110. See also Notes and Queries, Second Series, XI (1861), 424.

21. Dunton later claimed that the work had been reprinted as well at Oxford, Holland, Dublin, and Edinburgh (The Bull-Baiting, 1709, p. 1).

22. Jane Nicholas, Will, dated 14 October 1708, proved 18 October 1708 (see John Nichols, Literary Anecdotes of the Century [London, 1812-15], IX, 592).

23. John Nichols, Literary Anecdotes of the Eighteenth Century (London, 1812-18), IX, 592.

24. John Dunton, An Essay on Death-Bed-Charity, 1728, p. 2.

25. See Theodore M. Hatfield, The True Secret History of Mr. John Dunton, unpublished thesis (Harvard University, 1926) pp. 218-9; and relevant papers in Public Record Office, London (Bills brought into Chancery, 22 and 29 January 1709 [Bridges Division No. 236, bundle 26], and Orders in Chancery, 8 February 1709 [Entry Book A, 1708, p. 290]).

26. John Dunton, Stinking Fish, 1708, "From the Athenian Society", f. B_2v.

27. Bodleian Library, Ms. Rawlinson D 72, Nos. 15, 20, 31, 74.

28. Fleet Prison Commitment Books, No. 2 (Public Record Office, London).

29. Dated 21 June 1711. PRO, Price fol. 82.

30. The Monitor, No. 1, 22 April 1714 (Copy at Bodleian Library).

31. Neck or Nothing, 1713, Whigg Loyalty and The Impeachment, 1714, published by T. Warner, and The Conventicle, published by John Oldsworth in 1714, are the only works of the period which fall outside this pattern.

NOTES

32. John Dunton, Mordecai's Memorial, 1716, p. 5. See also John Dunton, The Mob-War, 1715, p. ix.

33. John Dunton, The Impeachment, 1714, advertisement.

34. Quoted by Robert J. Allen, The Clubs of Augustan London (Cambridge, Mass., 1933), p. 243.

35. Jonathan Swift, The Public Spirit of the Whigs (London, 1714), p. 2.

36. Books Lately Writ by Mr. John Dunton, 1715.

37. Edward Harley, Earl of Oxford, "Notes on Biographies" (Harl. Ms. 7544), Notes and Queries, Second Series, IX (1860), 418-9.

38. The Flying Post, No. 3799, 10 May 1716.

39. John Dunton, Royal Gratitude, 1716, p. 62.

40. The Fleet Prison Commitment Books for the period 1713-25 are lost.

41. Bodleian Library, Ms. Rawlinson D 72, No. 49.

42. Advertised in The Weekly Journal, 31 May 1718; no copy has been located.

43. Dated 10 September 1720 (John Dunton, Will, PRO, Price fol. 82).

44. Sarah Dunton died intestate; her estate was administered 31 October 1721 (Administrations Book, unpublished ms. at Somerset House).

45. John Dunton, Will, PRO, Price fol. 82.

46. Ibid.

47. Edward Harley, Earl of Oxford, "Notes on Biographies" (Harl. Ms. 7544), Notes and Queries, Second Series, IX (1860), 419.

NOTES

Appendix 1. Dunton and his Authors.

1. Frank A. Mumby, Publishing and Bookselling (4th edition, London, 1956), p. 126.

2. Life and Errors, p. 61.

3. Ibid., p. 72.

4. Edward Ward, The London Spy (ed. Arthur L. Hayward, London 1927), p. 13.

5. Life and Errors, p. 61.

6. George Wither, The Schollers Purgatory (c. 1625), in Miscellaneous Works of George Wither First Collection (Publications of the Spenser Society, Issue No. 12, 1872), pp. 9-10.

7. Ibid., p. 121.

8. James Lackington, Memoirs (7th edn., London, 1794), p. 223.

9. Life and Errors, p. 75.

10. Ibid., p. 201.

11. Ibid., pp. 61-2.

12. Ibid., pp. 182-3

13. Ibid., p. 294.

14. Ibid., p. 184.

15. Ibid., p. 180.

16. Dunton met Spademan in Rotterdam, and after his return to England Dunton sent Spademan English Books, and Spademan supplied Dunton with "books of a foreign growth which he thought might be serviceable in an English dress". Dunton was obliged to him for The History of the Famous Edict of

Nantes, as with Spademan's help he "prevented the London Booksellers that were going upon the same design" (Life and Errors, p. 141). A letter from Spademan is preserved in the Bodleian Library, Ms. Rawlinson D 72, Number 78, written from Rotterdam, September 8, 1695, in which he assured Dunton that "at present, these Parts, are very barren of any Discourses worthy of a Translation. When I know of any that are, you shall have timely notice"; and asked Dunton to send him a small number of books to his account.

17. Life and Errors, p. 168.

18. Ibid., p. 161.

19. Ibid., pp. 179; 160.

20. John Dunton, Will, PRO, Price fol. 82, p. 11.

21. Matthew Barker, Flores Intellectuales (London, 1691), preface.

22. Life and Errors, p. 178.

23. Henry Brougham, Reflections to a Late Book (London, 1694), epistle dedicatory, by William Offley.

24. Life and Errors, pp. 183-4.

25. Ibid., p. 185.

Appendix 2. Dunton and the Trade.

1. Adam Black, Memoirs (ed. Alexander Nicolson, 2nd edn., Edinburgh, 1885), p. 20.

2. Life and Errors, pp. 242-3.

3. John Dunton, The Informer's Doom, 1683, p. 125.

4. Life and Errors, p. 242.

5. John Dunton, Will, PRO, Price fol. 82, p. 11.

6. R. W. Chapman, "Eighteenth Century Imprints", in The Library, 4th Series, XI (1930-31), 503-4.

7. T. C. II, 474 (Michaelmas 1693). In partnership with Baldwin and two other booksellers, Dunton issued in 1692-4 a series of nine Quaker tracts (see A Farther Account, 1693, in checklist).

8. Leona Rostenberg wrote on Richard Baldwin but failed to note any connection between Dunton and Baldwin other than mere acquaintance ("Richard and Anne Baldwin, Whig Patriot Publishers", in Bibliographical Society of America Papers, XLVII (1953), 1-42).

Appendix 3. Pseudonymous Imprints.

1. See Advertisements, "Books Concerning the Quakers", in Dunton's Catalogue, 1694, and advertisements in each work and relevant entries in checklist. Dunton himself advertised only three of the seven Levis imprints.

2. John Dunton, A Voyage Round the World, 1691 (edition of 1762, II, 152-3).

3. Life and Errors, p. 182.

4. The authorship of this pamphlet is ascribed to Thompkins by Wing, T 997.

5. Not in Wing; copy in British Museum.

6. Wing P 322. In the same year, Randal Taylor published A Lash for the Parable-Makers (Wing L 462A), and J. Johnson published The Parable of the Bear-Baiting (Wing P 320); both of these imprints are genuine.

7. Wing M 2458.

8. Stationers' Company, Court Book F, 9 February 1690/1, f. 148v.

Appendix 4. The Conger.

1. Norma Hodgson and Cyprian Blagden, eds., The Notebook of Thomas Bennet and Henry Clements (Oxford, 1956).

2. A Voyage Round the World, 1691, II, 77.

3. *Life and Errors*, p. 204.

4. Hodgson and Blagden, *op. cit.*, p. 98; *Life and Errors*, p. 204.

5. *Life and Errors*, pp. 204-5.

6. *Ibid.*, p. 274.

7. *Ibid.*, p. 72.

8. See Hodgson and Blagden, *op. cit.*, pp. 91-4.

9. John Dunton, "Advertisement. To ... Honest Booksellers", in *The State Weathercocks* (London, [1719]).

INDEX